Y0-DWP-751

PROCEEDINGS OF SPIE

 SPIE—The International Society for Optical Engineering

Sensors and Controls for Intelligent Machining, Agile Manufacturing, and Mechatronics

Patrick F. Muir
Peter E. Orban
Chairs/Editors

4–5 November 1998
Boston, Massachusetts

Sponsored by
SPIE—The International Society for Optical Engineering

Endorsed by
SME—The Society of Manufacturing Engineers

Published by
SPIE—The International Society for Optical Engineering

Volume 3518

SPIE is an international technical society dedicated to advancing engineering and scientific
applications of optical, photonic, imaging, electronic, and optoelectronic technologies.

The papers appearing in this book comprise the proceedings of the meeting mentioned on the cover and title page. They reflect the authors' opinions and are published as presented and without change, in the interests of timely dissemination. Their inclusion in this publication does not necessarily constitute endorsement by the editors or by SPIE.

Please use the following format to cite material from this book:
    Author(s), "Title of paper," in *Sensors and Controls for Intelligent Machining, Agile Manufacturing, and Mechatronics,* Patrick F. Muir, Peter E. Orban, Editors, Proceedings of SPIE Vol. 3518, page numbers (1998).

ISSN 0277-786X
ISBN 0-8194-2979-1

Published by
SPIE—The International Society for Optical Engineering
P.O. Box 10, Bellingham, Washington 98227-0010 USA
Telephone 360/676-3290 (Pacific Time) • Fax 360/647-1445

Printed in the United States of America.

Contents

Conference Committees

Part A   Sensors and Controls for Intelligent Machining and Agile Manufacturing

Conference Chair

Peter E. Orban, National Research Council Canada

Program Committee

Yusuf Altintas, University of British Columbia (Canada)
Colin Bradley, National University of Singapore
Illés Dudás, University of Miskolc (Hungary)
M. A. Elbestawi, McMaster University (Canada)
Geza Haidegger, Computer Auto Research Institute (Hungary)
Robert B. Jerard, University of New Hampshire
Jin Jiang, University of Western Ontario (Canada)
George K. Knopf, University of Western Ontario (Canada)
John Mo, CSIRO—Commonwealth Scientific and Industrial Research Organisation (Australia)
Bartholomew O. Nnaji, University of Pittsburgh
Mark Olszewski, Omtronix Engineering (Canada)
Sanjay Sarma, Massachusetts Institute of Technology
Anbo Wang, Virginia Polytechnic Institute and State University
Ian Yellowley, University of British Columbia (Canada)
Millan K. Yeung, National Research Council Canada

Session Chairs

1   Sensors
Peter E. Orban, National Research Council Canada

2   Control Systems I
Peter E. Orban, National Research Council Canada

3   Control Systems II
Illés Dudás, University of Miskolc (Hungary)

4   System Integration
Evgueni V. Bordatchev, National Research Council Canada

5   Process Modeling and Control
Sanjay Sarma, Massachusetts Institute of Technology

Part B   Mechatronics

Conference Chair

Patrick F. Muir, Carnegie Mellon University

Program Committee

Kevin Dowling, PRI Automation Inc.
John S. Bay, Virginia Polytechnic Institute and State University
Jeffrey L. Ruckman, University of Rochester

Session Chairs

6   Mechatronics I
Patrick F. Muir, Carnegie Mellon University

7   Mechatronics II
John S. Bay, Virginia Polytechnic Institute and State University

8   Mechatronics III
Kevin Dowling, PRI Automation Inc.

Part A

SENSORS AND CONTROLS FOR INTELLIGENT MACHINING AND AGILE MANUFACTURING

Introduction

Modern production systems rely heavily on various sensors and control technologies to achieve higher productivity, better product quality, and lower production costs. The technology supporting intelligent manufacturing processes and systems went through tremendous change during the last decade. This progress affected all aspects of the production, from the hardware and software components to the algorithms and the thinking of the enterprises utilizing these technologies and production methods. The ongoing advancements in sensor and control technology and its applications will continue to have a major impact on manufacturing in the coming years.

As part of Photonics East '98, the conference on Sensors and Controls for Intelligent Machining and Agile Manufacturing brought together technology providers, control and automation professionals, manufacturing engineers, researchers, and users who discussed the latest technical knowledge, ideas, and experiences in the field. This selection of papers covers relevant theoretical, practical, and application issues.

Peter E. Orban

SESSION 1

Sensors

Data Fusion using a Hierarchy of Self-Organizing Feature Maps

George K. Knopf

Mechatronics Research Laboratory, Department of Mechanical & Materials Engineering,
Faculty of Engineering Science, University of Western Ontario,
London , Ontario, Canada , N6A 5B9

ABSTRACT

The *synergistic* use of data acquired from different sensors will enable autonomous manufacturing equipment to make faster and more intelligent decisions about the current status of the workspace. Multisensor data fusion deals with mathematical and statistical issues arising from the combination of different sources of sensory information into a single representational format. A fundamental problem in data fusion is associating the data captured by one sensor with that from another sensor or the same sensor at a different point in time. This paper describes a non-statistical unsupervised hierarchical clustering algorithm used to associate the complementary feature vectors extracted from different data sets. Each level in the hierarchy consists of one or more *self-organizing feature maps* that contain a small number of cluster units distributed in a linear array. The self-organizing feature map develops an internal ordered representation of the cluster units based on the combined feature set derived from the original data. The unsupervised learning algorithm ensures that "similar" feature vectors will be assigned to cluster units that lie in close spatial proximity in the feature map. If the sum-of-square error for the feature vectors associated with a cluster unit is greater than a predefined tolerance, then those vectors are used to create another feature map at the next level of the hierarchy. This growing procedure enables the feature set to control the number of cluster units generated. The hierarchical structure provides an efficient mechanism to deal with uncertainties in correct classification. Experimental studies are presented in order to illustrate the robustness of this technique.

Keywords: Self-organizing feature maps, hierarchical clustering, data association, data fusion.

1. INTRODUCTION

The manufacturing environment of the next century will involve a variety of intelligent production systems that perform their tasks with greater flexibility and speed. Important technologies for realizing such systems are smart sensors that operate with a high degree of autonomy and networks of autonomous sensors that can simultaneously monitor numerous locally distributed processes in a flexible manufacturing environment[13,14].

The *synergistic* use of information acquired from different sensors will enable autonomous manufacturing equipment to make intelligent decisions about the current status of the product and workspace. The information can originate from different sensory devices during a single period of time, or from a single sensor over an extended period of time. Two important advantages of using information from multiple sensors include data redundancy and complementary information. Fusion of redundant data from several similar sensors increases system accuracy and reliability by reducing uncertainty associated with the fidelity of any single sensor. In addition, different types of sensors monitoring the same physical phenomenon can provide complementary information that is impossible to acquire with a single type of sensor. The complementary information can either represent redundant data for enhanced system reliability or new information for increased discrimination of the sensory observations.

Multisensor data fusion deals with mathematical and statistical issues arising from the combination of different sources of sensory information into a single representational format[2,10,11]. This fusion can take place at either the signal, sampled data, object property or symbolic level. Signal-level fusion can be used in real-time applications and can be treated as another step in the overall processing of the signal. Data level fusion can be used to improve the performance of signal conditioning or intermediate processing tasks such as image segmentation in scene analysis applications. Property and symbol-level fusion can provide additional features to enhance recognition and interpretation capabilities. The different levels are distinguished by the type of information provided to the system, how the information is modeled, the degree of the

6

Part of the SPIE Conference on Sensors and Controls for Intelligent Machining and Agile Manufacturing
Boston, Massachusetts ● November 1998
SPIE Vol. 3518 ● 0277-786X/98/$10.00

sensor registration required for fusion, the methods used for fusion, and the means by which the fusion process can improve the "quality" of the information provided to the intelligent production system [2,14].

One unsolved problem in integrating and fusing redundant information from multiple sensors is that of *registration*. Registration is the process of associating the feature vectors extracted from the sampled data captured by one sensor with that from another sensor or the same sensor at a different point in time. The Initial Match Matrix (IMM) shown in Figure 1 illustrates the non uniqueness of the feature vector matches in the two data sets. In this example, numerous features extracted from the sampled data of sensor #1, $S_1(t)$, falsely match more than one feature vector arising from sensor #2, $S_2(t)$. The goal of any data fusion algorithm is, however, to find only one match per row and column. In order to achieve this a Final Match Matrix (FMM) is often generated using an optimization technique such as genetic algorithms, simulated annealing or competitive neural networks [1,5-7].

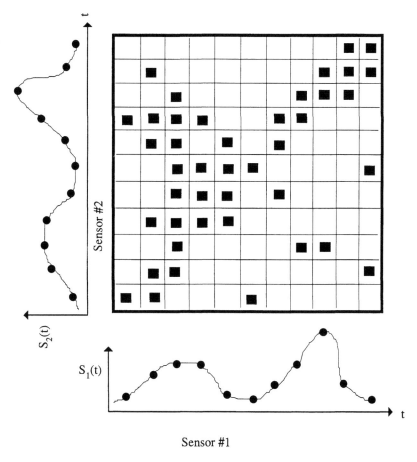

Figure 1.   An illustration of the data association problem for two time sampled signals $S_1(t)$ and $S_2(t)$. Note that the Initial Match Matrix (IMM) indicates that several features extracted from the discrete samples of sensor #1 match more than one feature from sensor #2.

The focus of this paper is on a non-statistical unsupervised hierarchical clustering algorithm used to associate the complementary feature vectors extracted from the same or different data sets. The feature vectors can represent information from the different levels and are classified as partitioned regions in a multidimensional feature space [3]. Each level in the classification hierarchy consists of one or more *self-organizing feature maps* [4,5,9] that contain a number of cluster units distributed in a linear array. In the studies reported in this paper only a 1-D array of cluster units will be considered. The number of cluster units assigned to each feature map is a function of the number of data vectors used for training. The self-organizing feature map develops an internal ordered representation of the cluster units based on the combined feature set derived from the original data. The unsupervised learning algorithm ensures that "similar" feature vectors will be assigned to cluster units that lie in close spatial proximity in the output layer. If the sum-of-square error for the feature vectors associated with a cluster unit is greater than a predefined tolerance, then those vectors are used to create a feature map at the next level of the hierarchy. This divide and expand strategy enables the feature set to control the location of cluster units in the feature space. Thus, the matching process occurs with little or no a priori knowledge of the data relationship. The hierarchical structure provides an efficient mechanism to deal with uncertainties in correct classification.

The following section is a brief description of the Kohonen self-organizing feature map and how this neural-like structure partitions data. Section 3 describes the self-organizing hierarchical architecture used to classify the features extracted from sensory data. It is important to realize that the system performance is only as good as the discrimination capabilities of the feature extraction processes. A poor set of features will result in poor association of the input data. Two simple experimental studies are presented in Section 4 to illustrate the data fusion capabilities of the proposed technique. Finally, concluding remarks are presented in Section 5.

2. SELF-ORGANIZING FEATURE MAP

The Kohonen self-organizing feature map is a competitive learning neural network that emulates the process by which topological feature maps are formed in the brain [4]. The self-organizing neural network shown in Figure 2 arranges the weights, w_{ij}, such that they reflect some physical characteristic of the external input X^p being applied, where $p = 1, 2, ..., P$ and P is the total number of training patterns. In essence, this two-layered network maps continuous valued input vectors into a 1D output space. The weights are adjusted with the application of each input vector. After enough input vectors have been presented to the network, the weights will specify cluster units (or cluster centers) in the feature space.

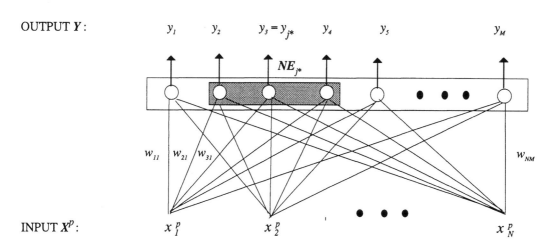

Figure 2. The basic structure of a Kohonen self-organizing feature map.

During the training process the weights will be organized such that topologically close cluster units in the output layer are sensitive to input vectors that are physically similar. Each cluster unit in this network, y_j, has an associated topological neighborhood NE_j with other cluster units in the layer. The weight adaptation algorithm is designed such that both the winning cluster unit and the units in the neighborhood of the winning unit are simultaneously updated. The size of the neighborhood decreases as the training procedure progresses, until the neighborhood consists of only one unit located at j. By using a variable neighborhood adaptation strategy the self-organizing network overcomes the problem of under utilized cluster units. Thus, the output responses are organized in a natural manner. For convenience, the magnitude of the feature vectors are normalized such that they reside within a unit hypercube.

The basic algorithm for generating a self-organizing feature map is as follows:

Step 0. Initialize the weights w_{ij} to small random values located inside the unit hypercube. Set the topological neighborhood parameter NE_j and fixed learning parameter μ. The size of the topological neighborhood is a function of the maximum number of cycles N_{cycle}, or epochs, through the training set. Typical rules to describe the shrinking neighborhood, NE_j, with respect to the # of cycles is presented in Step 6.

Step 1. While the stopping condition is false, do Steps 2 - 7.

 Step 2. Randomly select an input vector X^p from the training data set, where p = 1, 2, ..., P and P is the total number of training patterns. For each selected input vector, do Steps 3 -5.

  Step 3. Compute the error or difference $D_j(p)$ between the input and weight vectors for all cluster units in the array using

$$D_j(p) = \sum_{i=1}^{N} \left(x_i^p - w_{ji} \right)^2 \tag{1}$$

where x_i^p is the ith input, w_{ji} is the weight from the ith input to j^{th} cluster unit, and j = 1, 2, ...M.

  Step 4. Find the index j^* for the output unit with minimum distance $D_{j*}(p)$.

  Step 5. Update the weights to cluster unit j^* and all units residing within the specified neighborhood NE_{j*}, using

$$w_{ki}\ (new) = w_{ki}\ (old) + \alpha \left[x_i^p - w_{ki}\ (old) \right] \tag{2a}$$

where

$$\alpha = \mu \left[1 - \left(\text{\# of cycles}/ N_{cycle} \right) \right] \tag{2b}$$

$$\left(j^* - NE_{j*} \right) \leq k \leq \left(j^* + NE_{j*} \right) \tag{2c}$$
and $1 \leq i \leq N$.

Step 6. Reduce the radius of the topological neighborhood NE_j at specified times based on the maximum number of acceptable cycles through the training set, i.e. N_{cycle}.

 (i) If the number of cluster units in a layer is small then NE_j can be determined using

  If $\left(\text{\# of cycles .le.}(N_{cycle}/2) \right)$ **then** $NE_j = 1$

  If $\left(\text{\# of cycles .gt.}(N_{cycle}/2) \right)$ **then** $NE_j = 0$

 (ii) If the number of cluster units is large then NE_j can be given by

  If $\left(\text{\# of cycles .le.}(N_{cycle}/4) \right)$ **then** $NE_j = 3$

  If $\left((\text{\# of cycles .gt.}(N_{cycle}/4)).\text{and.}(\text{\# of cycles .le.}(N_{cycle}/2)) \right)$ **then** $NE_j = 2$

  If $\left((\text{\# of cycles .gt.}(N_{cycle}/2)).\text{and.}(\text{\# of cycles .le.}(3 \times N_{cycle}/4)) \right)$ **then** $NE_j = 1$

  If $\left(\text{\# of cycles .gt.}(3 \times N_{cycle}/4) \right)$ **then** $NE_j = 0$

Step 7. Test stopping condition. If the stopping condition is not satisfied then go to Step 1 and repeat the process.

Kohonen's network performs relatively well in noisy data because the number of classes is fixed, and adaptation stops after training has been completed. However, for data sets with a limited number of feature vectors the results may depend on the presentation order of the input data. Another common problem with this type of competitive learning algorithm is that all cluster units are not equally utilized during the training process. Often during training only a few cluster units will be updated and this leads to unwanted distortions and misclassifications.

The under utilization problem can be addressed by incorporating a measure of how frequently a unit has been declared a winner in the winner selection process (Step 4). The frequency sensitive competitive learning network [9] is similar to the one described above except that it incorporates a measure of how often a unit has been a winner. Each unit maintains a count u_j of the number of times it was a winning unit. The error measure that is used to select the winning unit, Eqn. (1), is modified to be

$$D_j(p) = F(u_j) \times \sum_{i=1}^{N} \left(x_i^p - w_{ji} \right)^2 \qquad (3)$$

where $F(u_j)$ is a non-decreasing function called the *fairness function*. The fairness function is a simple way of introducing a count-dependent weighting to the error measure. Typically, $F(u_j) = u_j$.

3. HIERARCHY OF FEATURE MAPS

Each level in the classification hierarchy consists of one or more *self-organizing feature maps* that contain a small number of cluster units distributed in a linear 1-D array. The self-organizing feature map develops an internal ordered representation of the cluster units based on the feature set derived from the original data. The data can be from one or more sensors. The only restriction is that the feature vectors represent the same type of information. The unsupervised learning algorithm ensures that "similar" feature vectors will be assigned to cluster units that lie in close spatial proximity in the feature space. If the sum-of-square error for the feature vectors associated with a cluster unit is greater than a predefined tolerance, then those vectors are used to create another feature map at the next level of the hierarchy. The hierarchical structure provides an efficient mechanism to deal with uncertainties in correct classification by ensuring similar vectors reside in neighboring regions of the output layer.

One of the main problems in this approach is selecting an appropriate number of cluster units for each level in the hierarchy. A pre-fixed number of units may not best represent the variability in the data set. Incorporating too few units at any particular level will result in many incorrect associations being formed. Alternatively, too many cluster units will both increase the computational time and diminish the discrimination ability of the network. For example, a feature map with a single cluster will result in all input vectors being assigned to the same unit. On the other hand, an equal number of cluster units to feature vectors will result in poor matching or association between the feature vectors because each input will be treated as a separate class.

For illustrative proposes, the hierarchy is restricted to the three levels shown in Figure 3. The number of cluster units in each level is dependent upon the number of feature vectors in the training set. If the training set contains P feature vectors then the first level will have $C \geq P^{1/3}$ cluster units. Correspondingly, the second level will have C^2 and the third C^3 cluster units.

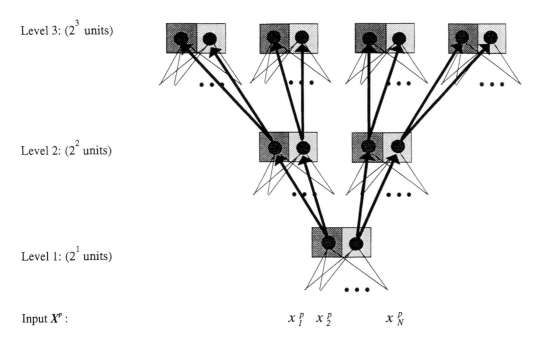

Level 3: (2^3 units)

Level 2: (2^2 units)

Level 1: (2^1 units)

Input X^p : x_1^p x_2^p x_N^p

Figure 3.   The basic structure of the three level data fusion algorithm that utilizes numerous self-organizing feature maps. In this simple illustration the number of feature vectors is restricted to eight and $C^3 = 8$.

Once the number of cluster units for the various levels have been determined then the weights for the units in the various levels are adjusted using the self-organizing learning algorithm described in the previous section. During training, the cluster units in level #1 are first adapted. Based on the cluster assignments the units in neighboring regions of the feature space in level #2 are adjusted for enhanced discrimination ability. The procedure is repeated for the third and final level. The entire training set is applied to the network during one cycle or epoch. The updating of the weights continues until no weight changes occur over the epoch, the total error is less than a pre-set amount, or a maximum number of epoch cycles has been reached.

Although, the number of units in level #3 is pre-set to be greater than or equal to the number of training vectors, there will be fewer active cluster units after training if there exist strong similarities between any of the training vectors. In many cases where there exists a correlation between the data sets, the number of active units will be small compared to the overall number of units that are available. If there exists *no similarity* between the feature vectors in the training data then all cluster units in level 3 will be activated. The immediate conclusion may be that the feature vectors are completely dissimilar, however, neighboring activation in the output layer can be used to make decisions as to *approximate* pattern associations.

4. EXPERIMENTAL RESULTS

The goal of the hierarchical self-organizing architecture is to match or associate local features extracted from one or more sensors. The initial experiment was to investigate the behavior of the approach when a string of 125 random numbers bounded by [0, 1] were applied to the hierarchy. This test was used to investigate the self-organizing feature map's ability to reorganize data based on *similarity*. For simplicity, the feature vectors used in this preliminary study contained only one element (i.e. $N = 1$). Since the training set consisted of 125 patterns (i.e. $P = 125$), the first layer contained 5 cluster units , the second layer 25 units and the third layer had 125 units.   The fixed learning rate parameter was set to 1.0 and the maximum cycles through the training patterns was $N_{cycle} = 2000$. Figure 4 represents the cluster units determined after the training procedure for the random inputs at N_{cycle} . Each cluster unit in level #1 controlled the activation of 5 neighboring units in level #2. Correspondingly, each unit in level #2 controlled the activation of 5 neighboring units in level #3. After training the cluster units were ordered in a sequence of decreasing magnitude. Note that no prior knowledge of an ordering scheme was imposed on the network.

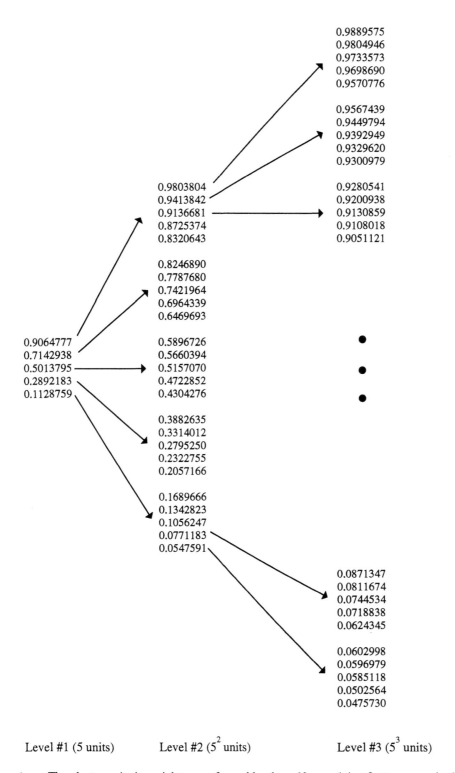

0.9889575
0.9804946
0.9733573
0.9698690
0.9570776

0.9567439
0.9449794
0.9392949
0.9329620
0.9300979

0.9280541
0.9200938
0.9130859
0.9108018
0.9051121

0.9803804
0.9413842
0.9136681
0.8725374
0.8320643

0.8246890
0.7787680
0.7421964
0.6964339
0.6469693

0.9064777
0.7142938
0.5013795
0.2892183
0.1128759

0.5896726
0.5660394
0.5157070
0.4722852
0.4304276

0.3882635
0.3314012
0.2795250
0.2322755
0.2057166

0.1689666
0.1342823
0.1056247
0.0771183
0.0547591

0.0871347
0.0811674
0.0744534
0.0718838
0.0624345

0.0602998
0.0596979
0.0585118
0.0502564
0.0475730

Level #1 (5 units)   Level #2 (5^2 units)   Level #3 (5^3 units)

Figure 4.   The cluster units in weight space formed by the self-organizing feature maps in the hierarchy for random inputs
bounded by [0, 1].

Figure 5 illustrates the frequency of cluster unit selection for the feature vectors once training had been completed. The histograms help illustrate the ordered partitioning of the feature vectors in each of the three levels. Figure 5 (a) shows that although the training data was random, more feature vectors resided near cluster units 1 and 2 than the others. Figure 5 (c) indicates that a small number of the feature vectors were incorrectly classified when an equal number of cluster units and training patterns were used. This implies that some feature vectors were located between the two adjoining cluster units.

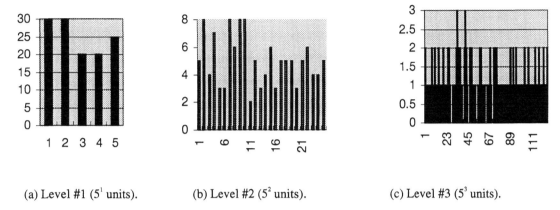

(a) Level #1 (5^1 units). (b) Level #2 (5^2 units). (c) Level #3 (5^3 units).

Figure 5.   Histograms displaying the frequency of feature vector classification for the cluster units in the various levels after training has been completed for random inputs.

The second experiment involved classifying 800 feature vectors extracted from the two 20x20 gray-level images shown in Figure 6. The primary objective for this study was to relate local features in the image pair for higher level motion or depth analysis [8,12]. The basic approach involved first extracting local or regional features from the individual images. One set of features for this type of application are the invariant moments described by Duda and Hart [3]. However, for this preliminary study the pixel intensity values that reside in a 3x3 local window were used. A 9-element feature vector (i.e. $N =$ 9) was computed at each pixel location in the image plane there was. The feature vectors extracted from the images were used to train the topologically ordered feature maps in the hierarchy. The Kohonen network determined cluster centers that best represent all the feature vectors. The self-organizing nature of the network caused cluster centers with similar feature values to be associated with cluster centers that lie in close topologically proximity in the output layer. After the training process had been completed, each image of the test sequence was re-introduced to the network and the classes for the features were identified. The process of association was, therefore, nothing more than scanning across the feature images and identifying where each cluster center was located in the image space.

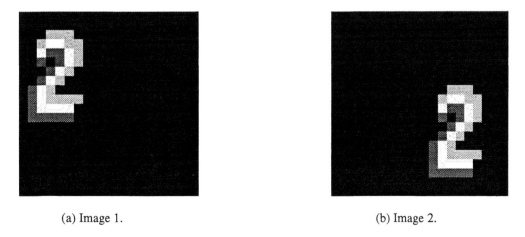

(a) Image 1.   (b) Image 2.

Figure 6.   The two 20x20 images used to generate the feature vectors for the data association experiment.

In this study the training set consisted of 800 feature vectors (i.e. $P = 800$). Correspondingly, the first layer contained 10 cluster units , the second layer 100 units and the third layer had 1000 units. The fixed learning rate parameter was set to 1.0 and the maximum cycles through the training patterns was $N_{cycle} = 2000$. Figure 7 shows the cluster units determined after the training procedure had been completed and Figure 8 shows the frequency of cluster unit selection for the training set.

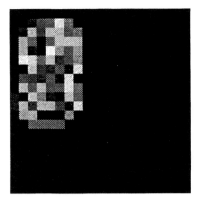

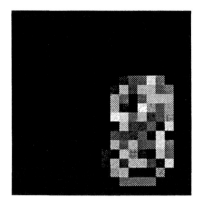

(a) Image 1.   (b) Image 2.

Figure 7.   The classifications according to the 10^3 cluster units in level #3 for the two 20x20 images. The pixel intensity corresponds to the cluster unit assignment. Some of the classes are indistinguishable because only 256 levels of gray are used for image display.

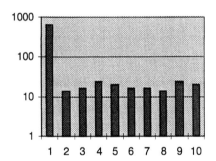

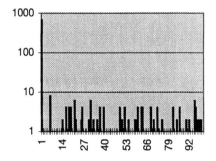

(a) Cluster assignments for level #1 (10^1 units).   (b) Cluster assignments for level #2 (10^2 units).

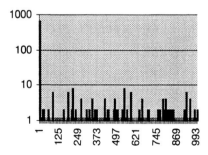

(c) Cluster assignments for level #3 (10^3 units).

Figure 8.   Histograms displaying the frequency of classification for the cluster units located in each level of the hierarchy after training had been completed. The 9-element feature vectors used in this study were the 3x3 local intensity values.

In the above example there were more cluster units in level #3 than feature vectors used for training. However, the selective nature of the hierarchical self-organizing feature map is such that only a limited range of cluster units were actually searched and weights updated. Each cluster unit in level #2 was activated only if the corresponding unit in level #1 was activated by the same input. Similarly, the units in level #3 were dependent upon the proper activation of related units in level #2. As a result, a significant number of cluster units in level #3 were unused during the data association stage after the training procedure had been completed (Figure 8(c)).

5. CONCLUSIONS

A self-organizing unsupervised hierarchical clustering algorithm for associating the data captured by one or more sensors was briefly described in this paper. Each level of the proposed hierarchical clustering algorithm consisted of a *self-organizing feature map* that contained a small number of cluster units distributed in a 1-D linear array. The self-organizing feature map developed an internal ordered representation of the feature vectors derived from the original sensor data. The unsupervised learning algorithm ensured that "similar" feature vectors are assigned to cluster units that lie in close spatial proximity in the feature space and output layer.

Two experiments were presented to illustrate the effectiveness of the approach. The first study demonstrated the ordering and discrimination capabilities of the self-organizing feature map and the hierarchical architecture. Furthermore, the histograms presented in Figure 5 illustrated that the architecture first performed coarse classification at level #1 and proceeded to perform finer classifications through levels #2 and #3. The second experiment involved matching features extracted from two sequential images. Again, the coarse-to-fine search strategy was demonstrated.

The success of the technique is, however, very dependent upon the features used for clustering. A poorly selected feature set can result in numerous incorrect classifications regardless of the effectiveness of the clustering algorithm employed. This will always be a problem because the garbage-in garbage-out principle of information processing.

Additional work and study is required in order to make this algorithm truly useful in intelligent manufacturing applications. The computational time required to achieve a usable result is significant and does not lend itself to real-time applications. The problems arising from selecting appropriate feature sets or incomplete feature sets must still be investigated. An important positive attribute of the technique is that no assumption is made about the underlying data structure. If there is no correlation between the features in the data set then the method results in as many cluster units as feature vectors. However, by tracking backwards through the hierarchy it is possible to determine similarities and use this information to derive viable conclusions about associations in the data set.

ACKNOWLEDGMENTS

This work has been supported, in part, by the Natural Sciences and Engineering Research Council of Canada.

REFERENCES

1. Abidi, M.A., "Fusion of multi-dimensional data using regularization", in *Data Fusion in Robotics and Machine Intelligence*, M.A. Abidi and R.C. Gonzalez (Eds.), Boston: Academic Press, Inc., pp. 415 - 455, 1992.

2. Abidi, M.A. and Gonzalez, R.C., Data Fusion in Robotics and Machine Intelligence. Boston: Academic Press, Inc., 1992.

3. Duda, R.O. and Hart, P.E., *Pattern Classification and Scene Analysis*. New York: John Wiley, 1973.

4. Fausett,L. , *Fundamentals of Neural Networks*. Englewood Cliffs, N.J. : Prentice Hall, 1994.

5. Haykin, S., *Neural Networks : A Comprehensive Foundation*. New York: Macmillan, 1994.

6. Huntsberger, T.L., "Data Fusion: a neural networks implementation", in *Data Fusion in Robotics and Machine Intelligence*, M.A. Abidi and R.C. Gonzalez (Eds.), Boston: Academic Press, Inc., pp. 507 - 535, 1992.

7. Hush,D.R. and Horne,B.G., " Progress in supervised neural networks", *IEEE Signal Processing Magazine*, vol. 10, no. 1, pp. 8 - 39, 1993.

8. Jain, R., Kasturi, R. and Schunck, B.G., *Machine Vision*. New York: McGraw-Hill, 1995.

9. Krishnamurthy, A.K., Ahalt, S.C., Melton, D.E., and Chen, P., "Neural networks for vector quantization of speech and images", *IEEE Journal on Selected Areas in Communication*, vol. 8, no. 8, pp. 1449 - 1457, 1990.

10. Luo, R.C. and Kay, M.G., "Multisensor integration and fusion in intelligent systems", *IEEE Transactions on Systems, Man, and Cybernetics*, vol. 19, no. 5, pp. 901 - 931, 1989.

11. Luo, R.C. and Kay, M.G., "Data fusion and sensor integration: state-of-the-art 1990's", in *Data Fusion in Robotics and Machine Intelligence*, M.A. Abidi and R.C. Gonzalez (Eds.), Boston: Academic Press, Inc., pp. 7 -135, 1992.

12. Marshall, A.D. and Martin, R.R., *Computer Vision, Models and Inspection*. Singapore: World Scientific, 1992.

13. Van der Spiegel, J., "Computational Sensors", in *Intelligent Sensors*, H. Yamasaki (Ed.), Amsterdam: Elsevier, pp. 19 - 38, 1996.

14. Yamasaki, H., "What are the Intelligent sensors", in *Intelligent Sensors*, H. Yamasaki (Ed.), Amsterdam: Elsevier, pp. 1 - 17, 1996.

Machine Vision Monitoring of Tool Wear

Y.S. Wong, W.K. Yuen, K. S. Lee, C. Bradley

Department of Mechanical and Production Engineering
National University of Singapore

ABSTRACT

Automated tool condition monitoring is an enabling technology in the push to develop fully unmanned machining centers. If this goal can be achieved across a broad range of machine tools, then researchers have assisted industry in moving one step closer to attaining truly flexible manufacturing work cells. Recent advances in the field of image processing technology have led to experimentation with machine vision as a potential means of directly evaluating tool condition. In this work, a machine vision system is employed that permits direct milling insert wear measurement to be accomplished in-cycle. The system is characterized by measurement flexibility, good spatial resolution and high accuracy. The flank wear monitoring system consists of an illumination source, CCD camera and high-resolution microscope lens. The extent of flank wear on the milling inserts was measured using the vision system and an image-processing algorithm. Two vision-based parameters were developed and their efficacy in directly quantifying insert flank wear was compared with measurements on a traditional toolmaker's microscope.

Keywords: CNC machining, machine vision, flank wear

1. INTRODUCTION

The development of a reliable cutting tool monitoring system is an important step for the development of unmanned, computer numerically controlled (CNC) machining centres. In the absence of a human operator, the automated machining system must compensate for the lack of the human's experience and judgement. To achieve full automation at the machining centre, sensor technology is being adopted to gather the tool wear data so that a "smart controller" can decide when a tool change should be made. Timely changes of the cutting tools nearer the end of their useful cutting life prevent inferior finish quality that can lead to additional scrap or re-work cost. In the literature, many single- and multiple-sensor strategies are being explored for reliable tool wear monitoring. Corresponding investigations into sensor data processing, sensor fusion and artificial intelligence techniques are also being undertaken.

A variety of experimental sensing techniques has been applied to the automated tool wear-monitoring problem. The particular sensor method employed can be described as performing either a direct or an indirect measurement. For example, a direct measurement method could employ machine vision to gauge the extent of the flank wear, essentially emulating the role of the human inspector armed with the toolmaker's microscope. The approach described in this paper is under the direct measurement category.

Indirect sensing techniques have predominantly been implemented, employing varied technologies such as acoustic emission monitoring[1, 2], spindle current measurement and cutting force determination. Tool wear generally creates small changes in the pertinent parameter derived from the sensing signal whereas alteration of the cutting conditions tends to affect the parameter being monitored in more significant way. A vast majority of this previous work has been restricted to tool wear monitoring on CNC turning centres. The tool wear monitoring problem is considerably more difficult to attempt for machining centres using indirect sensing techniques. For example, changes in the cutting forces on a milling tool are subject to frequent and large magnitude variation due to the varying cutter directions, feedrates and tool changes common in today's complex part manufacturing. It is difficult to get repeatable results for indirect methods across a wide range of milling machines, tooling, cutting conditions and part geometries commonly encountered.

Previous research has described the use of machine vision-based sensor systems for both tool breakage[3] detection and tool wear monitoring. Kurada and Bradley[4] employed an image texture analysis technique for flank wear monitoring of uncoated carbide tool inserts on a turning centre. A repeatable tool wear monitoring parameter was found to be the flank wear area

Part of the SPIE Conference on Sensors and Controls for Intelligent Machining and Agile Manufacturing
Boston, Massachusetts • November 1998
SPIE Vol. 3518 • 0277-786X/98/$10.00

17

obtained by first applying the Hurst operator to the grey level image. Weiss et al.[5] also employed a vision approach to monitoring the wear rate of cutter inserts on end mills; however, few details and results were documented. Park and Ulsoy[6] examined tool flank wear using a binary image analysis approach where scene illumination proved critical to achieving reliable image segmentation. The issue of tool and surface illumination was examined more closely by Leon[7] and recommendations were made for achieving suitable image contrast. Jeon and Kim[8] employed a laser beam to illuminate the tool's surface but encountered difficulties, using this structured light method, due to the surface irregularities found on the tool's surface. In this research, the flank wear on a milling tool insert is measured directly using a machine vision and illumination system.

2. TOOL WEAR PARAMETERS

There are two predominant wear mechanisms that limit the useful life of a cutting tool: flank wear and crater wear. Flank wear occurs on the relief face of the tool and is mainly attributed to the rubbing action of the tool on the machined surface. Crater wear occurs on the rake face of the tool and changes the chip-tool interface, thus affecting the cutting process. Tool wear increases progressively during machining, depending on the type of tool, material and cutting conditions. A typical flank wear profile is divided into three regions, as shown in Figure 1 and described below:

- Zone A – leading edge groove, which marks the outer end of the wear land.

- Zone B – A plateau consisting of uniform wear land.

- Zone C – Trailing groove which forms near the relief face and contributes to the surface roughness.

In traditional tool life monitoring, the maximum wear land width is used to measure the extent of the tool wear. The tool can continue to be used until the average value of V_B is greater than 0.3 mm. In this vision-based project, therefore, the tool wear is characterised by deriving the following morphological parameters from the wear image:

- Maximum wear land width, V_{Bmax}.

- Area of the wear land.

Both parameters are extracted from the CCD camera image by means of an image processing software package.

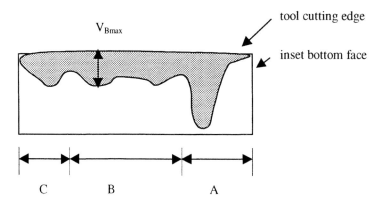

Figure 1. A typical flank wear profile.

3. EXPERIMENTAL SETUP

The video camera used in this project is a grey-level CCD camera with a ½-inch format, a pixel resolution of 752×582, and a minimal illumination classification of $\varnothing 2$ lux F1.2 (i.e., good performance even at low light levels). The camera was used in conjunction with a Tamron 75mm magnifying lens and at the focusing distance employed in this project (approximately 100 mm), the cutting tool edge occupied an area of 5mm by 5mm. The images were transferred to the video capture card mounted in a personal computer.

The sequence of steps employed to gather the images of the cutting tool insert and the manual wear measurements is described below:

- The images in the series were captured after each milling pass by moving the cutter (under CNC part program command) to a location in the work volume where the measurements were performed. At this location, the cutting tool's insert was correctly illuminated and in the precise position for the CCD camera to focus on the wear region.

- The wear image was captured and transferred to the computer via the image-capture card.

- The insert was removed from the end mill cutter and a manual tool wear measurement performed using a microscope.

- The insert was replaced in the cutter and the next milling pass was carried out.

- On completion of the entire milling process, the images were fed into the image processing software to perform the vision-based measurement of the wear parameters.

- Comparisons were then made between the traditional wear characteristic and the vision-based parameters.

During the image acquisition process, the insert was illuminated by a halogen lamp. The lamp was focused onto the wear region with minimum illumination of the rest of the insert's surface and the background. This was feasible by positioning the light source, outside of the machine tool's workspace, whereby it only illuminated the wear, as shown in Figure 2. The method is similar to that employed by Kurada and Bradley. As shown in the figure, the unworn insert surface area reflects light away from the lens giving the images illustrated in Figure 3.

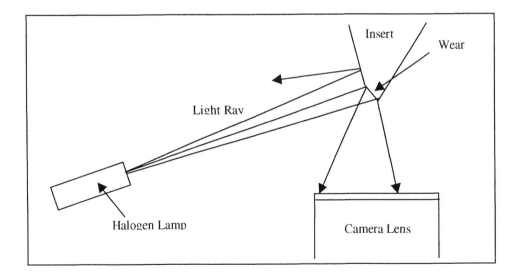

Figure 2. Position of light source for the illumination of the insert wear.

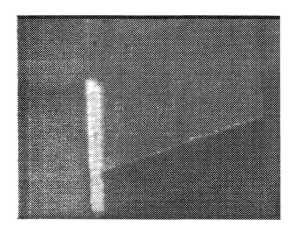

Figure 3. Image of tool insert with wear highlighted by halogen lamp illumination.

4. IMAGE PROCESSING

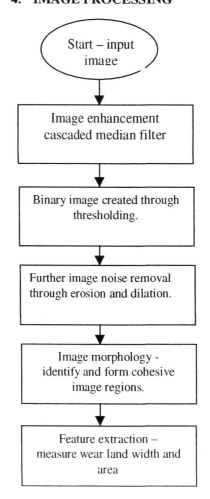

Figure 4. Flowchart of image processing algorithm.

The functions of the image processing modules, as illustrated in Figure 4, are to automatically isolate and measure the wear region in the following sequence of steps:

- The tool wear image was entered into the analysis software that initially performed an enhancement. A cascaded median filter (5x5 window) was applied to the image to remove the very bright and randomly located regions of specular reflection from the surface.

- The resulting image was applied to a thresholding algorithm to create a binary image. The still noisy image required further spatial domain processing before any quantitative analysis could be performed. A suitable threshold value was easily determined from several trial runs performed using the set-up.

- The erosion and dilation processes were performed consecutively on the binary image. These two operators had the net effect of removing remaining bright spots in the image. The number of erosion and dilation steps is dependent on the threshold value set previously. Again, after experimentation, the optimum number of iterations was readily determined.

- The image morphology process performed a connectivity analysis on the pixel run lengths present in the binary image. The algorithm proceeded at the top of the binary image and raster scanned to the bottom of the image collecting run lengths that represented a set of non-zero pixels. Any run length previously identified, and directly or diagonally above the current run-length, was considered part of the same object (i.e. 8-way connectivity). This process produced a binary "blob vector" where each element consists of a unique integer identifier and run length data described by a [start, end] X co-ordinate and row Y co-ordinate. The set of binary image blob vectors comprised the set of image features such as the tool wear region, remaining tool surface and any background pixels present.

- The feature extraction process examined the blob vectors and measured key features for each, such as centroid location, major and minor axes, bounding boxes, perimeter length etc. This step performed the measurement of the tool flank wear parameters, employed in this study, namely the maximum flank wear width and the wear area.

5. EXPERIMENTAL RESULTS

The experimental machining was performed on a Makino CNC milling machine using a Toshiba Tungaloy EGD 4450R 50-mm diameter milling cutter that takes up to four milling inserts. The milling inserts were Sumitomo SDEX 42MT-A30N tungsten carbide, suitable for milling steel. The workpiece material was ASSAB 718-grade pre-hardened and tempered mild steel.

The manually determined characteristics of the insert flank wear were compared with the corresponding vision system results. The vision system parameters employed were the maximum width M and the flank wear area A; both were determined in terms of image pixels. These two parameters were then compared against the flank wear measurement W measured using the microscope. Six separate experiments were carried out using either two or four inserts in the milling cutter and wear measurements performed on all the cutter inserts. The machining conditions are summarised in Table 1.

Table 1. Experimental conditions for the tool wear experiments.

	Spindle RPM	Feedrate (mm/min.)	Depth of Cut (mm)	Number of Inserts
1	1200	300	1	4
2	1200	350	1	4
3	900	350	1	2
4	900	250	1	2
5	1200	350	1	2
6	1200	250	1	2

The results of the six experiments have been combined and are summarised in Figure 5. The cutting tests were carried out with different machining parameters, in order to determine if the machine vision-deduced parameters emulated the tool wear measurements. The figure shows the average values, from each set of two or four inserts, of the vision parameters M and A, together with average values of the flank wear W, plotted against the cutting pass number. The inserts were inspected after every two cutting passes. To aid the visual comparison, the results have been plotted on a scaled graph.

The plots of Figure 5 indicate that both M and A exhibit a characteristic trend expected from a tool life measurement. Table 2 shows the average values for the maximum wear width M (in pixels) and the wear area A (presented as total number of pixels in the worn region) corresponding to a tool flank wear W of 0.3 mm.

Table 2. Average values for M and A when $W = 0.3$ mm.

Experiment No.	Vision Parameter	
	Maximum Width, M (Pixels)	Area, A (Pixels)
1	0.41	0.35
2	0.31	0.25
3	0.29	0.35
4	0.28	0.33
5	0.28	0.33
6	0.29	0.28

6. DISCUSSION OF RESULTS

An error analysis performed on the data has indicated that the maximum width parameter M is a more accurate and consistent wear predictor. Some of the major problems encountered in applying this method to flank wear measurement are discussed below:

- One source of error was the effect the rake face wear occasionally had on the flank wear measurement. The light source was positioned beneath the tool to give the most effective flank wear illumination. Since the rake face was also at the bottom of the tool, the presence of more severe rake face wear caused both the wear regions to be measured in the image.

- The flank wear process occasionally showed a tendency to erode into the insert; thereby removing areas of the illuminated flank wear region. Therefore, these darker regions in the flank wear area zone were not measured by the vision system. This is one reason for the area parameter to be less consistent than the maximum width.

- The presence of chips on the insert created black specks on the image, which were also included in the wear region. This caused the wear area measurement to be lower than actual and the problem was particularly acute near the worn-unworn interface, where most of the chips were gathered.

7. CONCLUSIONS

After appropriate image processing, two vision parameters were computed and employed in the measurement of tool wear based on the computer vision method: the maximum width M and area A parameters. From comparison with the actual measurement of the flank wear, the maximum width parameter was found to be a more accurate and consistent predictor of the flank wear than the area parameter.

REFERENCES

1. E. Kannatey-Asibu and D. A. Dornfield, "A Study of Tool Wear Using Statistical Analysis of Metal-Cutting Acoustic Emission", *Wear*, **76**, pp. 247-261, 1982

2. A. E. Diniz, J. J. Liu and D. A. Dornfield, "Correlating Tool Life, Tool Wear and Surface Roughness by Monitoring Acoustic Emission in Finish Turning", *Wear*, **152**, pp. 395-407, 1992

3. Jiri Tlusty and Y. S. Tarng, "Sensing Cutter Breakage in Milling", *Annals of the CIRP*, **37**, pp. 45-51, 1988

4. S. Kurada and C. Bradley, "A Machine Vision System for Tool Wear Assessment", *Tribology International*, **30**, No. 4, pp. 295-304, 1997

5. W. Weiss, A. Lengeling and V. Huntrup, "Automatisierte Werkzeuguberwachung und-vermessung beim Frasen mit Hilfbildverarbeitender Systeme", *Technisches Messen*, **61**, pp. 473-476, 1994.

6. J. J. Park and A. Galip Ulsoy, "On-line Flank Wear Estimation Using an Adaptive Observer and Computer Vision, Part 2: Experiment", *J. of Eng. For Ind.*, **115**, pp. 37-43, 1993.

7. F. Puente Leon, "Image Processing Methods for the Macroscopic Acquisition of High-Quality Images of Surfaces and Tools", *Proc. of 7th International Conference on Metrology and Properties of Engineering Surfaces*, pp. 252-259, 1997.

8. J.U. Jeon and S.W. Kim, "Optical Flank Wear Monitoring of Cutting Tools by Image Processing", *Wear*, **27**, pp. 207-217, 1988.

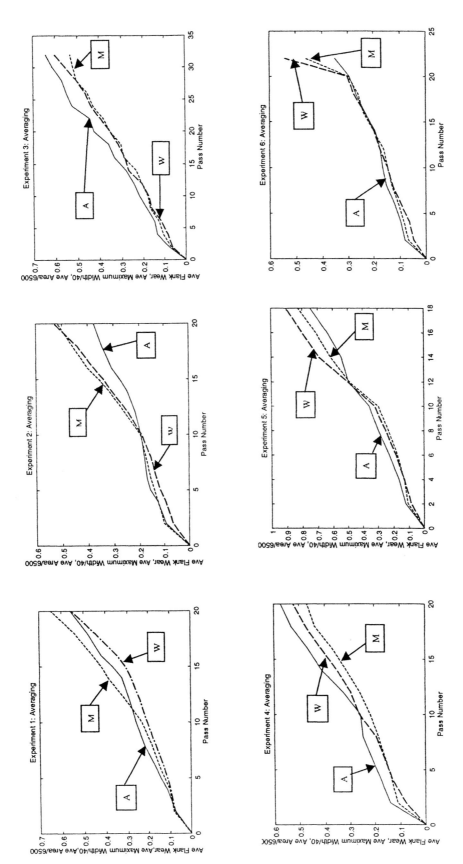

Figure 5. Summary of the results for the tool wear measuring experiments.

Fourier series analysis for in-process inspection of XFP SMT solder joints

Z. Zhang, J. C. Wang, and C. Lee

Manufacturing Engineering and Industrial Management, Department of Engineering
University of Liverpool, Brownlow Hill, Liverpool L69 3BX, UK

ABSTRACT

With the increased use of extra-fine-pitch (XFP) surface mounted components in electronic products, machine vision techniques for in-process inspection of solder joints during PCB assembly have become highly demanding. Existing algorithms for this purpose are mostly designed to perform inspection based on the analysis of 3-dimensional image profiles of individual solder joints. They are computation intensive and often result in expensive implementations. This work introduces a new approach to automated solder joint inspection. With this approach, the inspection problem is considered as a task of detecting textural distortions from the two-dimensional proper-view images of a printed circuit board. A real-time texture inspection algorithm based on Fourier Series Analysis is developed to carry out the inspection. The algorithm has been implemented and tested on a PC-based vision system. The results from the tests show that the proposed technique can perform practical PCB inspection successfully. This suggests that real-time and in-process inspection of XFP solder joints may be carried out by a low cost PC-based vision system. In this paper, the principles of Fourier Series Analysis are discussed and the proposed algorithm described. The usefulness of the algorithm in texture inspection in general, and PCB inspection in particular is investigated. The performances of the proposed technique are demonstrated on practical PCB inspection problems.

Keywords: Computer Vision, Texture Analysis, PCB Inspection, Image Processing, Electronics Manufacturing

1. INTRODUCTION

The rapid development of VLSI technology has enabled electronic circuit designers to come up with designs with higher device population and more I/O connections on a single printed circuit board than ever. One of the major breakthroughs, which have enabled such development, is the use of Surface Mount Devices (SMD) which are assembled to printed circuit boards without using through holes.

Recently, extra fine pitch (XFP) components based on Surface Mount Technology (SMT) have found wide spread use in electronic products, resulting in increasingly higher density of solder joints on PCBs. The advantage of using XFP is that the size and weight of an electronic product can be reduced through the increased density of joints. However, one of the major problems associated with the use of XFP components is the increased difficulty in performing solder joint inspection. It is claimed that the smaller the lead space and the stencil aperture, the more the solder defects. In order to ensure 100% reliability of the final products, it is important to incorporate in-process inspection in PCB manufacturing processes.

Solder joint inspection in PCB manufacture is mostly performed by human inspectors. High magnification optical equipment is used to assist human operators to inspect solder joints. PCBs are shifted and rotated during inspection to enable the inspectors to obtain important information. The images of solder joints are compared with a standard specification and individual joints classified into different categories such as good joints, shorts, excess solder, no solder, solder balls, and insufficient solder. This classification is also partly based on the knowledge and experience of inspectors. A study carried out by Fanelli and mentioned by Vanzetti and Traub[1] shows that one inspector, in examining the same PCB at two different times, came up with consistent judgements in only 44 % of cases. Two inspectors agree in 28% of cases,

Further author information –

Z.Z. (correspondence): Email: zhengwen.zhang@liv.ac.uk; WWW: http://www.liv.ac.uk/~indstud/staff/dzhang/dzhang.html; Telephone: (44) (0) 151-7944685; Fax: (44) (0) 151-7944693
J.C.W.: Email: jcw@liv.ac.uk; WWW: http://www.liv.ac.uk/~jcw
C.L.: Email: ching.lee@kla-tencor.com; Telephone: (1) 408-8755467; Fax: (1) 408-8752001

Part of the SPIE Conference on Sensors and Controls for Intelligent Machining and Agile Manufacturing
Boston, Massachusetts • November 1998
SPIE Vol. 3518 • 0277-786X/98/$10.00

25

three in 12%, and four in 6%. The repeatability of manual inspection is very low. Furthermore, the inspection results would vary with the mood, experience and personal interpretation skills of individual inspectors who are also venerable to eye fatigue, neck and back strain, etc.

In the last several years, techniques have been developed to automate solder joint inspection. These technologies may be broadly divided into four categories: stereo vision, structured light, X-ray, and dynamic characterisation.

With **stereo vision techniques,** inspection is typically performed by analysing PCB images captured from one or more CCD cameras. The two-dimensional shapes of individual solder joints being inspected are analysed to produce geometric measures (features) thought to correlate to the quality of joints. The features obtained from the image of a joint are compared with those of good joints to determine whether the joint is acceptable[2].

With **structured lighting techniques**, the 3D profiles of individual solder joints being inspected are obtained and compared with that of a good joint. The light sources used in detecting the 3D profiles of solder joints include laser and programmable LED banks. The techniques are based on the principle that the surface of a solder joint is specula and light projected to the surface will be reflected. The reflected light from the surface of a joint may be captured with a light sensor, such as a CCD camera. From the directions of the projected and reflected light, the surface orientation of a solder joint at various locations can be calculated and the 3D profile of the solder joint obtained. The geometrical characteristics of the solder joint can be measured from the 3D profile. Different systems have been introduced to collect data from the specula surface of solder joints. These include the colour highlight system[3,4,5,6,7], the LEDs array system[8], the fillet profile system[9,10,11,12,13], and the laser triangulation system[14,15,16].

With **X-ray techniques**, an X-ray beam is perpendicularly projected to a PCB and soldering defects detected by analysing the x-ray images obtained from the other side of the PCB. The techniques are based on the principle that solder joints attenuate the intensity of x-ray to a much greater degree than other parts of the circuit board and therefore the intensity variations in X-ray images can be analysed to determine the quality of solder joints. X-ray techniques provide a see-through ability, allowing faults such as voids in solder joints, broken internal traces, and other flaws to be detected. These defects would otherwise remain undetected by inspection schemes based on visible light or infrared light. Two different approaches to X-ray based inspection have been introduced in industry, transmission X-ray[17] and X-ray Laminography[18,19,20].

With **dynamic characterisation techniques**, the natural frequencies of individual solder joints are characterised and used as a basis for solder quality inspection. The natural frequencies of soldered and unsoldered leads of various types of chips (SOIC, PLCC, PQFP, etc.) are calculated using the finite element method[21] and experiments carried out to obtain the dynamic characteristics of the corresponding chips. It was shown that the fundamental frequency of all soldered leads is at least five times larger than those of unsoldered ones. Therefore vibration spectra could be used as an inspection criteria. By measuring the vibration of soldered leads under test using Laser Doppler Vibrometer (LDV), and comparing it with the natural frequencies of soldered leads, the quality of solder joints can be determined.

A common problem with the above techniques is that solder joints have to be inspected individually. Given that there are thousands of joints on a PCB, and this number is still growing with the development of ULSI technology, the computations involved can be prohibitive and the inspection process slow. This paper proposes to overcome the above problem based on textured image analysis. The two-dimensional images of a printed circuit board to be inspected are obtained using several CCD cameras. Solder joints of XFP components on the board are then inspected from the 2D images using a texture inspection algorithm based on Fourier Series Analysis.

2. FOURIER SERIES

Fourier texture descriptors have been widely used in digital image processing[22,23,24,25]. In the theorem of Fourier series[26,27], if $f(\theta)$ is a periodic function of θ, it is possible to find values of constants a_0, a_1, a_2,…a_n, b_1, b_2,…b_n so that

$$f(\theta) = \frac{a_0}{2} + a_1 \cos(\theta) + a_2 \cos(2\theta) + a_3 \cos(3\theta) + ... + a_n \cos(n\theta) +$$
$$b_1 \sin(\theta) + b_2 \sin(2\theta) + b_3 \sin(3\theta) + ... + b_n \sin(n\theta)$$

$$(1)$$

where n→∞. According to the above equation, a basic Fourier Series may be given as follows:

$$f(\theta) = \frac{a_0}{2} + \sum_{n=1}^{\infty} [a_n \cos(n\theta) + b_n \sin(n\theta)] \tag{2}$$

where

$$a_n = \frac{1}{\pi} \int_0^{2\pi} f(\theta) \cos(n\theta) d\theta \quad \text{where } n \geq 0 \tag{3}$$

$$b_n = \frac{1}{\pi} \int_0^{2\pi} f(\theta) \sin(n\theta) d\theta \quad \text{where } n \geq 1 \tag{4}$$

The above Fourier series function may be rewritten as:

$$\begin{aligned} f(\theta) = \frac{a_0}{2} &+ a_1 \cos(\theta) + b_1 \sin(\theta) + \\ &a_2 \cos(2\theta) + b_2 \sin(2\theta) + \\ &a_3 \cos(3\theta) + b_3 \sin(3\theta) + \dots\dots \end{aligned} \tag{5}$$

Let

$$S_0 = \frac{a_0}{2} = \frac{\int_0^{2\pi} f(\theta) d\theta}{2\pi} \tag{6}$$

$$S_n = a_n \cos(n\theta) + b_n \sin(n\theta) \tag{7}$$

and given $a_n = p_n \cos(\phi_n)$ and $b_n = p_n \sin(\phi_n)$ for n≥1, we have

$$\begin{aligned} S_n &= a_n \cos(n\theta) + b_n \sin(n\theta) \\ &= p_n \cos(\phi_n) \cos(n\theta) + p_n \sin(\phi_n) \sin(n\theta) \\ &= p_n \cos(n\theta - \phi_n) \end{aligned} \tag{8}$$

Function $f(\theta)$ can be presented as a series of cosine waves with different amplitudes (P_n), and different phase angles (ϕ_n). P_n and ϕ_n may be calculated from Equations (9) and (10)

$$p_n = \frac{a_n}{\cos(\phi_n)} \tag{9}$$

$$\phi_n = \tan^{-1}(\frac{b_n}{a_n}) \tag{10}$$

The above analysis has shown that any function in the period between 0 to 2π can be represented as a series of cosine waves with different amplitudes and phases angles, whose frequencies may vary from 0 to infinity.

3. THE EXTRACTION OF REGIONS OF SOLDER JOINTS FROM A PCB IMAGE

In order to apply Fourier Series Analysis to automated solder joint inspection, regions of solder joints have to be identified and obtained from a PCB image. This is carried out with an image processing algorithm shown in Figure 1. Various steps involved in the algorithm may be demonstrated using a test image shown in Figure 2, where the section of image (region) containing 30 solder joints (one side of a QFP chip) needs to be separated from other regions.

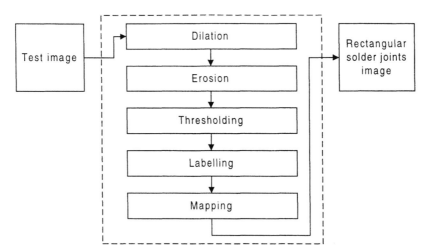

Figure 1. Extraction of regions of solder joints from a PCB image.

Figure 2. The image of a QFP chip on a PCB.

First, a dilation operation is carried out. This operation expands bright regions in the image and, as a result, connect solder joints together to form a single blob. Figure 3(a) shows the results after dilation, where all solder joints have been connected to form a white region. A problem with this operation is that the total size of the solder joint region is also expanded.

Following the dilation operation, an erosion operation is carried out. This operation expands the sizes of dark regions in an image. As a result, the solder joint region is restored to its original size, as shown in Figure 3(b).

The resulting image after dilation and erosion is a grey intensity image in which different objects fall into different ranges of intensities. The histogram of the image after dilation and erosion is shown in Figure 3(c). There are three types of intensity regions in the histogram:

➤ Dark regions representing the black plastic package of the QFP chip and the shadow of components on the PCB.
➤ Grey regions representing the PCB and the pad of solder joints which has no solder.
➤ Bright regions representing solder joints and labels (the written characters) on the PCB.

The region of interest is the section containing solder joints, which are farthest from other regions in the histogram. A thresholding operation is then applied to separate the solder joints regions from other regions. The result after thresholding is shown in Figure 3(d), where the white regions in the image represent one side of the QFP chip (solder joints), some individual solder joints and labels on the board.

Following the thresholding operation, the region of interest (i.e. solder joints on a side of QFP chip) needs to be distinguished from other bright regions. This is carried out by a labelling operation which assigns a number to each region in the image and lists up the number of pixels in each region. The region of interest (i.e., one side of a chip) will naturally correspond to the region with maximum number of pixels.

Once the quadrilateral region of solder joints has been selected, the four points corresponding to the top, bottom, left, and right corners of the region are identified by finding the pixel locations with minimum y, maximum y, minimum x, and maximum x in the image. With the four corner points, the quadrilateral region of the solder joints can be marked as shown in Figure 3(e). A rectangular image of the solder joint region can be reconstructed. The top-left corner of the new image corresponds to the left point of the quadrilateral region, the top-right corner of the new image to the top point of the quadrilateral region, the bottom-left corner of the new image to the bottom point of the quadrilateral region, and the bottom-right corner of the new image to the right point of the quadrilateral region. The resulting image is shown in Figure 3(f).

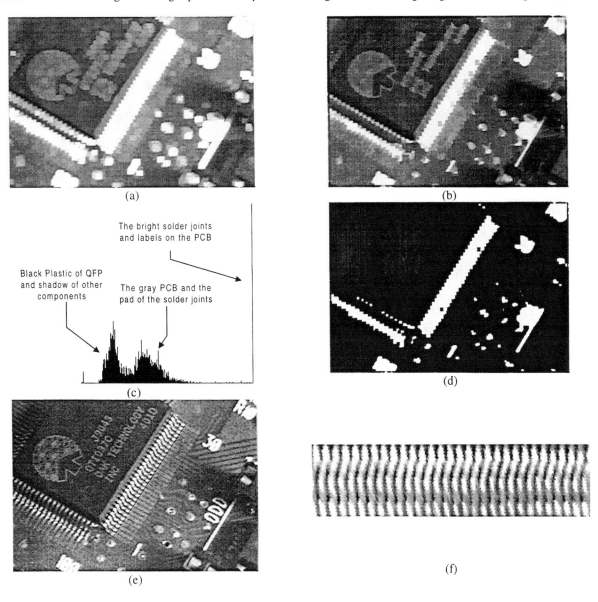

Figure 3. The steps involved in extracting regions of solder joints from the PCB image shown in Figure 2. (a) The image after dilation. (b) The image after erosion. (c) The histogram of the image in (b). (d) The image after thresholding. (e) The marked quadrilateral region of solder joints. (f) The reconstructed rectangular image of solder joints.

4. CHARACTERISING SOLDER JOINT IMAGES WITH FOURIER SERIES

As shown in Figure 3(f), the image of solder joints displays a property similar to that of a periodic function. The solder joint repeats itself in every pitch distance horizontally. Considering a row of pixels in the rectangular image, the intensity function along the row will be a perfect periodic function for normal solder joints. However, if defective joints are present in the image, pixels on the defects would appear as low frequency noises in the periodic function. These noises may be separated from other parts once the function is decomposed into cosine waves with various frequencies and phase angles. This suggests that solder joints could be characterised with Fourier series.

Figure 4(a) and Figure 4(b) show two 64×256 solder joints images, one with a bridge defect and the other defect-free. Following the theory discussed in section 2, the intensity function along each row in the two images may be represented by a series of cosine waves with frequencies varying from 0 to infinity. Theoretically, all frequencies from 0 to infinity need to be used to fully represent a function. In practice, a limited number of frequencies may be able to represent a function with sufficient accuracy.

Figure 4(c) and 4(d) show the amplitudes of the first 64 cosine waves (corresponding to frequencies from 0 to 63) of the intensity functions along the rows of the two images shown in Figure 4(a) and 4(b). It may be seen that the amplitudes of cosine waves with frequencies near 0 and 30 are greater. This is expected since the waves with frequencies near 0 represent the average values of the intensity functions while those with frequencies near 30 represent the textural patterns of solder joints (the number of solder joints along each row is 30). The cosine waves may therefore be broadly divided into four frequency ranges. The first set of waves, corresponding to frequencies from 0 to 2, represents average intensity in each intensity function. The second set, corresponding to frequencies from 3 to 20, represents the low frequency elements of each intensity function. The third set, corresponding to frequencies from 21 to 40, represents the textural property of solder joints in each function, and the fourth, corresponding to frequencies from 41 to 63, represents the high frequency elements of each intensity function.

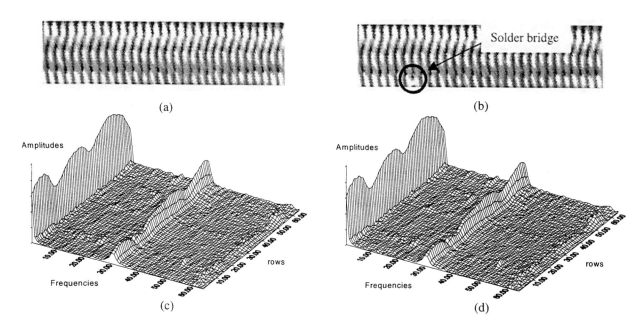

Figure 4. The intensity function and the frequency elements of the testing image. (a) is a solder joints image without defect. (b) is a solder joints image with a bridge defect. (c) is the frequency elements of the image in Figure 4(a). (d) is the frequency elements of the image in Figure 4(b).

Four new intensity functions may be created by adding together the cosine waves within each of the four frequency ranges, which may be defined here as the *Component Functions* of the original intensity function. Defects, if any, would appear as low frequency elements and therefore should be able to be identified from the *Component Function* corresponding to the low frequency range (3 to 20). This is confirmed in Figure 5, where two intensity functions corresponding to the 5th row (the location of the bridge defect in Figure 4(b)) of images shown in Figure 4(a) and (b), together with their corresponding *Component Functions* are plotted. It can be seen that the bridge defect in Figure 4(b) may be detected from the profile of the low frequency component function by thresholding, as shown in Figure 5(d).

To use the process discussed above for defect detection, the low frequency component function corresponding to every row of pixels in the original image must be calculated. These functions may then be used as rows to construct an image which can then be thresholded to detect the defects. One problem is that component functions corresponding to different rows in the original image may have different intensity levels therefore a global threshold value may not be appropriate. This problem may be solved by using different threshold values for different component functions. The threshold value for each component function is selected as a percentage of the maximum intensity value of the function (i.e., the sum of magnitudes of relevant cosine waves). In this way, the parameter used to control the thresholding operation will be the percentage value.

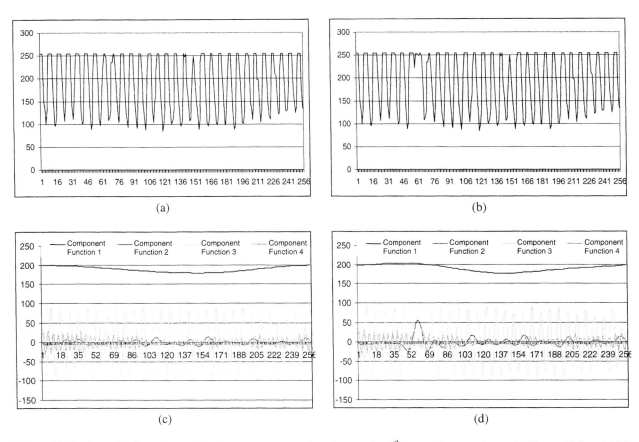

Figure 5. The intensity functions and relevant component functions at the 5th row of images shown in Figure 4(a) and 4(b). (a) is the intensity function of the image in Figure 4(a) at row 5. (b) is the intensity function of the image in Figure 4(b) at row 5. (c) is the profiles of component functions for the intensity function shown in (a). (d) is the profiles of component functions for the intensity function shown in (b).

Figure 6 shows the flow-chart of the algorithm discussed above. Two parameters need to be determined to set-up the algorithm for practical solder joint inspection problems. One is the low frequency range, and the other the percentage value to be used in the thresholding operation. Figure 7 shows the resulting images after applying the algorithm to images shown in Figure 4. The frequency range used was 3 to 20 and the threshold 75%.

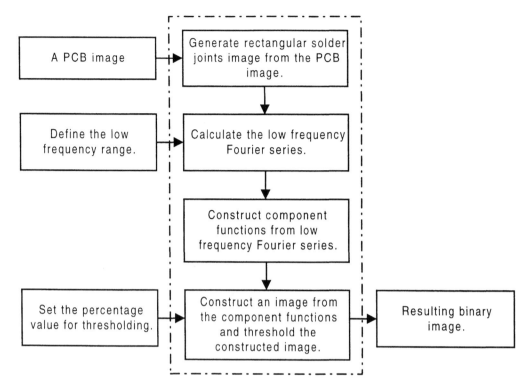

Figure 6. The flowchart of the inspection algorithm.

(a)   (b)

Figure 7. The result of the inspection. (a) is the result on the image shown in Figure 4(a). (b) is the result on the image shown in Figure 4(b). The frequency range used was 3-20 and threshold value 75%.

5. EXPERIMENTAL RESULTS

The algorithm proposed in the last section is tested for practical use in XFP solder joint inspection. Figure 8 shows two images of a soldered MC68360 XFP QFP taken from different direction. The images are processed according to the algorithm proposed in section 2 to obtain rectangular images of solder joints shown in Figure 9(a), 9(b), 9(c), and 9(d). For demonstration purposes, only the bottom 1/3 (where defects exist) instead of the full images of solder joints are shown. The selected low frequency range was 4 to 15 and the percentage value used in thresholding was 80%. The final results of inspection of the four sides of the MC68360 XFP QFP chip are shown in Figure 10(a), 10(b), 10(c), and 10(d).

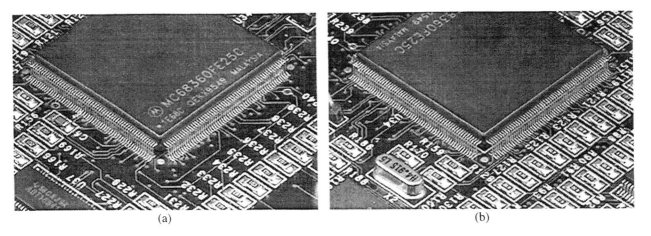

(a)   (b)

Figure 8. An XFP QFP chip. (a) shows two sides of solder joints and (b) shows two other sides of solder joints.

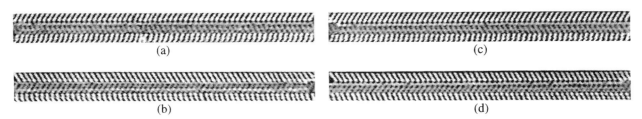

(a)   (c)

(b)   (d)

Figure 9. The reconstructed rectangular images of solder joints. (a) is the image of solder joints at the left side of the XFP chip shown in Figure 8(a). (b) is the image of solder joints at the right side of the XFP chip shown in Figure 8(a). (c) is the image of solder joints at the left side of the XFP chip shown in Figure 8(b). (d) is the The image of solder joints at the right side of the XFP chip shown in Figure 8(b).

(a)   (c)

(b)   (d)

Figure 10. The result of solder joint inspection. (a) is the inspection result on the image shown in Figure 9(a). (b) is the inspection result on the image shown in Figure 9(b). (c) is the inspection result on the image shown in Figure 9(c). (d) is the inspection result on the image shown in Figure 9(d).

As shown in Figure 10(a) and (d), two solder defects (one solder bridge and the other insufficient solder) have been detected successfully.

6. DISCUSSIONS AND CONCLUSIONS

An algorithm has been proposed to perform automated inspection of solder joints based on Fourier analysis and its performance demonstrated on practical inspection problems. The algorithm assumed that there were only few defects on each side of a soldered XFP QFP chip and the texture pattern of defects was different from that of normal solder joints. Defects were detected by analysing the low frequency elements of a Fourier series. The advantage of the algorithm is that joints on one side of a XFP chip can be inspected simultaneously therefore the speed of inspection can be high. Solder joint inspection may therefore be carried out with a low cost PC based vision system.

7. REFERENCES

1. R. Vanzetti and A. C. Traub, "Combining Soldering with Inspection", *IEEE Control Systems Magazine*, Oct., pp. 29-32, 1988.
2. S. Jagannathan, S. Balakrishnan, and N. Popplewell, "Visual inspection of soldered joints by using neural networks", *IEEE International Joint Conference on Neural Networks*, pp. 7-12, 1991.
3. S. Kobayashi, Y. Tanimura, and T. Yotsuya, "Identifying Solder Surface Orientation from Color Highlight Images", *IECON, 16th annual conf. of IEEE Industrial Electronics Society*, pp. 821-825, 1990.
4. H. H. Loh and M. S. Lu, "SMD Inspection Using Structured Light", IECON Proceedings, pp. 1076-1081, 1996.
5. J. H. Kim and H. S. Cho, "Neural network-based inspection of solder joints using a circular illumination", *Image and Vsion Computing*, Vol. 13, No. 6, August, pp. 479-490, 1995.
6. T. H. Kim, T. H. Cho, Y. S. Moon, and S. H. Park, "Automatic Inspection of Solder Joints Using Layered Illumination", *IEEE International Conference on Image Processing*, Vol. 2, pp. 645-648, 1996.
7. T. H. Kim, T. H. Cho, Y. S. Moon, and S. H. Park, "Automatic Inspection of Solder Joints Using 2D and 3D features", *IEEE Workshop on Applications of Computer Vision*, pp. 645-648, 1996.
8. S. K. Nayar, A. C. Sanderson, L. E. Weiss, and D. A. Simon, "Specular Surface Inspection Using Structured Highlight and Gaussian Images", *IEEE Transactions on Robotics and Automation*, Vol. 6, No. 2, pp. 208-218, 1990.
9. T. Muraoka and C. Rice, "Applications of Laser Systems in Post Solder Inspection Equipment", *IECON, 16th annual conf. of IEEE Industrial Electronics Society*, pp. 805-810, 1990.
10. Y. K. Ryu and H. S. Cho, "Visual inspection scheme for use in optical solder joint inspection system", *IEEE International Conference on Robotics and Automation*, Vol. 5, pp. 3259-3264, 1996.
11. Y. K. Ryu and H. S. Cho, "Neural Network Approach to Solder Joint Inspection on Printed Circuit Board", *Proceedings of the Japan/USA Symposium on Flexible Automation*, Vol. 2, pp. 1445-1452, 1996.
12. Y. K. Ryu and H. S. Cho, "Neural Network Approach to Extended Gaussian Image Based Solder Joint Inspection", *Mechatronics*, Vol. 7, No. 2, pp. 159-184, 1997.
13. Y. K. Ryu and H. S. Cho, "New optical measuring system for solder joint inspection", *Optics and Lasers in Engineering*, Vol. 26, No. 6, pp. 487-514, 1997.
14. K. Yoshimura and S. Okamoto, "A Three-Dimensional Sensor for Automatic Visual Inspection of Soldered Parts", *IECON, 15th annual conf. of IEEE Industrial Electronics Society*, pp. 562-567, 1989.
15. J. Yano, O. Yamada, E. Hiraoka, and K. Kaida, "3-D Visual Inspecter of PCB using Laser", *IECON, 16th annual conf. of IEEE Industrial Electronics Society*, pp. 811-814, 1990.
16. T. Doiron, D. D. Pinsky, S. Chen, and M. Plott, "An SPC Artifact for Automated Solder Joint Inspection", *Measurement: Journal of the International Measurement Conference*, Vol. 12, No. 1, pp. 1-8, 1993.
17. B. L. Pierce, D. J. Shelton, H. G. Longbotham, S. Baddipudi, and P. Yan, "Automated Inspection of Through Hole Solder Joints Utilizing X-ray Imaging", *IEEE Proceedings of AUTOTEXTCON*, pp. 191-196, 1993.
18. R. J. Kruse and R. H. Bossi, "X-ray Tomographic Inspection Techniques on Electrical Components and PWA's", *IECON, 17th annual conf. of IEEE Industrial Electronics Society*, pp. 1761-1769, 1991.
19. A. R. Kalukin, V. Sankaran, B. Chartrand, D. L. and Millard, "An Improved Method for Inspection of Solder Joints Using X-ray Laminography and X-ray Microtomography", *Proceedings of the IEEE/CPMT International Electronic Manufacturing Technology (IEMT) Symposium*, p.p. 438-445, 1996.
20. C. Neubauer, "Intelligent X-ray Inspection for Quality Control of Solder Joints", *IEEE Trans. on Components, Packaging, and Manufacturing Technology – Part C*, Vol. 20, No. 2, p.p. 111-120, 1997.
21. J. H. Lau and C. A. Keely, "Dynamic Characterization of Surface-Mount Component Leads for Solder Joint Inspection", *IEEE Trans. on Components, Hybrids, and Manufacturing Technology*, Vol. 12, No. 4, p.p. 594-602, 1989.
22. S. L. Tanimoto, "An Optimal Algorithm for Computing Fourier Texture Descriptors", *IEEE Trans. Computer*, No. 1, pp. 81-84, 1978.
23. C. R. Dyer and A. Rosenfeld, "Fourier Texture Features: Suppression of Aperture Effects", *IEEE Trans. Systems, Man. and Cybernetics*, pp. 703-705, 1976.
24. D. D. Day and D. Rogers, "Fourier-Based Texture Measures with Application to the Analysis of the Cell Structure of Baked Products", *Digital Signal Processing*, No. 3, pp. 138-144, 1996.
25. R. Azencott, J. P. Wang, and L. Younes, "Texture Classification Using Windowed Fourier Filters", *IEEE Trans. Pattern Analysis and Machine Intelligence*, No. 2, pp. 148-153, 1997.
26. A. Jeffrey, *Mathematics for Engineers and Scientists*, 4th Ed., Chapter 16, Chapman and Hall, 1989.
27. E. Kreyszig, *Advanced Engineering Mathematics*, 7th Ed., Chapter 10, John Wiley and Sons, New York, 1993.

A Low Cost, Digital Signal Processor Based
Optical Position Sensor And Its Application To Vibration Control

Timothy N. Chang and Thomas J. Spirock
Department of Electrical & Computer Engineering,
New Jersey Institute of Technology

Key words: vibration control, optical position sensor, digital signal processor, robot, flexible beam.

ABSTRACT

A low cost, Digital Signal Processor (DSP) based optical position sensor and control system was developed on this work for the vibration control of flexible structures and assembly workcells. This system is based on Texas Instruments' TL220/230 programmable light-to-frequency converters which are interfaced to a TI TMS320C25 DSP. The sensor is a standard 8-pin dip powered by a single DC supply so that it may be mounted on robots or other industrial machines without causing any loading or perturbations. Effects of additive noise are also minimized as the sensor output is pulse position modulated TTL signals.

1. INTRODUCTION

In vibration control problems, sensor selection and deployment can significantly affect the performance of the closed loop system. Factors such as sensor size/weight, bandwidth, stability, range/resolution, cost, and reliability determine, to a large extent, the selection of sensor. In this work, a low cost optoelectronic photodetector chip (the Texas Instruments TSL220 and TSL230) is adapted for use as position sensor for vibration control problems. Besides being non-contacting, this low cost photodetector chip possesses a number of advantages: 1) high stability, 2) frequency modulated TTL output, 3) high bandwidth. However, light intensity based position sensors generally required an optically stable environment to minimize interference. In an industrial environment, such "laboratory-type" condition is not always possible and pulse-modulated light may be used to reject interference from ambient lights. However, the corresponding analog modulation-demodulation process can be too costly for many applications. In this work, a fixed-point digital signal processor (the Texas Instruments TMS320C25) is coupled with several TSL220/230's to form a complete sensor system that can support multi-axis position detection. It is estimated a complete three-axis system can be realized with less than $100.

The organization of this paper is as follows: First, a description of the hardware is given (the optical sensor modules, the laser-diode - module, the DSP, and the test setup for the vibration control experiment). Second, software development is discussed (signal processing of sensor output, host interface, and program for the vibration control experiment). Third, test results of the sensor are presented (drift, short-range, and long-range properties). Finally, vibration control is acrried out on a flexible beam system and results summarized (transient characteristics and steady state-accuracy).

2. HARDWARE DEVELOPMENT

A block diagram of the experimental hardware is shown in Figure 1 . It consists of 1) laser diode source, 2) optoelectronic sensor module, 3) TMS320C25 based digital signal processing board, and 4) host PC. The stationary laser diode, power-modulated by a 500Hz sine wave, illuminates a mobile light sensor module. The light sensor module comprises of a TSL220 light sensor and interface electronics. The TMS320C25 Digital Signal Processor (DSP) performs the following tasks: 1) Modulate the laser diode, 2) Sample the signal from the sensor module, 3) Demodulate the sensor signal, and 4) Pass the results to the host PC for future signal processing.

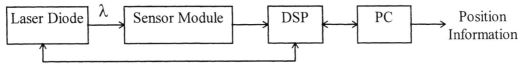

Figure 1: Hardware structure of the sensor system.

Part of the SPIE Conference on Sensors and Controls for Intelligent Machining and Agile Manufacturing
Boston, Massachusetts ● November 1998
SPIE Vol. 3518 ● 0277-786X/98/$10.00

2.1 Light Sensor Module

The heart of the sensor module is the TSL220 light intensity to frequency converter chip from Texas Instruments. The TSL220 consists of a photo-diode and a current-to-frequency converter. The output voltage is a pulse train whose frequency is directly proportional to the incident light intensity on the photodiode. The output frequency range is determined by an external capacitor; so that the desired output frequency is adjustable for a given intensity of light.

2.2 Laser Diode Module

The light source which illuminates the light sensor modules is a Panasonic LN9705 laser diode. The LN9705 is a visible red GaAlAs laser diode with a nominal illumination wavelength of 670nm. Automatic power control is possible by utilizing a built-in pin photodiode to monitor light power. The primary source of noise on the light sensor is the overhead fluorescent room lights which is left on to create a more realistic environment. The frequency of oscillation of the laser diode was chosen to be 500Hz so that it is sufficiently far enough away from the frequency of the room lights for demodulating purposes.The TMS320C25 Digital Signal Processor generates the signal to modulate the laser diode. The signal consists of a 500Hz sine wave with an amplitude of 0.2 volts and a 2.6 volt DC bias.

2.3 TMS320C25 Digital Signal Processor

The TMS320C25 Digital Signal Processor (DSP) from Texas Instruments is used for sensor signal demodulation and conditioning, laser modulation, and real time control. It is located on a development plug-in card in the host PC. The DSP development card has the following peripherals: An internal timer with 0.1us resolution, eight analog input channels multiplexed to an A/D, two independent analog output channels, 128K words of dual-ported memory which is simultaneously accessible to both the DSP and the host PC. The DSP program is executed concurrently with the host PC.

2.4 Data Sampling Interface

One advantage of the TSL220/230 optoelectronics sensor is its TTL output which can be transmitted over a relatively long distance without suffering signal degradation. At the DSP interface, the sensor signal can be processed by means of time sampling or analog sampling. The time sampling approach uses the DSP's internal timer to clock the pulse stream generated by the sensor. In the analog sampling method the pulse stream from the sensor is first passed through a 500Hz analog bandpass filter (BPF) to extract the carrier's fundamental harmonic which is then sampled by the A/D. Figures 2 and 3 illustrate the block diagrams of the two sampling schemes. Both sampling schemes have relative merits over the other. The main advantage of the time sampling scheme is that it samples the time between successive pulses from the TSL220/230down to the timer resolution with no external analog circuits. However, this method has two disadvantages, non-uniform sampling and signal inversion, which can be solved by implementing time consuming assembly codes. The analog sampling method, requires more external circuitry but is more flexible and quicker to prototype. This approach is used in this work to investigate the properties of the sensor system.

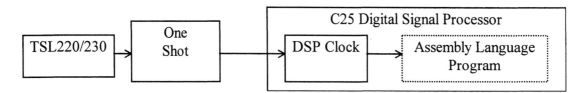

Figure 2: Block diagram of the Time Sampling scheme.

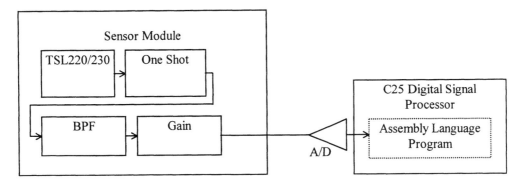

Figure 3: Block diagram of the Analog Sampling scheme.

2.5 Sensor Calibration

Sensor calibration is the first experiment to be performed. A block diagram of the setup that was used to test the sensor system is shown in Figure 4.

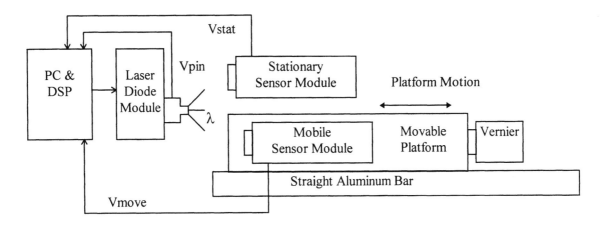

Figure 4: Block diagram of the one-dimensional testing setup.

The laser diode, modulated at 500 Hz by the DSP, illuminates two TSL220 sensor modules. One module is setup on a stationary mount which is used to monitor the intensity of the laser diode. The second module is mounted on a platform that can be moved towards and away from the laser diode for either short range or long range tests. For the short range test, the platform can be moved over a range of 12.5mm with a repeatability of approximately +/-0.01mm. For the long range test, the platform can be moved over a range of approximately 600mm with a repeatability of approximately +/-1mm.

2.6 Flexible Beam Control Experiment

The characteristics of the sensor is further tested in a flexible beam control experiment where a sensor module is mounted at the end of a type 304 flexible stainless steel beam, approximately 1500 mm long, 25 mm wide, and 6 mm thick. The position of the flexible beam is controlled by a brushless DC motor mounted in a vertical position on a platform as shown in Figure 5. The goal of control is to rotate the beam to a reference angle while suppressing flexural vibration and actuator transient response.

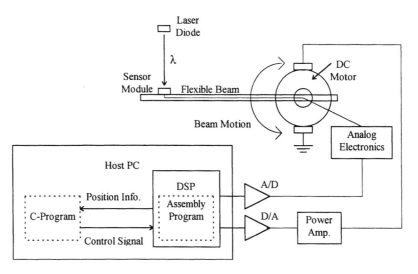

Figure 5: Block diagram of the flexible beam setup.

3. SOFTWARE DEVELOPMENT

3.1 General Description
The C25 Digital Signal Processor (DSP) executes the sensor signal demodulation program while synchronously pulsing the laser diode. The PC provides the interface between the user and the DSP by executing the DSP's debugger or a C-program which can access the information in the DSP's external data memory area.

3.2 C25 Digital Signal Processor Software
The main assembly language program in the DSP is responsible for modulating the laser diode intensity and demodulating the TSL220 light sensor signals. It is written in Texas Instruments C2x assembly language. Upon reset, the program sets up all of the necessary initialization and house keeping tasks such as: define and label memory locations; define the interrupt vector table; enable the proper interrupts; set the A/D sampling frequency; set up the sine table and sine table pointers; define the digital filter coefficients; and define the laser modulation voltages.

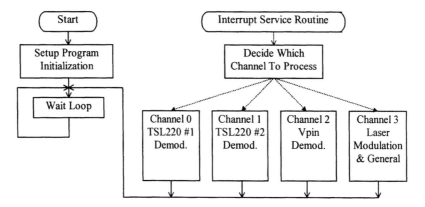

Figure 6: Structure of the DSP Software

All of the signal processing takes place in the interrupt service routine. After initialization, the DSP enters into a loop and waits for the interrupt trigger to occur. The interrupt trigger originates from the A/D. Its arrival signals the completion of the conversion process whose conversion rate is governed by an external programmable timer mapped to port zero of the DSP. There are four channels of program code. Each channel is executed, in succession, at 10KHz resulting in 25us/channel of loop time.

The first task of the interrupt service routine is to determine which channel to process during the current interrupt. A description of the tasks executed by the channels is as follows: Channel Zero and Channel One are responsible for the synchronous demodulation of the reference and target sensor module signals. Channel Two is responsible for the synchronous demodulation of the laser power feedback signal from the laser diode's built-in photodiode monitor. Finally, Channel Three is responsible for the modulation of the laser diode and communicating with the host PC. Functionally, the Channel Zero, One, and Two programs are identical. The only difference is that they sample and perform synchronous demodulation on different input signals. A flow chart for the Channel Zero, One and Two Programs is shown in Figure 7.

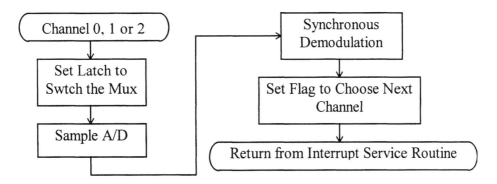

Figure 7: Flow chart of Channels Zero, One & Two.

The first operation of each channel is to set the input Multiplexer (Mux) to the next input channel. The Channel Zero program and the Channel One program read in the sampled signals via the A/D from the mobile and the stationary sensor modules respectively. The Channel Two program, on the other hand reads in the sampled feedback signal form the laser diode. A block diagram of the A/D's data acquisition system is shown in Figure 8.

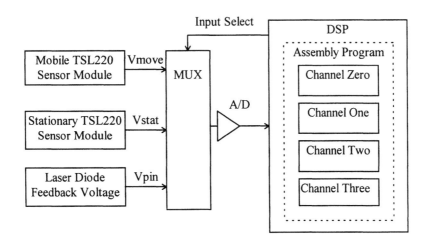

Figure 8: Block diagram of the data interface.

After sampling, synchronous demodulation is performed on each signal. The result is then stored in a memory location where it can be fetched by a C-program running on the host PC and stored on disk.

3.3 Synchronous Demodulation Implementation
The demodulation process recovers the incident laser intensity from the sensor module while rejecting ambient room light. The demodulator, shown in Figure 9, consists of five sets of sub-components: a bandpass filter, two multipliers, two lowpass filters, two elliptic filters, two squarers, and a summer.

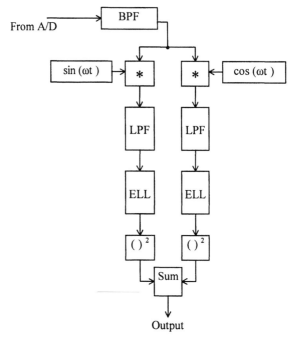

Figure 9: Structure of synchronous demodulation scheme.

The bandpass filter has a center frequency of 500Hz and Q=25. The transfer function of the bandpass filter is shown in (1):

$$\frac{Dout\_bpf(z)}{D\_in(z)} = \frac{0.006244 - 0.006244\,z^{-2}}{1 - 1.89027\,z^{-1} + 0.987511\,z^{-2}} \tag{1}$$

An elliptic filter is synthesized to remove the double carrier frequency component (1KHz). However, due to finite word length effects, it is necessary to add a lowpass prefilter to avoid signal saturation in the elliptic filter. The lowpass filter is a first order Butterworth filter with a cutoff frequency of 100Hz. The transfer function of the lowpass filter is shown in (2):

$$\frac{Vout\_lpf(z)}{Vin\_lpf(z)} = \frac{0.030468 + 0.030468\,z^{-1}}{1 - 0.939062\,z^{-1}} \tag{2}$$

At this point in the demodulation scheme, the signal consists of the desired DC component and the second harmonic component (1KHz). The purpose of the elliptic filter is to significantly attenuate the second harmonic component (1KHz). The elliptic filter is a second order filter with 3db of ripple in the passband, 20db of attenuation in the stopband and a notch frequency of 1KHz. The transfer function of the elliptic filter is given in (3):

$$\frac{Vout\_ell(z)}{Vout\_lpf(z)} = \frac{0.100783 - 0.162863\,z^{-1} + 0.100783\,z^{-2}}{1 - 1.795105\,z^{-1} + 0.849777\,z^{-2}} \tag{3}$$

3.4 Laser Modulation

Channel Three software is designed to modulate the laser diode at 500 Hz and to copy the outputs of the demodulation routines to the DSP's external memory where it can be accessed by a C-program running on the host PC. The laser diode is powered by a sine wave voltage with an amplitude of 0.2 volts added to a 2.6 volt DC bias. Within the fixed point DSP, the laser voltage is calculated according to (4) where 2048 is the bias value for the 12-bit DAC which has a range of −5 to +5 Volts mapped numerically from 0 to 4095. A block diagram illustrating the modulating algorithm is given in Figure 10.

$$V\_laser = \frac{80 \times \sin\theta}{4096} + 1077 + 2048 \tag{4}$$

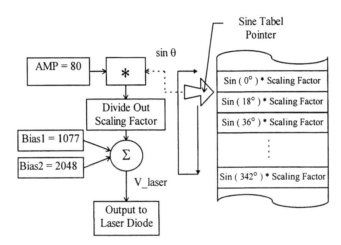

Figure 10: Block diagram of the laser diode modulation scheme.

3.5 Control Program

Two control algorithms are used: a standard Position, Integral and Derivative (PID) control and a variable gain PID. The standard PID is chosen as a benchmark algorithm because of its widespread usage in robot control. For faster response, methods such as robust servo-control [4] and optimal input shaper [5] can be applied. The equation of the standard PID is given in (5) and (6) where Y and Y_{REF} denote the sample position and reference position of the beam while U represents the output of the controller.

$$INT(i) = INT(i-1) + E(i) \tag{5}$$
$$U(i) = K_P [Y(i) - Y_{REF}] + K_D [D(i) - D(i-1)] + K_I [INT(i)] \tag{6}$$

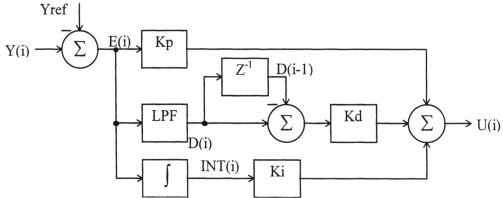

Figure 11: Structure of the standard PID control.

To improve the dynamic response of the flexible beam system, a variable gain control program was implemented. If the error signal is large, the PID gains will be small while if the error signal is small the PID gains will be large. This implementation will help improve transient response of the flexible beam if the error signal is large but will improve the steady state error of the position of the flexible beam when the error signal is small. To prevent division by zero in the variable gain equations, the current error value ($E(i)$) is replaced by the previous error value ($E(i-1)$) if it is zero. The equations for the variable PID gains are shown in (8), (10) and (12). Each gain is also upper and lower bounded by (9), (11) and (13).

$$\text{If } E(i) = 0 \text{ then } E(I) = E(i-1) \tag{7}$$
$$K_{PV}(i) = K_P / E(i) \tag{8}$$
$$K_P / 2 < K_{PV} < 2\,K_P \tag{9}$$
$$K_{DV}(i) = K_D / E(i) \tag{10}$$
$$K_D / 2 < K_{DV} < 2\,K_D \tag{11}$$
$$K_{IV}(i) = K_I / E(i) \tag{12}$$
$$K_I / 10 < K_{IV} < 10\,K_I \tag{13}$$
$$U(i) = K_{PV}\,[Y(I) - Y_{REF}] + K_{DV}\,[D(i) - D(i-1)] + K_{IV}\,[INT(i)] \tag{14}$$

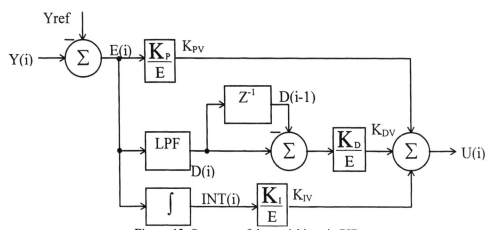

Figure 12: Structure of the variable gain PID

4. SENSOR CALIBRATION AND TESTING

A number of calibration tests are conducted to determine, quantitatively, the characteristics of the sensor modules. These tests include: 1) Time stability, 2) Short range accuracy, and 3) Long range accuracy. Two sensor modules are used: a stationary unit that monitors the intensity of the laser diode at a fixed distance and a second unit that is mounted on a mobile target. The position information is then derived ratiometrically. To check the time stability of the sensor, a drift test is performed at the same position over thirty minutes. Sensor noise sigma is found to be about 0.0006 which translates to a position uncertainty of 0.23 mm RMS. There are no detectable drifts in the sensor during repeated testing. Both the short and long range tests are then performed by applying polynomial interpolation to form a calibration curve which is checked against a new set of position data.

The short-range test is defined for a range of 12.5mm. The position repeatability of the calibration platform is +/-0.01mm. A 2nd order polynomial generated from the calibration data for the short range test is shown in (15). The calibration curve for the short-range test is shown in Figure 13. The solid line is constructed by linearly interpolating the verification data taken at positions indicated by the asterisks. The dashed line, on the other hand, is generated by (15). Pstat represents the ratiometric sensor output. The error between the predicted and the actual position, is plotted in Figure 14.

$$\text{Location (mm)} = 101.1071 \, \text{Pstat}^2 - 21.2036 \, \text{Pstat} - 41.1373 \tag{15}$$

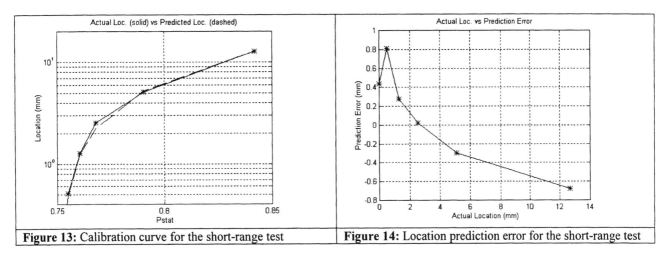

Figure 13: Calibration curve for the short-range test	Figure 14: Location prediction error for the short-range test

From the above standard deviation the location of the mobile sensor module can be predicted to within an uncertainty of approximately 0.5 mm.

The system is also tested for its ability to predict the position of the mobile sensor module over a range of approximately 600mm. In this case, the calibration platform has a position uncertainty of about +/- 1mm. The method for determining the calibration polynomial and prediction data set is the same as for the short range test. However, the order of the calibration polynomials has also been increased to the 4th power to better fit the data over the expanded operating range. A typical calibration polynomial is given in (16) and the corresponding calibration curve is shown in Figure 15. The solid lines are constructed by linearly interpolating the verification data taken at positions indicated by the asterisks. The dashed lines, on the other hand, were generated by (16). Figure 16 shows the error between the predicted and the actual position from the three calibration polynomials.

$$\text{Location (mm)} = -0.0164 \, \text{Pstat}^4 + 0.6944 \, \text{Pstat}^3 - 11.1875 \, \text{Pstat}^2 + 107.6895 \, \text{Pstat} - 15.9818 \tag{16}$$

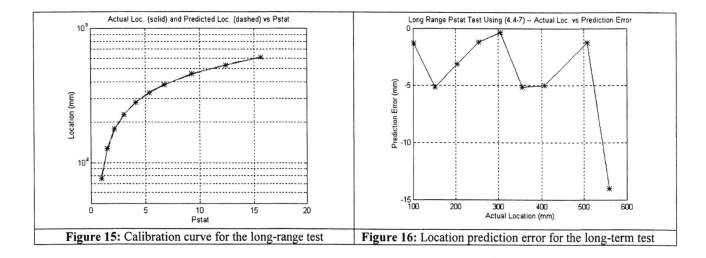

| **Figure 15:** Calibration curve for the long-range test | **Figure 16:** Location prediction error for the long-term test |

In summary,

1) The sensor was stable over during drift tests of 30 minutes or more.

2) Short term test revealed a sensor error of 0.53 mm RMS while the long range test indicated that the error had increased to 4.2 mm RMS.

3) There was a consistent deterioration of the sensor performance once the range exceeded 500mm. This is due to the effects of reduced signal-noise ratio brought about by the overhead fluorescent lights. Error for a range up to 500mm was 2.1 mm RMS, comparable to the +/- 1 mm repeatability of the calibration platform.

5. FLEXIBLE BEAM EXPERIMENT

5.1 Control Implementation

The control objective for flexible beam experiment is to position the end of the beam at a desired location, in minimum time and with minimum oscillation, using the output from the sensor module as the position feedback signal. The three performance indices used to monitor the relative responses of the control experiment for the standard PID and the variable gain PID algorithms are: 1) $\Sigma E(i)^2$ sum of the squared position error, 2) steady state position error , and 3) 5% settling time of the flexible beam. To perform each test, the end of the beam is located at 20 cm from the neutral axis, as the initial position. The beam is then commanded to move to the neutral position (0 mm) by the control program which also records the performance indices. A total of 10 test runs are conducted for each of the two control algorithms so that both the error and the RMS deviation can be calculated.

5.2 Test Results: Standard PID

Using on-line tuning, the optimal gains for the standard PID are found to be: $K_P = 10$, $K_D = 10$, and $K_I = 0.02$. The plant output Y, corresponding to the end position of the flexible beam, and the controller output U are plotted in Figure 17. It is observed that the effects of sensor noise has been increased by the use of derivative feedback. The average values of the performance indices are: $\Sigma E(i)^2 = 32.6$ cm^2 (standard deviation=2.1), steady error = -0.39 cm, and settling time=7.9 s.

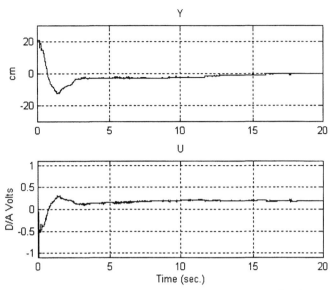

Figure 17: Typical beam position and controller output plots for the standard PID

5.3 Test Results: Variable Gain PID

The same PID parameters are used in the variable PID controller. A typical plot of the beam position and controller output are shown in Figure 18. The average values of the performance indices are: $\Sigma E(i)^2 = 33.8$ cm^2, steady state error=-0.31 cm, settling time = 3 s. It is observed the variable gain PID improves settling time by over 100%. Furthermore, sensor noise has not been amplified by the derivative action.

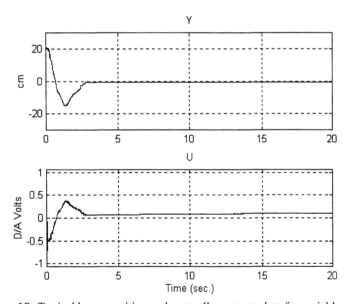

Figure 18: Typical beam position and controller output plots for variable gain PID

6. CONCLUSIONS

In this work, an optical position sensor has been implemented based on the Texas Instruments TSL220/230 photodetector and TMS320C25 digital signal processor. The DSP modulates a light source (a laser diode for this work) at 500Hz to decouple the effects of ambient light. No optical filters or shielding are required. Output of the TSL220/230 photodetector is a TTL pulse train whose frequency is proportional to the intensity of the incident light and therefore, can be transmitted over a relatively long distance without affecting signal/noise ratio. Upon sampled, the photodetector output is demodulated in the DSP to recapture the intensity signal. Calibration tests indicate that there is no detector drift, and the sensor resolution is 0.5 mm (short range) and 2mm (long range). To further test the sensor performance in applications such as vibration control, a flexible beam experiment is set up with two algorithms, standard and variable gain PID, applied to control the position of the beam. Test results verify the feasibility of using this sensor system for vibration control.

7. REFERENCES

[1] Davison, E. J. and Chang, T.N., *"Decentralized Controller Design Using Parameters Optimization Method,"*. Control-Theory and Advanced Technology. Vol. 2, No. 2, 131 - 154, 1986.

[2] Davison, E. J. and Chang, T.N., *"Decentralized Stabilization and Pole Assignment for General Proper Systems,"* IEEE Transactions on Automatic Control, June 1990, pp 652 - 664.

[3] Kwong, R. and T. Chang. *Development of Control; System Hardware Demonstration for Third Generation Spacecrafts.* Department of Electrical Engineering, University of Toronto, Toronto, Ontario. June, 1986.

[4] Chang,T.N., and Hou, E., "Synthesis of Approximately Spatially Round Controllers," Proceedings to the 1997 American Control Conference, Albuquerque, NM.

[5] Pao, L, Chang, T.N., and Hou, E., ``Input Shaper Design for Minimizing the Expected Level of Residual Vibration in Flexible Structures," Proceedings to the 1997 American Control Conference, Albuquerque, NM.

[6] Lewis, F., *Applied Optimal Control and Estimation: Digital Design and Implementation.* Englewood Cliffs, NJ: Prentice-Hall, 1992.

[7] Fraden, J., *Handbook of Modern Sensors*, 2nd Ed., American Institute of Physics, Woodbury, NY, 1997.

[8] Everett, H.R., *Sensors for Mobile Robots, Theory and Application*, A.K. peters Ltd., Wellesley , MA, 1995.

[9] Doebelin, E.O., *Measurement Systems, Application and Design*, McGraw-Hill Book Company, New York, NY.

[10] Malacara, D., *Optical Shop Testing*, John Wiley and Sons, Inc. New York, NY, 1992.

[11]Fowler, K. R., *Electronic Instrument Design, Architecture for the Life Cycle*, Oxford University Press Inc., New York, NY, 1996.

Automated and Intelligent On Line Quality Analysis
of Polymer Film

Lee F. Kaminski

Adaptive Optics Associates, Inc. / 54 Cambridgepark Drive / Cambridge, MA 02140

ABSTRACT

Ongoing emphasis on improving quality and reducing waste in polymer refining and converting has resulted in easy to use, cost effective instruments that can provide 100% quality analysis of polymer film. A brief tutorial of vision system technology, focusing on the inspection of polymer webs, will be provided by Adaptive Optics Associates Inc. (AOA), a world leader in high-speed commercial and industrial vision systems. The technique of building polymer-specific "intelligence" into a quality analysis vision system will be discussed. Included in this presentation will be specific examples from field use of the Advisor® web inspection system, as well as the lessons learned during the genesis of this application specific product.

Keywords: Vision Systems, Machine Vision, Inspection, Web, Quality, Analysis, Gel, Manufacturing, Converting

1. INTRODUCTION

This paper discusses the technique of designing an expert system for polymer quality analysis. A vision system overview is provided as a framework for the discussion of the expert system design. The paper concludes with examples from manufacturing installations of the vision instrument.

In 1995 AOA started development of a vision system to inspect a continuous sheet, or web, of plastic or converted polymer product. Above all the system had to be cost effective, detecting and classifying events and defects for a wide variety of applications for a reasonable cost. The system, the Advisor, was introduced in 1997. The utility and effectiveness of the product has validated the approach to this expert system design.

2. VISION SYSTEM OVERVIEW

2.1 Vision System Refresher

There are a variety of vision systems in the marketplace today. An informal one hour survey on the Internet produced over one hundred companies that manufacture equipment that can be described as machine vision, or vision systems. The purpose of this vision system refresher is twofold: 1) It is intended to provide a very brief overview for those new to this technology, and 2) for those already familiar with some form of imaging, this refresher provides a backdrop for the balance of the paper.

Examples of vision systems (figure 1) range from simple process monitoring to advanced statistical process control through analysis. A process *monitoring* vision system can consist of nothing more than a low cost camera and monitor that provide operators with a safe, detailed view of a critical stage in a manufacturing process. A *view and capture* system gives an operator more control of inspection with features such as pan/zoom, and typically includes image printing or archiving. To realize the benefit of these two system types, the full attention of an operator is required.

A machine vision system for *inspection* of piece parts, materials or processes is a more advanced tool that, in some cases, may not require any operator intervention at all. Image data from a camera is analyzed by a processing element, producing an objective description of the inspected object. The description may be in the form of a pass/fail tolerance measurement, a present/absent component location, or a relative quality grade compared to a known good, or golden, object. In addition to a report to an operator, an inspection system can provide accept/reject control to the manufacturing line.

Part of the SPIE Conference on Sensors and Controls for Intelligent Machining and Agile Manufacturing
Boston, Massachusetts ● November 1998
SPIE Vol. 3518 ● 0277-786X/98/$10.00

Figure 1: Examples of Vision Systems

An *analysis* instrument is an expert system that transcends the function of a traditional inspection system. Process-specific knowledge is incorporated into the vision system to provide more accurate and more relevant analysis. For these instruments structured lighting highlights specific, subtle events in the process that can go undetected using traditional light sources. The user interfaces are intuitive and typically use the vocabulary of the industry, rather than language of machine vision systems. These vision systems can be either advanced tools for an operator, or stand-alone equipment performing statistical analysis to optimize the performance of a process.

2.2 Vision System Tradeoffs For Web Inspection

The majority of challenges in providing web inspection solutions can be summarized as finding the right price/performance point. Some engineering tradeoffs directly impact the system architecture, other tradeoffs are less committal and can be addressed by reconfiguring the vision system. Some of the more common tradeoffs are addressed briefly below.

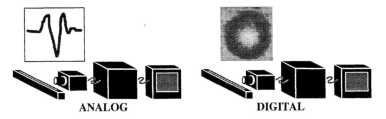

Figure 2: Analog vs. Digital Vision Systems

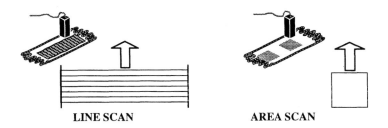

Figure 3: Linescan vs. Area scan Digital Vision Systems

The *front end* design of a vision system -- the lighting, optics and camera -- are critical. Smart design choices here will significantly improve the performance of a system. The majority of modern web inspection systems use digital linescan cameras for good reason. Digital cameras generally provide better access to data and better repeatability at a comparable cost (figure 2). Linescan cameras can provide 100% coverage of a web without involved synchronization to the line (figure 3). Note that a fast linescan camera without a sufficiently fast processor cannot perform continuous inspection.

3. A SOLUTION FOR POLYMER-SPECIFIC INTELLIGENCE

The concept of building polymer specific intelligence into a quality analysis vision system can be simply put: understand all the tasks an operator/inspector performs and make an instrument that improves the operators effectiveness. The reality of the development is somewhat more complex.

There are four functions the majority of line operators and inspectors perform with regards to manufacturing quality product:

1) detect events and defects (gels, holes, gas bubbles)
2) classify events and defects (size, type, severity)
3) troubleshoot and tune the process
4) create reports off line

3.1 Detect Events and Defects

Inspecting polymer or converted material is somewhat of a black art. Obvious defects such as large holes and black specs are easy to see on line for web speeds up to 100 feet per minute. More subtle objects such as gels, streaks, or unmelted polymer pellets require special lighting before being visible to the human eye. Defects as small as one micron are typically not seen.

Manufacturing and quality control representatives from major polymer manufacturers and converters have techniques for inspecting film for subtle defects. The inspection techniques were analyzed and recreated in the form of structured lighting for the vision system (figure 4). The structured light gives subtle defects more definition at the beginning of the inspection process.

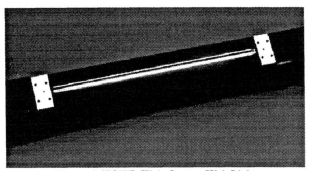

Figure 4: HOWL High Output Web Light

3.2 Classify Events and Defects

It seems every manufacturer has a unique library of names for describing defects and events. An amber to one producer is a fisheye to another producer, and is a glob to another. Each defect type is identified by an inspector based on visual clues such as tint and shape. Event types are then classified by subjective sizes: small/medium/large, tiny/small/medium/large/huge, don't-care/big.

The vision system starts with a digital image of an event and performs a detailed blob analysis. The result of the blob analysis is a set of metrics such as length, width, area, maximum intensity, minimum intensity and average intensity. The appropriate metrics are linked to a single term that describe an event or a defect.

As the vision system inspects material, events and defects are reported by type and size in the language of the industry. Additionally, the system can be configured to ignore objects or events that exist, but are non-events. Ultimately, operators are presented with the correct amount of useful information that accurately and concisely describes the material.

3.3 Tune Manufacturing Line

Line operators inspect product to understand the efficiency of the manufacturing line. The operators periodically make a visual analysis of material and tune the process accordingly. A vision system improves upon the tuning process in a number of ways: continuous inspection, immediate response, historical data, interface to factory control systems, interface to factory machinery.

A high performance vision system can provide continuous inspection of product and immediate notification of a change in product quality. The availability of historical data enables statistical process control via direct feedback to factory control systems and process machinery such as slitters and tab throwers. The description of the product is available in an intuitive user interface as well as printed reports.

3.4 Create Reports

As manufacturers remain focused on quality and compliance to the requirements of ISO9000, documentation is becoming increasingly important. Quality reports typically created by operators or QC personnel can be effectively generated by a vision system. Vision systems produce electronic archives of reports as well as providing printed reports on the factory floor.

4. REAL WORLD STORIES

The Advisor web inspection instrument was beta tested (figure 5) at two facilities for a total of 17 months before the formal product introduction in June 1997. Since that time units have been installed in a variety of applications. The following are some observations and some real world lessons learned from these installations.

Figure 5: The Advisor Web Inspection Instrument

4.1 Some Obvious Observations

-A vision system that is available in a variety of price/performance configurations can provide the right solution for the right price.
-100% continuous inspection ensures quality and provides fast statistical process control.
-An easy to use system is used often and effectively

4.2 Listen To The End Users

Line operators make product. Line operators use the equipment. Line operators understand their manufacturing process. Listen to the line operators. They often have common sense solutions to challenging problems regarding error reporting and the user interface. It makes sense to have line operators participate in the design of the user interface that line operators are going to use.

CASE 1: Operators asked for a setting to automatically stop inspection after a user programmable area of product had been analyzed. With this feature the line operator was free while the Advisor automatically collected the appropriate amount of data.

4.3 Vision Systems Are Objective

> CASE 2: Two operators looked at the same gel defect off line. One operator said the gel was small at less than 1/16". The other operator said the same gel was medium at greater than 1/16". The Advisor was set up to agree with the line supervisor, repeatably and reliably.

> CASE 3: Operators working in sunlit manufacturing space regularly reported more defects during daylight shifts because of enhanced lighting; the Advisor did not.

> CASE 4: On blind trials, the analysis of a QC team had a standard deviation four times greater than the analysis done by the Advisor.

4.4 System Confidence

Critical high performance components of the Advisor such as the vision engine and high output web light (HOWL) are designed, manufactured and tested in house. A diagnostic suite provides fault isolation for the modular system supporting a "0 hour" mean time to repair.

> CASE 5: Operators ran diagnostics on a seemingly broken Advisor system. The diagnostics recommended the operators check the HOWL. The factory power for the light had been switched off.

> CASE 6: An operator started to inspect a product and was warned by the Advisor that either the product had changed significantly, or the operator had incorrectly initiated an inspection. The product had changed significantly and the operator was properly warned.

5. CONCLUSION

The Advisor web inspection instrument was designed on a simple premise: understand all the tasks an operator/inspector performs and make an instrument that improves the operators effectiveness. A rigorous development based on this premise has resulted in an application specific product that is a critical component in efficient production of high quality polymer and converted material.

A New Digital Tomosynthesis System to monitor
the Soldering State of a Ball Grid Array

Sung T. Kang[a], Young O. Kim[a] and Hyung S. Cho[b]

[a]Korea Electronics Technology and Institute, 455-6 Masan-Ri, Jinwi-Myun,
Pyungtaek-Si, Kyunggi-Do, 451-860, Korea
[b]Korea Advanced Institute of Science and Technology, 373-1 Kusongdong,
Yusonggu, Taejon, Korea

ABSTRACT

This paper represents a new method to monitor the soldering state of a ball grid array by newly designed digital tomosynthesis system. Firstly, a new digital tomosynthesis (DTS) system, called object-detector synchronous rotation (ODSR), is suggested and designed to acquire images for the soldering state of a ball grid array. Secondly, the shape distortion of DTS images generated by an image intensifier is modeled. And a new synthesis algorithm, which overcomes the limitations of the existing synthesis algorithms, is suggested to improve the sharpness of the synthesized image. Also an artifact analysis of the DTS system is performed. Thirdly, the experiment to obtain the cross-sectional images of ball grid arrays is accomplished by the ODSR system.

Keywords: digital tomosynthesis, distortion, sharpness, artifact, ball grid array

1. INTRODUCTION

Fig.1 shows some defects generated in the manufacturing process of a ball grid array. Defects exist at solder joints formed between balls and printed circuit board. In X-ray inspection for monitoring the soldering quality of high density packages, such as a ball grid array, the inspection results using the cross-sectional images are more reliable than the results when using transmission images[1-2]. The reason is that the X-ray intensity, containing the information of the solder joints, is severely attenuated when passing through the solder ball, which has a high lead content. Hence, X-ray information about the solder joints cannot be extracted from the transmission image alone. On the other hand, in a cross-sectional image, the solder joint condition can be clearly seen. Therefore, producing the cross-sectional images effectively and efficiently is a very important research topic.

Digital tomosynthesis is a technology realizing a cross-sectional image of an object by synthesizing digital X-ray images of it. The digital tomosynthesis technology has been used for monitoring the state of cross-sectional planes of three-dimensional objects[3]. But DTS images can be distorted and blurred according to the surface shape of an image intensifier and to the synthesis method used[4]. These are the cause to deteriorate the image quality.

There have been some efforts to improve a DTS image quality[5-6]. Doi et al. performed mathematical modeling for compensating the shape distortion due to an image intensifier. They derived a formula of the distortion ratio using a geometric relation of X-ray projection on an image intensifier. The distortion is not symmetric to the vertical axis. Therefore, a new mathematical model for the case of the slant incidence of the source should be derived. Rooks and Sack suggested a synthesis algorithm to improve the sharpness for the DTS cross-sectional image. In this method, because only the maximum gray value is selected in the image, the domain steeply changed in the gray value of the object area exists. Therefore, a more effective algorithm to improve the sharpness is needed. Artifact is an artificial phenomenon appearing in synthesized image. Artifact is generated by the configuration between an X-ray source and an object. It also is a cause to deteriorate the image quality, therefore it should be analyzed and improved.

To realize a sharp and correct DTS image, a methodology to improve the image quality needs to be developed along with a method to evaluate the quality quantitatively. In this paper, firstly, a new DTS system is suggested and designed to acquire a DTS image set. Secondly, the shape distortion for the slant incidence of a source is modeled mathematically, and formulas to improve the quality are derived. And a new synthesis algorithm to improve the sharpness of a cross-sectional image is suggested. Also, the formulas expressing the artifact size are derived to improve the artifact. Thirdly, the experiment to obtain the cross-sectional images of ball grid arrays is accomplished by the ODSR system newly designed.

2. ODSR SYSTEM DESIGN

Three constituents to realize a cross-sectional image are an X-ray source, an object and a detector. During rotating synchronously any two elements among these elements, an image set is obtained. The acquired image set is synthesized by a

Part of the SPIE Conference on Sensors and Controls for Intelligent Machining and Agile Manufacturing
Boston, Massachusetts ● November 1998
SPIE Vol. 3518 ● 0277-786X/98/$10.00

computer, then the cross-sectional image is realized. In this paper, a new digital tomosynthesis system, called object-detector synchronous rotation (ODSR), is introduced. Fig.2 shows the ODSR DTS system. An object and a detector (CCD array) are synchronously rotated by two motors. To express the synthesis principle of DTS image, let a letter 'A' put on the focal plane of an object and a letter 'B' put on a out-of-focal plane. When the X-ray is irradiated to the object, the two letters are projected on the input surface of an image intensifier. During rotating synchronously the object and the CCD array, an image set (I_N) is acquired by the CCD array. The letter 'A' on the focal plane is projected at the same position of the CCD array, but 'B' on the out-of-focal plane is projected at one another positions. By synthesizing the image set, 'A' is superposed and becomes clear, while 'B' is blurred and not clear. Finally, the letter 'A' is obtained as a cross-sectional image.

In the ODSR system, an X-ray source is irradiated to the object with a tomographic angel (ψ). The X-ray beam passing through the object is transferred to a visible light by an image intensifier, and is focused onto the output window of an image intensifier. It passes a lens array and projected on the CCD array. The tomographic angle (ψ) of the source is related with the artifact of the system. The tomographic angle of the existing system can be adjusted up to about 30 degrees, while the ODSR system is designed to adjust the tomographic angle up to 60 degrees at the maximum. Hence, this system makes it possible to reduce the artifact. The rotating part of the object and the detector is designed by considering the moment of inertia of the part. By calculating the moment of inertia generated by the object and the turntable load, the motor 1 is selected to have a 1KW power. The ratio of the speed reduction of motor 1 to motor 2 is 9:1. A timing belt is used to rotate two gears at an accurate ratio. The rotating part of the detector, designed in order to tune the CCD array, uses a slip-ring to prevent the twisting of the signal lines, when the detector rotating. Some noise is formed to be included in the image signal passing through the slip-ring, but removed by a filtering circuit.

The ODSR system thus designed has some advantages compared with the existing systems. Firstly, because DTS images are acquired by the central domain of an image intensifier, the shape distortion is smaller than that of the existing systems which use the outer domain of an image intensifier. Secondly, by developing the new synthesis algorithm, the realization of the sharper cross-sectional image is achieved. Thirdly, because the tomographic angle(ψ) of the ODSR system is adjusted by large degrees, the artifact generated in the synthesized image can be reduced remarkably.

3. IMAGE QUALITY IMPROVEMENT METHODS OF ODSR SYSTEM

In this section, some methods to improve the image quality of ODSR system are suggested. A mathematical model to improve the shape distortion of the image is derived, and a new synthesis algorithm to improve the image sharpness is suggested. Also, the artifact of the ODSR system is improved.

3.1 Mathematical modeling of shape distortion

Fig. 3 represents a schematic diagram to model the shape distortion of the DTS image. It is assumed that the X-ray source is irradiated to an object with a uniform intensity. The input surface of an image intensifier is assumed to be sphere. In the figure, the plane 'A' depicts the horizontal plane tangential to the image intensifier surface, and the plane 'B' depicts the one including a projection point (Q) of the image intensifier surface. If the X-ray source is irradiated to an object with a tomographic angle(ψ), the point(M) on the line l_0 of the object is projected to the point Q on the surface of the image intensifier. Then, it is refracted with an angle θ in the surface and is projected to the point V on the line l_3 in the output window of the image intensifier. Therefore the line l_3 is a projection of the line $l_2(O_1U)$, not of the line $l_1(O_1P)$. It means that the image is distorted from l_1 to l_2 due to the spherical surface of the image intensifier. That is, the shape distortion is caused in the process of $l_1 \rightarrow l_2$.

To compensate for the shape distortion, the compensation length l_1 can be calculated from the distortion length l_2, using the following equation.

$$l_1 = \frac{1}{k_S} \cdot l_2 \tag{1}$$

where the shape distortion ratio k_s is defined as:

$$k_s = \left[\frac{h_2 + R(1 - \cos\phi)}{h_2} \right] \cdot \frac{\sin\beta}{\cos\phi} \cdot \frac{1}{\sin\alpha} \tag{2}$$

Therefore, the shape compensation to improve the image distortion can be achieved by the equations (1) and (2).

3.2 Sharpness improvement algorithm

Sharpness means the degree of clearness. An X-ray cross-sectional image is realized by the difference of relative sharpness between the inner area and the outer area of the edge line. Because the cross-sectional image is obtained by synthesizing the image set acquired for a focal plane of an object, the sharpness for the image is changed remarkably in according to the image synthesis method. In this paper, the existing synthesis methods such as an average method and a maximum method are described first, and then a new synthesis algorithm to improve the sharpness is proposed.

Average method: It is a method calculating the average value of pixels of the same position of the image set. This method is fast for calculation, but has a limitation that the sharpness for the image is decreased by simple averaging.

Maximum method: This method compares pixel values for the same position of an image set and selects the pixel of the maximum gray value. The pixels of an edge line are filled with the maximum value among the pixels. Because the difference of the gray value between the object area and the background area is high, the edge line becomes sharper than that of the average method. This method has an advantage of obtaining the cross-sectional image with a sharper edge, but has a limitation that the gray value in the object area is suddenly changed because of selecting only a maximum value.

Now, to solve the blurred edge problem in the average method and the changed gray value problem in the maximum method, we propose a new synthesis algorithm utilizing only the advantages of the above two methods. The root average value is calculated for the object area in the image, and the maximum value is selected for the background area. This algorithm is called 'Root-mean method', and can be realized by the equation:

$$I(i,j)_{rm} = (2^n - 1) - \sqrt[N]{(2^n - 1 - I_1) \times (2^n - 1 - I_2) \times \cdots \times (2^n - 1 - I_N)} \qquad (3)$$

where $I_N(i,j)$ is in the range of $0 \sim (2^n-1)$, and N is the number of image used. If any value among N pixels $(I_1 \sim I_N)$ is 255, the inside value of the root of the equation (13) becomes zero, and then I_{rm} has a maximum value 255. It means that the source does not pass through the object and becomes a background image. And if all values of N pixels $(I_1 \sim I_N)$ are not 255, the average value is obtained by the N-square root calculation. The outer area of the edge line is filled with the value 255 and the inner area of the edge line has the average value of N pixels. Therefore, a cross-sectional image with sharp edge and with nearly uniform brightness can be obtained by the root-mean algorithm.

3.3 Artifact analysis and improvement

Artifact image is an artificial one appearing by the shape of an object and by the configuration of the constituent items of a system. Fig.4 shows the artifact phenomenon generating in the cross-sectional image of a cone-type object. The four images $(I_1 \sim I_4)$, projected on the image plane from the X-ray source, are depicted as plane views for easy understanding. The common area becomes the cross-sectional image. The cross-sectional image of the radius r_c for the focal plane of the height h from the bottom should be realized, however the artifact image of the larger radius r_{ar} is obtained. It is generated because the original area for the focal plane is included in the image area formed by the bottom plane with a radius R_m. Geometrically, the artifact is formed when the angle ß, between the source and the vertex of the cone, is smaller than 1/2 of the vertex angle θ. That is, the condition of the artifact generation is $\beta < \theta/2$. The radius of artifact r_{ar} is derived as:

$$r_{ar} = \frac{h_2}{h_1 + h} \cdot \left(R_m - h \cdot \tan\psi \right) \qquad (4)$$

Equation (4) means that the artifact radius can be reduced by increasing the tomographic angle ψ of the X-ray source for the fixed values of h_1 and h_2.

4. IMAGE QUALITY IMPROVEMENT RESULTS BY EXPERIMENT

The experiments are performed to verify the improvement of image quality by using the equations expressed in previous sections. The object-detector synchronous rotation (ODSR) system newly designed in this work is used for experimentation.

4.1 Compensation of the shape distortion

Fig.5(a) shows the acquired image for the wire-grid sample by experiment and the compensated image from the acquired image. The grid sample has 32×32 wire grids of 4.5mm gap distance, which is enough to show the degree of distortion at the edge domain of an image intensifier of 145mm diameter. Fig.5(b) represents the distortion length (λ) measured from images of the figure (a). The solid lines in Fig.5(b) are the data of the original image, and the dotted lines are the data compensated from the original image. The data are represented only for the observed one in the image. To compare the distortion degree between an inner domain and an outer domain of an image intensifier, two bold dotted lines meaning the domain of an image intensifier are drawn in the original data. The one expresses the edge line (D) of the image intensifier, and the another one expresses the half line (D/2) of the image intensifier. The ODSR system uses mainly the half domain (D/2) of the image intensifier to acquire images, while the existing system uses the whole domain (D) of an image intensifier. From the original data, the distortion length at the half line is about 1/3 of that at the edge line of an image intensifier. Therefore, it shows that the ODSR system is superior to the existing system in acquirement of high quality images.

The figure (b) also shows that the original image is remarkably compensated for. The distortion length after compensation is about 13.3% of that of the original data. To evaluate the compensation degree quantitatively, the newly defined evaluation index E_L is used. The evaluation index E_L is calculated from the data of the figure (b), and the result is represented in figure (c). The curve shows that the index values are raised gradually according to the increase of the distance from the grid center. The figure also shows that the index values are decreased with great deal according to the increase of the distance of the j-axis. It means that the compensation can be achieved excellently in the grid center area.

4.2 Sharpness improvement

To evaluate the sharpness of a cross-sectional image, a cone type object represented as in Fig.6(a) is used. The diameter of the bottom is 10mm, and the focal plane is set at 3mm height from the bottom. The vertex angle (θ) varies from 30° to 60°. The distance (h_1) between the source (S) and the focal plane is 275mm, and the distance (h_2) between the source and the surface of the image intensifier is 584mm. The simulation and the experimental results of the cross-sectional image for the cone are shown in figure (b) and (c), respectively. The number of images used for synthesis is 8. The cross-sectional images are realized by the synthesis algorithms previously expressed. It shows that the blurred domain exists around the edge line of the focal plane by the average method, and that the gray value changed domain exists in the image by the maximum method, where the cross-sectional image for the focal plane becomes sharp by the root-mean method.

Fig.6(d) represents the evaluation result for the sharpness of the realized images. The newly defined evaluation index E_{SH} is used. It shows that the index value of the root-mean method is highest among those of the synthesis methods. As the result of simulation, the evaluation index by the root-mean method is increased by 32.4% compared with that by the average method and 20.5% by the maximum method. The result of experiment well agrees with that of simulation. It means that the root-mean method is more superior to the other two methods. Therefore, the sharpness of the cross-sectional image can be improved remarkably by the root-mean method.

4.3 Artifact improvement

The artifact is estimated for the same object as the cone shown in Fig.6(a). Fig.7 is the result of artifact evaluation according to the X-ray tomographic angle ψ. Fig.7(a) shows that the value of the evaluation index is decreased rapidly for the fixed height of h=3 according to the increase of the angle ψ. It means that the artifact can be reduced by increasing the tomographic angle. As an example, for θ=110°, the evaluation index E_{AR} is 0.91 at ψ=15° in a simulation result. It is decreased according to the angle ψ, and becomes 0.55 at ψ=60°. The reduction of 39.6% of the index value is achieved. For the lower angle than θ=110°, the artifact is reduced more largely. Because the area of the focal plane in Fig.7(a) becomes bigger according to decrease of the vertex angle θ. The trend of experimental result well agrees with that of simulation.

Fig.7(b) shows the variation of the artifact index for the fixed angle of θ=70°. The index is decreased rapidly according to the increase of the tomographic angle ψ. As an example, for h=3, the index is 0.78 at ψ=10° in a simulation result. It falls to 0.05 at ψ=40°, and the reduction of 93.5% is obtained. Therefore, it is shown that the artifact generated in the cross-sectional image can be improved greatly by increasing the tomographic angle ψ.

5. EXPERIMENT : DEFECTS DETECTION FOR BALL GRID ARRAY SOLDER JOINTS

Fig.8 shows a cross-sectional view of a ball grid array used in this experiment. 119 balls are arrayed on the printed circuit board with 22mm×9.5mm area. The balls were collapsed by pressure in the soldering process. 8 images are acquired for the focal plane of h=0.4mm. Fig.9(a) shows the acquired image set. Field of view(FOV) is 6.5mm×6.5mm. The image set shows that the array shape of balls is distorted according to the X-ray projection direction. It means pin-cushion distortion by the surface of the image intensifier. The distortion is increased according to the distance from the source. These distorted images should be compensated. Fig.9(b) represents the compensation process. First, shape compensation is accomplished by the previous derived equation (1). Next, the image is filtered by 3×3 median filter for removing the error (small white circles) generated in the shape compensation process. Then aspect ratio of the image is corrected. Because the size of CCD array is 6.4mm×4.8mm, i axis of the image is multiplied by 3/4. Consequently, the well-compensated result is obtained.

Next, cross-sectional images are obtained for solder joints. The height h of desired solder plane is set to 0.1mm. The cross-sectional image for insufficient, excess and void defects are obtained, and compared with the normal image. Fig.10 shows the results. The open defect is considered as a kind of the insufficient defect. The solder areas of the cross-sectional images are obviously changed according to defects. Therefore, it shows that the defects generated in solder part of a ball grid array can be detected using the cross-sectional images obtained by the ODSR system. It is remained as a further work that the development of inspection method by neural network using features as area, centroid, and moment etc. for the acquired image profile.

6. CONCLUSIONS

This paper represented a new method to monitor the soldering states of a ball grid array by newly designed ODSR system. Firstly, the object-detector synchronous rotation system was newly designed to acquire the DTS images. Secondly, the shape distortion generated by an image intensifier was modeled and the compensation formulas were derived. And a new synthesis algorithm to solve some limitations of the existing algorithms was proposed, and the artifact analysis was performed. Also the Performance improvement results by experiment were shown. Thirdly, the experiment to obtain the cross-sectional images of ball grid arrays is accomplished by the ODSR system newly designed, and it shows that the defects generated in solder joint of a ball grid array can be detected well using the cross-sectional images obtained by the ODSR system.

7. REFERENCES

1. S. Rooks and T. Sack, "X-ray inspection of Flip Chip Attach using Digital Tomosynthesis," *Circuit World,* Vol. 21, No. 3, 1995, pp. 51-55.
2. S. Rooks, M. Okimura and D. Urban, "Inspection of very-fine-pitch connections on PCMCIA cards," *Proc. NEPCON West 93,* 1993, pp. 752-762.
3. Z. Kolitsi and G. Panayiotakis, "A Multical Projection Method For Digital Tomosynthesis," *Medical Physics*, Vol. 19, No. 4, 1992, pp. 1045-1050.
4. P. Chakaborty, "Image Intensifier Distortion Correction," *Med. Phys.*, Vol. 14, No. 2, 1987, pp. 249-252.
5. H. Doi, Y. Suzuki and Y. Hara, "Real-time X-ray Inspection of 3-D Defects in Circuit Board Patterns," Fifth International Conference on Computer Vision(ICCV'95), June 1995, pp. 575-582.
6. S. Rooks, B. Benhabib and K.Smith, "Development of an Inspection Process for Ball Grid-Array Technology Using Scanned-Beam X-ray Laminography," *IEEE Trans. On Components, Packaging, and Manufacturing Technology-Part A.* Vol. 18, No. 4, 1995, pp. 851-861.

S.T.K.(correspondence): E-mail: kangst@nuri.keti.re.kr; www:http//www.keti.re.kr/~premech; Telephone: +82-333-610-4328
Y.O.K: E-mail: youngok@nuri.keti.re.kr; Telephone: +82-333-610-4109
H.S.C.: E-mail: hscho@lca.kaist.ac.kr; Telephone: +82-42-869-3213

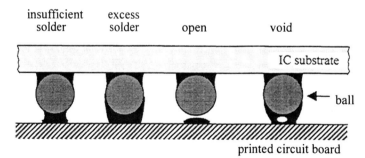

Fig.1 Defects of ball grid array joints

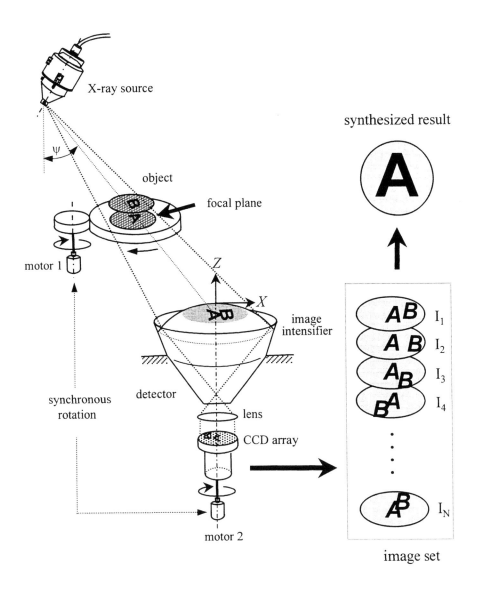

Fig.2 Object detector synchronous notation system

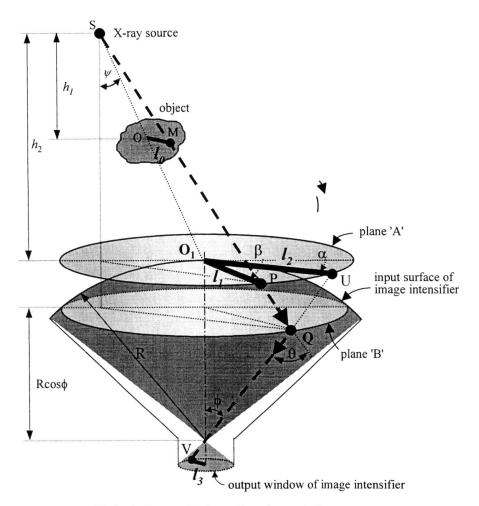

Fig.3   A diagram for shape distortion analysis

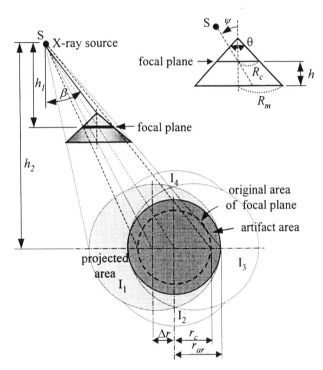

Fig.4 Artifact generation of a cone-type object
　　　 (The projected images are represented as plane views)

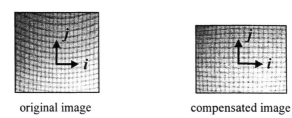

original image   compensated image

(a) original image and compensated image

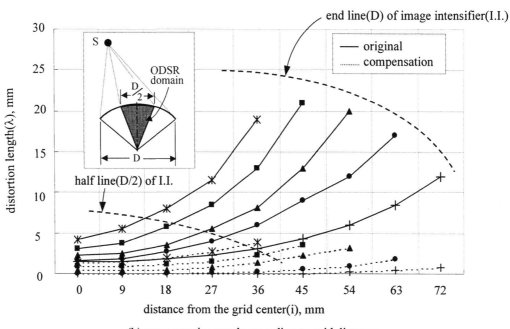

(b) compensation result according to grid distance

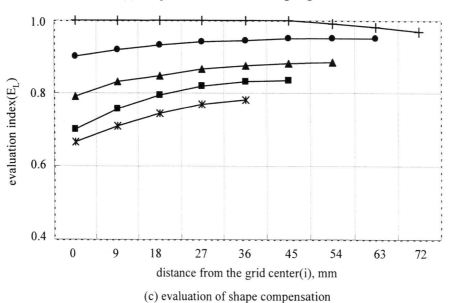

(c) evaluation of shape compensation

Fig.5 Compensation and evaluation of an experimental image ($\psi = 30°$)
(+:j=0, ●:j=2, ▲:j=4, ■:j=6, ∗:j=8)

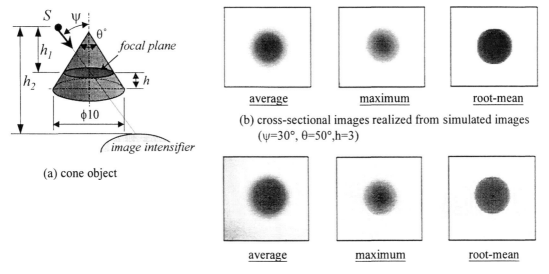

(a) cone object

average   maximum   root-mean

(b) cross-sectional images realized from simulated images
(ψ=30°, θ=50°, h=3)

average   maximum   root-mean

(c) cross-sectional images realized from experimental images
(ψ = 30°, θ = 50°, h=3)

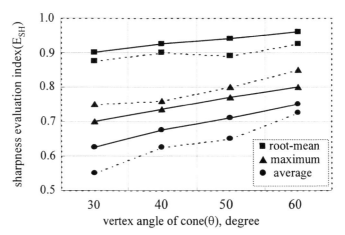

(d) sharpness evaluation according to the vertex angle of the
cone (— simulation, --- experiment)

Fig.6 Sharpness evaluation for the cross-sectional images of a cone

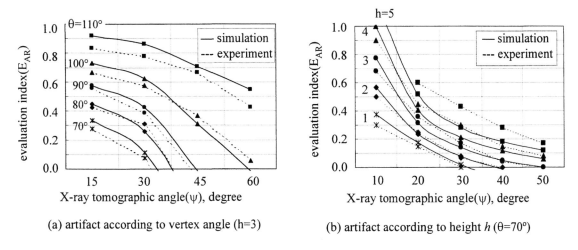

(a) artifact according to vertex angle (h=3)

(b) artifact according to height h (θ=70°)

Fig.7 Artifact evaluation for a cone according to an X-ray tomographic angle

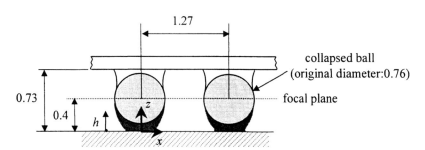

Fig.8 Dimensions of a ball grid array used in experiment

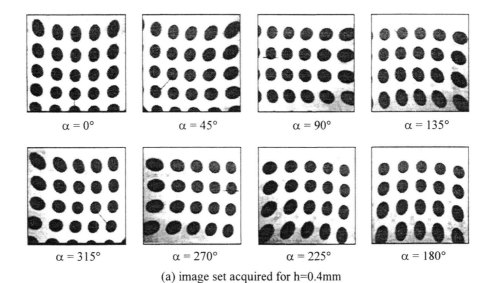

$\alpha = 0°$ $\alpha = 45°$ $\alpha = 90°$ $\alpha = 135°$

$\alpha = 315°$ $\alpha = 270°$ $\alpha = 225°$ $\alpha = 180°$

(a) image set acquired for h=0.4mm

original image   shape compensation 3×3 median filtering   aspect ratio compensation

(b)example of compensation process ($\alpha = 0°$)

Fig. 9 Compensation of a ball grid array image set ($\psi=30°$, $h_1=44$mm, $h_2=584$mm)

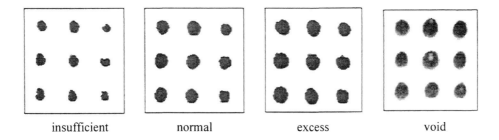

insufficient   normal   excess   void

Fig.10 Comparison of normal joint with defect joints for 3×3 balls (h=0.1mm)

SESSION 2

Control Systems I

Reliable servo system design with redundant sensors

Qing Zhao [a], Jin Jiang [a], Peter E. Orban [b]

[a] Department of Electrical and Computer Engineering
University of Western Ontario, London, Ont., N6A 5B9, Canada

[b] Integrated Manufacturing Technology Institute
National Research Council Canada, London, Ont. N6G 4X8, Canada

ABSTRACT

A reliable servo system design scheme against sensor failures in the speed control loop is proposed. In the proposed reliable control system structure, in addition to the primary output sensor, redundant dissimilar sensors are used to measure different system variables which are more easily accessible and dynamically related to the desired system output. In the event of output sensor failure, the measured signal from the redundant sensor can still maintain the system stability and certain performance, such as, tracking ability.

Keywords: Servo system, speed control loop, machining, reliable control.

1. INTRODUCTION

Servo systems have found wide applications in modern automated machine tools. They are utilized for controlling the axes as well as the spindle of the machine tool. The slides of numerically controlled machines that are suitable for contouring are based on positional servo systems [1]. While the problem of accurate contouring of the machine tool has been thoroughly addressed in the literature [2], very little attention has been paid to the reliable operation of these servo systems. To maintain the integrity and performance of the servo systems is an ever-important consideration. The satisfactory operation of the servo system has a direct bearing on the quality of the part being produced and on the "health" of the machine tool. Failures in the servo system usually results in damage to the part being machined and in catastrophic cases, it can cause significant damage to the machine tool as well. Therefore, having fault tolerant servo systems can help prevent economic losses in production systems.

In practical control systems, the requirement on the reliability of the feedback loop is usually very high. A failure in the feedback path may result in the deviation of system outputs from the desired values, or even worse, to cause instability of the entire control system. Therefore, the design of a reliable control system which can tolerate failures in the feedback path is of extreme importance. In the literature, a control system designed to tolerate failures in sensors (or actuators), while maintaining the closed-loop stability and an acceptable performance, is known as a reliable control system, [3], or a control system possessing integrity against sensor (actuator) failures, [4], [5].

Generally speaking, the output sensor plays a very important role in the entire system. On the other hand, sensors are relatively vulnerable and easily subject to failures. As mentioned above, sensor failure can cause very serious problem. For this reason, redundant sensors are often used in systems with high reliability requirement. In fact, using triple or quadruple sensor redundancy in such systems is a very common technique in practice. Usually, at the sensor outputs, a voting scheme is used to distinguish the normal sensor reading from the abnormal ones and a switching device is used to feedback the proper signal, [6]. By and large, such scheme is effective in increasing the reliability against sensor failures. However, in some cases, due to the sensor size, the extra cost and the increased complexity of the entire control system, such scheme may not be applicable.

In this paper, a reliable servo system design scheme against speed sensor faults are proposed. In addition to the system speed sensor, redundant dissimilar sensors are used to measure the related system variables which are accessible. Then the

Part of the SPIE Conference on Sensors and Controls for Intelligent Machining and Agile Manufacturing
Boston, Massachusetts ● November 1998
SPIE Vol. 3518 ● 0277-786X/98/$10.00

system output can be indirectly obtained or estimated from these additional measurements. When the primary output sensor fails, the indirectly measured output signal can be used instead. There is no switching action in the proposed control strategy since both the output sensor and the redundant dissimilar sensors are used during the entire system operation. When properly selected, the redundant sensors usually have smaller size, lower cost and higher reliability compared to the primary output sensor. Such indirect output measurement technique has already been applied in the sensorless DC motor design in motor drive systems, [7], [8]. The objective of using this technique is to save space, cost and also to increase the reliability.

The paper is organized as follows: the problem formulation and the reliable control system design is illustrated in section II. The design simulation results are given in section III followed by the conclusion in section IV.

2. DESIGN OF RELIABLE SERVO SYSTEM

2.1 Problem Formulation

The servo systems of machine tools are usually based on PID control loops, using DC motors. In addition to position control, speed control is an important issue in most of servo systems. By using speed control, the system stability and damping property can be improved. In the machining process, the speed of the spindle is closely related to the quality of the cutting surface of the workpiece. Accurate speed control allows high quality cutting surface. In the positional servo system, the servo amplifier itself has speed and current inner control loops utilizing analogue techniques [9]. In these cases, failure of the speed control loop can result in unacceptable dynamic performance of the axis positioning system. By applying a fault tolerant speed control loop in the system, the positioning performance of the system will still be acceptable regardless of speed loop failure. In this paper, the sensor failure is of our main concern. As mentioned above, it may cause severe consequence.

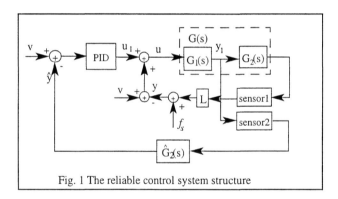

Fig. 1 The reliable control system structure

Consider a SISO LTI system with the input u and the output y, a reliable control system structure is shown in Fig. 1. In addition to the primary output sensor (sensor 1), another sensor (sensor 2) is also used to measure a properly chosen intermediate state variable, y_1. From y_1, the system output can be estimated and used as the feedback signal to the controller. From Fig. 1, the system transfer function $G(s)$ can be written into:

$$G(s) = G_1(s) G_2(s) \tag{1}$$

and

$$\frac{Y_1(s)}{U(s)} = G_1(s) \tag{2}$$

$$Y(s) = LG_2(s)Y_1(s) + f_s(s) \tag{3}$$

The sensor failure is represented in Eq.3, where $f_s(s) = \dfrac{d_f}{s}$ is the sensor reading deviation due to the failure, which in time domain is a constant term d_f, and L is used to model the operation modes of the output sensor.

$$L = \begin{cases} 1 & normal \\ 0 & failure \end{cases} \tag{4}$$

By assuming that $G_2(s)$ is known, one can model it as $\hat{G}_2(s)$. Through $\hat{G}_2(s)$, the system output can be estimated using the signal y_1.

Given such a system structure, now the problem is how to design the controller such that, under both normal and sensor failure cases, the closed-loop stability and certain performance can be maintained. It should be mentioned that in the servo system, the tracking ability of the control system is guaranteed by using a PID controller.

2.2 Design of the Controller

From Fig. 1, by simple manipulation of the block diagram, the transfer function of closed-loop system can be obtained:

$$\begin{aligned} Y(s) &= \frac{(G_{pid}(s) + 1)G_1(s)G_2(s)}{1 + G_1(s)\hat{G}_2(s)G_{pid}(s) + LG_1(s)G_2(s)} \cdot V(s) + \frac{G_1(s)G_2(s)}{1 + G_1(s)\hat{G}_2(s)G_{pid}(s) + LG_1(s)G_2(s)} f_s(s) \\ &= G_c(s)V(s) + D_f(s) \end{aligned} \tag{5}$$

where $G_{pid} = k_p + \dfrac{k_i}{s} + k_d s$.

From Eq. 5, one can further obtain that:

$$G_c(s) = \frac{\{k_d s^2 + (k_p + 1)s + k_i\}G_1(s)G_2(s)}{k_d G_1(s)\hat{G}_2(s)s^2 + (k_p G_1(s)\hat{G}_2(s) + LG_1(s)G_2(s) + 1)s + k_i G_1(s)\hat{G}_2(s)} \tag{6}$$

$$D_f(s) = \frac{G_1(s)G_2(s)}{k_d G_1(s)\hat{G}_2(s)s^2 + (k_p G_1(s)\hat{G}_2(s) + LG_1(s)G_2(s) + 1)s + k_i G_1(s)\hat{G}_2(s)} \cdot \frac{d_f}{s}$$

Therefore, in the system steady-state:

$$K_\infty = G_c(s)\big|_{s \to 0} = \frac{G_2(s)\big|_{s \to 0}}{\hat{G}_2(s)\big|_{s \to 0}} \tag{7}$$

and

$$D_{f,\infty} = \lim_{s \to 0} s \cdot \frac{d_f}{s} \cdot \frac{G_1(s)G_2(s) \cdot s}{k_d G_1(s)\hat{G}_2(s)s^2 + (k_p G_1(s)\hat{G}_2(s) + LG_1(s)G_2(s) + 1)s + k_i G_1(s)\hat{G}_2(s)} = 0 \tag{8}$$

where K_∞ is the DC-gain of the closed-loop system. One can see clearly that the sensor failure, which is modelled in L, does not affect the steady state of the system response at all. By assuming that $\hat{G}_2 = G_2$, the DC-gain can be maintained at unity independent of L. From Eq.7, the sensor reading bias is also eliminated by the PID controller. Therefore, using the above control system structure can indeed guarantee the system steady-state performance regardless of the output sensor failure. However, it can be seen from Eq. 6, that L does affect the denominator of the closed-loop transfer function, i.e. the system characteristic equation. In other words, the sensor failure can actually affect the system transient performance, and even the system stability. Hence, the controller needs to be carefully designed in order for the system to retain the stability even if the output sensor fails.

By substituting $G_1(s)$ and $G_2(s)$ in Eq. 5, $G_c(s)$ can be written as:

$$G_c(s) = \frac{n(s)}{d(s)} \tag{9}$$

The characteristic equation of the closed-loop system can then be obtained:

$$d(s) = s^q + \alpha_1 s^{q-1} + \alpha_2 s^{q-2} + \ldots + \alpha_q \tag{10}$$

where q is the order of the closed-loop system, and α_i, $i = 1, \ldots, q$ are the coefficients of the closed-loop system:

$$\alpha_i = \alpha_i\left(a, \hat{a}_2, k_i, k_p, k_d, L\right) \quad i = 1, 2, \ldots, q \tag{11}$$

where a is a vector which contains parameters of dynamic system, $G(s)$, and $\hat{a}_2$ is the parameter vector of $\hat{G}_2$.

When the output sensor fails, i.e. L changes from 1 to 0, the closed-loop characteristic equation is also changed:

$$\begin{aligned} \alpha_{i, normal} &= \alpha_i\left(a, \hat{a}_2, k_i, k_p, k_d, 1\right) \\ \alpha_{i, failure} &= \alpha_i\left(a, \hat{a}_2, k_i, k_p, k_d, 0\right) \end{aligned} \quad i = 1, 2, \ldots, q \tag{12}$$

In order to stabilize the closed-loop system under both normal and sensor failure cases, some robust control techniques can be utilized in choosing k_i, k_p, k_d, such as simultaneous stabilization technique [10], and robust eigenvalue assignment technique [5]. Both methods can guarantee the system stability under normal and sensor failure cases, the latter can also assign the eigenvalues of the above two characteristic equations in the desired stability region in the s-plane.

Therefore, with the proposed system structure, by choosing the PID parameters properly, the closed-loop system stability and the tracking ability can be maintained.

In the above analysis, it is implied that $G_2(s)$ and its equivalence $\hat{G}_2(s)$ should be asymptotically stable. This condition is very restrictive and may not be satisfied in many situations. In fact, when the above control system is implemented in practice, $\hat{G}_2(s)$ can be replaced by an observer, which is shown in Fig. 2. By using the observer, the restrictive condition on $G_2(s)$ can be relieved.

Another assumption of the proposed scheme is that the system dynamic model is known exactly. However, the modelling error always exists in practice. In this case, the effect of the modelling error can be examined through sensitivity and robustness analysis.

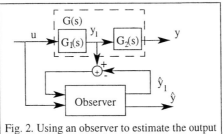

Fig. 2. Using an observer to estimate the output

3. APPLICATION AND SIMULATION RESULTS

3.1 Reliable speed control servo system

The above design scheme is implemented in a lab-scale DC motor servo system. The system block diagram is shown in Fig. 3. The motor parameters are given as below:

$$\begin{aligned}
L_a &= 0.08H \\
R_a &= 4.0\Omega \\
K_{me} &= K_{mt} = 0.46 \\
J_m &= 0.012 \\
f &= 0.002
\end{aligned} \tag{13}$$

The speed signal is measured by a tachometer which might be subject to malfunctions. The armature current is measured by the redundant current sensor and is used to estimate the speed signal through an observer. Both the speed signal and its estimated equivalence are fed back. With the properly designed PID controller, the system stability and the tracking performance are maintained even in the presence of the tachometer failure. The sampling frequency is 500 Hz.

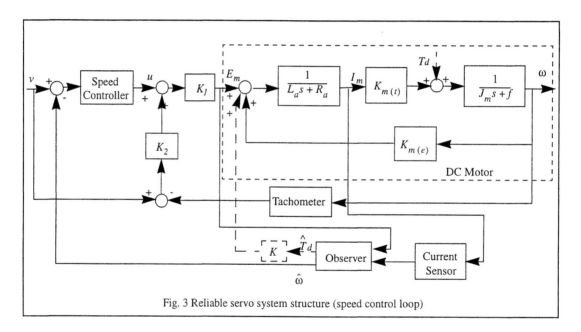

Fig. 3 Reliable servo system structure (speed control loop)

Based on the motor model, a state observer can be used to estimate the motor speed signal. However, in practice, there usually exists some unknown disturbance load in the motor, and it can affect the accuracy of the estimation. In this case, one can treat such an unknown disturbance load as an extra system state, and then design an observer based on the augmented system model. Hence, the disturbance load can be estimated using such an observer. By assuming that there exists a constant disturbance load, the observer used in Fig. 3 is given as follows:

$$\begin{bmatrix} \dot{I}_m(t) \\ \dot{\hat{\omega}}(t) \\ \dot{\hat{T}}_d(t) \end{bmatrix} = \begin{bmatrix} -\dfrac{R_a}{L_a} & -\dfrac{K_{m(e)}}{L_a} & 0 \\ \dfrac{K_{m(t)}}{J_m} & -\dfrac{f}{J_m} & -\dfrac{1}{J_m} \\ 0 & 0 & 0 \end{bmatrix} \begin{bmatrix} I_m(t) \\ \hat{\omega}(t) \\ \hat{T}_d(t) \end{bmatrix} + \begin{bmatrix} \dfrac{1}{L_a} \\ 0 \\ 0 \end{bmatrix} E_m(t) + H \left(I_m(t) - \begin{bmatrix} 1 & 0 & 0 \end{bmatrix} \begin{bmatrix} I_m(t) \\ \hat{\omega}(t) \\ \hat{T}_d(t) \end{bmatrix} \right) \tag{14}$$

where H is a 3×1 column vector, which is called the observer gain vector. By properly choose H, theoretically, the estimated states will converge to the real system states, i.e. $\hat{\omega}(t) \rightarrow \omega(t)$, and $\hat{T}_d(t) \rightarrow T_d(t)$.

3.2 Simulation results

Fig. 4 shows the system response (motor speed) under normal operation, and the system response when the tachometer malfunctions is shown in Fig. 5. In order to examine the effect of the sensor failure, the fault induced transient is shown in Fig. 6 (sensor failure is simulated at $t = 4\ sec$). The observer estimation error is shown in Fig 7.

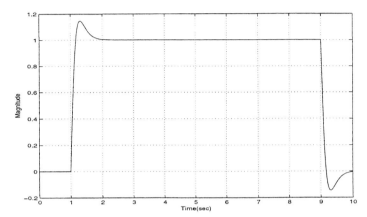

Fig.4. System step response (normal operation)

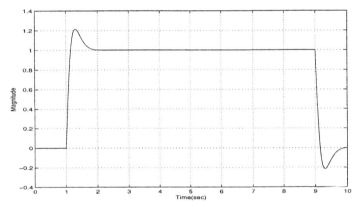

Fig. 5. System step response (sensor failure)

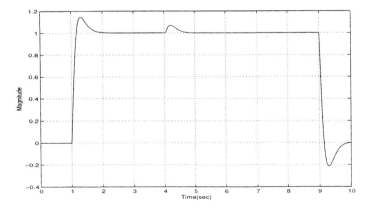

Fig. 6. Fault induced transients

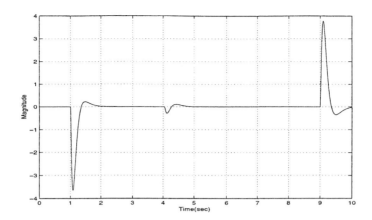

Fig. 7. Estimation error from observer

It is clear that the system are stable in both normal and sensor failure cases, and the fault-induced transient is small. This is due to the fast convergence rate of the observer.

4. CONCLUSION

A reliable control system structure and the design scheme against sensor failure are proposed. The proposed scheme can be applied to the servo system design in the machining process to achieve a reliable operation. Although current work is mainly focused on the reliable speed control loop design, the same concept can also be applied to the position control loop design.

5. REFERENCES

[1] Spalla, L. J. "DC servo design made simple", *Control Engineering,* February 1971, pp. 56 - 59.

[2] Koren, Y. and C.C. Lo, "Advanced controllers for feed drives", *Annals of CIRP*, vol. 4/2/1992, pp. 689 - 698.

[3] Veillette, R. J., J.V. Medanic and W. R. Perkins, "Design of reliable control systems," *IEEE Trans. Auto. Contr.,* vol. 37, no. 3, pp. 290-304, 1992.

[4] Fujita, M. and E. Shimemura, "Integrity against arbitrary feedback-loop failures in linear multivariable control systems," *Automatica*, vol. 24, no. 6, pp. 765-772. 1988.

[5] Zhao, Q. and J. Jiang, "Reliable control system design against feedback failures with applications to aircraft control," *Proceedings of 1996 IEEE Conference on Control Applications,* Dearborn, U.S.A., pp. 994-999, Sept., 1996.

[6] Clark, R. N., "State estimation schemes for instrument fault detection," in *Fault Diagnosis in Dynamic Systems, Theory and Applications,* (edited by R. Patton, P. M. Frank and R. Clark), Prentice Hall, New York, 1989.

[7] Matsui, N., "Sensorless PM brushless DC motor drives," *IEEE Trans. Ind. Electron.,* vol. 43, no. 2., 1996.

[8] Lee, T. H., T. S. Low, K. J. Tseng and H. K. Lim, "An intelligent indirect dynamic torque sensor for permanent magnet brushless DC drives," *IEEE Trans. Ind. Electron.,* vol. 41, No. 2, 1994.

[9] Weck, M., *Handbook of Machine Tools*, vol. 3, *Automation and Control*, John Wiley & sons, 1984.

[10] Ackermann, J., *Robust Control: Systems with Uncertain Physical Parameters,* Springer-Verlag, New York, 1993.

User-friendly method for tuning fuzzy logic controllers

Hakan Gürocak

Washington State University
Manufacturing Engineering Program
14204 NE Salmon Creek Ave.
Vancouver, WA 98686, USA

ABSTRACT

Design of a fuzzy logic controller (FLC) is generally based on trial-and-error because no standard method exists for developing the rule base of an FLC directly from human knowledge. Consequently, the performance of an initial design attempt will, in general, not be satisfactory in terms of certain design criteria such as steady state error and/or the oscillatory behavior of the system. In this paper, a method to tune the rule base of such an initial design attempt is presented. The method is based on a novel formulation of an objective function which can then be used in a conventional optimization algorithm. Results of two experiments are reported.

Keywords: Fuzzy logic control, tuning, optimization, engineering

1.   INTRODUCTION

Fuzzy logic controllers (FLC) are the most significant and fruitful application for fuzzy logic and fuzzy set theory. In the past few years, advances in the microprocessor and hardware technologies have resulted in FLCs appearing in many commercial products such as automatic transmissions, anti-skid brakes, camcorders and washing machines[1].

FLC design starts with heuristics and human expertise. For many practical control problems (e.g. process control) it is difficult to have an accurate mathematical model yet there are experienced human operators who can provide heuristics and rules-of-thumb for successfully controlling the process. In such cases an FLC can be designed by converting the operator's expertise into a set of IF-THEN rules forming the rule base of the controller. The design is finalized with the help of fuzzy sets to define vague terms such as "hot" or "medium" used in these rules and fuzzy inference mechanisms. However, when the controller is tested in the real system the performance will, in general, not be satisfactory in terms of certain design criteria such as steady state error of the controller and/or the oscillatory behavior of the system. At this point the designer has two choices: (1) he needs to tune the rules using numerous, time consuming trial-and-error cycles; or (2) some kind of an optimization technique needs to be used to improve the performance. Today the literature contains many attempts at automatic FLC tuning, using various techniques including reinforced learning[2], neural networks[3,4], non-linear optimization techniques[5,6] and genetic algorithms[7,8,9]. In this paper, a FLC rule base tuning method is presented. The method is based on a new way of formulating an objective function. The function can then be used in a conventional optimization algorithm.

2.   TUNING METHOD

As mentioned earlier, the performance of the FLC can be improved by either going through numerous trial-and-error attempts or by using some type of an optimization technique. If the optimization approach is chosen, an algorithm is used to minimize or maximize an objective function that describes the FLC's performance. Since the rule base contains a fuzzy inference mechanism (MAX, MIN operators), it is not possible to use algorithms that require differentiation of the objective function. Consequently, a direct

Part of the SPIE Conference on Sensors and Controls for Intelligent Machining and Agile Manufacturing
Boston, Massachusetts ● November 1998
SPIE Vol. 3518 ● 0277-786X/98/$10.00

73

search technique - a technique that evaluates only the function without using its derivatives needs to be selected as the optimization algorithm. There are quite a few direct search techniques available in the literature[10,11]. They differ from each other in their computational performance. However, they all are able to solve a multivariable optimization problem given an objective function to be optimized. The biggest issue then is not so much the choice of the algorithm but the formulation of the objective function so that it correctly represents the problem to be solved. The main emphasis of this paper is on defining an objective function. The optimization algorithm used in the study is a simple strategy that is easily programmed, and has been reported to be extremely useful in a wide variety of applications[10,11].

2.1. OBJECTIVE FUNCTION DEFINITION

Figure 1a shows an unsatisfactory initial attempt at a FLC design while aiming for a response as shown in Figure 1b. The response indicates performance of a feedback position control system with the FLC as the controller. Such a design can be improved using an optimization algorithm which requires definition of an objective function.

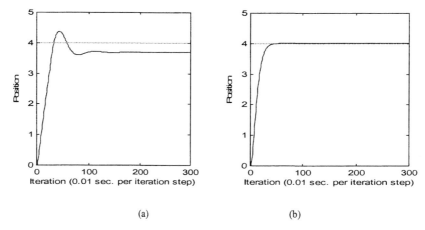

(a)   (b)

Figure 1.   (a) Unsatisfactory initial FLC design attempt, (b) desired FLC performance.

First, an approximate desired response ($y_d(t)$) is defined using two line segments (Fig. 2):

$$y_d(t) = \begin{cases} \dfrac{y_1 - y_0}{t_1 - t_0}(t - t_0) + y_0 & \text{for } t_0 \le t < t_1 \\[2mm] \dfrac{y_2 - y_1}{t_2 - t_1}(t - t_1) + y_1 & \text{for } t_1 \le t < t_2 \end{cases} \tag{1}$$

where (t_0, y_0) is the initial condition, (t_1, y_1) and (t_2, y_2) are two points specified by the designer.

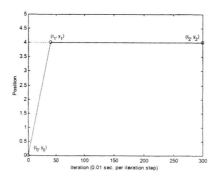

Figure 2.   Desired response definition.

Then, the objective function is defined by a 3D fuzzy set (Fig. 3) straddling the desired response (Fig. 2). The 3D fuzzy set is constructed by stacking 2D fuzzy sets side-by-side along the time (iteration) axis of the response curve:

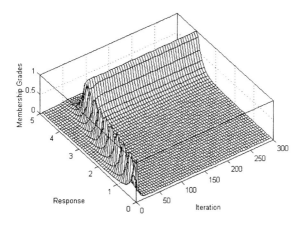

Figure 3.   3D fuzzy set.

$$\mu_{3D} = \frac{a_{3D}}{a_{3D} + b_{3D} \cdot [y - y_d(t)]^2} \tag{2}$$

where

y is the response (output of the controlled system)

a_{3D} is the spread of a 2D fuzzy set

b_{3D} is a coefficient to adjust the slope of the 2D fuzzy sets

$y_d(t)$ is the desired response at time t

The performance of the initial FLC is evaluated at every sampling time t by computing μ_{3D}. If the FLC response is not following the desired one, the optimization algorithm is called. The algorithm maximizes μ_{3D} by shifting the peak locations of all the fuzzy sets used in the rule base. This makes the response of the system under control of the FLC approach the desired one. In other words, the algorithm forces the system response to follow the crest of the hill created by μ_{3D} over the desired response.

However, this requires the optimization algorithm (explained later in section 3.3) to be used at every sampling instant t of the response. To reduce the frequency of usage of the algorithm a region around the desired response called the "response envelope" was defined. The boundary of the region is formed by the intersection of (2) with the following logistic function (Fig. 4):

$$\alpha(t) = \frac{a_\alpha}{1 + e^{-b_\alpha(t-t_i)}} + c_\alpha \tag{3}$$

where

a_α is the upper limit of the function

b_α is a coefficient to adjust the slope at the inflection point

c_α is the lower limit of the function

t_i is the inflection point of the function

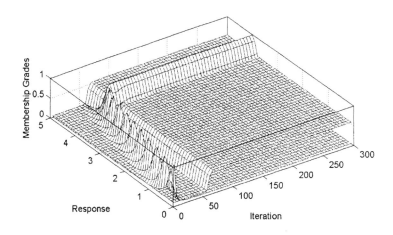

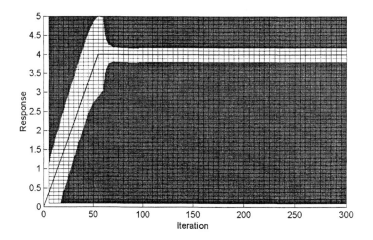

(Top view)

Figure 4.   Response envelope.

After this modification, the objective function is still evaluated at every sampling instant t to monitor the performance but the optimization algorithm is called only when the response goes outside the envelope:

$$\mu_{3D} < \alpha(t) \tag{4}$$

The algorithm then forces the response back towards the crest of the hill inside the envelope. The width of the resulting envelope can be controlled by adjusting a_α, b_α, c_α and the inflection point t_i of (3).

3.2.   TUNING RANGE
The method improves the FLC design by shifting the peak locations of the fuzzy sets in the rule base. However, if the movements of the fuzzy sets are left unconstrained the tuned system may have linguistically meaningless sets. Therefore, a set of inequality constraints called the "tuning range" were

developed. The tuning range is the part of the universe of discourse in which the manipulation of the peak location of a fuzzy set is permitted (Fig. 5). The tuning range for each fuzzy set in the design is defined using a lower and an upper limit. The optimization algorithm requires a vector of parameters (z^k) to be optimized. The vector is formed by the peak locations of the input and those of the output fuzzy sets. Similar vectors for the lower and upper tuning range limits are also formed (l_L^k and l_U^k). The size of each vector is (t_p x 1) and is determined by the total number of fuzzy sets used in the design (t_p). The objective function is augmented with the tuning ranges as:

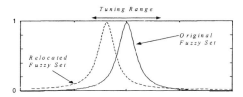

Figure 5.   Tuning range.

$$\mu_{3D} = \frac{a_{3D}}{a_{3D} + b_{3D} \cdot [y - y_d(t)]^2} - C \cdot \sum_{k=1}^{t_p} P^k \qquad (5)$$

where

$$P^k = \begin{cases} \left| z^k - l_U^k \right| & \text{if } z^k > l_U^k \\ \left| z^k - l_L^k \right| & \text{if } z^k < l_L^k \\ 0 & \text{if } l_L^k \leq z^k \leq l_U^k \end{cases} \qquad (6)$$

The added term, scaled by a constant C, is a global penalty function that reduces the value of μ_{3D} dramatically if the fuzzy sets are pushed beyond the limits of the tuning ranges. Since the algorithm tries to maximize the objective function, the dramatic drop in the value of the objective function causes it to move the sets back inside the tuning ranges and explore other solutions.

3.3.   DIRECT SEARCH ALGORITHM

This optimization algorithm[10] consists of two subdivisions called exploratory and pattern moves. To initiate the algorithm first a unit vector e^k ($k = 1, 2, \ldots, t_p$) is formed such that it contains all zeros except for a unity in the k th position. Then, the peak locations for the input and those for the output linguistic values are placed in the parameter vector z^k. Next, a perturbation with magnitude "s" is specified. Finally, the iteration and the parameter numbers are set as $i = 1$ and $k = 1$, respectively.

Exploratory moves are made about a point z_b^k called "base point". The first base point is chosen to be the parameter vector z_1^k containing the peak locations of the fuzzy sets used in the initial FLC design attempt. The exploration starts by perturbing the k th parameter in the forward direction

$$z = z_i^k + s \cdot e^k \qquad (7)$$

If the probe is successful, i.e.

$$\mu_{3D}(z) > \mu_{3D}(z_i^k) \tag{8}$$

then the perturbed value of the k th parameter is saved in a new vector to be used later

$$z_{i+1}^k = z \tag{9}$$

and a new parameter $(k + 1)$ is explored by computing z (7) and by repeating the above test (8). If the probe is unsuccessful, the same parameter k is explored in reverse direction:

$$z = z_i^k - s \cdot e^k \tag{10}$$

The above test (8) is then repeated and if it is successful the perturbed value is saved,

$$z_{i+1}^k = z \tag{11}$$

Otherwise the original value of the k th parameter is kept

$$z_{i+1}^k = z_i^k \tag{12}$$

and the next parameter $(k + 1)$ is explored in the same fashion. The exploration is completed when all the t_p parameters have been probed.

Pattern move is initiated by determining whether the exploratory moves were successful or not. If the exploration was successful, i.e.,

$$\mu_{3D}(z) > \mu_{3D}(z_b^k) \tag{13}$$

a pattern move is made and a new base point is established:

$$z_b^k = z_1^k + 2 \cdot (z - z_1^k)$$
$$z_1^k = z_b^k \qquad\qquad i = 1, k = 1 \tag{14}$$

Exploratory moves about the new base point are restarted. If condition (13) is not satisfied, and if

$$z \neq z_b^k \tag{15}$$

then exploration is repeated, however the step magnitude "s" is reduced for a finer search pattern:

$$s = s / 2 \tag{16}$$

The iteration terminates when "s" is reduced below a predetermined value "ε" and the optimized peak locations for the fuzzy sets are contained in z.

4.   RESULTS

To evaluate the performance of the proposed method two experiments were conducted. The first one is the simulation of position control of an inverted pendulum. This was chosen due to its popularity among the researchers in the field as a benchmark test system. The second experiment involves an educational control system hardware.

The simulations and tuning were performed using a software package that was developed by the author. The software runs under Windows operating system and allows the designer to enter the fuzzy sets, the rules, the system parameters, the tuning ranges and all the necessary optimization parameters using keyboard/mouse combinations. In addition, the designer can draw the desired response line segments (2) using the mouse. In all of the experiments the fuzzy sets used in the FLC designs were bell-shaped whose membership functions were computed by:

$$\mu(x) = \frac{a}{a + b \cdot (x - x_0)^2} \tag{17}$$

where "a" and "b" are constants used to control the spread and slope of the fuzzy set, respectively and x_0 is the peak location of the set.

4.1. POSITION CONTROL OF AN INVERTED PENDULUM

The vertical balancing of an inverted pendulum has been a very popular choice among the fuzzy control researchers, making it almost a benchmark test. Therefore, the method was used to tune an FLC controlling a simulated inverted pendulum in a closed loop system. Assuming no friction, the non-linear equations of motion for the inverted pendulum in state space form are:

$$\dot{x}_1 = x_2$$

$$\dot{x}_2 = \frac{g \cdot \sin x_1 + \cos x_1 \cdot \left(\dfrac{-f - m_p L(x_2)^2 \sin(x_1)}{m_c + m_p} \right)}{L \cdot \left(\dfrac{4}{3} - \dfrac{m_p \cos^2(x_1)}{m_c + m_p} \right)} \tag{18}$$

where "g" is the gravity, "f" is the control input, m_c is the cart mass, m_p is the pole mass, "L" is the pole length (Fig 6).

The states are: x_1 for the angular position of the pole measured in radians from the vertical and x_2 for the angular velocity of the pole (rad/s). The system parameters were chosen to be $m_c = 1$ kg, $m_p = 0.1$ kg and $L = 0.5$ m. The regions of interest for the angular error (in radians), change of error and control were chosen as [-1.05, 1.05], [-21, 21], and [-1100, 1100], respectively. The FLC used in this control system employs the rules given in Table 1. The untuned FLC has a minor overshoot with no steady state error, but it is slow (Fig. 6).

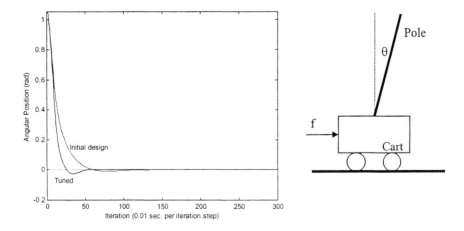

Figure 6.   Inverted pendulum response before and after tuning.

Error	Chg. of Error		
	NB	ZE	PB
NB	NB	NM	ZE
ZE	NM	ZE	PM
PB	ZE	PM	PB

Table 1.   Rule base.

To speed up the response, the controller was tuned using $a_\alpha = 0.8$, $b_\alpha = 1$, $c_\alpha = 0.04$, $t_i = 40$. The system response became faster, with the expense of a slight overshoot, and still with no steady state error (Fig. 6). Table 2 gives the peak locations of the fuzzy sets before and after the tuning.

Fuzzy Sets	Peak Points Initial	Peak Points Tuned	Membership Functions	Tuning Ranges	
				Lower	Upper
NB (error)	-1.05	-0.819	$a = 2.1, b = 100$	-1.05	-0.525
ZE (error)	0	0.084	$a = 2.1, b = 100$	-0.525	0.525
PB (error)	1.05	0.861	$a = 2.1, b = 100$	0.525	1.05
NB (chg. of err.)	-21	-16.38	$a = 42, b = 2$	-21	-10.5
ZE (chg. of err.)	0	2.52	$a = 42, b = 20$	-10.5	10.5
PB (chg. of err.)	21	17.22	$a = 42, b = 2$	10.5	21
NB (control)	-1100	-981.2	$a = 2200, b = 1$	-1100	-800
NM (control)	-500	-500	$a = 2200, b = 0.5$	-800	-250
ZE (control)	0	0	$a = 2200, b = 5$	-250	250
PM (control)	500	500	$a = 2200, b = 0.5$	250	800
PB (control)	1100	1020.8	$a = 2200, b = 1$	800	1100

Table 2.   Peak locations before and after tuning the inverted pendulum system.

4.1.   FUZZY LOGIC CONTROL OF AN EDUCATIONAL CONTROL SYSTEM

To test the method with actual hardware, an educational control system (Photograph 1) by Feedback, Inc. was used. The system consists of a DC motor, a tachometer, position sensor, inertial load, drive electronics, and a PC equipped with an interface card with A/D and D/A. The same rule base given in Table 1 was also used in this experiment. The goal of the control system is to control the angular position of an inertial load. The angular position, angular velocity, control input and desired position are all scaled to voltage signals. For example, if the load needs to be turned a quarter turn clockwise, the corresponding desired position command would be +4 volts.

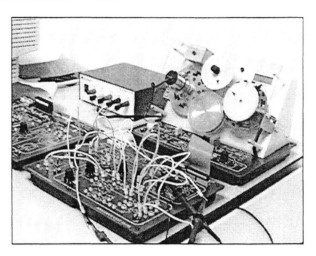

Photograph 1.   Educational control system.

In an initial FLC design attempt the peak locations given in Table 3 were chosen for the fuzzy sets. The universes of discourse for error, change of error and control were chosen to be [-8, 8], [-14, 14] and [-12, 12] volts, respectively. When the system is commanded to turn the load a quarter of a turn clockwise (+4 volts) it responds with an overshoot (Fig. 7), oscillations and a large steady state error (-2.084 volts which is about 1/8 of a turn). As is the case in general, the initial FLC design attempt has a poor performance.

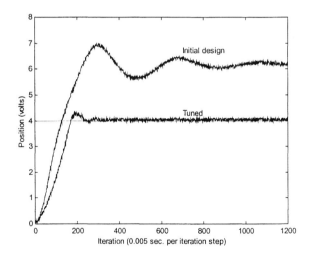

Figure 7.   Educational control system response with FLC before and after tuning.

To improve the performance of the FLC the software is run in the optimization mode. However, since neither the software nor the optimization algorithm is suitable for real-time tuning due to the computational overhead, first a system identification experiment was conducted and the following transfer function for the system was found:

$$G(s) = \frac{6.7335}{s(s+2)} \qquad (19)$$

Then, the transfer function was used in the software to tune the FLC by simulation. The resulting fuzzy set peaks are given in Table 3. After tuning, the system response improved drastically (Fig. 7). The overshoot was reduced to a negligible level. The sustained oscillations were eliminated and the steady state error became negligible (0.035 volts). In the tuning process the following parameters were used: $a_\alpha = 0.5$, $b_\alpha = 1$, $c_\alpha = 0.01$, $t_i = 240$.

Fuzzy Sets	Peak Points Initial	Peak Points Tuned	Membership Functions	Tuning Ranges	
				Lower	Upper
NB (error)	-8	-0.3	a = 16, b =50	-8	-0.3
ZE (error)	0	0.18	a = 16, b =200	-0.2	0.2
PB (error)	8	0.49	a = 16, b =50	0.3	8
NB (chg. of err.)	-14	-2.4	a = 28, b = 3	-14	-5.6
ZE (chg. of err.)	0	1.44	a = 28, b = 10	-1.6	1.6
PB (chg. of err.)	14	3.92	a = 28, b = 3	5.6	14
NB (control)	-12	-9.72	a = 24, b = 10	-12	-9.6
NM (control)	-6	-4.56	a = 24, b = 20	--8.4	-3.6
ZE (control)	0	0.72	a = 24, b = 20	-2.4	2.4
PM (control)	6	7.44	a = 24, b = 20	3.6	8.4
PB (control)	12	11.88	a = 24, b = 10	9.6	12

Table 3.   Peak locations before and after tuning the educational control system with FLC.

5. CONCLUSIONS

In this paper, an FLC tuning method was presented. The main emphasis of the study is on the definition of an objective function to be optimized. The proposed function can be used in many standard optimization techniques. In this study, a direct search algorithm was chosen.

The performance of the method was evaluated through two experiments. The first one, position control of an inverted pendulum, was chosen due to its popularity among the researchers in the field as a benchmark test system. The second one, position control of an educational control system hardware, was chosen to test the performance of the method with actual hardware. In both experiments, the method improved the initial design of the FLC.

The method is quite user-friendly. To tune an FLC all the designer needs to do is to draw two line segments indicating the desired response and enter a few parameters for the definition of the response envelope.

In this study, the shapes of the fuzzy sets were not altered in the tuning process. Currently, the method is being expanded to include optimization of the shapes as well.

6. REFERENCES

1. T. J. Ross, *Fuzzy Logic with Engineering Applications* , McGraw-Hill, Inc., New York, 1995.
2. H. R. Berenji and P. Khedkar, "Learning and tuning fuzzy logic controllers through reinforcements", *IEEE Trans. Neural Networks* vol. 3, 724-740, 1992.
3. C. Chao and C. Teng, "A PD-like self-tuning controller without steady-state error", *Fuzzy Sets and Systems* vol. 87, 141-154, 1997.
4. J. Shing and R. Jang, "ANFIS: Adaptive-network-based fuzzy inference system", *IEEE Trans. Sys., Man, and Cyb.,* vol. 23, 665-685, 1993.
5. T. Iwasaki, A. Morita and H. Maruyama, "Plant identification with fuzzy inference and its application to auto-tuning", *EME Int. Journal* vol. 38, 457-462, 1995.
6. P. Ramaswamy, R. M. Edwards and K. Y. Lee, "An automatic tuning method of a fuzzy logic controller for nuclear reactors", *IEEE Trans. Nuclear Sci.* vol. 40, 1253-1262, 1993.
7. H. B. Gurocak, "A genetic algorithm based method for tuning fuzzy logic controllers", *Fuzzy Sets and Systems* (in press).
8. F. Herrera, M. Lozano and J. L. Verdegay, "Tuning fuzzy controllers by genetic algorithms", *Inter. Journal of Approximate Reasoning*, vol. 12, 299-315, 1995.
9. J. C. Wu and T. S. Liu, "Fuzzy control of rider-motorcycle system using a genetic algorithm and auto tuning", *Mechatronics*, vol. 5, 441-455, 1995.
10. L.R. Foulds, *Optimization Techniques*, Springer, Berlin 1981.
11. P.E. Gill, W. Murray and M.H. Wright, *Practical Optimization*, Academic Press, 1981.

Study On Sliding Mode Controller For Positioning

Servo-Systems With Parameter Perturbances

Kai Xu*   Yan Lin**   Yonghua Li***

*Department of Electrical and Computer Engineering, Rutgers University, New Jersey
**Guangzhou Communication Institute, Guangzhou, P.R. China
***Department of Electronic and Electric Engineering, Wuhan Automotive Polytechnic University, Wuhan, P.R. China

Abstract

In general, the commutating voltage for a DC Pulse Width Modulator (PWM) fluctuates along with the power supply voltage changes. Therefore, when we describe the mathematical model of a PWM by a first order inertia unit, the gain of PWM unit will vary, e.g. the parameter of current loop will be perturbed. Additionally, in order to raise the safety coefficient of the resist voltage capacity of a large power transistor, the DC supply voltage is usually designed on a low level. As a consequence it causes a low fullness coefficient of starting current in the transient interval. Particularly when the PWM system is in a high velocity setting, the fullness coefficient of starting current is even lower, thus the designed maximum acceleration of system can not be guaranteed, and the transient process slows down. Therefore, when the setting is changed the parameter perturbance of PWM can not be ignored. Using the system identification technique to establish the mathematical model of the PWM system, we also observed that when the load of the positioning servo-system is an eccentric rotating plant, the change of the loading moment along with the angle displacement causes the parameter variation of the PWM system.

In this paper, we propose a new design method for the Discrete Sliding Mode Controller (DSMC) for the position servo loop that considers the influence of parameter perturbances. Different from the conventional design method, the probable variety region of parameter is taken into account in the computation. The result of this new design method eliminates the over-shoot and guarantees the stable, fast and precise positioning behavior of the controlled system in the presence of parameter perturbances. To verify the effectiveness of the proposed design method, a series of simulations for a positioning servo-system were conducted using both the conventional and proposed methods. The results have shown that the difference is obvious, and in various operating modes the proposed method produced better results.

The proposed design method has also been applied to a real industrial positioning servo-system consists of a 16 bit industrial microprocessor, a DC wide modulate servo-motor, a current regulator, a velocity regulator, a photoelectric encoder and a D/A converter. The DSMC of the position servo loop is performed by software. In order to obtain the parameter perturbance region of the controlled plant (a PWM velocity governing system, using pseudo random binary signal (PRBS) as the exciting signal), the Generalized Least Square Estimation (GLSE) algorithm was adopted for modeling in various loading conditions, power supply voltage levels and setting values. The DSMC was designed in accordance with the perturbance region of estimated parameters. The running results in situ proved that the system had a high quality behavior in various operating modes. Several graphs and curves of the system are presented in the paper.

Part of the SPIE Conference on Sensors and Controls for Intelligent Machining and Agile Manufacturing
Boston, Massachusetts ● November 1998
SPIE Vol. 3518 ● 0277-786X/98/$10.00

1. TWO DESIGN PRINCIPLES OF DSMC
FOR MODEL CERTAINTY AND UNCERTAINTY.

Generally, the designed method of discrete sliding mode controller (DSMC) is on the basis of plant model certainty (simply named: methed 1). In fact, the uncertainty of the controlled plant is a reality and unavoidable. Consequently, using method 1 to design DSMC, some unacceptable bad behaviors even unstability of the control system may occure. So the designed method based on model uncertainty (simply named: method 2) appears as more importance for applying the DSMC to industrial situ. In the paper, the authors choose the parameter perturbances of controlled plant as a measure of the model uncertainty to discuss the differences of two design methods, and reveal the different control effects of two kinds DSMC.

1.1 Model Certainty Design Principle of Discrete Sliding Model Controllers (DSMC) – Method 1
Considering a SISO discrete control system, the state equation and output equation can be described by Eqn. (1)

$$\begin{cases} X(k+1) = \Phi X(k) + \Gamma u(k) \\ y(k) = CX(k) \end{cases} \tag{1}$$

where $X(k)$ is n dimentional state vector, $u(k)$、$y(k)$ are single input and single output respectively.

Supposing the sliding hyperplane $s(k)$ as follows

$$s(k) = \{X \mid GX(k) = 0\} \tag{2}$$

and dividing the designed parameters into two parts. At first, we discuss the case that the system is operating in sliding mode stage, because the motion rests on the hyperplane, it satisfies the equation $s(k+1) = s(k)$, thus the equivalent control $u_e(k)$ can be deduced by Eqn. (1) and Eqn. (2), that is

$$u_e(k) = -(G\Gamma)^{-1}G(\Phi - I)X(k) \tag{3}$$

Substituting Eqn. (3) for $u(k)$ of Eqn. (1), yield

$$X(k+1) = [\Phi - \Gamma(G\Gamma)^{-1}G(\Phi - I)]X(k) \tag{4}$$

In this case, substantially, the system is a linear state feedback control system. The designed principle of vector $G = (g_1, g_2, \cdots, g_n)$ should ensure the stability of discrete system described by following Eqn. (5)

$$\begin{cases} X(k+1) = [\Phi - \Gamma(G\Gamma)^{-1}G(\Phi - I)]X(k) \\ GX(k) = 0 \end{cases} \tag{5}$$

Next, we research the existence condition of discrete sliding motion, it means that in state space an arbitrarily state vector of the system can be moved to rest on the hyperplane by the action of DSMC.

Choosing $v(k) = s^2(k)$ as Liapunov function, the existence condition of sliding mode motion is given is following

$$v(k+1) < v(k) \tag{6}$$

Assuming the output $u(k)$ of controller as follows

$$u(k) = (\Psi_e + \Psi)X(k) - \psi_0 s(k) \tag{7}$$

where, $\Psi_e = -(G\Gamma)^{-1}G(\Phi - I)$; Switching vector $\Psi = (\psi_1, \psi_2, \cdots, \psi_n)$; gain ψ_0. As long as the vector G is determined, the Ψ_e is determined. It is noted that the selection of Ψ and ψ_0 should staisfy the existence condition of sliding mode motion, namely Eqn. (6)

If the designed values Ψ and ψ_0 satisfy the following conditions [3]

(1)
$$0 < \rho < 1 \tag{8}$$

where
$$\rho \triangleq \psi_0(G\Gamma)$$

(2)
$$\psi_i = \begin{cases} f_0 & \text{if} \quad G\Gamma x_i(k)s(k) < -\delta_i \\ 0 & \text{if} \quad \mid G\Gamma x_i(k)s(k) \mid \leqslant \delta_i \\ -f_0 & \text{if} \quad G\Gamma x_i(k)s(k) > \delta_i \end{cases} \tag{9}$$

where $i = 1, 2, \cdots, n$

$$\delta_i = \frac{f_0(G\Gamma)^2}{2(1-\rho)} \mid x_i(k) \mid \sum_{j=1}^{n} \mid x_j(k) \mid \tag{10}$$

$$0 < f_0 < \frac{2(1-\rho) \mid s(k) \mid}{\mid G\Gamma \mid \sum_{j=1}^{n} \mid x_i(k) \mid} \tag{11}$$

thus the existence condition of sliding mode motion, namely Eqn. (6), is satisfied (The proof is omitted).

1.2 Model Uncertainty Design Principle of Discrete Sliding Mode Controller (DSMC) – Method 2

Considering the existence of parameter perturbances of controlled plant, correspondingly, assume the increment $\Delta\Phi$ of state matrix Φ in the discrete state equation (1) as follows:

$$\Delta\Phi = \Gamma D \tag{12}$$

$$D = [d_1 d_2 \cdots d_n], \mid d_i \mid < \bar{d} \ (i = 1, 2, \cdots, n) \tag{13}$$

thus the Eqn. (1) turns to Eqn. (14)

$$\begin{cases} X(k+1) = (\Psi + \Delta\Psi)X(k) + \Gamma u(k) \\ y(k) = CX(k) \end{cases}$$

and Eqns. (9). (10). (11) are modified by Eqns. (15). (16). (17) respectively [4]

$$\psi_i = \begin{cases} f_0 & \text{if} \quad G\Gamma x_i(k)s(k) < -\delta'_i \\ 0 & \text{if} \quad \mid G\Gamma x_i(k)s(k) \mid \leqslant \delta'_i \\ -f_0 & \text{if} \quad G\Gamma x_i(k)s(k) > \delta'_i \end{cases} \tag{15}$$

where $i = 1, 2, \cdots, n$

$$\delta'_i = \frac{(G\Gamma)^2}{2(1-\rho)} \mid x_i(k) \mid \sum_{j=1}^{n} \mid x_j(k) \mid (f_0 + \bar{d}) \tag{16}$$

$$\bar{d} < f_0 < \frac{2(1-\rho) \mid s(k) \mid}{\mid G\Gamma \mid \sum_{j=1}^{n} \mid x_i(k) \mid} - \bar{d} \tag{17}$$

2. THE COMPARATIVE SIMULATION RESEARCH OF TWO DESIGN METHODS

For the controlled plant model being perturbed by parameter perturbances, the comparative research work of two design methods mentioned in section 1 is conducted. It is found the robustness of system designed by method 2 is better than that designed by method 1 either of stability and quality.

Now, the positioning servo-system for comparative simulation is illustrated in following figure.

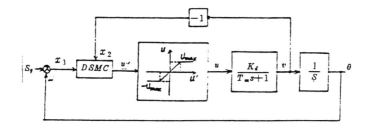

Fig. 1 Block diagram of the real discrete sliding mode control system

In Fig. 1, the control output u' of discrete sliding mode controller (DSMC) is transformed into output u by the amplitute limiter unit ($\pm u_{max}$), then u acts on the PWM velocity governing system. The transfer function of PWM is described in $\dfrac{K_d}{T_m S + 1}$ from [5]. Suppose that the parameter perturbance value of time constant T_m is 50%, namely $\Delta T_m = \pm 0.5 T_m$, and assume the state variables

$$
\begin{cases}
x_1 = s_g - \theta \\
\quad \text{position error} \\
x_2 = \dot{x}_1 = -\dot{\theta} = -v \\
\quad \text{velocity (negative value)}
\end{cases}
\tag{18}
$$

$$\text{(19)}$$

Correspondingly, the state equation of the continous system is

$$\dot{X} = AX + Bu \tag{20}$$

where

$$
A = \begin{bmatrix} 0 & 1 \\ 0 & -\dfrac{1}{T_m} \end{bmatrix};
$$

$$
B = \begin{bmatrix} 0 \\ -\dfrac{K_d}{T_m} \end{bmatrix}
\tag{21}
$$

setting the sampling period T_s, the discretization state equation of the system is given by

$$X(k+1) = \Phi X(k) + \Gamma u \tag{22}$$

where

$$
\Phi = \begin{bmatrix} 1 & T_m - T_m e^{-\frac{T_s}{T_m}} \\ 0 & e^{-\frac{T_s}{T_m}} \end{bmatrix}
$$

$$\Gamma = \begin{bmatrix} -K_d T_s + K_d T_m (1 - e^{-\frac{T_s}{T_m}}) \\ -K_d (1 - e^{-\frac{T_s}{T_m}}) \end{bmatrix}$$

Setting $\qquad G = [g_1 \quad 1]$

As mentioned above, the principle of the selection of value g_1 is to ensure the stability of Eqn. (5).

Substituting following real values of the system into the equations, that is $T_m = 0.083s, \Delta T_m \doteq \pm 0.5 T_m$ (correspanding to $D = [0, \pm 0.2]), K_d = 5.488, T_s = 0.008s, \pm u_{max} = \pm 0.205$, and choosing the eigen value of system $z = 0.9$, $\rho = 0.5$, We respectively use method 1 and 2 to design the DSMC. The results are obtained, and the superiority of method 2 can be illustrated by the system response curves $v(t); \theta(t)$; phase plane figure and Table 1.

Table 1

Orginal values of the controlled plant	Parameter perturbance D	Design method 1 Eqns. (9),(10), (11),$\bar{d}=0$		Design method 2 Eqns,(15),(16), (17),$\bar{d}=0.5$	
		Number of phase plane figure $v(t)$, $\theta(t)$	Control effect	Number of phase plane figure $v(t)$, $\theta(t)$	Control effect
$T_s = 0.008s$ $T_m = 0.083s$ $K_d = 5.488$	$D = [0 \quad +0.2]$	Fig. 2	$v(t)$ Chattering	Fig. 3	Positioning smoothing
	$D = [0 \quad -0.1]$	Fig. 4	Positioning overshoot	Fig. 5	Positioning non-overshoot
	$D = [0 \quad -0.2]$	Fig. 6	Unstable system Phase plane curve divergence	Fig. 7	Stable system Phase plane curve convergence

3. ILLUSTRATION OF A REAL SYSTEM

The real positioning servo-system is shown in Fig. 8, it is configured by a 16 bit industrial control microprocessor; PWM velocity governing system; photoelectric encoder; D/A convertor; phase discriminator and other interface devices. The DSMC designed by method 2 is performed by software of the 16 bit control microprocessor. The feedback

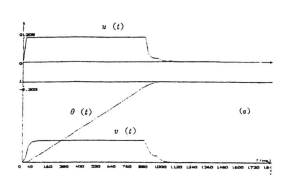

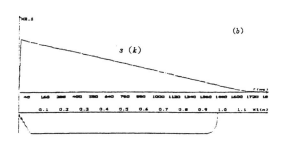

Fig. 2 **a.** u (t), v (t), θ (t) curves

b. s (t) trajectory on phase plane

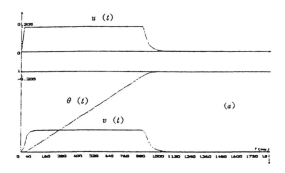

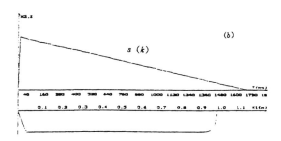

Fig. 3 **a.** u (t), v (t), θ (t) curves

b. s (t) trajectory on phase plane

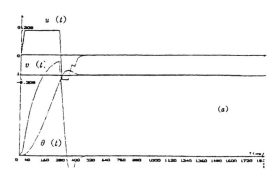

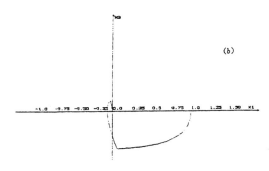

Fig. 4 **a.** u (t), v (t), θ (t) curves

θ (t) has overshoot ovbiously

b. Trajectory on phase plane

(passing through Ⅱ, Ⅲ, Ⅳ quadrants)

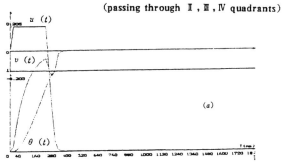

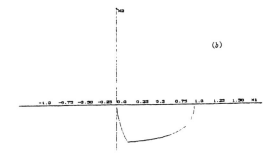

Fig. 5 **a.** u (t), v (t), θ (t) curves

b. Traijectory on phase plane

(passing througn Ⅳ quadrant)

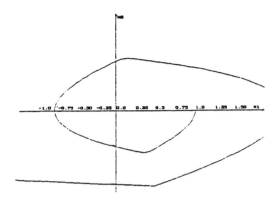
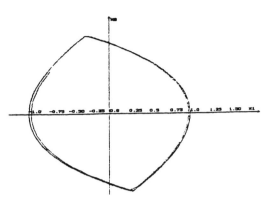

Fig. 6 Curves divergence on phase plane   Fig. 7 Curves convergence on phase plane

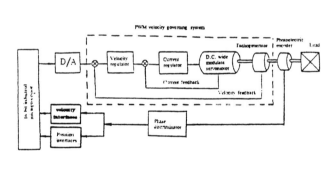

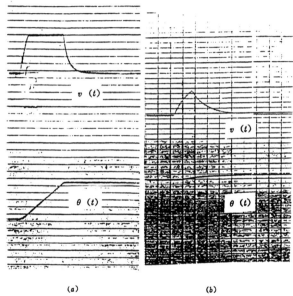

(a)   (b)

Fig. 8 A real positioning servo – system

Fig. 9 a. $v(t) . \theta(t)$ curves at large setting
b. at small setting

values of position and velocity are sampled and generated by the photoelectric encoder in pulsed form, and input to the 16 bit control microprocessor by means of the phase discriminator and both velocity and position interfaces.

The experimental results are given by Fig. 9a and Fig. 9b, where Fig. 9a shows the velocity and position curves at large setting $s_g = 1.94$m. In this case the velocity figure is a rectangle waveform, meanwhile the displacement figure is smooth and non – overshoot, Fig. 9b shows the same items at small setting $s_g = 0.52$m, where the velocity is triangular, and the displacement is smooth and non – overshoot as well.

4. CONCLUSION

By the comparative research of two design methods, the result revealed that using the DSMC designed by method 1 the system may occur bad response behavior and even instability under the action of parameter perturbances, however, under the same condition, using the DSMC designed by method 2 the system presents the satisfactory robustness and stability. Finally, authors successfully applied the DSMC designed by method 2 to a real positioning servo-system, the experimental results showed that the system had good quality in various operating states.

REFERENCES

1. Xu Fangtong et al, "Identification of Dynamic Model of Double Loop DC. PWM Speed Control System", ELECTRIC DRIVE (in Chinese), pp. 36-41, Vol. 23, No. 2, 1993
2. Li Yonghua et al, "Dynamic Behavior Identification of SR System For Variable Load", ELECTRICAL AUTOMATION (in Chinese), pp. 43-44, Vol. 16, No. 4, 1994
3. C.Y. Chan, "Servo-Systems With Discrete Variable Structure Control", SYSTEMS & CONTROL LETTERS 17, pp. 321-325, 1991
4. Katsuisa Furuta, "Sliding Mode Control of A Discrete System", SYSTEMS & CONTROL LETTERS 14, pp. 145-152, 1990
5. Wang Lijiu et al, "Automatic Control Systems of Electrical Drive (in Chinese), Press of Huazhong University of Science and Technology, pp. 310, 1991

SESSION 3

Control Systems II

Development and Implementation of An Application Programming Interface for PC/DSP Based Motion Control System[1]

Timothy Chang, Kedar Godbole, Murat Eren, Zhiming Ji, Reggie Caudill
New Jersey Institute of Technology
Newark, NJ 07201

ABSTRACT

This paper presents the results of a low cost, PC-DSP based motion control system development. The Texas Instruments TMS320C31 floating point Digital Signal Processor is selected for the real-time hardware platform while code development and user interface tasks reside on a standard, non real-time PC platform such as the Pentium/Windows 95 systems. An Application Programming Interface (API) has been implemented to facilitate open architecture code development. Finally, application to the control of an Adept linear robotic workcell is made with 2 input shaper designs serving as the test algorithms.

Keywords: motion control, robot, application programming interface, digital signal processor, real-time control

1. INTRODUCTION

Until recently, motion control hardware and software are highly proprietary and supplier dependent. Code portability and cross-platform interconnect are virtually non-existent.
Push towards open architecture (e.g. NIST [1] and NEMI [2]) lead to effort in establishing standard API for motion and machine control. For example:

- Cimetrix CODE API integrates robot and machine with motion control.
- ASAP ASIC100 combines PLC programming with RS-274 motion control.
- NEMI Low Cost API which provides an operating system independent Common API. The use of ANSI C also ensures full portability of code to and from different hardware platforms.
- Spectron Microsystems SPOX real-time kernel/OS generates hooks into the real-time environment, allowing the DSP to become the master processor that has full access to all peripherals on the PC.

However, most existing APIs are expensive, require large run-time overhead and initial outlay of training effort. In this work, we present a simple API which is easy to use, code efficient, and ANSI C compatible. Such API is particular suitable for University R&D work where rapid prototyping and control benchmarking are of prime interest. A PC-DSP based control platform is chosen for the following reasons: 1) Wide user base of PCs, 2) New PC bus structures such as PC/104 and CompactPCI have significantly improved the data rate, 3) The ever plummeting prices of the PC systems offer new possibility for low cost control, and 4) High bandwidth and low cost of floating point signal processors such as the TMS320C3x series further enhance throughput of the control hardware.

However, the lack of hardware standard and interface protocol between the PC and the DSP remains a development bottleneck for motion control systems based on such hardware platform. In this paper, results on implementing an Application Programming Interface and the relevant test results will be presented.

2. HARDWARE DESCRIPTION

The experimental system consists of the following hardware:

- An Adept Technology two-axis linear robotic workcell with MV-8 VME controller [7].
- Pentium PC with Windows 95.

[1] This work is supported, in part, by a NIST ATP Grant NO. 70NANB5H1092 and the Multi-lifecycle Engineering and Research Center, NJIT.

- Dalanco-Spry Model 310B Digital Signal Processor Board with TMS320C31 processor [3].
- Tech80 Encoder Interface Board.

Control system for the robot is centered around the Pentium PC. The MV-8 VME controller is used only for performance comparison. The DSP system and an encoder interface card are added as cards into the expansion bus for the PC.

An actual view of the system is shown in Figure 1 while the system block diagram is shown in Figure 2.

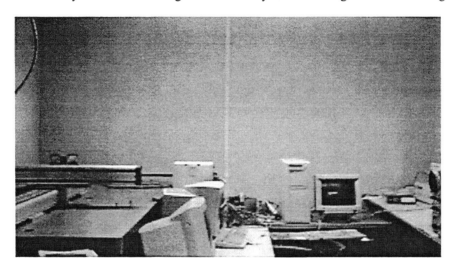

Figure1 PC-DSP Based Robot Control

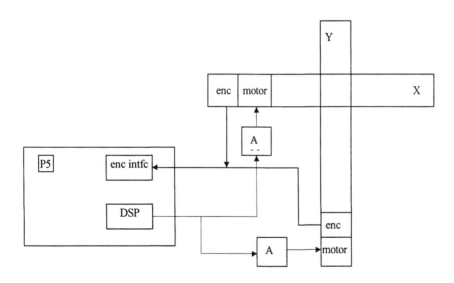

Figure 2 Block Diagram of the Workcell

2.1. ROBOTIC WORKCELL

The Adept robot consists of two linear modules: a type H module and a smaller type M module mounted on the type H module. The module basically is a precision ground ball-screw drive mechanism, with linear guides for the slide. The screw is driven by an AC servo motor. Each module also has sensors for detecting the positive or negative over-travel.

2.1.1 H-module
The H-module is the largest module in the series and offers the highest load handling capability. Standard H-modules have stroke lengths from 300 mm to 1000 mm. The H-module consists of a 20 mm pitch ball screw, with 25 mm linear guides and a 300 W motor. The H-module is 180 mm wide and 90 mm high. The standard H-modules are supplied with direct-mount motors, while extended stroke H-modules are supplied with side-mount motors. The H modules are intended to carry the M, and other smaller modules.

2.1.2 M-module
The M-module is a smaller module, with stroke lengths ranging from 250 mm to 950 mm and special order stroke lengths from 1150 mm to 1550 mm. The M module also has a 20 mm pitch ball-screw but with a single 50 mm linear guide. The ball-screw is again driven by a 300 W motor. The M-module also does not have a holding brake and is intended for use in the horizontal plane only. Some selected specifications of the modules are detailed in Table 1.

Table 1: Specifications of H and M Modules

Module Type	Stroke (mm)	Max. Speed (mm/sec)	Repeat-Ability (mm)	Ball Screw Pitch (mm)	Max. Payload (kg)	Motor mount	Rated Thrust Force (N)
H-module	1000	1200	0.01	20	60	Direct	300
M-module	550	1200	0.01	20	60	Direct	300

Table 2: Motor and Encoder specifications

Motor	300 W AC servo-motor
Position Feedback	2000 lines/revolution Maximum frequency: 150kHz.
Max. motor speed	3600 rpm
Power	1170 VA max. (at max. torque.) Single Phase 180-240 V

With the matching power amplifier for the motor, the robot module can be viewed as a DC servo motor with an inertial load attached to it. Since the leadscrew is a ball-screw mechanism the frictional effects are small and can be neglected. The mass on the slider can be reflected onto the motor shaft as a rotational inertia. Thus the problem is reduced to modeling the DC servo motor problem, and the translation of the linear quantities into the angular quantities. Experimentally, it was determined the lowest order model representing each of the H (X) and M (Y) modules is given by:

$$\frac{X(s)}{V(s)} = \frac{a}{s(s+b)} \tag{1}$$

The parameters a and b were computed for a variety of load conditions using transient response test, i.e. by closing the loop with proportional control and determining the overshoot and ringing period. Under nominal conditions, for the H module, a=4930.8, b=7.1577 while for the M module, a=16559, b=0.8372, where the dimensions of X and Y are expressed in counts (scale factors for X and V are, respectively, 2.5 microns/count and 2.5 mV/count).

2.2 The PC
A block diagram for the system hardware is shown in Figure 2. The PC is a standard Intel Pentium based system. The system has a 100MHz P5, with 16M RAM. The DSP card and the encoder counter card are installed in the PC as ISA add-on cards. In our system the position data is transferred to the DSP system via the PC. This imposes a restriction on the sampling rate, if the processor is not fast enough. The PC may use

any generic operating system such as MS DOS or Microsoft Windows '95 etc. No real time O/S is used or is necessary. Timing and synchronization are achieved in the DSP system.

2.3 The Digital Signal Processor

The DSP system used for this project was the 'Dalanco-Spry' Data Acquisition and Signal Processing Board - Model 310B. Block diagram of the Model 310B is shown in Figure 3 below [3]:

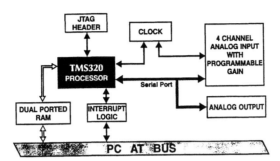

Figure 3: Architecture of the Model 310B DSP Card

The DSP board has a Texas Instruments' TMS320C31 DSP chip running at 50MHz, two 12-bit DAC, a 14-bit ADC with a four channel differential multiplexer, and 128k words of memory. The memory on the DSP board is dual ported, i.e. it is accessible at any time to the DSP as well as to the PC via the bus interface. The ADC and the DAC are however accessible only to the DSP. Any data from the ADC and to the DAC must pass through the C31. The DAC is capable of outputting at a maximum rate of 140kHz. The ADC has a maximum conversion rate of 300kHz and has a programmable gain amplifier that gives a software programmable gain, ranging from 1 to 1000, facilitating the handling of signals with small amplitudes.

2.4 TMS320C31 DSP

The C31 is a simplified version of the C30. A block diagram of the internal architecture is given in Figure 4 below [6]:

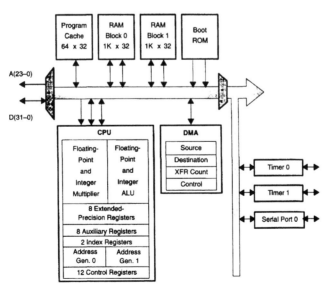

Figure 4: Architecture of the TMS320C31

In the Model310B, the serial port is assigned to communication with the ADC and DAC while other key components are utilized as:

- Timers 0 and 1: Timer 0 is used to trigger conversion on the ADC. The primary sampling rate is embedded into the conversion rate of the ADC whose serial transmission is framed by an external 5 MHz clock. Secondary control signal timing can be realized by programming timer 1.
- Internal RAM blocks 0 and 1: Variables, stack, and heap.
- Interrupts: INT0 is used for PC interrupt to the DSP while INT1 to INT3 are connected to monitor external asynchronous events such as robot over-travel, etc.
- External Memory: Code and data storage.

A memory map of the C31 is given in Figure 5:

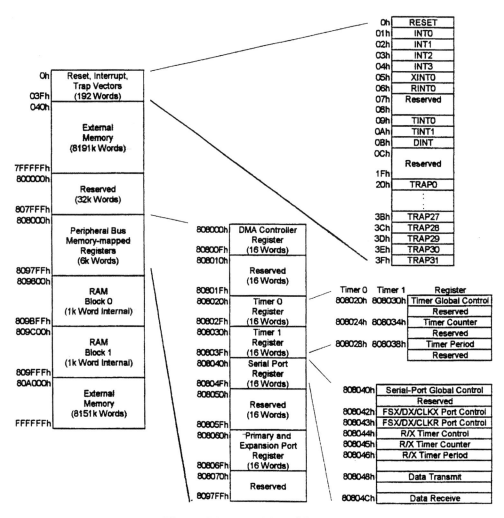

Figure 5: Memory Map of the TMS320C31

2.5 Encoder Based Position Sensing

The encoders are mounted on the motor shaft driving the ball-screw. The encoder is a rotary encoder and actually measures the angular position of the shaft. With a 2 cm pitch and encoder resolution of 2000 pulses per revolution, the equivalent linear resolution is 100,000 counts per meter. This scale factor is further enhanced by using the quadrature mode thus giving 400,000 counts per meter, or 2.5 microns per count. However the overall position accuracy is limited by the mechanical precision of the ball-screw and other mechanical tolerances, giving a repeatability of about 10 microns. The encoder interface card keeps track of the robot module positions. The encoder board is basically a set of counters. The inputs are filtered by a digital filter before the counters. The digital filter has a programmable cut-off frequency, which may be optimized to suit each application. The filtered inputs are applied to 24-bit counters. In this experimental system, a cut-off frequency of 5MHz was found satisfactory. The lowest frequency compatible with the highest input rate expected gives the best noise rejection while still ensuring the recording of data.

3. SOFTWARE DEVELOPMENT

The TI DSP software development environment supports the Common Object File Format (COFF) and ANSI C language, thus significantly simplifying code development on the PC for the DSP. The software tools used in this project include:

- TI C compiler, assembler, linker for floating point C3x/C4x DSP.
- Borland C/C++ Complier for the PC.
- Dalanco-Spry debugger, loader, and library functions.

3.1 C Programming on the DSP

Central to the C code development for the DSP is the suitable utilization of the Common Object File Format (COFF) where each object file consists of a file header, section headers, raw data, relocation information, line numbers, a symbol table, and a string table.

For the C31, the most common sections are .text (code), .data (initialized data),.bss (uninitialized variables), and name sections such as the interrupt vector table.

Input object files are combined by the linker to create an executable output file according to the memory and section directives specified in the linker command file.

A sample linker command file is shown in Figure 6:

```
-c                                    /* LINK USING C CONVENTIONS    */
-stack 0x400                          /* 1K STACK                    */
vecs.obj
window.obj
c30int.obj
-heap  0x400                          /* 1K HEAP                     */
-1 rts30.lib                          /* GET RUN-TIME SUPPORT        */


/* SPECIFY THE SYSTEM MEMORY MAP */

MEMORY
{
   RAMVECS: org = 0x0   len = 0x40   /* EXTERNAL MEMORY for vector table */
   WINDOW:  org = 0x40  len = 0x20 /*EXTERNAL MEMORY for PC-TMS320 sharing*/
   EXT0:    org = 0x60  len = 0x7fA0 /* EXTERNAL MEMORY for 32K system    */
   RAM0:    org = 0x809800 len = 0x400    /* RAM BLOCK 0              */
   RAM1:    org = 0x809c00 len = 0x400    /* RAM BLOCK 1              */
}

/* SPECIFY THE SECTIONS ALLOCATION INTO MEMORY */

SECTIONS
{
   "vecs"   : {} > RAMVECS
   "window" : {} > WINDOW
   .text:   > EXT0                    /* CODE                       */
   .cinit:  > EXT0                    /* INITIALIZATION TABLES      */
   .const:  > EXT0                    /* CONSTANTS                  */
   .stack:  > RAM0                    /* SYSTEM STACK               */
/* .sysmem: > RAM1                    DYNAMIC MEMORY - DELETE IF NOT USED */
   .bss:    > EXT0, block 0x10000              /* VARIABLES          */
}
```

Figure 6: Sample Linker Command File

In the linker command file, the interrupt jump table is supplied by vecs.obj which is loaded at locations 0 to 3Fh. The function c30int.obj handles all interrupts except RESET which is vectored to _ c_ int00. Linkage of this label to boot.ob j in rts30.lib enables the following tasks to be executed: 1) definition of .stack section for system stack, 2) setting up initial stack and frame pointer, 3) initialization of global variables by copying data from .cinit to .bss section, 4) setting up page pointer to .bss, and 5) calling main() to begin execution.

3.2 System Interaction

The software for this project was developed completely in 'C', with the exception of some assembly language embedded in C for implementing a C language interface library for the DSP card. The software programs in this project ran simultaneously on both platforms: the control algorithms were executed on the DSP. The programs on the PC performed the functions of data acquisition and supervisory functions. The position of the encoder is read from the encoder interface card by the PC, which is then put into the memory of the DSP by the PC. The DSP then accesses this position and then calculates the servo command. The hardware interface to the encoder card and the DSP card is through the PC-ISA bus. Figure 7 shows the data flow . The hardware interface to the encoder card and the DSP card is through the PC-ISA bus.

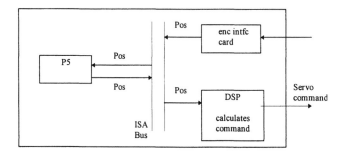

Figure 7: Data Flow Between the PC and the DSP

3.3 API for the Digital Signal Processing Card

The Dalanco-Spry Model 310 B Data Acquisition and Signal Processing card has four analog input channels and two analog output channels. The programmers interface to these analog inputs and outputs through assembly language is both time consuming and complex. This typically tends to complicate the software development and the effort on part of the programmer has to be concentrated on the program development rather than the development of the control algorithm or other application at hand. It was therefore necessary to develop a C language library which would encapsulate the entire card into a generic device, and frees the user from the need to know any internal details or the need to spend time and effort to learn the assembler for the DSP.

3.3.1 Description of the API

The following sections describe the function calls which form the entire user interface to the signal processing card. To make use of these calls it is necessary to include the file 'd310bio.h' as a header at the start of the program.

3.3.2 Initialization

The Dalanco Board needs initialization at startup. The ADC connects to the serial port on the DSP. So the serial port and timer must be set up, and also the latch on the Dalanco Spry Board must be set up. For this the *InitDSP()* function is implemented. The function call prototype is

void InitDSP(void);

The function begins by setting up a few pointers. The latch in the Dalanco Spry Board contains the ADC channel number and the gain for the programmable gain amplifier (PGA). This latch is set up, as a default, to set the ADC channel to 0 and a unity gain for the programmable gain amplifier. These are just the defaults, by accessing the latch before each conversion the user can set the gain for the PGA as well as set the channel. The function ReadAdc takes care of the function of setting the channel. The word format for the LATCH_VAL word is shown in Figure 8.

B3	B2	B1	B0
g_1	g_0	m_1	m_0

Figure 8: Word Format for the ADC Latch

The bits g_1 and g_0 set the gain of the programmable gain amplifier (PGA),while the bits m_1 and m_0 set the channel for the ADC multiplexer. The PGA gain is set by the value of the word g_1g_0, i.e. 00=>1, 01=>10, 10=>100 and 11=>1000. The ADC channel gets set to the value of the word m_1m_0, i.e. 00=0, 01=1, 10=2 and 11=3. The other bits in the LATCH_VAL are 'don't cares'. Following this the function now sets up the DSP chip registers itself. The registers set up are the Timer registers, and the Serial port control registers. In the C31 these are memory mapped. To do this a pointer is set up to the register area which in the C31 is at 808000_{16} and the values are written to the registers. This sets up the DSP to ADC communication on the serial port. The ReadAdc and WriteDAC functions can now be called, to perform analog I/O as desired.

3.2.3 Analog Output
The output to the analog channels is written via the DAC. The function call for this is *WriteDAC(..)*. The C prototype for this is

int WriteDAC(int value, int channel);

This outputs the value to the DAC channel specified. Since the DAC has two channels legal values for *channel* are 0 and 1. The value passed as *value* may be in the range -2047 to 2047. If the value is greater than 2047 it is clamped off to 2047, and if less than -2047, is also restricted to -2047. This clamping is done by the function WriteDAC and need not be performed by the user. This is to avoid problems associated with 'roll over'. If the value is greater than 2047, then it cannot be properly expressed in 12 bits and leads to wrong interpretation of the value. This also ensures that the saturation associated with the DAC output is properly reflected in the software. Thus if a value of 4096 is output to the DAC with an intended output value of 10V, it gets clamped to 5V only, since the DAC output is restricted to 5V. Similar clamping occurs on the negative side. The function WriteDAC retains the value output to the DAC channel 0 and channel 1. For this reason the declaration for channel_value[] is prefixed with static. The reason for maintaining the last value is that every write essentially modifies both the DACs. In C, it is made to appear as if each DAC is written to separately. While this is more convenient to use, it means that the function WriteDAC must know the value of the other DAC previously written. If this value is not stored, then when one DAC is written the other DAC output will be trashed. Clearly this would be unacceptable, and this is overcome by storing the previously output values. So actually the function WriteDAC always updates both the DACs, and effectively makes it appear as if only one DAC is updated every time. The value for the DAC channel 1 must be put into the upper 16 bits, i.e. right justified in the upper 16 bit word. This shifting is done, and then the values for the two channels are 'OR'ed together and then output via the serial port. Obviously if both the converters are to be updated, then it is more efficient to do so in one call and for this another function call, *WriteDACS(..)* is available. This function call updates both the DAC channels in one call. The prototype for this function is

int WriteDACS(int value0, int value1);

The channels 0 and 1 are updated with the values *value1* and *value2*. This is more efficient if both the converters are to be updated. For instance in our work, the controller writes both the servo commands by calling this function, two calls to WriteDAC are not used.

3.2.4 Analog Input
To input analog values from the ADC the function *ReadAdc()* is called. The prototype for this function is

int ReadAdc(int channel);

This reads the value from the ADC for the voltage applied on the specified channel. The function returns values ranging from -2048 to 2047 for voltages ranging from -5V to 5V. The integer data type 'int' on the C31 DSP is 32 bits, while the conversion result is 12 bits. The necessary sign extension is performed internally and the user does not need to perform any such extension. To read from more than one channel multiple calls to ReadAdc are necessary. Since the ADC on the card has four channels, legal values for *channel* are from 0 to 3. If the voltage at the ADC input is to be calculated then the ADC output is simply multiplied by the scaling factor 5/2047. The function begins by writing the channel (and the default gain of unity) to the latch. Once the latch is set the function waits for the conversion to be triggered by the TCLK0 pin toggling. This pin is the output of the Timer 0. Whenever the count is complete the pin goes high, stays high for a clock period and then goes low. This event is used for triggering the ADC in hardware. This also is used to synchronize the software to a time source. The timer runs off the DSP clock, in the timer mode, and its accuracy is determined by the resolution of the DSP clock, which is very stable to a few nanoseconds. This is the source of timing in all the control programs written with this library.

3.2.5 Sampling Rate Determination

To use the above function calls include the file 'd310bio.h' at the start of the program. The example program in Appendix A. shows a very basic example. Also it is necessary to define the sampling rate for the system. This is done by defining the constant TIMPER0. The functions WriteDAC and ReadAdc both detect the falling edge of the TCLK signal in the C31 DSP (the output of the on-chip timer), and the read or write event is synchronized to this falling edge. A sequence RWWRRW synchronizes up as

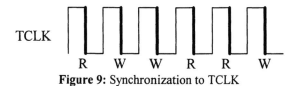

Figure 9: Synchronization to TCLK

This means that the sampling rate is determined by the value loaded into the Timer 0 of the C31. Also since these functions wait for the falling edge, all the reads and writes get synchronized to these falling edges. Figure 9 shows a arbitrary sequence of reads and writes as it would get executed. The function InitDSP puts TIMPER0 into the Timer 0 count register. The constant must be defined before the file d310bio.h is included, so that the default value is not picked up. The value of TIMPER0 is calculated from the formula

$$\text{Sample Rate} = \frac{\text{System Clock}}{(\text{TIMPER0})(\text{numcalls})(8)}$$

where System Clock=50MHz. The factor numcalls is the total number of calls to the functions ReadAdc and WriteDAC in one execution of the control loop. This is to account for the fact that both the ReadAdc and WriteDAC function wait for the falling edge of TCLK. So, for example if TCLK has a frequency of 1kHz, and if the control loop has one ReadAdc and one WriteDAC, then the loop will run 500 times per second.

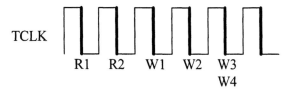

Figure 10: Successive Read and Write Events

The functions WriteDAC and WriteDACS must be distinguished with care. Refer to Figure 10, write outputs W1 and W2 are made using WriteDAC. The writes W3 and W4 are made with the function WriteDACS. Owing to the architecture of the board, such paired writes may be made but paired reads are not possible. The functions thus isolate the user from the unnecessary details of the board architecture but reflect the restrictions that the architecture imposes on the operations to be performed. The sampling rate may also be set dynamically as explained in the following section.

3.2.6 Runtime Sampling Rate Determination

As explained in the previous sub-section, the sampling rate is determined by the count in the Timer 0 Period Register of the C31. This value is set up by InitDSP, but it can also be altered within the program if the need arises. For this the memory mapped Timer Period Register must be altered. This can be done very simply as follows:

```
int *period;
period=(int *)0x8008028;
*period=TIMER_PERIOD_DESIRED;
```

This changes the rate at which TCLK0 pulses and sets the rate for the reads and writes. Note that if this is to be done repeatedly, e.g. to generate a rectangular wave (duty cycle not 50%) at the output of the DAC, then for good accuracy it would be necessary to start and stop the timer while this is done and also to synchronize the modifications with TCLK itself.

3.3.7 Other Interface Routines

A number of interface routines are supplied by Dalanco-Spry for general I/O handling. These are:

- int320: sends interrupt INT0 to the C31
- go320: runs the C31
- hlt320: halts the C31
- sendio: sends data from PC to the C31.
- recevio: receives data from DSP to PC.

4. Robot Control and Test Results

Two input shapers were selected for test purposes: 1) Zero Vibration (ZV) and 2) Zero Vibration and Derivative. The theory of operation of the shapers may be found in e.g. [8], [9]. For a second order underdamped system with peak overshoot M_p and ringing period T_d, the ZV Shaper, the impulse strength and switch time are given by:

$$A_1 = 1/(1+M_p), A_2 = Mp/(1+M_p), \Delta T=T_d/2$$

While for the ZVD shaper, the impulse strength and switch times are given by:

$$A_1=1/(1+M_p)^2, A_2=2M_p/(1+M_p)^2 , A_3=M_p^2/(1+M_p)_2 , \Delta T=T_d/2$$

Now since the robot is a type-1 system, a PD loop is first synthesized to stabilize the two axes. However, instead of achieving smooth transient response as in most applications, the PD control used in this test is designed to minimize the ringing period of the robots so that fast switch time can be achieved. Furthermore, since the dynamics of the two robots are similar, the test focuses on the Y module which has a higher ringing frequency and thus poses a more stringent requirement on the switch time of the shaper.
With the PD feedbcak in place, the shaper parameters are calculated as:
(I) ZV Shaper:

$$A_1 = 0.6027, A_2 = 0.3973, \Delta T=0.1025$$

(II) ZVD Shaper:

$$A_1=0.3633, A_2=0.4789, A_3=0.1578, \Delta T=0.1025$$

It is observed that, in order to realize the precision of the switch time, the DSP timer resolution should be better than 5 KHz. The actual rate used in the experiments is 10KHz.

4.1 Step Response Test

Step response test, with PD inner loop and an input shaper, is set up as follows:
First, the DSP card is initialized for the following tasks: 1) to set up the sampling rate to 10kHz, 2) to fetch controller parameters from the dual port memory placed by the host program running on the PC, 3) to command to robot to the home position.
Second, the main program executes the shaper algorithms by updating the DAC at the switch time(s). Third, the encoder data are acquired and transfer to the PC for analysis.

4.2. Test Results

The robots were tested for a period of five consecutive days under "identical" laboratory conditions, e.g. temperature, load, home position, etc. The same ZV and ZVD shapers were used for the entire test process without readjustment. This way, sensitivity of the shaper to intrinsic plant parameter variations can be assessed. Measurements of the encoder output were made at 2 ΔT, 3 ΔT, 4 ΔT, and the corresponding RMS errors were calculated. Results of the ZV shaper are shown in Figure 11 and Table 3 while those of the ZVD shaper are shown in Figure 12 and Table 4. It is observed that the ZV shaper, with only one switch time, attains the steady level more rapidly than the ZVD. However, it is also more sensitive as evident in the higher RMS values and %residual vibration.

Table 3: Summary.of ZV Step Responses

ZV	2ΔT	3ΔT	4ΔT
#1	+0.2600	+0.2425	+0.2425
#2	+0.7350	-0.5400	-0.5375
#3	+0.3375	+0.3300	-0.3300
#4	+0.2250	+0.2200	-0.2200
#5	+0.5875	-0.4850	-0.4825
RMS	0.2114	0.1724	0.1718
% Vibration	0.8457	0.6895	0.6872

Table 4: Summary of ZVD Step Responses

ZVD	2ΔT	3ΔT	4ΔT
#1	+0.4675	+0.0050	+0.0050
#2	+0.5150	-0.1200	-0.1200
#3	+0.0000	-0.1400	-0.1375
#4	+0.1775	-0.2625	-0.2625
#5	+0.5525	-0.3875	-0.3875
RMS	0.1812	0.1006	0.1005
% Vibration	0.7247	0.4025	0.4019

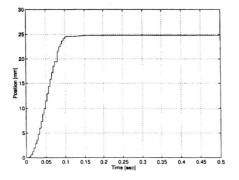 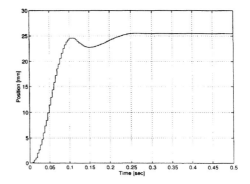

Figure 11: Nominal (left) and Worst Case (right) ZV Step Response

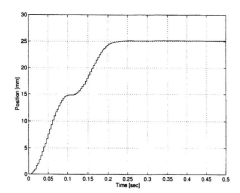 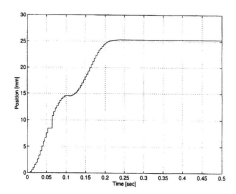

Figure 12: Nominal (left) and Worst Case (right) ZVD Step Response

5. CONCLUSIONS

In this work, a low cost DSP/PC motion control system has been developed and implemented. An ANSI C compatible application programming interface was written for open architecture controller realization. Two input shaper algorithms were implemented and tested on an Adept linear robotic workcell. The results indicate the feasibility of the PC/DSP system for motion control.

6. SELECTED REFERENCES

[1] National Institute of Standards and Technology, Open Architecture Enhanced Machine Controller, Manufacturing Engineering Laboratory, 1996.

[2] National Electronics Manufacturing Initiative, Low Cost Controller API Specifications Version 1.1, Final Assembly Technical Implementation Group, 1996.

[3] Model 310B User's guide, Dalanco-Spry, 89 Westland Ave., Rochester, NY 14618.

[4] TMS320 Floating Point DSP Assembly Language Tools User's Guide, Texas Instruments.

[5] TMS320 Floating Point DSP Optimizing C Compiler User's Guide, Texas Instruments.

[6] TMS320 DSP Development Support Reference Guide, Texas Instruments.

[7] Adept MV Controller Developer's Guide, Adept Technology,Inc., 150 Rose Orchard Way, San Jose, CA 95134.

[8] Singer, N. and Seering, W., "Preshaping Comand Inputs to reduce System Vibration," ASME J. on Dynamic Systems, Measurement, and Control, 1990.

[9] Pao, L.Y., Chang, T.N., Hou, E., "Input Shaper Design for Minimizing the Expected Level of Residual Vibration in Flexible Systems," Proceedings to the 1997 American Control Conference, Albuquerque, NM, pp. 3542-3546.

[10] Astrom, C. and Wittenmark, B, "Computer-Controlled Systems, Theory and Design", 3rd Ed., Prentice-Hall, 1997.

[11] Eren, M., "Vibration Control of Robotic Modules Using Input Shaping Algorithms," M.A.Sc. Thesis, Department of Electrical & Computer Engineering, New Jersey Institute of Technology, 1997.

[12] Godbole, K, "Performance Enhancement of Linear Robotic Workcell Using DSP Based Control," M.A.Sc. Thesis, Department of Electrical & Computer Engineering, New Jersey Institute of Technology, 1998.

Modeling and parameter identification of the impulse response matrix of mechanical systems

Evgueni V. Bordatchev[1]

Don State Technical University, 1, Gagarin Sq., Rostov-on-Don, 344010 Russia

ABSTRACT

A method for studying the problem of modeling, identification and analysis of mechanical system dynamic characteristic in view of the impulse response matrix for the purpose of adaptive control is developed here. Two types of the impulse response matrices are considered: (*i*) on displacement, which describes the space-coupled relationship between vectors of the force and simulated displacement and (*ii*) on acceleration, which also describes the space-coupled relationship between the vectors of the force and measured acceleration. The idea of identification consists of: (*a*) the practical obtaining of the impulse response matrix on acceleration by "impact-response" technique; (*b*) the modelling and parameter estimation of the each impulse response function on acceleration through the fundamental representation of the impulse response function on displacement as a sum of the damped sine curves applying linear and non-linear least square methods; (*c*) simulating the impulse response function on displacement using pre-identified parameters, such as amplitudes, time constants, and frequencies, which provides the additional possibility to calculate masses, damper and spring constants. The damped natural frequencies are used as *a priori* information and are found through the standard FFT analysis. The problem of double numerical integration is avoided by taking two derivations of the fundamental dynamic model of a mechanical system as a linear combination of the mass-damper-spring subsystems. The identified impulse response matrix on displacement represents the dynamic properties of the mechanical system. From the engineering point of view, this matrix can be also understood as a "dynamic passport" of the mechanical system and can be used for dynamic certification and analysis of the dynamic quality. In addition, the suggested approach mathematically re-produces amplitude-frequency response matrix in a low-frequency band and on zero frequency. This allows the possibility of determining the matrix of the static stiffness due to dynamic testing over the time of 10-15 minutes. As a practical example, the dynamic properties in view of the impulse and frequency response matrices of the lathe spindle are obtained, identified and investigated. The developed approach for modelling and parameter identification appears promising for a wide range of industrial applications; for example, rotary systems.

Keywords: Mechanical coupled system, dynamics, mathematical modelling, impulse response matrix, identification

1. INTRODUCTION

Recently, dynamic characteristics of the mechanical system have played an important role in developing a control system. It is obvious that the fundamental system dynamic characteristics such as transfer function, impulse and step response functions, *etc.* can be obtained by mathematical modeling or by experimental identification. But in practice, very often the mathematical model does not match the actual dynamic behavior of the existing system. The sources of difference between actual and modeled system characteristics are non-adequate model structure and inaccurate numerical values of model parameters such as masses, stiffness and damper constants, *etc.* The main reason for this is that a mechanical system is a complex coupled dynamic system with *a priori* unknown mass, damping and stiffness properties of its sub-elements, such as bearings, springs, mechanical and frictional joints and contacts, *etc.* In addition, any dynamic model of a real mechanical system has to take into account space-coupled displacements. Identification of the system dynamic characteristics allows the ascertainment of accurate numerical values of the model parameters, and the adoption of the structure of the mathematical model as an actual dynamic behavior of a real mechanical system.

Various methods are known for identifying system dynamic characteristics and modal parameters such as natural frequencies and eigenvectors, which play an important role in the system dynamic analysis [1, 2]. From a theoretical and practical point of view, the transfer function $H(j\omega)$ is one of the most appropriate dynamic characteristics for completely describing dynamic properties of the mechanical system. The reason for the identification of the exact transfer function is the engineering comprehension of the physical meaning of this function, because one part of a mechanical system transfer function (an amplitude frequency response function) is dynamic compliance. In general, dynamic compliance can be defined as both the ratio of displacement amplitude to force amplitude at a certain vibration frequency, and as the inverse characteristic at dynamic

[1] now with Integrated Manufacturing Technologies Institute, National Research Council of Canada, 800 Collip Circle, London, Ontario, Canada N6G 4X8

106

Part of the SPIE Conference on Sensors and Controls for Intelligent Machining and Agile Manufacturing
Boston, Massachusetts • November 1998
SPIE Vol. 3518 • 0277-786X/98/$10.00

stiffness. Another reason for the identification of the exact transfer function is that the frequency response function can be well-determined in practice as a Fourier transformation of the impulse response function [3].

The aim of the present paper is to evaluate the possibility of engineering parameter identification and analysis of the dynamic properties of the dynamic model of the mechanical system using an "impact-response" testing technique. The developed approach is applied to the machine tool spindle mechanical system, which is one of the well-known examples of the dynamically coupled systems [4-7].

Typically, the identification of machine tool dynamic properties consists of determining natural frequencies and damping rations. For example, natural frequencies are taken from the non-parametric frequency response of the machine tool mechanical system, and natural frequencies are calculated through ARMA modelling vibration data [8]. But one main problem that is usually avoided is that measured data is acceleration, not displacement, which deals with the dynamic compliance. Here the problem of double integration arises.

In addition to the fundamental methods of identifying dynamic properties of the machine tool mechanical system [3-6, 8], the developed approach takes into account the dynamically coupled system in view of the impulse and amplitude frequency response matrices. The sequence of the suggested identification procedure includes:
- measuring the force impact and impulse responses in space directions several times
- determining the statistically best data due to the calculated matrix of the correlation coefficients
- calculating amplitude frequency response from each impulse response on acceleration using FFT transformation in order to determine damped natural frequencies
- estimating and correcting parameters of the model of each impulse response function on acceleration by applying linear and non-linear least square methods
- simulating impulse response matrix on displacement

Data from real (not simulated) experiments are used to illustrate the contents of the paper; specifically, the impulse response matrix of the machine-tool spindle was investigated and identified.

2. THEORETICAL BASIS

It is well-known that the dynamics of a mechanical system is based on the analysis of transformation of the force vector-column $\mathbf{F}(t)$ to the vector-column of displacement (vibrations) $\mathbf{x}(t)$ in time domain. In general, the transfer matrix $\mathbf{W}(D)$ mathematically describes this transformation as

$$\mathbf{x}(t) = \mathbf{W}(D)\mathbf{F}(t) \tag{1}$$

where $D = \dfrac{d}{dt}$ is the differential operator.

Let us consider a mechanical system as a "two inputs - two coupled outputs" system; i.e., $\mathbf{F}(t) = \{F_1(t), F_2(t)\}^{\mathrm{T}}$, $\mathbf{x}(t) = \{x_1(t), x_2(t)\}^{\mathrm{T}}$. In this case, the dynamic structure of the system can be represented by Fig. 1, and Eq. 1 shown respectively as:

$$\begin{Bmatrix} x_1(t) \\ x_2(t) \end{Bmatrix} = \begin{bmatrix} W_{1,1}(D) & W_{1,2}(D) \\ W_{2,1}(D) & W_{2,1}(D) \end{bmatrix} \begin{Bmatrix} F_1(t) \\ F_2(t) \end{Bmatrix} \tag{2}$$

or

$$\begin{cases} x_1(t) = W_{1,1}(D)F_1(t) + W_{1,2}(D)F_2(t) = x_{1,1}(t) + x_{1,2}(t) \\ x_2(t) = W_{2,1}(D)F_1(t) + W_{2,2}(D)F_2(t) = x_{2,1}(t) + x_{2,2}(t) \end{cases} \tag{3}$$

where $W_{i,j}(D)$ is the transfer function which forms i-direction displacement $x_{i,j}(t)$ under applied j-direction force $F_j(t)$, and $i, j = 1,2$ are the space directions.

The existing non-diagonal elements $W_{1,2}(D)$ and $W_{2,1}(D)$ show the inner coupling of the system; i.e., how displacements $x_1(t)$ and $x_2(t)$ influence each other.

The other fundamental representation of mechanical system dynamics as a linear and time invariant system in time domain is the convolution integral:

$$\begin{cases} x_1(t) = \int\limits_0^t h_{1,1}(t-\tau)F_1(t)d\tau + \int\limits_0^t h_{1,2}(t-\tau)F_2(t)d\tau \\ x_2(t) = \int\limits_0^t h_{2,1}(t-\tau)F_1(t)d\tau + \int\limits_0^t h_{2,2}(t-\tau)F_2(t)d\tau \end{cases} \tag{4}$$

where $h_{i,j}(t)$ is the impulse response function which forms i-direction displacement $x_{i,j}(t)$ under applied j-direction force $F_j(t)$, and $i,j = 1,2$. Impulse response functions $h_{i,j}(t)$ form the impulse response matrix $\mathbf{h}(t) = \left\| h_{i,j}(t) \right\|_{i,j=1,2}$.

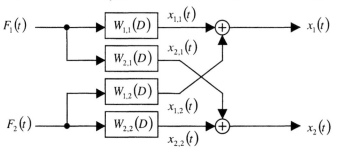

Fig. 1. Dynamic structure of the "two inputs - two coupled outputs" mechanical system.

It is also necessary to take into account the fact that the impulse response function and transfer function are interrelated through Laplace and Fourier transformations:

$$h(t) \xrightarrow{\;L(\cdot)\;} W(s) \xrightarrow{\;F(\cdot)\;} W(\mathbf{j}\omega) \tag{5}$$

where $L(\cdot)$ is the Laplace transformation, $F(\cdot)$ is the Fourier transformation, s is the Laplace operator that forms s-domain, $\mathbf{j}\omega$ is the Fourier operator that forms frequency domain, ω is the angular frequency [rad/sec], and $\mathbf{j} = \sqrt{-1}$.

The classical method of identification of the impulse response function, which is called the impact testing technique, consists of measuring the system response to δ-impulse (Dirac's function) impact (Fig. 2).

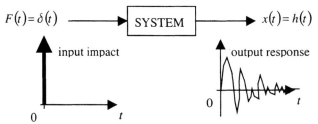

Fig. 2. Impact testing technique for determining impulse response function.

In practice, the input impact is formed by impulse-force vibro-hammer, and the response signal is measured by an accelerometer that is connected to the vibration-input channel, for example, the FFT analyzer. Here the problem of transforming the acceleration into displacement arises. This problem can be generally solved only in a low-frequency band (up to 10-20 Hz) using electronic hardware for double integration. Thus impulse response on acceleration can be taken into a consideration when acceleration is measured. This function transforms the force into system response in view of measured acceleration. Conversely, the impulse response function on displacement describes the transformation of force into system displacement (vibrations).

The suggested approach is based on this impact testing technique adding parameter identification and modeling of the impulse response function on acceleration and impulse response function on displacement. In this paper, the problem of double integration is avoided using parameters, like amplitude, damping, and natural frequencies, identified from the impulse response function on acceleration to simulate the impulse response function on displacement.

3. EXPERIMENTAL SETUP

The spindle subsystem of the machine tool (in this case, the lathe) was used as a real example of a coupled mechanical system whose dynamic properties in view of the impulse response matrix was investigated and the parameters of mathematical models were identified.

In this study the accelerations of the spindle in horizontal (x_1) and vertical (x_2) directions are used to measure the spindle responses to the force impulses formed by the force-impulse vibro-hammer, as shown in Fig. 3. The accelerations are measured by two accelerators (DN-4-1M, Russian type, frequency range up to 12,500 Hz) mounted on a small workpiece fixed in the spindle of the CNC lathe (YT16F3, Russian type, medium-size). The force-impulse vibro-hammer with the force piezoelectric sensor DS-1M (frequency range up to 100 Hz) is manufactured by "PRIBOI" (Taganrog, Russia) and has a mass equal to 0.67 kg. The piezoelectric signal produced by each accelerator during the response to the force impulse is low-pass filtered and amplified by charge amplifiers (Kistler type 5004), and is afterwards converted to a voltage signal in a data acquisition board (type DASH-16).

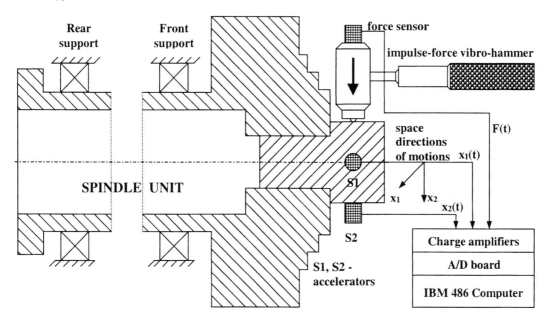

Fig. 3. Experimental set-up.

The experimental procedure consists of applying the force impulse by hand and on-line acquisition of the spindle response time series (2048 samples, sample period 0.012 msec) in the space directions x_1 and x_2. Also, the actual force impulse time series is collected in a similar way.

4. DETERMINING THE IMPULSE RESPONSE MATRIX ON ACCELERATION

The "two inputs - two coupled outputs", linear, time-invariant mechanical system has the impulse response matrix on displacement with 2×2 symmetrical (in theory) structure as

$$\mathbf{h}(t) = \begin{bmatrix} h_{1,1}(t) & h_{1,2}(t) \\ h_{2,1}(t) & h_{2,2}(t) \end{bmatrix} \tag{6}$$

where each impulse response function $h_{i,j}(t)$ represents the dynamic transformation of force $F_j(t)$ into displacement $x_{i,j}(t)$. In the case where acceleration is measured, the impulse response matrix on acceleration is

$$\mathbf{h}^{(a)}(t) = \begin{bmatrix} h_{1,1}^{(a)}(t) & h_{1,2}^{(a)}(t) \\ h_{2,1}^{(a)}(t) & h_{2,2}^{(a)}(t) \end{bmatrix} \tag{7}$$

where each function $h_{i,j}^{(a)}(t)$ dynamically transforms force $F_j(t)$ into acceleration $a_{i,j}(t)$ and the equation of the mechanical system dynamics will be represented by the following:

$$
\begin{cases}
a_1(t) = \int_0^t h_{1,1}^{(a)}(t-\tau)F_1(t)d\tau + \int_0^t h_{1,2}^{(a)}(t-\tau)F_2(t)d\tau \\
a_2(t) = \int_0^t h_{2,1}^{(a)}(t-\tau)F_1(t)d\tau + \int_0^t h_{2,2}^{(a)}(t-\tau)F_2(t)d\tau
\end{cases}
\tag{8}
$$

or in view of transfer functions as

$$
\begin{cases}
a_1(t) = W_{1,1}^{(a)}(D)F_1(t) + W_{1,2}^{(a)}(D)F_2(t) = a_{1,1}(t) + a_{1,2}(t) \\
a_2(t) = W_{2,1}^{(a)}(D)F_1(t) + W_{2,2}^{(a)}(D)F_2(t) = a_{2,1}(t) + a_{2,2}(t)
\end{cases}
\tag{9}
$$

Taking into account the structure of the matrix $\mathbf{h}^{(a)}(t)$ (7), it is obvious that the first matrix column ($h_{1,1}^{(a)}(t)$ and $h_{2,1}^{(a)}(t)$) is formed by the system reactions to the force impulse impact $F_1(t)$. In the same way, the second matrix column ($h_{1,2}^{(a)}(t)$ and $h_{2,2}^{(a)}(t)$) is formed by the system reactions to the force impulse impact $F_2(t)$.

The above gives us the possibility of experimentally obtaining the impulse response matrix on acceleration $\mathbf{h}^{(a)}(t)$ for the "two inputs - two coupled outputs" mechanical system in two steps:

- applying the force impulse impact $F_1(t)$ in direction x_1 while simultaneously measuring the time series of force $F_1(t)$ and system responses $h_{1,1}^{(a)}(t)$ and $h_{2,1}^{(a)}(t)$. In this step the first column of the matrix $\mathbf{h}^{(a)}(t)$ will be determined

- applying the force impulse impact $F_2(t)$ in direction x_2 while simultaneously measuring the time series of force $F_2(t)$ and system responses $h_{1,2}^{(a)}(t)$ and $h_{2,2}^{(a)}(t)$. In this step the second column of the matrix $\mathbf{h}^{(a)}(t)$ will be obtained

A weak point of this procedure is that the amplitude and space orientation of the force impulse impact is formed by hand. Here the repeatability of the amplitude and space orientation represents a "quality" of the impulse force impact. The amplitude is selected experimentally to instigate small displacements, which enable us to find a linear dynamic model of the mechanical system. In practice, each experiment (force impulse impact and the corresponding system responses) is repeated several times (usually 11 times) and the statistically best data is estimated from the matrix of the correlation coefficients [9] between different experimental data, viz.

$$
\rho_{i,j}^{(k)} = \frac{Cov\left[h_{k,i}^{(a)}, h_{k,j}^{(a)}\right]}{\sqrt{var\left[h_{k,i}^{(a)}\right]var\left[h_{k,j}^{(a)}\right]}}, \quad i,j = 1\dots11, \quad k = 1,2
\tag{10}
$$

where $\rho_{i,j}^{(k)}$ is the correlation coefficient between impulse responses $h_{k,i}^{(a)}$ and $h_{k,j}^{(a)}$, i, j denote the experiment number, k is the space direction, $Cov[\cdot]$ is the covariance, and $var[\cdot]$ is the variance.

This is applied to each element (impulse response function) of matrix $\mathbf{h}^{(a)}(t)$.

Usually, experimental time series have amplitude in volts, but physically represent force and acceleration. Hence it is necessary to transform the time series of the force impact in N, and the time series of the system response in $[m/sec^2]$ or $[g]$ by utilizing technical characteristics (for example, the ratio of transformation) of used transducers.

Finally, in order to obtain the impulse response matrix on acceleration, the time series of the system responses have to be normalized at the respective amplitude of the force impulse impact. The impulse response functions will have the unit $[m/sec^2/N]$ only after following this procedure.

The results of the experimental investigations of the spindle unit of machine tool YT16F3 (# 132, 1981) are represented by:
- Fig. 4, where actual data of force impulses $F_1(t)$ and $F_2(t)$ in directions x_1 and x_2 are shown
- Fig. 5, where the impulse response matrix on acceleration $\mathbf{h}^{(a)}(t) = h_{i,j}^{(a)}(t)\big|_{i,j=1,2}$ illustrates the spindle responses to the force

impulses $F_1(t)$ and $F_2(t)$

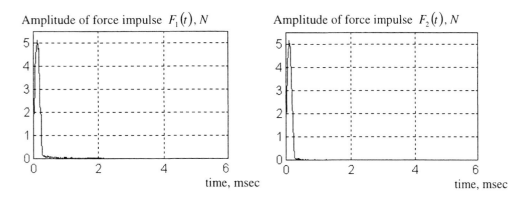

Fig. 4. Actual data of force impulse impacts.

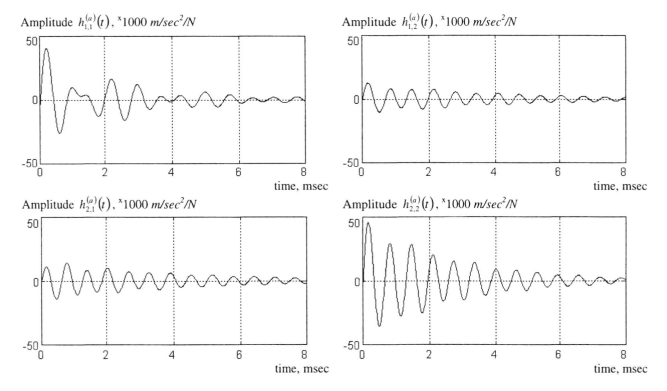

Fig. 5. Impulse response matrix on acceleration.

Further, it is necessary to extract the impulse response matrix on displacement from the experimentally obtained impulse response matrix on acceleration.

5. PARAMETER IDENTIFICATION OF THE IMPULSE RESPONSE FUNCTION

The fundamentals of the dynamic modelling of a linear mechanical system [10] say that each degree of freedom is represented by a mechanical resonance contour in view of the spring-mass-damper system, which has an impulse response function in view of damped sine curve as

$$h(t) = A\exp(-t/\tau)\sin(\Omega^* t) = A\exp(-\alpha t)\sin(\Omega^* t) = \frac{\exp(-\xi\Omega t)}{m\Omega\sqrt{1-\xi^2}}\sin\left(t\Omega\sqrt{1-\xi^2}\right) \quad (11)$$

where A is the amplitude, *[m/N]*, τ is the time constant *[sec]*, $\alpha = 1/\tau$, Ω^* is the damped natural frequency *[rad/sec]*, Ω is the undamped natural frequency or, for simplicity, natural frequency *[rad/sec]*, m is the mass, *[N]*, and ξ is the damping ratio, *[dimensionless]*.

The impulse response function on displacement of the system with n mechanical resonance contours is mathematically described as

$$h(t) = \sum_{i=1}^{n} \frac{\exp\left(-\xi_i \Omega_i t\right)}{m_i \Omega_i \sqrt{1-\xi_i^2}} \sin\left(t\Omega_i \sqrt{1-\xi_i^2}\right) \tag{12}$$

Eq. (12) represents each elements of the impulse response matrix on displacement $\mathbf{h}(t)$ (6).

After taking two derivations of Eq. (11), the following result

$$h^{(a)}(t) = A\exp(-\alpha t)\left[\left(\alpha^2 - \Omega^{*2}\right)\sin\left(\Omega^* t\right) - 2\alpha\Omega^* \cos\left(\Omega^* t\right)\right] \tag{13}$$

represents the mathematical model of the impulse response function on acceleration.

The mechanical system with n-degree-of-freedom will have the following impulse response function on acceleration

$$h^{(a)}(t) = \sum_{i=1}^{n} A_i \exp(-\alpha_i t)\left[\left(\alpha_i^2 - \Omega_i^{*2}\right)\sin\left(\Omega_i^* t\right) - 2\alpha_i\Omega_i^* \cos\left(\Omega_i^* t\right)\right] \tag{14}$$

which we need for parameter identification of the impulse response matrix on acceleration $\mathbf{h}^{(a)}(t)$ (7).

The idea for the determination of $\mathbf{h}(t)$ (6) consists of the parameter identification of $\mathbf{h}^{(a)}(t)$ and the use of identified parameters A_i, τ_i, α_i, Ω_i^*, Ω_i, m_i, ξ_i for the digital simulation of $\mathbf{h}(t)$. The common procedure for determining matrix $\mathbf{h}(t)$, including the determination of the impulse response matrix on acceleration and parameter identification of the each impulse response function, is presented by Fig. 6.

This common procedure of parameter identification of the each impulse response function $h^{(a)}(t)$, in addition to determining matrix $\mathbf{h}^{(a)}(t)$, includes:

- taking FFT transformation to calculate amplitude frequency response function (Fig. 7)
- determining number n and values of damped natural frequencies Ω^*; moreover, n additionally represents the number of mechanical resonance contours of the modeled system and will mainly influence the quality of identification
- identifying parameters $\hat{A}_i$ and $\hat{\alpha}_i$ from (14) using the linear least square method [11]

$$\left\|h^{(a)}(t) - \hat{h}^{(a)}(t)\right\|_{\Omega_i^*} \to \min_{\hat{A}_i, \hat{\alpha}_i} \tag{15}$$

where $\wedge$ represents the estimation

- correcting parameters $\hat{A}_i$, $\hat{\Omega}_i^*$, and $\hat{\alpha}_i$ using the non-linear least square method [12]

$$\left\|h^{(a)}(t) - \hat{h}^{(a)}(t)\right\| \to \min_{\hat{A}_i, \hat{\alpha}_i, \hat{\Omega}_i^*} \tag{16}$$

- calculating parameters $\hat{\Omega}_i$, $\hat{m}_i$, $\hat{\xi}_i$ based on fundamental relations [10]

$$\hat{\Omega}_i^* = \hat{\Omega}_i \sqrt{1-\hat{\xi}_i^2}, \quad \hat{\alpha}_i = \hat{\xi}_i \hat{\Omega}_i, \quad \hat{A}_i = \frac{1}{\hat{m}_i \hat{\Omega}_i \sqrt{1-\hat{\xi}_i^2}} \tag{17}$$

- simulating impulse response function on displacement

$$\hat{h}(t) = \sum_{i=1}^{n} \frac{\exp\left(-\hat{\xi}_i \hat{\Omega}_i t\right)}{\hat{m}_i \hat{\Omega}_i \sqrt{1-\hat{\xi}_i^2}} \sin\left(t\hat{\Omega}_i \sqrt{1-\hat{\xi}_i^2}\right) \tag{18}$$

Further, based on the experimental data of the impulse response matrix on acceleration (Fig. 5):

- the amplitude-frequency response matrix on acceleration $\mathbf{A}^{(a)}(\omega) = \mathrm{A}_{i,j}^{(a)}(\omega)\Big|_{i,j=1,2}$ (Fig. 7), which illustrates the frequency structure of the impulse responses $h_{i,j}^{(a)}(t)$, was calculated

- parameters $\hat{A}_i$, $\hat{\Omega}_i^*$, $\hat{\alpha}_i$ were identified and parameters $\hat{\Omega}_i$, $\hat{m}_i$, $\hat{\xi}_i$ were calculated for each $\hat{h}_{i,j}(t)$ (see Table 1)

- using the identified parameters $\hat{A}_i$, $\hat{\Omega}_i^*$, $\hat{\alpha}_i$ the time series of the impulse response matrix on displacement $\hat{\mathbf{h}}(t)$ of the spindle mechanical system was simulated (Fig. 8)

Table 1. Identified parameters

	$\hat{h}_{1,1}(t)$		$\hat{h}_{1,2}(t)$		$\hat{h}_{2,1}(t)$		$\hat{h}_{2,2}(t)$	
Amplitude, $\hat{A}$, m/N, x10^{-4}	-6.411	-2.082	-0.477	-1.230	0.993	-1.379	-1.412	-4.632
Time constant, $\hat{\tau}$, sec	0.0020	0.0034	0.0029	0.0041	0.0025	0.0044	0.0027	0.0027
Damped natural frequency, $\hat{\Omega}^*$, Hz	1069.0	1450.0	1070.0	1524.0	924.0	1600.0	958.0	1560.0
Undamped natural frequency, $\hat{\Omega}$, Hz	1073.0	1450.8	1070.1	1525.5	927.2	1600.4	961.9	1561.1
Mass, $\hat{m}$, N	0.232	0.527	3.121	0.848	1.733	0.721	1.174	0.220
Damping ratio, $\hat{\xi}$, $dimensionless$	0.466	0.203	0.322	0.160	0.431	0.142	0.385	0.237

The simulation results cannot visually be distinguished from the (real) experimental results, so there is no point in presenting them. That they are virtually indistinguishable are moreover confirmed by the correlational coefficients (see Table 2 below).

The quality of the identification can be determined by the correlation coefficient between $\mathbf{h}(t)$ and $\hat{\mathbf{h}}(t)$ and the mean-square error $\left\| h_{i,j}^{(a)}(t) - \hat{h}_{i,j}^{(a)}(t) \right\|$. The results from this are shown in Table 2.

Table 2. Estimations of identification quality

	$h_{1,1}(t)$	$h_{1,2}(t)$	$h_{2,1}(t)$	$h_{2,2}(t)$
Correlation coefficient, $dimensionless$	0.96	0.97	0.92	0.95
Mean-square error, $^x 1000$ $m/sec^2/N$	257.774	33.75	2341.7	1116.8

Common time that was spent on practical impacts, measuring and parameter identification of the impulse response matrix for the machine tool spindle does not exceed 15 minutes.

Additionally, the transfer matrix of the mechanical system can be calculated, where each element of this matrix $\mathbf{W}(s) = [W_{i,j}(s)]$ will have the classical form of

$$W_{i,j}(s) = \sum_{k=1}^{n} \frac{1/m_k}{s^2 + 2\xi_k \Omega_k s + \Omega_k^2} = \sum_{k=1}^{n} \frac{1}{m_k s^2 + h_k s + c_k} \tag{19}$$

where h_i, c_i are damper and spring constants respectively, which can be calculated [10] as

$$c_k = m_k \Omega_k^2, \quad h_k = 2\xi_k \sqrt{c_k m_k} = 2\xi_k \Omega_k m_k \tag{20}$$

6. SUMMARY AND CONCLUSION

An engineering approach to the modelling and identification of the impulse response matrices on acceleration and on displacement has been developed using experimental data and a method for parameter identification.

The suggested approach avoids the double integration of acceleration using fundamental representation of the mechanical system as a linear combination of n mechanical resonance contours, where each contour represents the mass-damper-spring system. The mathematical model of the impulse response function was differentiated two times and the parameters of the resulting form, such as amplitudes, time constants, damped and undamped natural frequencies, masses, and damper and spring constants, were identified. Further, the identified parameters were used for the modelling and simulation of the impulse response matrix on displacement.

The impulse response matrix on displacement represents the dynamic properties of the investigated system, and shows, for example, how the displacements are coupled. From the engineering point of view, the impulse response matrix on displacement can be understood as the "dynamic passport" of the mechanical system and can be used for dynamic certification and analysis of the dynamic quality, as it was proposed for machine tools [13, 14].

Another important result of the suggested approach is the mathematical regeneration of the amplitude-frequency response matrix in low-frequency band and on zero frequency that gives us the practical possibility of determining the matrix of static stiffness due to dynamic testing.

Finally, the suggested approach to modelling and identification seems promising for a wide range of industrial applications, such as rotary systems.

7. REFERENCES

1. A. Fasana, and B.A.D. Piombo, "Identification of linear mechanical systems by deconvolution techniques", *Mechanical Systems and Signal Processing,* pp.351-373, No. 3, Vol. 11, 1997
2. C.-P. Fritzen, "Identification of mass, damping, and stiffness matrices of mechanical systems", *Transaction of the ASME, J. of Vibration, Acoustics, Stress, and Reliability in Design.,* pp. 9-16, Vol. 108, 1986
3. W.G. Halvorsen, and D.L. Brown, "Impulse technique for structural frequency response testing", *Sound and Vibration*, pp. 8-21, No.11, Vol. 11, 1977
4. J. Tlusty, and F. Ismail, "Dynamic Structural Identification Tasks and Methods", *Annals of the CIRP*, pp. 251-255, No. 1, Vol. 29, 1980
5. Y.C. Shin, K.F. Eman, and S.M. Wu, "Experimental complex modal analysis of machine tool structures ", *Transaction of the ASME, J. of Engineering for Industry*, pp. 116-124, Vol. 111, 1989
6. M.U. Jen, E.B. Magrab, "The dynamic interaction of the cutting process, workpiece, and lathe's structure in facing", *Transaction of the ASME, J. of Manufacturing Science and Engineering,* pp. 348-358, Vol. 118, 1996
7. E.V. Bordatchev, "Parametrical identification of the machine tool dynamic characteristics", *Proc. of the 3-rd Int. Conf. Computer Science for Design and Technology*, Moscow State Technical University "STANKIN", pp. 33-34, 1996
8. K.J. Kim, K.F. Eman, and S.M. Wu, "Identification of natural frequencies and damping ratios of machine tool structures by the dynamic data system approach", Int. J. Mach. Tool Des. Res., pp. 161-169, No. 3, Vol. 24, 1984
9. E.R. Dougherty, *Probability and Statistics for the Engineering, Computing, and Physical Sciences.* Prentice-Hall International, Inc., 1990
10. R.L. Woods, and K.L. Lawrence, *Modelling and simulation of dynamic systems.* Prentice-Hall International, Inc., 1997
11. N.R. Draper, and H. Smith, *Applied regression analysis*, New York, Wiley, 1981
12. Y. Bard, *Non-linear parameter estimation*, Academic Press, 1974
13. E.V. Bordatchev, and V.L. Zakovorotny, "Modern Multi-functional Monitoring of the Machine Tool Dynamic Quality", *Proc. of the 13-th Int. Conf. on "Computer-Aided Production Engineering"*, Warsaw, Poland, pp.133-141, 1997
14. V.L. Zakovorotny, and E.V. Bordatchev, "Prediction and Diagnostics of Workpiece Machining Quality in Machine Tools, based on Dynamic Simulation". *Proc. of the 31-th Int. MATADOR Conference*, UMIST, Manchester, pp. 315-320, 1995

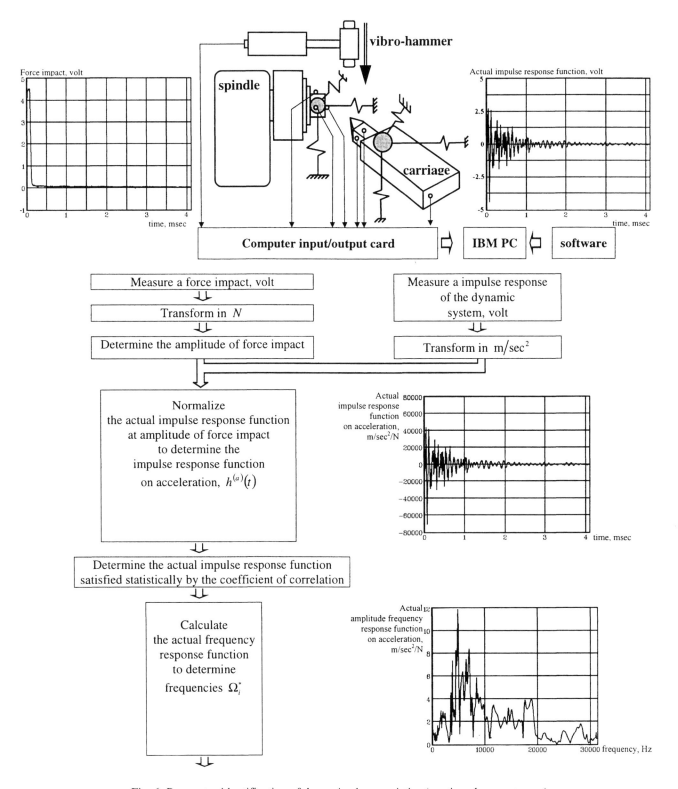

Fig. 6. Parameter identification of dynamic characteristics (continued on next page).

(continued)

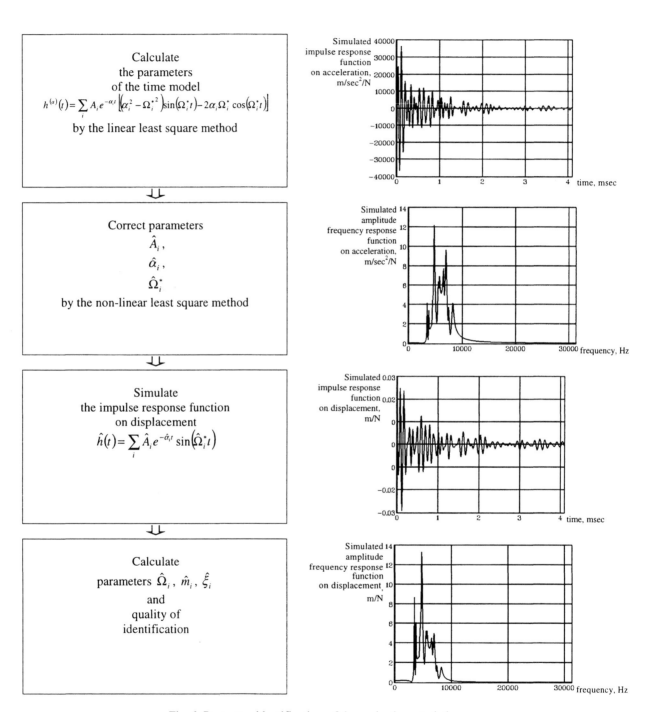

Fig. 6. Parameter identification of dynamic characteristics.

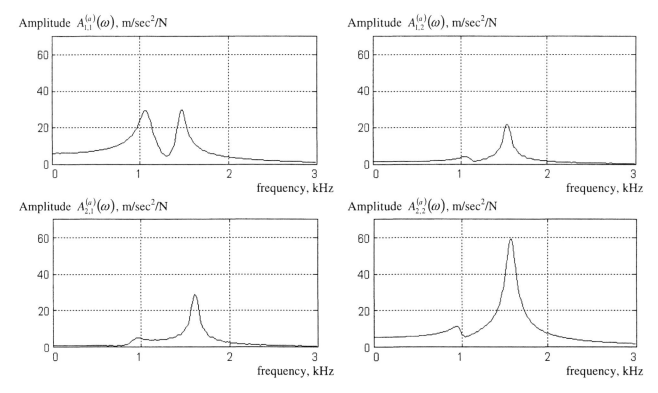

Fig. 7. Amplitude-frequency response matrix on acceleration (spindle of the lathe YT16F3, #132, 1981).

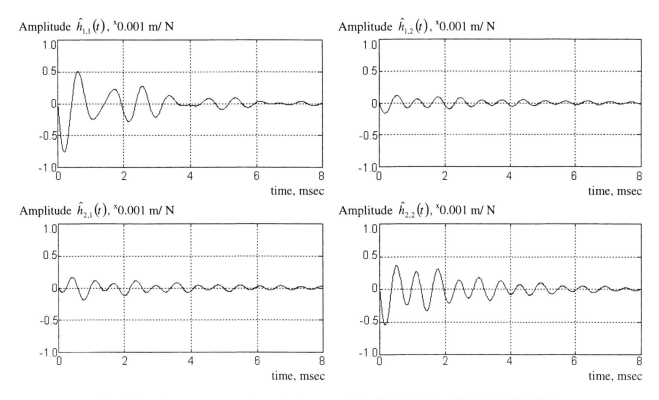

Fig. 8. Impulse response matrix on displacement (spindle of the lathe YT16F3, #132, 1981).

Market-Based Control of Active Surfaces

Andrew A. Berlin[a], Tad Hogg[a], Warren Jackson[a]

[a]Xerox Palo Alto Research Center

ABSTRACT

This paper describes a market-based approach to controlling a smart matter-based object transport system, in which an array of distributed air jets applies forces to levitate and control the motion of a planar object. In the smart matter regime, the effects of spatial and temporal variation of operating parameters among a multiplicity of sensors, actuators, and controllers make it desirable for a control strategy to exhibit a minimal dependence on system models, and to be able to arbitrate among conflicting goals. A market-based strategy is introduced that aggregates the control requests of multiple relatively simple local controllers, each of which seeks to optimize the performance of the system within a limited spatial and temporal range. These local controllers act as the market's consumers, and two sets of distributed air jets (one set aimed forwards and one set aimed backwards) act as the producers. Experiments are performed comparing the performance of the market-based strategy to a near-optimal model-derived benchmark, as well as to a hand-tuned PD controller. Results indicate that even though the local controllers in the market are not based on a detailed model of the system dynamics, the market is able to effectively approximate the performance of the model-based benchmark. In certain specialized cases, such as tracking a step trajectory, the performance of the market surpasses the performance of the model-based benchmark by balancing the needs of conflicting control goals. A brief overview of the active surface smart matter prototype being developed at Xerox PARC that is the motivation behind this work is also presented.

1. INTRODUCTION

Recent advances in batch fabrication technologies such as MEMS make it possible to mass-produce dense arrays of integrated sensors, actuators, and computational elements, which we call 'Smart matter'. These dense arrays, which may be embedded within structures, distributed over surfaces, or spread throughout the environment, provide the ability to interact with and manipulate the physical world in a very fine-grained, spatially distributed manner.[1, 2] Control programs for smart matter use measurements of the response of a system to compute appropriate control inputs to the system, such as forces or electric fields, which are then imposed on the system by actuators that manipulate the physical world. Parameters of smart matter systems vary spatially from component to component, and vary over time as individual components fail. Hence the dominant model-based optimization approach used for design of controllers for smart structures does not scale well to the smart matter regime because such models are not robust, exhibiting an extreme sensitivity to deviations in parameter values as the number of sensors and actuators in the system grows large. Moreover, in a system composed of components spread over a large area, a control action taken in one part of the system may adversely affect other parts of the system over the course of time. This spatio-temporal coupling leads to conflicts and the need for coordination of multiple controllers with minimal communication. This paper explores a strategy for using markets to achieve this coordination while reducing dependence on the model-based optimization approach to controller design.

Consider the control of an object transport system based on smart matter (see Figure 1), in which an array of air jets is used to levitate and apply distributed control forces to transport a planar object, such as a sheet of paper, over distances of several meters.[3, 4]. As the transported object moves spatially along the surface, variations in system parameters (for instance, from jet to jet) and in control goals (for instance, from region to region) add a degree of unpredictability to the control problem. Conflicts between goals arise, where a control action taken in one region of the surface may impart momentum or trigger actuator delays that will have a detrimental effect when the object reaches a different region of the surface, creating the need for collaboration between regional controllers.

Further author information:

Andrew Berlin: Email: berlin@parc.xerox.com; WWW: http://www.parc.xerox.com/berlin; Telephone: 650-812-4372
Tad Hogg: Email: hogg@parc.xerox.com; WWW: http://www.parc.xerox.com/hogg; Telephone: 650-812-4166
Warren Jackson: Email: wjackson@parc.xerox.com; Telephone: 650-812-4196

118

Part of the SPIE Conference on Sensors and Controls for Intelligent Machining and Agile Manufacturing
Boston, Massachusetts ● November 1998
SPIE Vol. 3518 ● 0277-786X/98/$10.00

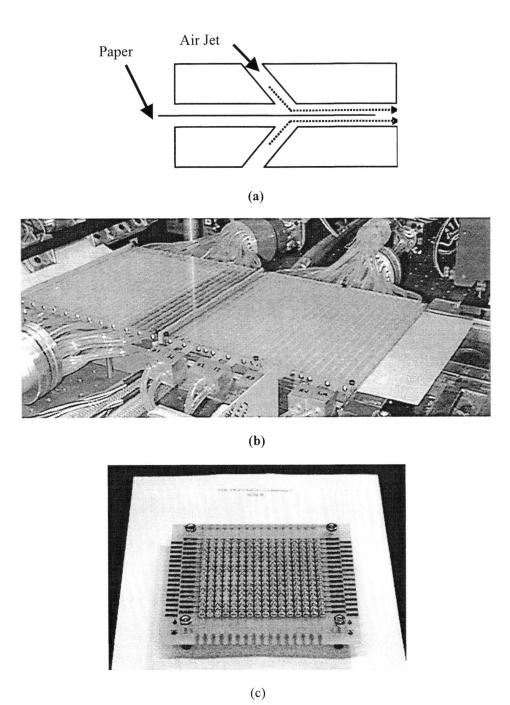

(a)

(b)

(c)

Figure 1: **(a)** Schematic of air jet object transport. An array of angled jets levitates and applies directed forces to a planar object being transported, such as a sheet of paper.

(b) Photograph of air jet array of the type used to generate the dynamical models used in this paper. This model uses a handful of macro-scale valves to control many jets in aggregate

(c) Photograph of batch fabricated air jet array with an integrated valve for each jet. This model, not yet operational, allows each of 256 jets to be controlled independently.

The intent of this work is to move towards the collaborative, model-insensitive control style required by the smart matter regime. A market-based perspective was selected because the market creates a setting in which arbitration among conflicting goals can occur naturally in a way easily understood and adjusted by human designers. Rather than jumping immediately to smart matter problems involving thousands individually controlled actuators, this paper focuses on a problem domain that employs a relatively small number of actuation decision options (forward, reverse, or glide). This permits comparison to model-based approaches to be used as a meaningful metric in evaluating the performance of the market-based systems.

This paper presents a set of simulation experiments that employ a market-based approach to coordinate the actions of multiple local controllers. Previously, market-based paradigms have shown promise to achieve robust, adaptable and scalable coordination of many independent entities. Markets have been used in network resource allocation[5], control of unstable structural systems[6], and in a variety of other settings[7]. The air jet control problem described above is used as the motivating application for this paper, with the goal of moving an object along a pre-specified trajectory using an array of controllers located spatio-temporally along the trajectory. These local controllers act as the market's consumers, and two sets of distributed air jets (one set aimed forwards and one set aimed backwards) act as the producers. Each local controller communicates its control decisions to a centralized market, which sends a collective control decision to the air jet array. The trajectory tracking performance of this market-based strategy is compared to that of a near-optimal search-derived benchmark, as well as to that of a hand-tuned PD controller.

Although this paper focuses on creating some initial results in the active surface domain, the concept of using markets to aggregate local agent-based controllers is potentially applicable in many settings. Some possibilities involving the use of distributed sensors, computers, and actuators include: controlling traffic flow in cities[8], regulating office environments[9], active stabilization of structural materials[10], structural vibration control[11], reducing fluid turbulence[12], controlling spacecraft[13] and adjusting optical responses [14]. In the long run, the continuing development of micrometer-scale machines[15] and proposals for even smaller devices[16] constructed with atomically precise manipulations [17-20] offer further possibilities for designing materials whose properties can be modified under program control[21]. These advances will further stress the scaling limits of controls technology, creating the need for alternative approaches.

2. SIMULATION OF AIR JET ARRAY DYNAMICS

Dynamic models for the simulation experiments presented in this paper were generated via physical experiments performed using the first-generation prototype of an air jet-driven object mover being developed at Xerox PARC, similar to the one pictured in Figure 1b.[1] The first generation prototype does not provide individual control of jets. Rather, the jet array is segmented into two sets of jets: one set angled forwards, and one set angled backwards. The control system has three options:

1. Turn all of the forward directed jets on
2. Turn all of the reverse-directed jets on
3. Turn both the forward-directed and the reverse-directed jets on, creating an air bearing that allows the transported object to glide without applying significant net acceleration (to a first approximation, the accelerating effects of the forward and reverse jets balance one another).

The physical system was observed operating under a variety of conditions, ranging from application of boxcar-shaped steps in acceleration to closed-loop performance of a PD controller. From these observations, the model of dynamics shown below was derived, and implemented in a simulator to support experiments with alternative control strategies. For the operating regime of interest, in which the velocity of the supporting air flow is substantially larger than the rate of object motion, the system dynamics (for transporting a sheet of average weight paper) were measured to be:

$$\ddot{x}(t) = a(t) - f(\dot{x}) \tag{1}$$

$\ddot{x}(t)$ is the position of the leading edge of the object being transported, $a(t)$ is the acceleration applied by the actuators, and f is the friction, given by

---

[1] Xerox PARC's active surfaces research is described in [3, 4] and at http://www.parc.xerox.com/mems-actl. Other work on active surfaces includes [22, 23].

$$f(v) = \begin{cases} \gamma_{viscous}\dot{x} & \text{if } |\dot{x}| < T_{drag} \\ \gamma \, \text{sign}(\dot{x}) & \text{otherwise} \end{cases} \tag{2}$$

with $\gamma = 7.5\dfrac{m}{s^2}$, $\gamma_{viscous} = 375\dfrac{1}{s}$ and $T_{drag} = 0.02\,m/s$. In this model of the dynamics, $\gamma_{viscous}T_{drag} = \gamma$, so the acceleration due to friction is a continuous function of velocity. The control acceleration a(t) is piecewise constant and selects among just three values: a, -a, and 0. For the simulations performed in this paper, a = 10 meters per second.

From a control perspective, these dynamics are somewhat unusual. Over a substantial portion of the operating range of the system, the magnitude of the drag force induced by friction does not depend on the magnitude of the velocity (Equation 2). However, over other parts of the operating range, the magnitude of the velocity does play a role. The switch-over point between these two regimes lies within the operating range of the simulation experiments presented in this paper.

The dynamics of actuation are further complicated by a switching delay δ between the time a new value for the actuator force is requested and the time it actually takes place. This delay simulates the observed behavior of the physical system, in which a build-up of current in the valve must be initiated a few milliseconds prior to the valve actually switching. Once this build-up of current has begun, it can damage the valve if it is interrupted, so once a valve switch is requested, it is not possible to abort it until after the switch has occurred. For simulation purposes, this effect was modeled as follows: During the period of time δ from the moment a valve transition is requested until the time it occurs, the applied acceleration retains its previous value and then instantaneously jumps to its new value at the end of the delay period. During the delay period, any subsequent requests by the controller to change the applied acceleration are ignored by the simulator, i.e., once the change in control is started, it runs to completion before further changes are possible.

For simulation purposes, we used a simple discrete version of this system:

$$\dot{x}(t_{i+1}) = \dot{x}(t_i) + \Delta(a(t_i) - f(\dot{x}(t_i))) \tag{3}$$

$$x(t_{i+1}) = x(t_i) + \dot{x}(t_i)\Delta + \frac{1}{2}(a(t_i) - f(\dot{x}(t_i)))\Delta^2 \tag{4}$$

where $t_i = i\Delta$ is the ith time step. Position information is input to the controllers directly from the state variables in the simulator. As the focus of this first simulation study is on actuation, detailed properties of the sensor subsystem, such as the spatially discrete nature of sensor elements, and issues sensor noise, are not included in the simulation model.

Initial conditions were $x(0) = 0$ and $\dot{x}(0) = 0$, with the time step $\Delta = 1$ millisecond and the valve delay δ=4 milliseconds.

3. MARKET STRUCTURE

1. Market Design Options

Analogies between computational processes and economic markets come in many different forms, and can serve a variety of functions. Structuring a complex system in terms of producers and consumers interacting in a market can be desirable as a means for expressing tradeoffs in a way that is intuitive for humans to understand and to make adjustments to. Transmitting a relatively small amount of information (prices or bids), markets can provide a graceful way to distribute a computation among multiple locations using minimal communication. This distribution of computation among multiple 'producers' or 'consumers' may be desirable for performance reasons, as in the case of parallel computation of a complex decision. Alternatively, this distribution may be desirable for reasons of limited communication bandwidth, as in situations where spatially distributed agents locally sense and react to their own environment, while receiving a limited amount of information about what actions the rest of the system would like them to take.

There are many options available when designing a control system using analogies to economic markets. The selection of what goods to trade includes a broad range of possibilities, such as the use of specific sensors and actuators, the use of computational resources (e.g., to do look-ahead behavior prediction), the use of finite resources such as energy, or even the selection of optimization goals. The key aspects of a market design are selection of which aspects of the system will act producers, which will act as consumers, and the mechanisms by which requests for supply and demand will interact. Markets may be open, where agents know one another's bids; or closed, where agents only know the aggregate going rate for a commodity, or perhaps only know whether their offer was accepted by the market. A wide variety of funding schemes are possible as well. For example, the market may be used as an optimization mechanism, rewarding agents for making decisions that correlate with good system performance, and taking funds away from those that make poor decisions. Alternatively, the market may be used primarily as a coordination mechanism, providing agents with unlimited or continuously refreshed funds, with the market serving as a means to balance the conflicting requests of the various components of a system.

Some possible consumers and producers for the air jet system include agents concerned with the behavior of the system at specific locations, agents focused on specific performance or optimization goals, agents controlling specific sensors or actuators, or agents representing control strategies. For example, an agent concerned with minimizing the number of valve transitions (so as to extend the lifetime of the system) would bid against any acceleration that required a valve transition. An agent concerned with the arrival time at a particular location would bid for control actions that provide the necessary amount of acceleration to achieve that goal. As many of these goals will conflict, the art of designing the market lies in selecting the relative weights (effectively the amount of funds) assigned to each agent, and in determining what mechanisms will be used to aggregate the desires of the various agents to form decisions.

In the examples used in this paper, controllers associated with space-time regions act as consumers, and a market is used to aggregate the demands from the various regional controllers to determine what the appropriate action for the shared actuators should be. The various regions interact with one another through a shared set of actuators, and through the dynamics of the object being transported as it moves from place to place. Various regions of the air jet surface will often have different targets for the position-velocity-time trajectory that the transported object should follow in that region. For instance, a typical trajectory would be to accelerate the object in one portion of the air jet array, hold the velocity constant, and then decelerate that object in a different portion of the array to arrive at a given location at a pre-specified time and velocity.

2. Market Design Decisions

In this work, agents representing points in time act as the consumers, and the air jets act as the producer. Each of the consumers is associated with a different moment in time (the agent's 'control time'), and strives to have the system reach a specific state (position and velocity of the transported object) at that moment in time. To experiment with reducing reliance on system models, the individual consumers do not have detailed knowledge of the system dynamics. For example, they are not aware of valve delay times, the drag coefficient of the system, or the amount of acceleration that will result from a forward or reverse control action. The only feedback that the individual consumers receive is the current position and velocity of the transported object. To reduce reliance on communication, the market is closed, meaning that the consumers are not aware of one another, and are not aware of the current state of the actuation subsystem (forward, reverse, or glide). Thus each agent does not know what effect the current state of the actuation system will have on the transported object, or what magnitude of affect requesting a change will have.

When an actuation decision is to be made, each agent bids for the system to go either faster or slower. Since the agents lack the knowledge of system dynamics and status that is necessary to extrapolate from the current state of the system to the system state at the moment in time that the agent is trying to optimize, each agent uses a simple guide: each agent strives to adjust the velocity of the transported object to arrive at the agent's 'control time' at the appropriate position using a constant velocity approach. This simple guide allows the agent to make decisions based on whether the current position and velocity of the object will allow it to arrive at the desired location at the desired velocity. Once an agent's 'control time' has passed, that agent stops bidding. This leads to a somewhat unusual market structure in which the number of consumers declines over time.

Each agent's resources are fully replenished after each decision cycle. In the examples in this paper, during each decision cycle the agents bid *all* of their resources on one of two options: going 'faster' or of going 'slower'. At the start of each decision cycle, agents are allocated resources based on an exponential discount factor related to the distance of their 'control time' from the current time. Thus agents whose time is far from the current time give relatively less contribution to overall utility. Specifically, a *discount factor* is used when allocating resources to agents: $e^{-\frac{R}{\tau}}$ where R is the amount of time remaining until an agent's 'control time is reached, and τ is the characteristic discount time. Based on typical velocities in the system, $\tau = 0.08$, 0.16, and 1 for high, moderate, and low amounts of time discounting. The effect of the amount of time discounting on the tracking ability is shown in Figure 2. Based on comparing the current position and velocity to its locally desired value, each agent computes a desired velocity shift:

$$s = W_x \Delta x + W_v \Delta v \qquad\qquad (5)$$

If s>0, the agent wants to slow down the system, otherwise speed it up. The weights W_x and W_v give the relative importance to matching position and velocity. For the results presented below, W_x=7500 while W_v=130, so as to weight the position tracking ability more heavily than the velocity tracking ability. The market sums over all of the active agents (those whose time has not yet passed) to give overall utilities for going faster and for going slower. The decision with the largest aggregate utility is selected by the market. The market's selection leads to changes in the air jet array status in a stepwise manner:

Current actuator array status	Aggregate market request	New state
Forward	Faster	Forward
Glide	Faster	Forward
Reverse	Faster	Glide
Forward	Slower	Glide
Glide	Slower	Reverse
Reverse	Slower	Reverse

4. SIMULATION RESULTS

1. Comparison Benchmarks

The trajectory tracking performance of the market-based controller using a moderate value for the time discount factor (τ=0.16) was compared to a near-optimal model-based benchmark and to the trajectory tracking performance of a single PD controller, as illustrated in Figures 3 and 4. The model-based benchmark was derived using a search mechanism that at *each* decision point examined the effects of the next 22 possible decisions through via brute force simulation that included valve delays and other parameters of the dynamics. Based on the simulation results, the benchmark selected the control decision that led to the best overall performance. In effect, the search-based benchmark represents the best sequence of actions that *any* controller could take, given the system dynamics, to track the target trajectory. The search-based benchmark is not optimal, but is near-optimal: only a controller (such as the market-based system) that intentionally introduced errors early on in the trajectory to achieve better performance at a later stage (beyond 22 decisions forward in time) could do better. Unlike the market-based controller, which is constrained to alter actuation directions based on the table shown above, the model-based benchmark is willing to jump directly from forwards to reverse without going through glide, or to remain in glide mode indefinitely as it deems appropriate.

The PD controller used in the comparisons uses the same position and velocity weightings as each of the agents in the market-based controller, namely W_x=7500 while W_v=130. However, rather than operating based on the target position and velocity at the 'control time' of an agent, the PD controller makes decisions at each instant based on the target position and velocity specified for the current time in the target trajectory. For the PD controller, the weighted sum of position and velocity errors is thresholded to determine a 'faster' or 'slower' decision that is implemented in the same manner as the market actuation decision (based on the table shown above).

To evaluate the ability of markets to mediate between conflicting goals, a step function was used as the target trajectory in Figures 2-4. Agents whose time location is earlier than the step that occurs at 200msec have a goal of tracking a constant-velocity trajectory that starts at a position of 0.01 meters at time 0. Agents whose time location is subsequent to 200ms have the same constant velocity target, but have position targets that are 0.02 meters larger than the agents located prior to time=200ms. This creates conflicts in the control goals between the need to accelerate early on to reach achieve the larger displacement desired by the >200ms agents, versus maintaining the smaller displacement desired by the <200ms agents as well as the constant velocity trajectory desired by all of the agents.

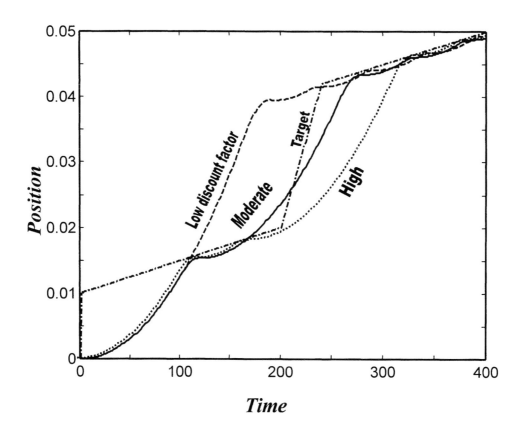

Figure 2: Effect of discount factor on market performance while tracking a step function. An excessively low discount factor causes the desires of the agents corresponding to later points in time to dominate, while an excessively high discount factor causes the system to operate 'in the moment'. The moderate value of the discount factor blends a focus on the present with anticipation of future needs. The 'control time' of ten consumer agents was distributed evenly over the 400 millisecond duration of the experiment (40 milliseconds between consumers).

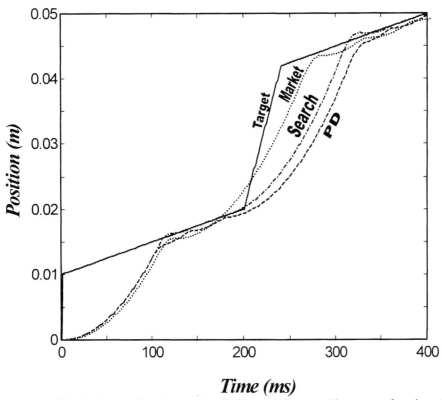

Figure 3: Comparison of Market-based, Search-based, and PD controllers tracking a step function. Note how the search-based benchmark, which has full knowledge of the valve delays, is able to track the trajectory most accurately (indistinguishable from the plot of the 'target' line) during the period from 100-175 msec. During the period 175-260msec, the market-based controller's consideration of future performance allows it to anticipate the step in the target trajectory by a substantial margin. Conflicts between agents decisions took place 61 times, primarily during the 85 decision cycles that occurred from 175-260milliseconds.

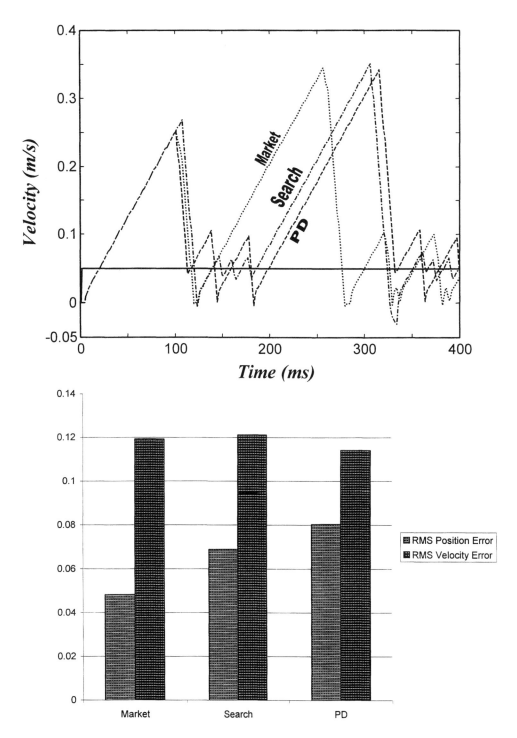

Figure 4: Comparison of Market-based, Search-based, and PD controllers tracking a step function. Note how the market-based controllers consideration of future performance allows it to anticipate the step in the target trajectory by a substantial margin, giving it performance superior to that of the search-based controller, even though the search-based controller has full knowledge of the system dynamics and valve delays. The PD controller does not anticipate the step at all, while the search based controller anticipates by only a few milliseconds.

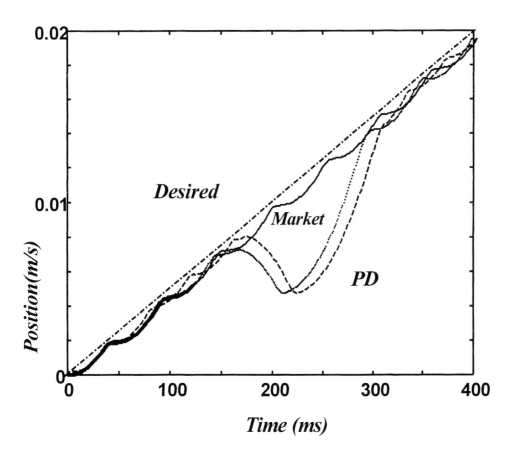

Figure 5: The market allocation of control is robust to failure by individual agents. Consider the control problem of controlling the trajectory to a constant velocity trajectory by a group of ten controllers. The trajectory to be tracked is indicated by the dot-dashed line. Suppose that one controller (the fifth one) is malfunctioning in that while the object is in its region of control, the controller tries to move the object position to zero. If this controller is given complete control, the object deviates as indicated by the dashed line. Only when the object leaves the control of the fifth controller does the object return to its correct trajectory. The market however is robust to such failures as indicated by the solid line when many controllers are involved in the market. The other controllers have a different goal than the failed controller and override its faulty control to yield a robust control close to the desire trajectory. When the time discount factor is decreased so that other controllers are in effect removed from the market, the market control reverts to that similar to the PD controller (dotted line).

5. CONCLUSIONS

It is remarkable that the market-based system did reasonably well in comparison to the search-based benchmark. Each agent communicated only a very small amount of information to the market: a preference for 'faster' or 'slower', with no indication of how badly that agent desired a change in actuation to occur. Each agent had no detailed knowledge of the system dynamics. For instance, the individual controllers had no knowledge of the coulombic friction effect, the valve delays, or of the quantitative amount of acceleration that would result from an actuation decision. The market could not change directly from forwards to reverse, but rather had to change from forwards to glide, and then from glide to reverse, thereby decreasing the effective control bandwidth and increasing the impact of the valve switching delays. In contrast, the search-based benchmark was permitted to switch directly from forwards to reverse, and had exact knowledge of the system dynamics, as well as the benefit of a substantial 22 decision look-ahead capability.

One way to view markets is as an abstraction mechanism. One could view the market controller presented here as a weighted sum of PD controllers with somewhat bizarre look-ahead terms. However, adjusting those somewhat bizarre terms and their weightings without the market analogy is very unintuitive. Another way to view this work is in terms of the possibilities that are opened up by synthesizing complex controllers through coordination of numerous relatively simple controllers. One interesting direction for future work is to explore a market optimization approach to the examples presented in this paper. In that approach, controllers that correlate positively with system performance would be rewarded with more funds.

Markets are an interesting way to think about setting up and tuning controllers for systems where it is not practical to use a model-based optimization approach. In cases such as the step function, where the various local controllers had conflicting goals, the market proved to be an effective mechanism for balancing the requests of the various controllers. Rather than being sensitive to particular model parameters, the market was found to be sensitive to variables affecting the aggregated behavior and balance between the agents, such as the time discount factor τ. From the perspective of scaling to more complex smart matter systems, the concept of tuning aggregation properties rather than model properties is very attractive.

The key question for future work is whether this approach can be scaled to the regime of thousands of independently addressable sensors and actuators. In that regime, it becomes essential to utilize a principled abstraction mechanism to structure and expose conflicts (and communication) in a way that is easily understood and adjusted by a human designer. Using markets to combine multiple simple controllers, each of which is concerned with an understandable set of subgoals, appears to hold promise as a means for structuring large-scale smart matter systems.

6. ACKNOWLEDGEMENT

The work described in this paper was performed as part of the Distributed Smart Matter Control and Integrated Smart Stuff projects at the Xerox Palo Alto Research Center. These projects are sponsored in part by the Defense Advanced Research Projects Agency under contract DABT630095C-025, 'MEMS-based Active Control of Macro-Scale Objects'. The content of the information does not necessarily reflect the position or the policy of the Government and no official endorsement should be inferred.

7. REFERENCES

1. Berlin, A.A., *et al. Distributed Information Systems for MEMS*. 1995: Information Science and Technology Study Group.
2. Berlin, A.A. and K.J. Gabriel, *Distributed MEMS: New Challenges for Computation*, in *Computational Science and Engineering*. 1997. p. 12-16.
3. Biegelsen, D., *et al. Air Jet Arrays for Precision Positional Control of Flexible Media*. in *International Conference on Micromechatronics for Information And Precision Equipment (MIPE'97)*. 1997. Tokyo.
4. Cheung, P., *et al.*, *Batch Fabrication of Pneumatic Valve Arrays by Combining MEMS with Printed Circuit Board Technology*, in *Proc. of the Symposium on Micro-Mechanical Systems*. 1997.
5. Waldspurger, C.A., *et al.*, *Spawn: A Distributed Computational Economy*. IEEE Trans. on Software Engineering, 1992. **18**(2): p. 103-117.
6. Guenther, O., T. Hogg, and B.A. Huberman, *Controls for Unstable Structures*, in *Proc. of SPIE Conf. on Smart Structures and Materials*, V.V.V.a.J. Chandra, Editor. 1997. p. 754--763.
7. *Market-Based Control: A Paradigm for Distributed Resource Allocation*, ed. S.H. Clearwater. 1996, Singapore.
8. Mahmassani, H.S., J.C. Williams, and R. Herman, *Transportation and Traffic Theory*, in *Performance of Urban Traffic Networks*, N.G.a.H. Wilson, Editor. 1987: Amsterdam.
9. Huberman, B. and S.H. Clearwater, *A Multi-Agent System for Controlling Building Environments*, in *Proc. of the 1st International Conference on Multiagent Systems (ICMAS95)*, V. Lesser, Editor. 1995: Menlo Park, CA. p. 171-176.
10. Berlin, A.A., *Towards Intelligent Structures: Active Control of Buckling*. 1994.
11. How, J.P. and S.R. Hall, *Local Control Design Methodologies for a Hierarchic Control Architecture*. J. of Guidance, Control, and Dynamics, 1992. **15**(3): p. 654-663.
12. Ho, C.M. and Y.C. Tai, *MEMS and its Applications for Flow Control*. Journal of Fluids Engineering, 1996. **118**: p. 437-447.
13. Williams, B.C. and P.P. Nayak, *A Model-based Approach to Reactive Self-Configuring Systems*, in *Proc. of the 13th Natl. Conf. on Artificial Intelligence (AAAI96)*. 1996: Menlo Park, CA. p. 971-978.
14. Mcmanamon, P.F., *Optical Phased Array Technology*. Proc. of the IEEE, 1996. **84**(2): p. 268-298.
15. Bryzek, J., K. Petersen, and W. McCulley, *Micromachines on the March*, in *IEEE Spectrum*. 1994. p. 20--31.

16.   Drexler, K.E., *Nanosystems: Molecular Machinery, Manufacturing, and Computation.* 1992.

17.   Bell, T.W., *Molecular Trees: A New Branch of Chemistry.* Science, 1996. **271**: p. 1077-1078.

18.   Eigler, D.M. and E.K. Schweizer, *Positioning Single Atoms with a Scanning Tunnelling Microscope.* Nature, 1990. **344**: p. 524-526.

19.   Jung, T.A., *et al.*, *Controlled Room-Temperature Positioning of Individual Molecules: Molecular Flexure and Motion.* Science, 1996. **271**: p. 181-184.

20.   Shen, T.C., *et al.*, *Atomic-Scale Desorption Through Electronic and Vibrational Excitation Mechanisms.* Science, 1995. **268**: p. 1590-1592.

21.   Kersey, A.D., *Prolog to the Special Section on Smart Structures.* Proc. of the IEEE, 1996. **84**: p. 57-59.

22.   Bohringer, K.-F., B.R. Donald, and N.C. MacDonald, *Upper and Lower Bounds for Programmable Vector Fields with Applications to MEMS and Vibratory Plate Part Feeders.* 1996.

23.   Bohringer, K.F., *et al.*, *Computational Methods for Design and Control of MEMS Micromanipulator Arrays*, in *Computational Science and Engineering.* 1997. p. 17-29.

SESSION 4

System Integration

A Framework for component-based CNC Machines

John Michaloski[a], Sushil Birla[b], George Weinert[c], and C. Jerry Yen[d]

[a]National Institute of Standards and Technology, Gaithersburg, MD

[b] General Motors North American Operations, Warren, MI

[c] Lawrence Livermore National Laboratories, Livermore, CA

[d] General Motors Power Train Headquarters, Pontiac, MI

ABSTRACT

Open architecture technology is ushering in new advances in the world of computer numerically controlled (CNC) machines. Yet, some major benefits of open architecture technology have failed to materialize due to the lack of a standard open architecture specification. We propose an open architecture framework to fill the specification void. The proposed framework supports component-based technology by specifying a control class hierarchy, plug-and-play components and a design framework. This framework can be used to build applications ranging from a single-axis device to a multi-arm robot. An example application applying the framework is documented.

Keywords: API, architecture, classes, CNC, control, framework, object-oriented

1. BACKGROUND

A major advance is underway within the CNC community toward open, component-based, controller technology.[1] Much as openness revolutionized the PC industry, openness has the potential to revolutionize the CNC industry. Currently many controllers are marketed as open. However, to truly realize open architecture benefits, standardization of controller components and interfaces must be established. An open architecture standard allows integrators to mix and match components from different vendors. With an open architecture standard, controllers can be built from best value components from best in class services. For parts manufacturing, this ability leads to better integration of process improvements and increased satisfaction of application requirements.

The "Open Modular Architecture Controller" (OMAC) white paper spells out the industry requirements for an open architecture controller to meet the manufacturing needs of the automotive industry.[2] In response to these requirements, the OMAC Application Programming Interface (API) workgroup was formed. As members of the Open Modular Architecture Controller (OMAC) API workgroup, our goal has been to define a specification for open, component-based controllers. On the basis of our evaluation, we believe that a specification based on an object-oriented framework offers the best hope in achieving open, component-based controllers.

In this work we describe an object-oriented framework for designing and implementing open architecture control systems. In our context, the term *framework* is used to mean a specification for an integrated set of software components. An *open system framework* is a framework that promotes *interface reuse* based on a public interface specification.[3] In the OMAC framework, classes define components of the system. Class instances or *objects* are used to implement the components. The framework classes are derived from decomposing a generic controller into a class hierarchy. Framework classes are then grouped into OMAC API modules that become plug-and-play components. Within the framework, a controller design is generated by selecting from different implementations of the OMAC modules.

A survey of the industry finds other open-architecture standardization efforts. OSACA is a message-based open architecture effort that has developed a reference architecture and communication scheme directed at equipment controllers.[4] OSEC has also produced a message-based, open architecture specification based on the Factory Automation Equipment Description Language (FADL) as the basis for exchanging messages in a distributed, agent-based, networked environment.[5] These efforts use a *message-based* approach to specification. Message-based communication is at a lower level of abstraction than an API-based framework. In the OMAC API framework, communication between objects is achieved by method invocation; or when distributed communication is needed, a *proxy agent* is used to cross a domain boundary.[6] We feel this approach hides the lower-level communication details thus improving software quality. The proxy-based approach offers a model conducive to both local and remote object interaction.

132

Part of the SPIE Conference on Sensors and Controls for Intelligent Machining and Agile Manufacturing
Boston, Massachusetts ● November 1998
SPIE Vol. 3518 ● 0277-786X/98/$10.00

In the following sections, we will review major aspects of the OMAC framework. First, we start by describing the notion of a framework and why it is useful. We then apply information modeling to the application domain leading to a class hierarchy and the concept of a "module" as a necessary prerequisite for plug-and-play. Following this discussion, architecture design and detail design within the OMAC framework will be reviewed. We then look at the behavior model for the framework including discussion on finite state machines, events, and collaboration.

2. FRAMEWORK MODEL

An object-oriented framework builds controllers as a collection of objects that encapsulate algorithms and data representations. This is in contrast to procedural software approach where the behavioral procedures and the data structures exist as separate entities and are only loosely connected. The benefits of modularity, reusability and extensibility were decisive in selecting an object-oriented framework as the specification approach. This contrasts with the procedural approach where there is difficulty extending and specializing functionality; difficulty in factoring out common functionality; difficulty in reusing functionality that results in duplication of effort; and difficulty in maintaining the non-encapsulated functionality.

Frameworks enhance modularity by encapsulating volatile implementation details behind stable interfaces. Modularity is based on information hiding where an object has a public API that other objects can use to communicate with it. The object can maintain a private representation that can be changed at any time without affecting the other objects that depend on it. Further, you don't need to understand the inner object workings in order to use it. Ultimately, framework modularity improves software quality by localizing design and implementation changes.

Frameworks provide extensibility by allowing new or modified objects to be developed. Using inheritance, frameworks allow you to modify or change any object's behavior. Frameworks provide the specifications for new objects allowing you to build new components out of smaller objects. Frameworks allow you to integrate components system-tailored for your particular application. Assimilating the new or modified objects within the framework is achieved by three principal mechanisms: associations (relationship between different types), subtypes (relationship between like types including inheritance) and aggregation (subpart relationship within a larger part).

Frameworks promote reusability so that application developers do not have to start over each time. Frameworks are built from a collection of objects. Given standard object interfaces, reuse of both the design and the code of a framework is possible. Additionally, frameworks define the environment in which the objects operate. Since each object makes assumptions about its environment, these assumptions must be the same or there is no way of using them together. Frameworks define an environment containing a range of standard mechanisms including data exchange data, error handling, and interobject cooperation.

3. INFORMATION MODELING

The domain of interest is discrete parts manufacturing where the applications range from low-end single axis machines to high-end machines requiring multi-axis, coordinated motion control and sensor-based process control. A high end machine controller makes decisions regarding part sequencing, tooling, part locations, and monitors the operation of the machine under its control. Representative applications include Computer Numerical Control (CNC) machines for cutting, inspecting and grinding. Although these applications differ in terms of their processes, from a control point of view there is a great deal of overlap of functionality in motion and process control.

3.1. Class Hierarchy

A framework embodies generalized domain functionality based on analysis and synthesis of a wide range domain applications. Frameworks use a *class hierarchy* for domain modeling. Class hierarchies define static relationships between classes sharing common behavior. At the lowest level, the definition of the software class closely corresponds to the physical objects in the application domain. More abstract classes are defined in terms of the lower classes. Ultimately, all classes are members of a hierarchy of classes united via inheritance or association relationships.

To derive a class hierarchy, a decomposition of generic controller is performed. The decomposition of a generic controller into classes spans many levels of abstraction and has elements for motion control and discrete logic necessary to coordinate machining, mill parts, and sequence operations. Figure 1 portrays the class hierarchy derived from a controller decomposition.

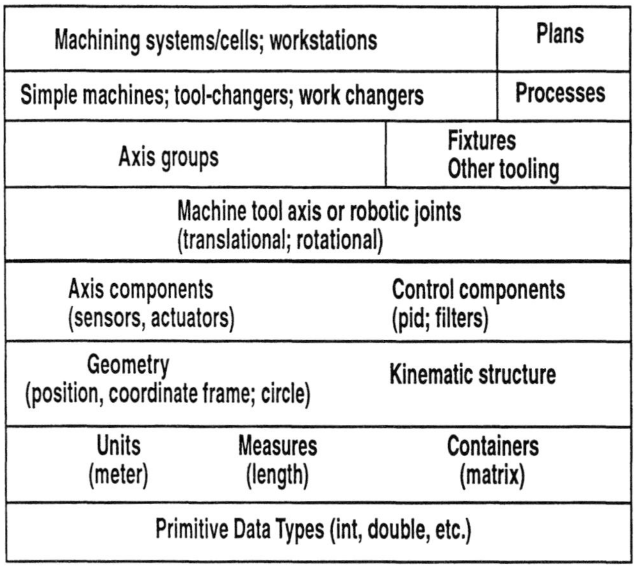

Machining systems/cells; workstations		Plans
Simple machines; tool-changers; work changers		Processes
Axis groups		Fixtures Other tooling
Machine tool axis or robotic joints (translational; rotational)		
Axis components (sensors, actuators)		Control components (pid; filters)
Geometry (position, coordinate frame; circle)		Kinematic structure
Units (meter)	Measures (length)	Containers (matrix)
Primitive Data Types (int, double, etc.)		

Figure 1. Controller Class Hierarchy

At the lower levels, the classes are the building blocks that may be found in multiple modules. For example, the class definition of a Geometry "position" would be found in most modules. As one moves up the hierarchy, framework classes broaden their scope to define device abstractions for such motion components as sensors, actuators, and PID control laws. As the scope broadens however, not all software objects have physical equivalents. Objects such as axis groups are only logical entities. Axis groups hold the knowledge about the axes whose motion is to be coordinated and how that coordination is to be performed. Services of the appropriate axis group are invoked by user-supplied plans.

Object-oriented techniques can greatly help in defining a specification. We found the object-oriented feature of inheritance crucial in managing complexity. For example, when defining a control law class, there exist many options to implementing control laws including PID, Fuzzy Logic, Neural Nets, and Nonlinear. Each control law option has different nomenclature and features. The question arises, "When do we stop defining our class definitions?"

We used object-oriented inheritance to control the breadth and scope of class definitions. Inheritance is a specialization mechanism which allows a derived class to inherit properties of a base class. Inheritance has many benefits. It helps manage the scope of capabilities which reduces complexity. It allows differing terminology (e.g., weights versus gains) based on need. Specialization provides a technique to handle evolving technology by allowing new derived class to be defined when necessary. Objects of the derived class have access to data and methods of base class without the need to redefine them. We started by defining base classes that modeled the general data and behavior. Subsequently, only highly-demanded subclasses, such as PID in our case, were derived with the knowledge that inheritance offers a straightforward mechanism for expanding the specification.

Inheritance was also used to institute levels of conformance. Level 1 classes constitute base functionality seen in current practice. Level 2 classes inherited all the data and behavior of the level 1 class definitions, but added extensions to handle advanced functionality. Higher levels constitute functional capability seen in emerging technology, but unnecessary for simple applications. Levels of complexity was seen as critical in allowing different specification conformance levels.

3.2. Modules

A primary goal of the OMAC API specification was to enable "plug-and-play." Plug-and-play on a per-class basis as defined in a class hierarchy is not economically feasible since the level of granularity of a class is too fine. Instead, a coarser granularity component, which we call a *module*, is necessary for realizing plug-and-play. To be plug-and-play, a module must satisfy the following requirements. (1) A module must be a significant piece of software used in a component-based controller. (2) A module contains a grouping of similar classes. (3) A module must support a well-defined API, states, and state transitions. (4) A module must be replaceable by any piece of software that implements the API, states, and state transitions.

The OMAC API framework extracts fourteen modules from the class hierarchy. The set of OMAC Modules and their general responsibilities include:

Axis Modules responsible for servo control of axis motion, transforming incoming motion setpoints into setpoints for the corresponding actuators.

Axis Group Modules responsible for coordinating the motions of individual axes, transforming an incoming motion segment specification into a sequence of equi-time-spaced setpoints for the coordinated axes.

OMAC Base Class Base class for control OMAC modules providing uniform state model with methods for start-up and shutdown, uniform name and type declaration, and error-logging interface.

Capability Object derived from Control Plan Units to which the Task Coordinator delegates for specific modes of operation that correspond to traditional operating modes (AUTO, MANUAL, and MDI).

Control Law Components responsible for servo control loop calculations to reach commanded setpoints.

Control Plan Units Derived from FSM class. When the FSM is passed between modules it is called a `ControlPlanUnit`. Received ControlPlanUnits are then used within a module for control flow.

Control Plan Generator Modules responsible for translating part programs into a Control Plan.

Discrete Logic Modules responsible for implementing discrete control logic or rules characterized by a Boolean function that maps input and internal state variables to output and internal state variables.

Kinematic Model Modules responsible for kinematic mechanisms, connections, coordinate frame transformations and kinematic solutions.

Human Machine Interface Modules responsible for remotely handling data, command, and event service of an internal controller module.

I/O Points Collection of IO responsible for the reading of input devices and writing of output devices through a generic read/write interface.

Machine-to-Machine Modules responsible for connecting and communicating to controllers across different domains.

Process Model Component containing dynamic data models to be integrated with the control system.

Task Coordinator Modules responsible for sequencing operations and coordinating the various motion, sensing, and event-driven control processes.

Modules have other characteristics that clarify its intent within the framework. Interchangeable modules may differ in their performance levels. Modules may provide more functionality (added value) than required in the specification. Specialization of a module interfaces is the mechanism to achieve additional functionality. A controller may have more than one instance of a module. Modules can be explicitly control-related (e.g., Axis) or be inheritance-related encapsulating common functionality (e.g., OMAC Base Class.) Modules can run as separate threads and contain multiple threads of execution. Modules do not need to run as separate threads so systems can be built from a single thread of execution. Modules may be used to build other components. For example, a discrete mechanism, such as a tool changer component, can be built using OMAC modules.

4. DESIGN ISSUES

A system design is divided into two phases. The first phase is *architectural design* and deals with system decomposition into OMAC Modules. The second phase is called *detailed design* and is responsible for detailing individual object API, that is, the object attributes and methods. In this case, the design uses the published object API or extends the API to suit the application.

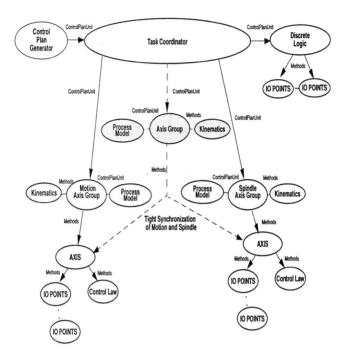

Figure 2. Drilling Example

4.1. Architecture Design

The design architecture describes the decomposition of the application into individual modules. A design architecture highlights the static relationship between modules (as opposed to the data flow.) The OMAC framework does not specify a reference architecture so composing a design architecture from OMAC modules is left to the developer. We felt it was imperative that the framework be scalable and allow the designer the freedom to build any size system. With this freedom, OMAC systems can start small, stay small, or be pieced together into a larger system. For example, an embedded system with a small footprint is possible. Another system possibility is to start with an operator controlling several IO points, add an axis at a time, integrate the axes into an axis group to eventually evolve into a full-blown 5-axis controller. This design freedom offers much flexibility, but without guidance, can be perplexing.

4.2. Architecture Example

An example describing a programmed CNC for one-axis drilling will be developed. A typical one-axis drilling workstation would perform some hole-working operations, e.g., drilling with a spindle drill-head, boring a precision bore, counter-boring the bored hole, probing the (axial) location of the counterbored shoulder. Figure 2 illustrates the module and component relationships for a drilling application. One Axis module is necessary for motion control and another Axis module is required for Spindle control. Spindle drive components are assumed to provide a facility for setting spindle speed and direction and to start and stop spindle rotation. Coordinated motion of the motion and spindle is supplied by three Axis Group modules. One Axis Group independently controls controls the motion and one Axis Group independently controls the Spindle. The final Axis Group supercedes the first two to synchronize coupled control of the Motion and Spindle (shown as shaded with dashed line connections). Generally, the Spindle Axis will not need a Control Law, however, when it is synchronized with motion it will require servoed control.

In the diagram, a Task Coordinator exists to provide program control. A Control Plan Generator module translates a part program into Control Plan Units. The primary command communication between modules is reflected in the diagrams by showing the keyword "Method" or "ControlPlanUnits" (which uses a method to pass it) next to an arrow. A Discrete Logic Module exists for handling part loading and unloading, as well as machine state (e.g., temperature, estop). To improve predictability and reduce variation, a Process Model module exists to integrate sensing and control to detect tool breakage by monitoring spindle torques and thrust forces. A Kinematics module exists to model the workspace and handle different tool offsets and part placements.

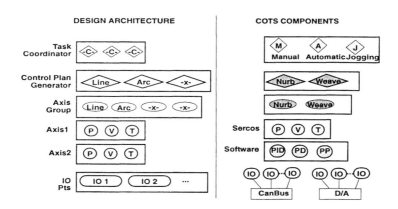

Figure 3. Design Framework

4.3. Detail Design

The detailed design is concerned with the component assembly especially integration and configuration. The detailed design configures module responsibilities, performance, timing, and logical to physical mappings. Controllers are integrated as a set of connected module instances that use other module services through the published API. Much of module integration depends on an *infrastructure* which is defined as the services that tie the modules together and allow modules to use platform services.

4.4. Infrastructure

An *infrastructure* is defined as the services that tie modules together and allow modules to use platform services. The infrastructure is intended to hide specific hardware and platform dependence; however, this is often difficult to achieve. The infrastructure deals primarily with the computing environment including platform services, operating system, and programming tools. Platform services include such items as timers, interrupt handlers, and inter-process communications. Programming tools include compilers, linkers, and debuggers.

The OMAC API does not specify an infrastructure because many of the infrastructural issues are outside the controller domain and are better handled by the domain experts. Further, it is more cost-effective to leverage industry efforts rather than to reinvent these technologies. Because there are so many competing infrastructure technologies, OMAC API has chosen to let the market decide the course of the infrastructure definition. As such, to achieve plug-and-play module interchangeability, a commitment to a *Platform + Operating System + Compiler + Loader + Infrastructure* suite is necessary for it to be possible to swap OMAC modules.

4.5. Detail Design Example

We will consider the detailed design for the drilling example discussed previously. We assume that the detailed design is the responsibility of the system integrator who analyzes individual modules for performance and functional requirements. Based on this analysis, the system integrator selects modules and module components from the available commercial off-the-shelf (COTS) technology. Figure 3 illustrates the design framework with the "Design Architecture" enumerating the necessary modules and module components and the "COTS Components" giving the available technology. If desired modules are not available as COTS technology or are available but do not meet the requirements, then the system integrator must develop modules on their own. Once the pieces are in place, the application developer configures the modules and "puts the pieces together" by linking the purchased COTS ".o" object files.

Modules are configured based on their reference mapping to other modules. For the Axis modules in the example, the application developer has the possibility to select position (P), velocity (V) or torque (T) Control Law modules in software, hardware or some combination of hardware and software. For software P control, a Control Law object from the Software set is selected. For hardware P control, a Control Law object from the Sercos[7] set is selected. The applications developer is also responsible for mapping the logical IO points onto physical devices.

Modules are also configured based on the selection of Control Plan Units (CPU) to define a module responsibilities. Within the example, there is a Task Coordinator module which has containers for inserting Capability CPU (in the figure represented by a -C- framed by a diamond). The Capabilities include Manual, Automatic or Jogging. The application developer is free to put one or more of these Capabilities into the Task Coordinator or develop a unique Capability. For Control Plan Generator and Axis Group, the application developer is already provided Line and Arc CPU but can plug in a Non-uniform Rational B-spline (NURB) CPU or a Weave CPU.

5. BEHAVIOR MODEL

Building a controller is based on assembling instances of OMAC modules into a system. In general practice, controllers are modeled as a distributed system of concurrently active objects – although in implementation a single thread of execution is possible. *Active objects* do not need to receive a message to be in the "active" state and govern their execution by internally managing one or more independent threads of control. To reinforce the notion of plug-and-play, we use the term *active module* in lieu of "active object." Examples of controller active modules include: (1) Axis modules, (2) Axis Group modules, (3) Discrete Logic modules, and (4) Task Coordinator modules. Active modules may delegate to *passive modules* that do not possess threads of control and that depend on an active module for the execution of their functions. Examples of passive modules include (1) Kinematic Model modules, and (2) Control Law modules.

5.1. State Machine Model

The behavior of an active module is modeled as a Finite State Machine (FSM). In the FSM model, the world is thought of as being in a definite state at any given time. The set of the possible states is known as the state-space. Time itself is discretized to a sequence of relevant moments. There exists the notion of changing from one state to another between moments. The concept of change is expressed in terms of state transitions from one state to another state as time passes. Typically, there is a set of allowed transitions from any given state. For our domain, we assume that a controller has a finite set of states, so that the term Finite State Machine more accurately describes our model. We further assume that a controller can be modeled as deterministic FSM whereby states can exhibit only one transition sequence for a given state and a given input.

The OMAC framework assumes that complex FSM can be simplified by grouping states into a hierarchical FSM.[8] A "flat" FSM can suffer from combinatorial growth of state transitions, such as in the case where every normal state has a state transition to an error state in the FSM. The hierarchical FSM can be used to simplify the error state combinatorics by nesting all the states that have error transition inside a higher-level "normal" state. Hierarchical FSM help reduce an excessive amount of state transitions.

Of greater interest to the OMAC framework is the *recursive nesting* of FSM. This functionality differs from a hierarchical FSM and more closely resembles running a program within a job control shell. In the shell, suspending the shell causes the program to suspend also. A good example of this job control model can be found in the Sematech "Job Manager/Managed Job" model.[9] In the recursive nesting model, both the shell and the job are FSM, but the shell FSM is a supervisor to the job FSM.

OMAC API does not dictate the number of levels of recursive nesting. In general, an outer *administrative* FSM exists to handle activities that include initialization, startup, shutdown, and, if relevant, power enabling. OMAC API defines the OMAC Base Class module to provide a uniform administrative state model across modules. To enter into a lower FSM, the module enters into the "executing" state. In the "executing" state, client/server coordination uses a lower FSM for coordination. This lower FSM is module- and application-dependent. This lower FSM, in turn, can have a FSM embedded within it so that further nesting of embedded FSMs is possible.

Figure 4 shows the nesting of FSM levels. Within the figure, the FSM icon is represented by a rectangle inside a diamond. The dotted FSM icon represents an optional FSM. The nesting of one or more lower level *operational* FSMs is possible depending on system complexity. Within the nesting of the FSM shown in Figure 4, the operational FSM handles different CNC modes corresponding to "auto," or "manual." The designer of a particular control system determines the number of nested FSM levels, depending upon the complexity and organization of the controlled system. For example, at the operation level for part programming, there may be even another FSM level to handle a family of parts. The lowest level FSM or *dominion* FSM monitors the current focus of control. The dominion FSM "rule" over lower level objects. There may be one or more dominion FSM at the lowest level within an OMAC module, which will be covered later in the computational model section.

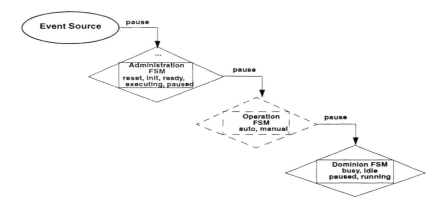

Figure 4. Recursive Nesting of FSM

5.2. Events

Within a FSM, actions are associated with states and/or state transitions. Associating an action with a state is categorized as a Moore machine. Associating an action with a state transition is categorized as a Mealy machine. We adopt the Mealy machine as our model since it better suited for an event-driven system. Event-driven systems correlate actions to discrete changes in the world. We characterize change to be modeled as an event, which triggers a state transition.

For OMAC API, method invocations cause events to be propagated from the client to the server. Events are evaluated within the highest level FSM and then recursively forwarded through each lower level FSM. For example, we will assume that the Administrative FSM in Figure 4 is in the "executing" state and the "executing" state accepts a "pause" event to trigger a state transition to the state "paused." Referring to Figure 4, the receipt of a "pause" event at the highest Administration level causes the state transition to "paused." If the Operation FSM supports a "pause" method then this method is invoked and the event evaluated. This event evaluation and recursive forwarding of the event may cross module boundaries and propagate all the way to the "bottom" FSM in the application controller.

Overall, event dispatching is both distributed as well as recursive. Such event dispatching contrasts to traditional frameworks characterized by centralized event handling known as inversion of control.[10]

5.3. Computational Model

A general computational model exists for characterizing all OMAC active modules. Figure 5 illustrates the general computational model. The general computational model supports a mechanism to receive and queue client requests. Client requests can be either events or FSM. FSM received by a server can replace existing FSM or be added to the dominion list. The next section on Control Plan Units covers the concept of collaboration using FSM.

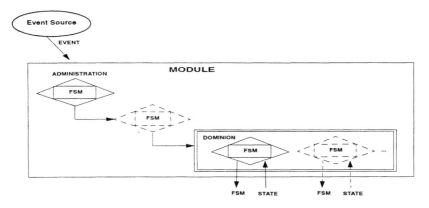

Figure 5. Module Computational Paradigm

As outlined previously, each OMAC module can support levels of recursive FSM. The OMAC API module may also have one or more FSM simultaneously executing on a dominion FSM list. Each FSM on the dominion list is conceptually equivalent to a concurrent thread of state logic. FSM on the dominion list can operate independently or have dependencies between them.

The ability to have multiple FSM executing concurrently is especially useful for process modeling. Within the Axis Group module for example, the dominion list could contain a FSM for motion control as well as a FSM for sensor integration. Additionally, FSM can be added to the dominion list that are "task-independent," such as data logging. Further, the dominion list could support more complex architectures, such as RCS,[11] with FSM for sensor processing, world modeling, planning, value judgment and behavior generation.

The OMAC framework identifies three types of FSM that can exist on the dominion list:

Transient FSM perform a fixed amount of work within a certain period. Transient FSM execute cyclically and are removed from the dominion list when an internal condition is satisfied. An example of a transient FSM is a motion segment FSM which has a beginning and an end. When the FSM "is done", the FSM is removed from the dominion list.

Resident-Cyclic FSM execute "forever" and perform a function periodically. Resident-cyclic FSM execute repeatedly with no internal completion condition. One example of a resident-cyclic FSM is a programmable logic controller (PLC) operation to turn the oil/slides pump on/off every five minutes.

Resident-Event-driven FSM execute once when an event triggers their execution. An example of a Resident-Event-driven FSM is turning an IO point on or off.

Applying these concepts to the Axis Group for example, *transient* FSM are used for controlling different motions (e.g., line, arc) while *resident-cyclic* FSM are used to integrate probe readings or handle data logging.

Different OMAC API modules have different FSM dominion list sizes and different types of FSM. The Discrete Logic module has a multi-item FSM list containing resident-cyclic and resident-event-driven FSM. The Discrete Logic multi-item dominion list is analogous to a PLC scan list to handle IO. The Axis Group has a multi-item dominion list with one or more transient motion FSM and potentially one or more resident-cyclic Process FSM. The Axis module has a one-item transient motion FSM dominion list.

5.4. FSM Distribution

Equivalent application functionality can be achieved with different distributions of FSM within a controller. Depending on the circumstances, *tight coupling* or *loose coupling* can be used to coordinate logic and motion. Tight coupling is achieved by placing *resident-cyclic* FSM on the dominion list. Loose coupling is achieved by placing *resident-cyclic* FSM in a separate thread under the scheduler used for all the other OMAC modules (which are resident-cyclic FSM.)

As an example, consider the integration of a Probe sensor data with an Axis Group to modify motion control. There are at least three ways for incorporating the Probe FSM into the system. (1) The Probe FSM is placed in the Discrete Logic module to be run at a given period. The probe could running at the same period as the Axis Group or be oversampled. This is an example of loose coupling. (2) The Probe could be a Process Model resident-cyclic FSM that runs inside of the Axis Group at the same frequency as the Axis Group. This is an example of tight coupling and is illustrated in Figure 6. (3) The probe could run as standalone resident-cyclic FSM scheduled like other OMAC modules. The probe FSM could run at a slower, faster or the same frequency as the Axis Group. This is an example of loose coupling and is illustrated in Figure 7.

5.5. Collaboration

In the OMAC framework, *FSM are used for controlling behavior and also serve as data.* When events are sent from the client to the server and contain FSM as data, the FSM data is called a *ControlPlanUnit* (CPU). A ControlPlanUnit is a FSM, but the internal representation is not important to the OMAC framework. Instead, CPU are defined with a simple state management API hiding unnecessary FSM details. The crux of the CPU class is a few fundamental methods as seen in the following Interface Definition Language[12] (IDL) code:

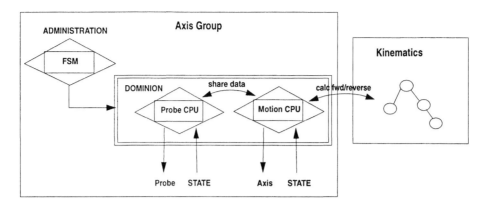

Figure 6. Example Tight Coupling Probe Architecture

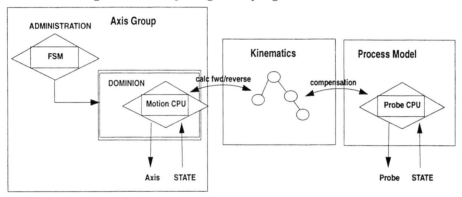

Figure 7. Example Loose Coupling Probe Architecture

```
interface ControlPlanUnit
{  ControlPlanUnit executeUnit();
   boolean isDone();
};
```

The `ControlPlanUnit` is an example of the Command pattern.[13] To evaluate the current state, an active module invokes the `executeUnit()` method, which causes the FSM to perform a state evaluation. Examples of modules derived from Control Plan Unit include: (1) *Capability*, which is a CPU to which the Task Coordinator delegates for specific modes of operation corresponding to traditional CNC operating modes (AUTO or MANUAL); (2) *Motion Segment*, which is a transient CPU used by the Axis Group module for motion control; and (3) *Discrete Logic Unit*, which is a transient or resident-cyclic CPU for discrete logic control.

A series of linked CPUs forms a Control Plan. A *Control Plan* is a general-purpose representation of a control program. OMAC API defines the *Control Plan Generator* module, which is responsible for translating programs written in application-specific languages (e.g., CNC RS274D[14] part programs) into the more general Control Plan. To enable program translation, program logic CPU are defined to mimic control constructs such as if/then, or while statements.

CPUs serve as data by being passed between active modules. Subsequently, such CPUs then serve as the FSM logic within the behavior model. A `ControlPlanUnit` can contain other ControlPlanUnits. When activated, a CPU can send embedded CPU to lower level servers. Thus, CPU contain "intelligence" and understand how to coordinate and sequence the lower level logic and motion modules.

Figure 8 illustrates the collaboration model as a CPU propagates through a simplified control system. In step (a) the Control Plan Generator module translates a part program written in RS274D into a Control Plan. In step (b) the Task Coordinator uses `getNextControlPlanUnit` to retrieve a CPU. In step (c) the Task Coordinator does

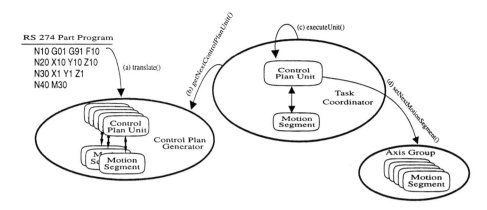

Figure 8. Collaboration Model

an `executeUnit` on this CPU. Step (c) may be repeated several times as in the case where the CPU may have to synchronize with lower level modules (e.g., such as waiting until all current Motion Segments have first completed). After synchronization, step (d) occurs whereby the CPU running within the Task Coordinator appends a reference to the Motion Segment CPU onto the Axis Group motion queue using the method `setNextMotionSegment`. This is an example of an embedded CPU being passed to a subordinate module. Once the Motion Segment CPU is loaded onto the Axis Group queue, it waits for activation. Once activated, the Axis Group periodically calls the Motion Segment CPU `executeUnit()` method until the `isDone()` condition is true.

6. DISCUSSION

Defining an open-architecture controller specification that is flexible and extensible is hard. Making it cost-effective and real-time is even harder. In tackling this challenge, we used an object-oriented framework to define our open architecture specification. We used a framework largely due to its advantages in enabling COTS plug-and-play component technology where modules can be added, replaced, reconfigured, or extended based on the functionality and performance required. This paper highlighted only some of the more important aspects of the OMAC framework. Interested readers can find more information about the framework at the OMAC API website.[15]

Choosing a framework for defining the open-architecture specification is not without risks. Frameworks are an object-oriented technology that have been used successfully elsewhere for some time but are only now starting to make in-roads in the manufacturing domain. We recognize that industry has found it difficult to adopt the framework paradigm, due to entrenchment in the legacy of prior implementations, the "comfort zone" of past practice and culture, the investment hurdle to effect change, and the shortage of skilled resources. However, the future is bright as more and more manufacturing companies are shifting to this paradigm.

REFERENCES

1. F. Proctor and J. Albus, "Open-architecture controllers," *IEEE Spectrum* **34**, pp. 60–64, June 1997.
2. Chrysler, Ford Motor Co., and General Motors, *Requirements of Open, Modular, Architecture Controllers for Applications in the Automotive Industry*, Dec. 1994. White Paper – Version 1.1.
3. R. E. Johnson, "Frameworks = (Components + Patterns)," *CACM* **40**(10), pp. 39–42, 1997.
4. OSACA, "Open System Architecture for Controls within Automation Systems." See Web URL: http://www.osaca.org, 1996.
5. OSEC, "Open System Environment Consortium." See Web URL: http://www.sml.co.jp/OSEC, 1996.
6. M.Shapiro, "Structure and Encapsulation in Distributed Systems: The Proxy Principle," in *6th International Conference on Distributed Computing Systems, IEEE 6th International Conference on Distributed Computing Systems* , pp. 198–204, IEEE Computer Society Press, May 1986.
7. IEC, *IEC1491 - SERCOS (SErial Real-time COmmunications System) Interface Standard.* International Electrical Commission, Geneva, 1995.
8. D. Harel, "On Visual Formalisms," *CACM* **31**(5), pp. 514–530, 1988.

9. SEMATECH, *Computer Integrated Manufacturing (CIM) Application Framework Specification 1.5.* SEMAT-ECH, 2706 Montopolis Drive, Austin, TX 78741 U.S.A., 1997.

10. M. Fayad and D. C. Schmidt, "Object-Oriented Application Frameworks - Introduction," *CACM* **40**(10), pp. 32–38, 1997.

11. J. S. Albus, "Outline for a theory of intelligence," *IEEE Transactions on Systems, Man, and Cybernetics* **21**, pp. 473–509, May-June 1991.

12. Object Management Group, Framingham, MA, *The Common Object Request Broker: Architecture and Specification, Revision 2.0*, July 1995.

13. E. Gamma, R. Helm, R. Johnson, and J. Vlissides, *Design Patterns: Elements of Reusable Object-Oriented Software*, Addison Wesley, Reading, MA, Oct. 1994.

14. Engineering Industries Association, Washington, D.C., *EIA Standard - EIA-274-D, Interchangeable Variable, Block Data Format for Positioning, Contouring, and Contouring/Positioning Numerically Controlled Machines*, February 1979.

15. OMAC API Workgroup, *OMAC API Set.* See Web URL: http://isd.cme.nist.gov/info/omacapi.

-- INTRODUCTION TO MIMIC ENGINEERING --
CONCEPT OF HOLONIC CONTROL

Shigeki Sugiyama

(Foundation)Softopia Japan,
4-7-1, Kagano, Ogaki City, Gifu-Ken, Japan
E-Mail:sugiyama@vsl.gifu-u.ac.jp, sugiyama@gifu-irtc.go.jp

ABSTRACT
Here introduces a concept of Holonic Control in the field of broad sense of control.

Nowadays there are many much more complicated things than before in this world, waited to be controlled intelligently for getting a goods' production rate better at a factory or getting things clearer in a complex system or getting a help in a sense of analysing a system, etc. In a today's control field, for having these complicated things accomplished, we have tried to understand the target system to be controlled clearly, accurately, and precisely. After having got these information, it is ready to control for many purposes. But usually this method gives us further complexed problems,more time consuming because of the size of a system, and comparatively lower robustnesses. These are used by lack of a flexibility against a sudden change of a system's behaviour, giving too much redundant attention to a system, and lack of intelligence.

So in order to overcome these problems, here introduces the concept of HOLONIC CONTROL method which always introduces the necessary figures and functions of a system in the whole system to be controlled.

Keywords: control, production control, system, intelligent system, holon, holonic control, VR

1. INTRODUCTION
In the history of human beings, we have been taking ideas and physical powers from the nature and animals (including human beings) by having a MIMICal attitude to those behaviours and phenomenons of them as examples shown below;

1)Mechanisms of the animals' movements and behaviours;

Horse,Cow → Horse Riding → Horse Carriage → Steam Engine Locomotive → Diesel Engine Locomotive → Electric Motor Locomotive (Train)→ Linear Motor Train

Bird → Balloon → Airplane, Glider → Rocket → · · ·

Human beings → Ideas of Control → Semi Automatic Machine → Automatic Machine → Walking Robot
→ · · ·

· · ·

2)Phenomenons of nature in order to apply them for extracting power or productions;

Water → River → Mill Wheel → Cogwheel → Transmission

Wind → Wind Mill → Cogwheel → Mechanical Transmission → Electrical Transmission → Computer
→ Artificial Intelligence · · ·

Fire → Metal Manufacturing → Steam Engine → · · ·

Sun → Heat → Electric Power

· · ·

From above lines of sequences, we can feel and see some sort of meaning flow in the developments of technologies even though these are just put onto sequences in a line.

So as it is mentioned above, in a broad sense, we can say that our culture has been developed by the mimical watching, attitudes, and investigation towards the nature.

144

Part of the SPIE Conference on Sensors and Controls for Intelligent Machining and Agile Manufacturing
Boston, Massachusetts ● November 1998
SPIE Vol. 3518 ● 0277-786X/98/$10.00

As a result of this perspective, it is worth while mentioning that some scientific approach for categorization, definition, and process to our MIMIC attitudes has made possible today's scientific world.

So here introduces a general definition and concept of mimical attitudes (MIMIC ENGINEERING), and this idea will be expanded to a human behaviour of HOLON, and HOLON will be extended into a Concept of HOLONIC CONTROL.

2. GENERAL CONCEPT OF SYSTEM

2.1 System in General

Everything which has a some sort of "Organism" or "Pattern of Behaviour" or "Regulated Phenomenon" or " Relations" inside or in itself can be defined as "SYSTEM",referring to 1). In this case Behaviours or phenomenon of the creatures and the nature will be closely defined by an equilibrium theory or the laws of dynamics or the laws of thermodynamics (referring to 2)), but here only intererests in behaviours (phenomenon) of things.

According to "The Structure and Function of Organization" by J.Feibleman and J.W.Friend (referring to 3)), the study of organization must be approached from two standpoints - that of statics and that of dynamics. Static treats of organizations as independent of their environment and therefore as isolated from problems of interaction with other organizations. Dynamics treats of organizations as dependent to some extent upon their environment and therefore as interactive with other organizations. As mentioned above, in this case the interest is only focused into the behaviour of an organization itself, so Static will be only concerned. In one sense the system that we treat is Open system which attains a time-independent state where the system remains constant as a whole and in its phases, though there is a continuous flow of the component materials, referring to 4).

2.2 The General Concept of Statics Organization

2.2.1 The Basis of Organization

J. Feibleman and J.W. Friend have stated the Statics as;

In treating of structure we first regard the organization itself as a whole. The whole obviously analyses into parts. These parts themselves have parts, which we shall term subparts.

Thus there are two levels of analysis;

  1)Wholes(from which is analysis is made),

  2)Parts and Subparts.

So from this, we can have a following conjecture.

Conjecture I

Any Statics Organization can be recognized as a Whole and the Whole can be treated as a System of static. The System has parts, and parts are consist of subparts. The subparts have their each individual sub-subparts. This phenomenon goes on.

When we think about this world, we can easily face the following phenomenon

At one time, the whole is the main function in a System, but at another time subpart will function as a main of the system. This occurs at any part or subpart of the system.

So we can have the next conjecture.

Conjecture II

In a system, at one moment, "HOLOS" can be a main function which explains the whole behaviour of the system, and at an other moment "ON" can be a main function which explains the whole behaviour of the system. This HOLOS and ON comes one after another randomly in a situation by situation. So generally speaking the phenomenon of "HOLOS-ON → HOLON" is a function which can be found in every system.

Here describes the elements of relations (referring to 4));

There is another factor in the analysis of organization which we may temporarily describe as the ways in which parts exist in combination with other parts to form the structure of the whole.

Here shows the kinds of relations between parts, the ways in which parts combine. The elements of relations which exist between parts of an organization form a certain group of relations, listed as follows:

1)Transitivity

If one relates two parts to a middle part, it relates the extreme parts to each other.

2)Connexity

This is the relation of two parts without the mediation of a third part.

3)Symmetry

This is the relation in which the interchange of the parts does not involve any change in the relation.

4)Seriality

This is the relation which is transitive, asymmetrical, and connected.

5)Correlation

(one-many, one-one, many-one, many-many) is the relation between two series such that for every part of one series there is a corresponding part in the other series and no part of either series is without a corresponding part in the other.

6)Addition

This is the relation of the joining of parts so as to increase their number.

7)Multiplication

This is the relation of the joining of parts so as to involve them with each other.

8)Association

This is the relation which is commutative and connected.

9)Distribution

This is the relation which is commutative and intransitive.

10)Dependence

This is the relation in which the existence of one part is conditioned by some other part.

2.2.2 Rules of Organization

We now have the basis of organization, i.e. wholes, parts and subparts, and we also have the elements of relations between parts. But these are not sufficient to define or determine any given organization. In addition to them we need certain rules in terms of which parts and their relations are constitutive of organizations.

1)Structure is the sharing of subparts between parts.

The linkage of parts is accomplished by means of common subparts and not by mere juxtaposition or external linkage. The joining of two parts is effected by a subpart which they have in common, and this is the basis upon which all structures are constituted.

2)Organization is the one controlling order of structure.

It is not simply the fact of linkages but rather the principle according to which all linkages fall together into one controlling order, which makes an organization.

3)One more level is needed to constitute an organization than is contained in its parts and subparts.

No number of subparts and parts constitutes an organization, which essentially a property of the whole. The organization is one level above its analytic parts and subparts, and thus the whole involves another level.

4)In every organization there must be a serial relation.

The serial relation is the essential one in every organization. Other relations may and usually do exist in organizations but they are not necessary to the constitution of an organization. In the analysis of every whole there must be found a controlling relation which is asymmetrical, transitive, and connexive.

5) All parts are shared parts.

There is nothing in an organization except parts which have subparts in common. Ant item which is not so shared is extraneous to the organization and not a part.

6) Things in an organization which are related to parts of the organization are themselves parts of the organization.

Anything in an organization which is related to part of that organization is, by virtue of that relation, itself part of the organization, and not a foreign body.

7) Things in an organization which are related to related parts of the organization are themselves parts of the organization.

Sometimes there are things in an organization which are not related to any single part of the organization, but which may be related to any single part of the organization, but which may be related to two or more parts.

8) The number of parts and of their relations constitutes complexity.

The number of parts and of their relations, i.e. subparts, constitutes the complexity of an organization. This rule and the yardstick of integrality, or kinds of organization [Statics] form a pair of criteria. Complexity is seen to reduce to a mere matter of counting parts and subparts.

2.2.3 Kinds of Organization

The kinds of organization constitute degrees of integrality as follows;

1) Agglutinative

The governing relations are aseriality, where parts have intransitivity, connexity and symmetry.

2) Participative

The governing relations are seriality. Participative organizations subdivide into three kinds;

a) Adjunctive

The governing relations is symmetrical independence. The sharing subparts is not necessary to either of the parts. Parts can survive their separation.

b) Subjective

The governing relations is asymmetrical dependence. The sharing of parts is necessary to one of the parts but not to both.

c) Complemental

The governing relations is symmetrical dependence. The sharing of parts is necessary to both of the parts. Neither part can survive separation.

3. THE CONCEPT OF SYSTEM

Generally speaking, we can define the System of any Organization with the conjecture I above as mentioned below.

An organization has the whole and its parts. And parts have their subparts. And this phenomenon goes on and on into inside subparts. So, we can define a system as shown below.

Definition I

$U=\{U|U\}$ U :Universe

$P=\{P,p|p \in \Sigma\ P,\ \Sigma\ P \subseteq U\}$ P :Parts

$SP_0=\{SP_0,sp_0|x\ sp_0 \in \Sigma\ SP_0, \Sigma\ SP_0 \subseteq P\}$ p :Elements

$SP_1=\{SP_1,sp_1|x\ sp_1 \in \Sigma\ SP_1, \Sigma\ SP_1 \subseteq SP\}$ SP:Subparts

$\cdots$ sp:Elements in Subparts

$SP_n=\{SP_n,sp_n|sp_n \in \Sigma\ SP_n, \Sigma\ SP_n \subseteq SP_{n-1}\}$

And these parts and subparts etc will have a relationship among them as described in the 2.2.1 Basis of Organization above;

These are "transitivity, connexity, symmetry, seriality, correlation, addition, multiplication, commutation, association, distribution, dependence". These relationships are categorized into Relation, Function, and Connection between Parts and Subparts.

RELATION   : transitivity, connexity, symmetry, seriality

FUNCTION   : addition, multiplication, commutation, association, dependence

CONNECTION : correlation

From above it can be said that an organization has, generally speaking, factors of RELATION, FUNCTION, and CONNECTION. And these factors are related with that;

1)RELATION [R] specifies how to transfer,

2)FUNCTION [F] specifies a quantity to be transferred,

3)CONNECTION [C] specifies a route to transfer.

So from the facts of a System (Definition I) and an organization mentioned above, we can define a System of Organization (SO) as shown below.

Definition II

$SO(X) = \{X \mid [R],[F],[C],U,P,SP_1,...,SP_n\}$

$SO(U,P,SP,...) = \{[R],[F],[C]\}$

        $[R] = f(t,c,sy,se)$ t:transitivity, c:connexity, sy:symmetry, se:seriality

        $[F] = f(add,m,c,ass,d)$ add:addition, m:multiplication, c:commutation,

                                        ass:association, d:dependence

        $[C] = f(r)$ r:route

From above the elements of RELATION will be specified by FUNCTION [F] and this information goes to with the route defined by CONNECTION [C]. So this can be rewritten as

$U = f([R([F])])_{[C]}$

$P = f([R([F])])_{[C]}$

$SP_1 = f([R([F])])_{[C]}$

...

$SP_n = f([R([F])])_{[C]}$

So we can define a System of Organization as follows;

$SO(X,Y,Z,...) = f(U(X),P(Y),SP_1(Z_1),...,SP_n(Z_n))$ ---------(1)

4. THE CONCEPT OF HOLONIC CONTROL

In the field of control we have been trying to expand a robustness because a system to be controlled has become huge and too complexed. So this causes the problems of out of controllability, of sudden stop of a whole system, of lost way for control, of reducing a reliability to a system, and so forth. For reducing this problem, a lot of things have been introduced like enhance an intelligence on a system etc. But it is rather difficult to give us satisfaction on this. Because the method of today' control still has an idea that the mechanism of control has to have an ability to control a whole system all the time. When we think about human or living creatures, we use only necessary functions as they are required.The others are left vague or redundant until they are in needs. We can apply this idea to the control of present situation for reducing a complexity and increasing a reliability to a system to control. This is, so called, HOLON.

In the previous section System of Organization has been defined mathematically, so it is now possible to MIMIC a function of any System of Organization of living creatures. So here mimics the idea of HOLON, and here introduces HOLONIC idea.

4.1 Holonic Idea for Control

HOLON is firstly used in the book called "The Ghost in the Machine",London, 1967 by Auther Kestler. And he introduced the idea of "Self-regulating Open Hierarchic Order (SOHO)". This can be expressed as "YANUS", too. (Referring to 5).)

This has characteristics as;

① Living creatures are not simply consist of sets of parts and are not consist of uni-motivated chains.

② The whole of each creatures is branched into sub-wholes one after another autonomously and itself has a hierarchy of multi-levels.

③ Self-regulating Open Hierarchic Order;YANUS

④ Autonomy and integrality

⑤ Hierarchy and networkings

⑥ Regulation and targeted

⑦ The hierarchy has its own ordering regulations

And Shimizu Hiroshi has an another idea for ② of a hierarchy of multi-levels. That is to say, a whole is the whole of a system at usual and at the same time a sub-whole can be the whole of a system at another time; HOLOS-ON and ON-HOLOS $\rightarrow$ HOLON.

So it can be concluded that HOLON has characters as follows;

① HOLON, ② Fluctuation, ③ Self-organizing, ④ Entrainment, ⑤ YANUS, ⑥ Rhythm, ⑦ Distributive

These characters are expressed logically as;

① HOLON is defined mathematically as

$$\{ \Sigma\ P \subseteq U \}$$

② Fluctuation is defined by a probability or a distribution.

③ Self-organizing is U or P or SP or SP_0 or ... or SP_n.

④ Entrainment is a behaviour of mimicking a behaviour of neighbours.

⑤ YANUS is a behaviour of $\{ \Sigma\ P \subseteq U \} \cup \{ U \subseteq P \}$.

⑥ Rhythm is defined by an input rate or a dispatching rate or a production rate.

⑦ Distributive is defined by;

$$SO(X)=\{X \mid [R],[F],[C],U,P,SP_1,...,SP_n\}$$
$$SO(U,P,SP,...)=\{[R],[F],[C]\}$$

These phenomenon can be used for reducing the complexity of a system and increasing its reliability.

In the following section the Concept of Holonic Control will be discussed and defined.

4.2 Concept of Holonic SYSTEM & Control

Here the properties picked up above will be defined one by one.

Definition III

① HOLON is defined mathematically as

$$\{ \Sigma\ P \subseteq U \} \qquad \text{---------(2)}$$

This is stated in the Definition I .

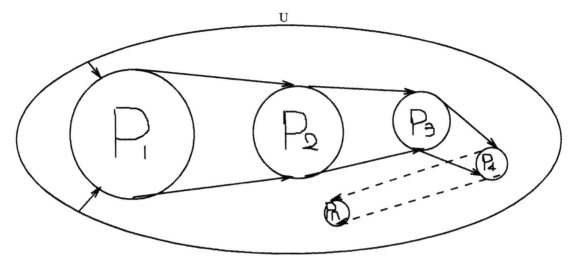

Definition IV

② Fluctuation is defined by a probability or a distribution.

Heart of human does not keep exactly the same pace for beating itself but it has some fluctuation. We have the same kind of properties in very organisms of our body.And what it more, Fluctuation is contained in every creat uresin this world.

So [F] is defined by;

[F]={regulated [r] and fluctuated behaviours [f],probabilistic [p] and distributive actions [d]}

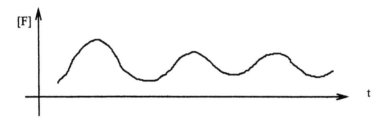

Definition V

③ Self-organizing is U or P or SP or SP_0 or ... or SPn.

Every part has its own self-organizing properties. And we can find this properties in every organisms in creatures.

And this can be simply defined by SO(X)={X | [R],[F],[C],U,P,SP_1,...,SPn} ----------(3)

Definition VI

④ Entrainment is a behaviour of mimicking a behaviour of neighbours.

We have been behaving this behaviour autonomously without self-recognition, and again this behaviour can be found in every animals.

This can be defined as;

f([F])m={[f(([F]n) $\cup$ f([F]n-1) $\cup$ f([F]n-2) $\cup$ ... $\cup$ f([F]1}   ----------(4)

Definition VII

⑤ YANUS is a behaviour of {Σ P $\subseteq$ U} $\cup$ {U $\subseteq$ P} as it is. This is mathematically equals to U=P, but in this case it has another meaning, that is to say, every function in a system has a moment to be the whole [U] of it and at that instance the whole becomes as a part [P].

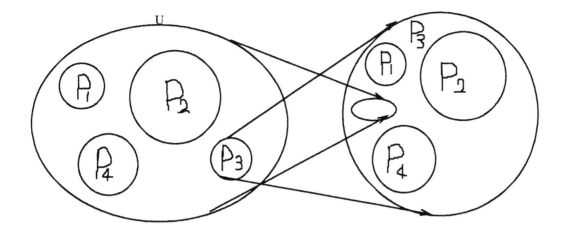

Definition VIII

⑥ Rhythm is defined by an input rate (IR) or a dispatching rate (DR) or a production rate (PR).
[R]={input rate, dispatching rate, production rate}

Definition IX

⑦ Distributive is defined by;

$$SO(X)=\{X \mid X \in [R], X \in [F], X \in [C], X \in U, X \in P, X \in SP_1,...,X \in SPn\} \quad ----------(5)$$

and

$$SO(U(X),P(X),SP(X),...)=\{X \in [R], X \in [F], X \in [C]\} \quad ----------(6)$$

Definition X

HOLONIC SYSTEM is a system which has properties defined by Definitions I ~ IX.

Definition X I

HOLONIC CONTROL is a method which treats the HOLONIC SYSTEM.

Here restates the System of Organization by using the definitions above.

By using the definitions I, II, VIII, and IX described above, we have a general expression of a System of Organization as shown below.

$$SO(X,Y,Z)=f[U(X),P(Y),SP_1(Z_1),...,SPn(Zn)] \quad ----------(7)$$

$$U =f([R([F])])_{[C]}$$
$$P =f([R([F])])_{[C]}$$
$$SP_1=f([R([F])])_{[C]}$$
$$\cdots$$
$$SPn=f([R([F])])_{[C]}$$

And by using and combining the definitions III, V, and VII, we can restate the system which has both properties as the HOLONIC. And expressed as;

$$SO(X,Y,Z)_H=f[U(X),P(Y),SP_1(Z_1),...,SPn(Zn)]_H \quad ----------(8)$$

And this can be rewritten as

$$SO(X \cup Y \cup Z)_H=\{U_H=f([R([F])])_{[C]H} \cup P_H=f([R([F])])_{[C]H} \cup SP_{1H}=f([R([F])])_{[C]H} \cup \cdots \cup SPn=f([R([F])])_{[C]}\} \quad (9)$$

And by using the definition IV, input quantities or properties are certain amount of tolerations. And they can be defined by [r], [f],[p], and [d]. These attributes are restated as [F] as used in the above equation.

And by using the definition VI, we can restate the system as;

$$SO(X,Y,Z)m=f[U(X)m,P(Y)m,SP_1(Z_1)m,...,SPn(Zn)m]$$ ----------(10)

$$Um =f([R([F]m)])_{[C]}$$

$$Pm =f([R([F]m)])_{[C]}$$

$$SPm_1=f([R([F]m)])_{[C]}$$

$$\cdots$$

$$SPmn=f([R([F]m)])_{[C]}$$

So here by using above results, we can have the theory of the HOLONIC SYSTEM.

Theory I

HOLONIC SYSTEM is a system which has attributions of System Organizations and can be defined by the equations shown below.

$$SO(\alpha)=\{SO(X,Y,Z)m \cup SO(X \cup Y \cup Z)_H\}$$ ----------(11)

[Proof]

This is obvious from the definitions I ~ IX.

We can state the normal System of Organization as;

$$SO(X,Y,Z)=f[U(X),P(Y),SP_1(Z_1),...,SPn(Zn)]$$

$$U =f([R([F])])_{[C]}$$

$$P =f([R([F])])_{[C]}$$

$$SP_1=f([R([F])])_{[C]}$$

$$\cdots$$

$$SPn=f([R([F])])_{[C]}$$

And we can restate above by adding the HOLONIC System as;

$$SO(X,Y,Z)m=f[U(X)m,P(Y)m,SP_1(Z_1)m,...,SPn(Zn)m]$$ ----------(12)

$$Um =f([R([F]m)])_{[C]}$$

$$Pm =f([R([F]m)])_{[C]}$$

$$SPm_1=f([R([F]m)])_{[C]}$$

$$\cdots$$

$$SPmn=f([R([F]m)])_{[C]}$$

And we can state the HOLONIC System as;

$$SO(X \cup Y \cup Z)_H=\{U_H=f([R([F])])_{[C]H} \cup P_H=f([R([F])])_{[C]H} \cup SP_{1H}=f([R([F])])_{[C]H} \cup \cdots \cup SPn=f([R([F])])_{[C]}\}$$
----------(13)

From these two equations we can easily get the following result simply by adding two attributes;

$$SO(\alpha)=\{SO(X,Y,Z)m \cup SO(X \cup Y \cup Z)_H\}$$ ----------(14)

[Proof End]

Theory II

The HOLONIC SYSTEM can be cotrolled well by using the HOLONIC CONTROL.

[Proof]

$SO(\alpha)$ is defined by the equation (14). Let put the attribute of Towards-In (TI) and Towards-Out (TO) for $SO(\alpha)$ as the behaviour of control area or control size by looking at the outputs rates of a system that we are thinking about. That is to say, if the output rate of U has a tendency of decreasing, start taking the action of TI. And this TI will find the ill part of the system by examining [R] of P. And this goes deeper into the system by examining $SP1 \Rightarrow SPn$ by the evaluation factor (E).

This examination will be done as follows.

Every system of behaviour [R] of P can be expressed by the first order differential equation 1form;

$$\overset{\circ}{X}(t)=AX(t)+bu(t) \qquad\qquad ----------(15)$$

This can easily handled by the present method of control. And every [R] of P can be enhanced and be expressed as;

$$\dot{X}(t)_1=AX(t)_1+bu(t)_1$$

$$\dot{X}(t)_2=AX(t)_2+bu(t)_2$$

. . .

$$\dot{X}(t)n=AX(t)n+bu(t)n$$

And if V is a linear vector space and X is some subset of the set of objects comprising V, then X is said to be a subspace of V if

$$X(t)_1, X(t)_2 \in X \text{ implies that } X(t)_1+X(t)_2 \in X. \qquad ---------(16)$$

So these all equations can be expressed by using the above equation (16),

$$\Sigma\, X(t)n = \Sigma\, AX(t)n + \Sigma\, bu(t)n$$

And this can be rewritten as

$$\overset{\circ}{X}(t)n=A\overset{\scriptstyle ' \, '}{X}(t)n+b\overset{\scriptstyle ' \, '}{u}(t)n \qquad\qquad ---------(17)$$

This can be easily treated by the present control method. And this shows that if something happens in the system U, this value will begin to change. So if we only watch the change, we can see the change of U.

And if we put certain value for these equations, we have series of values sequence ; the vector Ω. So if we watch the values' change of vector Ω, we can see which part of P will be changed or changing. This can be done simply by differenciating $\dfrac{d(\Omega(t))}{dt}$.

By this we can estimate estimated part P which will have some irregularity.

And if this changing really happens, we can fluctuate the value of P by taking a value from a besinity of Ps.

[Proof End]

5. CONCLUSION

Here the concept of HOLONIC CONTROL has been introduced theoretically. And it has been shown that it is possible to control very complexed one, very huge one, and very time consuming one by taking large and overall view when it is necessary to see an overview, and by taking small and detailed view when some troubles come out at Pn. And it has been found that this is the most important and eminent idea for the control of today.

The results got here are simple and general, so it is quite necessary to have much more endevoured theories, and full of results for real use. For doing these, it is quite necessary to have cleared the whole system.

As a future work, it is necessary to expand these concepts and definitions shown here much more in order to be able to use the real world.

REFERENCES

1)A.Angyal, Foundation for a Science of Personality, Havard University Press, 1941.

2)W.Koehler, The Place of Valures in the World of Fact, Liveright, 1938.

3)J.Feibleman and J.W.Friend,The structure and function of organization,Philosophical Review,Vol.54, 1945.

4)L.von Bertalanffy, The theory of open systems in physics and biology, Science vol.111, 1950.

5)Taro Nawa, Holonic Management Revolution, Sohko-sha publishing co., 1988.

6)R. Saucedo,E.E.Schiring, Introduction to continuous and digital control systems, Machmillan Publishing Co.,1968.

7)A.G.J.MacFarlane,Dynamical system models, George G.Harrap & co.,1970

SESSION 5

Process Modeling and Control

A Feature-based Machining System using STEP

Frederick M. Proctor and Thomas R. Kramer

National Institute of Standards and Technology
Building 220, Room B124
Gaithersburg, MD 20899-0001

ABSTRACT

Discrete part manufacturing flows from a design phase in which product information is defined to a manufacturing phase in which the processes are planned and executed. Process planning typically culminates with the generation of numerical control (NC) programs for specific equipment, such as machining centers or turning centers. These NC programs are written in the dialects of the various equipment vendors, for the specific mechanical configuration of the target machine. As a result, porting programs between machines is difficult. Worse, NC programs contain little if any of the product design information. The lack of this information at run time limits any adaptive control that could direct the process so that final parts more closely conform to the original design.

The authors have developed a prototype machining system in which product and process data replaces NC programs at run time. In this system, information models built in the EXPRESS information modeling language are used for all types of data, and data files are all in STEP Part 21 format; each Part 21 file is understandable by making reference to one of the EXPRESS models. The EXPRESS schemas of tool models proposed to ISO is used. An EXPRESS schema for ALPS (A Language for Process Specification, developed by NIST) is used for process planning. Ad hoc EXPRESS schemas are used for machining options, setup descriptions, shop and workstation operations, and tool usage rules. The system has been demonstrated on a three-axis machining center.

Keywords: STEP, manufacturing features, process planning, numerical control

1. THE USE OF FEATURES IN MANUFACTURING

A machining feature is a closed volume in space which is related to a machining operation as follows: when the operation is finished, there must be no material remaining inside the feature, and the operation may remove no material outside the feature. In use, the machining features are defined so that a boolean subtraction of the features from the original workpiece (stock or a partially finished part) will result in the desired final shape for the workpiece (finished or partially finished part). Examples of machining features include faces, pockets, slots, bosses, and holes, some of which are shown in Figure 1.

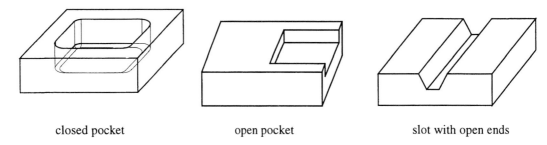

closed pocket   open pocket   slot with open ends

Figure 1.   Examples of machining features.

The machining features used to make a specific part may be instances of a fixed library of parametrically defined features, or they may be defined without a library by making boundary or constructive solid geometry representations. There are, of course, many alternative definitions of machining features[1]. To machine a part, both the machining features and the machining operations must be defined, and the operations must be sequenced. In our Feature-Based Inspection and Control

Part of the SPIE Conference on Sensors and Controls for Intelligent Machining and Agile Manufacturing
Boston, Massachusetts • November 1998
SPIE Vol. 3518 • 0277-786X/98/$10.00

System (FBICS), we have used operations that are instances of parametrically defined operations from a fixed library of operations.

2. THE STEP APPROACH

STEP is the common name for standard 10303 of the International Organization for Standardization (ISO). This standard is composed of individual documents known as STEP "Parts". STEP Part 11 defines the EXPRESS data modeling language. An EXPRESS model definition is contained in one or more constructs called EXPRESS "schemas". STEP Part 21 defines an exchange file format for transmitting instances of data which has been modeled in EXPRESS schemas. STEP also provides data models for various domains. The models fall in several classes. The class of model intended to be used is called an "Application Protocol" (AP).

2.1.   AP 203
STEP Application Protocol 203 (AP 203), entitled "Configuration Controlled Design", provides a representation for the shape of a product and related data regarding versions, approvals, authors, etc. AP 203 contains several methods of specifying shape. The AP 203 method most commonly used (and the only one used in the FBICS) is boundary representation, or b-rep.
In a b-rep, shape is expressed using both geometry and topology. The b-rep describes a shape by defining its bounding faces. Each face is a portion of a geometric surface, defined by its bounding edges. Each edge is a portion of a geometric curve, defined by bounding vertices. AP 203 geometry and topology are taken largely from STEP Part 42, the STEP basic resource for shape representation.

The FBICS is able to read AP 203 STEP Part 21 files, but since the FBICS does not include software for converting AP 203 to Parasolid (the solid modeler used in the FBICS), no further use is made of AP 203 models. Such software is commercially available.

2.2.   AP 213 and A Language for Process Specification (ALPS)
STEP Application Protocol 213 (AP 213) is entitled "Numerical Control (NC) Process Plans for Machined Parts." AP 213 provides a method of describing sequential process plans. At the finest level of detail the description of operations is made in terms of text strings, so that the meaning of a plan is not computer-sensible. AP 213 provides for resource description but not resource allocation. AP 213 provides for describing alternatives but not for methods of deciding among them. Because of the missing capabilities just mentioned and other shortcomings, AP 213 is not used in the FBICS.

ALPS[2] (A Language for Process Specification) is a generic language for representing plans for discrete processes. It is based on a directed graph representation. ALPS includes modeling constructs to represent concepts needed in plans for discrete processes, including: sequence, parallelism, alternatives, synchronization, resource allocation, and time. Variables and expressions are included so that tests may be made for deciding among alternatives and to add flexibility in plan specification.

In ALPS, a plan consists of a set of nodes arranged in a directed graph. The directedness is expressed by the use of the successor relation among nodes. Alternatives and parallelism are expressed by split nodes which branch out to several successors. Each split node is matched by a join node which gathers the alternatives or parallel activities back together before the plan proceeds. ALPS, developed at NIST, was originally modeled in NIAM and did not include a specification for the syntax of plans. It was later modeled in the EXPRESS language. As a consequence of being modeled in EXPRESS, a syntax specification for ALPS process plans in STEP Part 21 files is available automatically. The FBICS uses plans written in STEP Part 21 files.

For the FBICS, two significant enhancements to generic ALPS were made: expressions were modeled in EXPRESS and a new type of split node was added, providing for the use of preconditions. Earlier versions of ALPS included support for three stages of a process plan. These stages are not used in the FBICS. The additional items defined to support the stages have been removed from the version of ALPS used in the FBICS. In the FBICS, ALPS is used for process plans at both the Shop level and the Workstation level. At each of those levels, subtypes of the ALPS primitive_task appropriate to the level are defined in extensions to the generic ALPS EXPRESS schema.

2.3.   AP 224

A proposed standard set of machining features is defined in STEP AP 224, "Mechanical Product Definition for Process Planning Using Machining Features"[3]. This is largely a parametric library of machining features, but also provides for defining machining features in terms of a boundary representation and provides for related data, such as design_exceptions and requisitions. AP 224 provides definitions of base shapes and 51 parametric "manufacturing_features" including, for example: boss, chamfer, circular_pattern, compound_feature, counterbore_hole, countersunk_hole, edge_round, fillet, general_pattern, general_pocket, groove, hole, pocket, rectangular_pattern, rectangular_pocket, slot, spherical cap, thread. The AP 224 feature library provides rich methods of describing details of features. Thirteen types of (planar) feature_profile are provided, for example. Feature_profiles may be swept in various ways to produce manufacturing_features. Twenty-nine types of feature_definition_item are provided. This includes feature details such as hole_bottom_condition, path, and taper. Having features defined in terms of a boundary representation is less useful because it is very difficult, if not completely infeasible, to identify machining operations for making entities found in boundary representations without grouping the entities (i.e., recognizing features). It is correspondingly difficult to generate tool paths.

The FBICS uses AP 224 for representing the shapes of designs and workpieces, as well as for machining features. The FBICS software drives the Parasolid modeler from AP 224 models. AP 203 is now widely used for exchanging shape descriptions. In the long run, it would be desirable in the FBICS to have an AP 203 to Parasolid converter, and to add the capability to generate a machinable AP 224 shape description from an AP 203 file describing the same shape. At least one automatic AP 203 to AP 224 converter is said to be commercially available.

3. THE FEATURE-BASED INSPECTION AND CONTROL SYSTEM

3.1.   Earlier Work

In the Vertical Workstation of the NIST Automated Manufacturing Research Facility[4], a primitive CAD system was used with a design protocol[5]. This system constrained the user to design in terms of machining features (although the features did not conform fully to the definition just given, because several operations might be required to make one feature). The operations for cutting the features were automatically defined and partially sequenced by a generative process planner[6]. The individual components of this system were unsophisticated but they were very well integrated. Within a limited range of design, a part could be designed and cut within an hour using this system. An NC-code generator, controllers, and a feature recognition module which could extract features of the required sort from a boundary representation were included[7]. The Vertical Workstation System stopped just short of feature-based control, using short turnaround off-line NC code generation instead.

From experience with the Vertical Workstation, it became apparent that using machining features for design, while a good technique for a few special situations, is not a general solution for piece part manufacture. It is common to be able to machine a part more effectively (faster, cheaper, tighter tolerances, etc.) if machining features may be used which are not explicit in the design. Many other researchers have come to the same conclusion.

We then started work on the Off-Line Programming System (OLPS), an NC-code generation system which is intended to be used in a larger system in which machining features are defined separately from the design[8]. A library of parametric machining features was defined for use with OLPS[9].

3.2.   The Current System

The current Feature-Based Inspection and Control System is a hierarchy of planners and executors which transform a high-level, feature-based description of a piece part into a sequence of plans that are executed to achieve material removal. The primary purposes of the FBICS are:

1.   to demonstrate feature-based control in an open-architecture control system.
2.   to serve as a testbed for solving problems in feature-based manufacturing, particularly the partitioning of manufacturing activities into separate activities and the definition of interfaces between activities.
3.   to test the usability of STEP methods and models.

The FBICS is based on the NIST Real-Time Control Systems (RCS) reference model architecture[10, 11, 12]. RCS specifies a task-oriented problem analysis that results in a hierarchy of control modules, each which decomposes higher-level tasks into lower-level actions. Control modules at the bottom of the hierarchy interface directly to sensors and actuators. The FBICS architecture, shown in Figure 2, follows the RCS reference model.

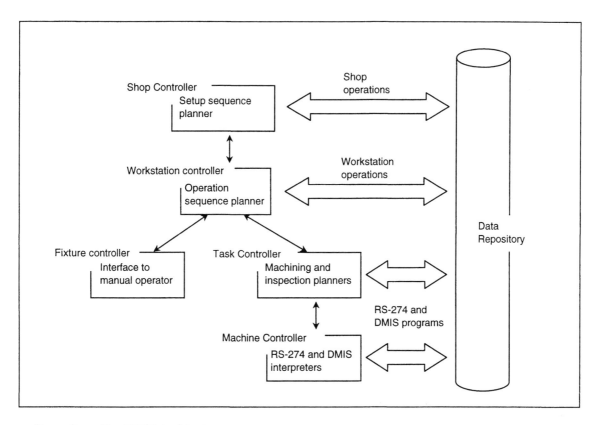

Figure 2.   The FBICS Architecture.

The lowest FBICS control module, the Machine Controller, corresponds to a conventional numerical control machine with direct numerical control (DNC) and networked file system capabilities. DNC allows the Task Controller to send requests to the Machine Controller to run RS-274 numerical control (NC) programs for machining[13], or DMIS[14] programs for inspection. The Data Repository is simply a set of files available via a networked file system.

3.3.   Data Types
Twelve different data sets drive the FBICS. The first five sets of data are independent of the part to be machined. The other seven types of data depend upon the work being done in a specific setup of a part. These files are listed in Table 1, and their description is detailed in the subsequent text.

Data Type	Description
Shop Option	preferences for inspection strategies
Task Options	preferences for inspection (number of points, etc.) and machining
Tool Catalog	a catalog of types of tools that are usually available
Tool Inventory	an inventory of specific tools that are currently actually available
Tool Use Rules	rules for setting speed, feed, stepover, pass depth, and coolant use
Machining Features	a description of the machining features to be cut away
Shop Process Plan	a plan for one of several setups
Workstation Process Plan	a plan which includes at least one operation to make each machining feature in a setup
Fixture	a description of the fixture which holds the workpiece being machined
Workpiece	a description of the shape of the workpiece as it is before machining is begun
Design	a description of the intended shape of the workpiece after machining
Setup	a list of files associated with a setup; locations of fixtures, workpiece, design, and features

Table 1.   Data types used in the FBICS.

In addition to the data types liste in Table 1, all of which are modeled in EXPRESS, data files are also used for executable operations (EXPRESS), NC code (RS-274), inspection code (DMIS), and graphics (non-standard).

Shop Options include four inspection options: what to do if a feature is out of tolerance, what to inspect, when to inspect, and how intensively to inspect.

Task Options include machining options and inspection options. Machining options describe user preferences for retract height, tool change position, and other information specific to a particular machine or process. Inspection options include the number of points to use for each feature at each level of inspection intensity (low, medium, or high).

The *Tool Catalog* describes the kinds of tools found in the facility, some or all of which may be found on the particular machine. This includes the tool type (e.g., end mill, twist drill), nominal dimensions (e.g., length and diameter), material from which the tool is made, materials which the tool can cut, number of flutes, maximum rotational speed, and maximum number of reworks.

The *Tool Inventory* lists the tools available for use on the particular machine. In addition to the information in the Tool Catalog, each instance of a tool in the Tool Inventory includes the unique tool identifying number, the location in the machine carousel, the actual dimensions, the time in service, and the number of reworks.

Tool Use Rules are expressions written in terms of tool and material variables (diameter, number of flutes, etc.) that are evaluated during operation planning to determine feed rate, spindle speed, horizontal stepover, vertical pass depth, and coolant use.

Machining Features are the basic features to be machined, as described earlier.

The *Shop Process Plan* is a sequence of run-setup operations, as described earlier.

The *Workstation Process Plan* is a sequence of machining and inspection operations to be performed at the Workstation level in the control hierarchy, as described earlier.

Fixture information includes the geometric description of the fixturing devices.

The *Workpiece* description includes the shape of the part before processing. This is the "as is" description.

The *Design* description includes the shape of the part after processing. This is the "to be" description.

Setup information describes the files needed by the Workstation and Task Controllers in each setup, and the transformations relating coordinates of features, fixture, workpiece, and design to world coordinates.

Each type of data is contained in a file globally accessible in the Data Repository shown in Figure 2. Currently, this is simply a networked file system. Files in the Data Repository are STEP Part 21 exchange files. For each file type, there is an EXPRESS schema providing a model of data of that type. Four types of data are prepared using STEP standards. The remaining five types do not have STEP standard representations. For consistency, they are defined in the FBICS in EXPRESS, following the STEP philosophy. The file types are listed in Table 2.

Data Type	EXPRESS Schema
Shop Options	a special-purpose schema written for the FBICS system
Task Options	a special-purpose schema written for the FBICS system
Tool Catalog	a subset of the ISO 13399 model with probes added
Tool Inventory	Tool Catalog with a tool_instance entity added
Tool Use Rules	expressions plus a special-purpose schema written for the FBICS
Machining Features	STEP AP 224
Shop Process Plan	ALPS plus run_setup
Workstation Process Plan	ALPS plus three-axis machining and inspection operations
Fixture	STEP AP 203

Workpiece	STEP AP 224
Design	STEP AP 224
Setup	a special-purpose schema written for the FBICS system

Table 2.   Data representation for FBICS files.

The EXPRESS schema used in the FBCS for STEP AP 203 is the AP 203 schema provided by STEPTools Inc. with functions and "where" clauses removed. STEPTools, Inc. is a commercial venture which provides tools for dealing with STEP methods, models, and data. The EXPRESS schema used in the FBCS for STEP AP 224 is a schema provided by Len Slovensky, owner of AP 224. In STEP terms it is an Application Resource Model (ARM) type of model. The Tool Catalog and Tool Inventory are a subset of the model built in EXPRESS by the NIST Manufacturing Systems Integration Division and contractors of that division[15], with probes and a tool_instance entity added.

4. SCENARIO

To understand the interaction of control modules in the FBICS and the use of STEP data throughout the feature-based machining and inspection process, it is helpful to follow an example scenario. Figure 3 shows a sample part (a clevis) that is to be machined and inspected during this scenario. Manufacturing begins with the definition of all the data required to specify the part and the resources required to make it, as listed in Table 1, in the file formats listed in Table 2. This would typically be done using computer-aided design/manufacturing (CAD/CAM) software. However, since commercial programs that generate files in the various FBICS formats are not available, this data is generated by hand using a text editor.

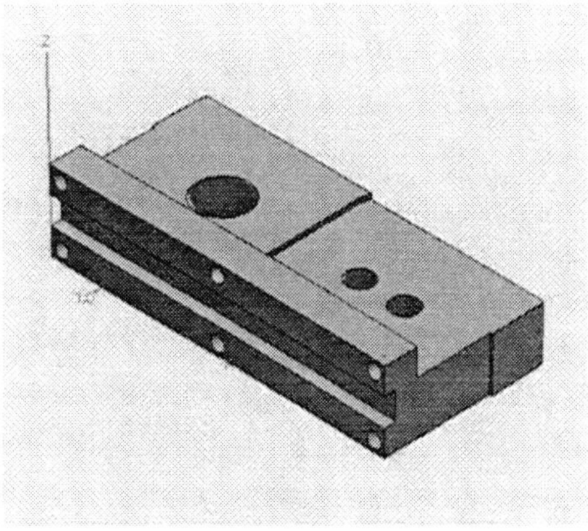

Figure 3. Sample part (a clevis) referenced in the scenario.

At the top level of the FBICS, shown as the Shop Controller in Figure 2, the user submits a request to plan the part. The request includes the files containing the STEP data definitions for the part and resources available. At the top-level prompt, this looks like:

```
SHOP => plan_part(data/clevis2/out2_224.stp, ON,
data/clevis2/in1_224.stp, pl1, fe1, fi1, se1)
```

The first argument to the plan_part request is the STEP Part 21 file containing the AP 224 features for the part to be made. The second argument means that the file that is the third argument already exists. If the second argument of "OFF" the file will be generated automatically. The third argument is the AP 224 description of the raw stock, in this case a 6.5-inch by 3.0-inch by 1.5-inch block of aluminum. The remaining arguments are the prefixes to use for files generated for process plans, feature assignments, fixturing, and setup.

The Shop Controller plans a series of setups and a series of tasks for each setup. Multiple setups may be required to access all the features given the kinematic configuration of the machine and the tooling available. The output of the planning phase of the Shop Controller is data, including a process plan for the Shop Controller and one or more process plans for the Workstation Controller, for the setups required to machine and inspect the entire part. In the FBICS, the process plan is described using the EXPRESS schema for ALPS, and written in STEP Part 21 physical file (ASCII) format. An example of the Shop-level process plan for the clevis part is shown in Listing 1.

The Shop Controller executes this process plan, and sends commands to the Workstation Controller to execute the plan for each setup. Data used by the Workstation Controller includes descriptions of each setup, as shown in Listing 2, and process plans containing references to the individual features able to be machined or inspected at each setup, as shown in Listing 3. Currently, FBICS fixturing is done manually, but is indicated architecturally as a "man in the loop" box labeled "Fixturing Controller" in Figure 2.

```
#10 = PLAN('pl1_shop','version 1',(),(),'SHOP','','',(#20,#30,#40,#50,#60,#70,#80));
#20 = START_PLAN_NODE(#10,1,$,$,(#30),());
#30 = PRECONDITION_SPLIT_NODE(#10,2,$,$,(#40),());
```

```
#40  =  RUN_SETUP(#10,3,$,$,(#50),(),1,'sel_1.stp',());
#50  =  RUN_SETUP(#10,4,$,$,(#60),(),1,'sel_2.stp',());
#60  =  RUN_SETUP(#10,5,$,$,(#70),(),1,'sel_3.stp',());
#70  =  PRECONDITION_JOIN_NODE(#10,6,$,$,(#80),());
#80  =  END_PLAN_NODE(#10,7,$,$,(),());
```

Listing 1. Shop process plan for complete clevis part, calling for three independent fixturing setups.

```
#10  =  CARTESIAN_POINT_SETUP(0.,0.,0.);
#20  =  CARTESIAN_POINT_SETUP(6.5,1.5,3.);
#30  =  CARTESIAN_POINT_SETUP(0.,0.,0.);
#40  =  DIRECTION_SETUP(1.,0.,0.);
#50  =  DIRECTION_SETUP(0.,0.,1.);
#60  =  AXIS2_PLACEMENT_SETUP(#30,#50,#40);
#70  =  AXIS2_PLACEMENT_SETUP(#100,#90,#80);
...
#190 =  BOX_SETUP(#10,#20);
#200 =  FILE_NAMES('sel_1.stp','data/clevis2/out2_224_1.stp','fil.stp',
         'pll_1.stp','fel_1.stp','data/clevis2/in1_224.stp',$,$);
#210 =  SETUP_SPEC(#200,#70,#110,#150,#60,#190);
```

Listing 2. Setup description for the first fixturing, which includes coordinate geometry and bounding box. Ellipses indicate information similar to that already provided, omitted for brevity.

```
#10  =  PLAN('pll_1','version 1',(),(),'WORK','a part','generated by FBICS', (#20,#30, …));
#20  =  START_PLAN_NODE(#10,1,$,$,(#30),());
#30  =  PARAMETERIZED_SPLIT_NODE(#10,2,$,$,(#50,#70, …),(),0,.SPLIT_TIMING_SERIAL.);
#40  =  PATH_JOIN_NODE(#10,3,$,$,(#270),());
#50  =  FINISH_MILL(#10,4,'',$,(#60),(),1,(),'END-MILL-0.5-2',
         0,3437,17.189240808531,.T.,.F.,0.25,0.25);
#60  =  INSPECT_FEATURE_GEOMETRY(#10,5,'',$,(#40),(),1,.MEDIUM.,(),
         'PROBE-2.5-0.12', 0,10.);
...
#150 =  TWIST_DRILLING(#10,14,'',$,(#160),(),1,(),
         'DRILL-0.1966-2',5,5200,5.1116,.T.,.F.,0.1966);
...
#410 =  END_PLAN_NODE(#10,40,$,$,(),());
```

Listing 3. Workstation process plan for clevis part, first setup.

The Workstation Controller traverses its process plan (such as shown in Listing 3) and sends descriptions of individual machining or inspection operations to the Task Controller. The Task Controller takes each operation description, associates tool usage rules and other user preferences for process parameters (e.g., retract height) to each feature accessible in this fixturing setup, and generates NC code for machining or DMIS code for inspection. The machining or inspection code is stored to the Data Repository, and requests to the machine tool controller are made to run the programs.

5. SUMMARY

The FBICS is a feature-based control system that interfaces with controllers to legacy machine tools programmed in RS-274 for machining or DMIS for inspection. It provides the ability to program machining and inspection using manufacturing features as defined in ISO standard 10303 (STEP), Application Protocol 224. The purposes of the FBICS are to demonstrate feature-based control in an open-architecture control system; to serve as a testbed for solving problems in feature-based manufacturing; and to test the usability of STEP methods and models. The FBICS philosophy is to use STEP standards where they exist, and to create data formats consistent with the STEP approach where they do not exist. A prototype system has been built that addresses simple 3-axis machining and inspection.

6. REFERENCES

1. Kramer, Thomas R.; *Issues Concerning Material Removal Shape Element Volumes (MRSEVs)*; International Journal of Computer Integrated Manufacturing; Vol. 7, No. 3; 1994; pp. 139-151; (also published as NISTIR 4804; National Institute of Standards and Technology; March 1992)

2. Catron, Bryan; Ray, Steven R.; *ALPS - A Language for Process Specification*; International Journal of Computer Integrated Manufacturing; Vol. 4, No. 2; 1991; pp 105 -113

3. Slovensky, Len; *Industrial Automation Systems and Integration - Product Data Representation and Exchange - Part 224: Application Protocol: Mechanical Product Definition for Process Planning Using Machining Features*; Committee Draft; International Organization for Standardization; 1995

4. Kramer, Thomas R.; Jun, Jau-Shi; *Software for an Automated Machining Workstation*; Proceedings of the 1986 International Machine Tool Technical Conference; September 1986; Chicago, Illinois; National Machine Tool Builders Association; 1986; pp. 12-9 through 12-44

5. Kramer, Thomas R.; Jun, Jau-Shi; *The Design Protocol, Part Design Editor, and Geometry Library of the Vertical Workstation of the Automated Manufacturing Research Facility at the National Bureau of Standards*; NBSIR 88-3717; National Institute of Standards and Technology (formerly National Bureau of Standards), January 1988

6. Kramer, Thomas R.; *Process Plan Expression, Generation, and Enhancement for the Vertical Workstation Milling Machine in the Automated Manufacturing Research Facility at the National Bureau of Standards*; NBSIR 87 - 3678; National Institute of Standards and Technology (formerly National Bureau of Standards); November 1987

7. Kramer, Thomas R.; *A Parser that Converts a Boundary Representation into a Features Representation*; International Journal of Computer Integrated Manufacturing; Vol. 2, No. 3, May-June 1989; pp. 154-163; (also published as NISTIR 88-3864; National Institute of Standards and Technology; September 1988)

8. Kramer, Thomas R.; *The Off-Line Programming System (OLPS): A Prototype STEP-Based NC-Program Generator*, proceedings of a seminar Product Data Exchange for the 1990's; New Orleans, Louisiana; NCGA; February 1991; Vol. 2

9. Kramer, Thomas R.; *A Library of Material Removal Shape Element Volumes (MRSEVs)*; NISTIR 4809; National Institute of Standards and Technology; March 1992

10. Albus, James S.; *A Theory of Intelligent Systems*; Control and Dynamic Systems; Vol. 45; 1991; pp. 197 - 248

11. Albus, James S.; McCain, Harry G.; Lumia, Ronald; *NASA/NBS Standard Reference Model for Telerobot Control System Architecture (NASREM)*; NIST Technical Note 1235, 1989 Edition; National Institute of Standards and Technology; April 1989

12. Albus, James S.; *A Reference Model Architecture for Intelligent Systems Design*; NISTIR 5502; National Institute of Standards and Technology; September 1994

13. National Center for Manufacturing Sciences; *The Next Generation Controller Part Programming Functional Specification (RS-274/NGC)*; Draft; NCMS; August 1994

14. CAM-I, Inc., *Dimensional Measuring Interface Standard*, Revision 3.0, ANSI/CAM-I 101-1995, 1995

15. Jurrens, Kevin K.; Fowler, James E.; Algeo, Mary E.; *Modeling of Manufacturing Resource Information*; NISTIR 5707; National Institute of Standards and Technology; July 1995

Multivariate process modeling of a high volume manufacturing of consumer electronics

Stefan Asp and Peter Wide

Department of Technology and Science
Örebro University
S-701 82 Örebro, Sweden

ABSTRACT

As production volumes continue to increase and the global market for consumer electronics is getting fiercer, the need for a reliable and essentially fault-free production process is becoming a necessity to survive. The manufacturing processes of today are highly complex and the increasing amount of process data produced is making it hard to unravel the useful information extracted from a huge data set. We have used multivariate and nonlinear process modeling to examine the surface mount production process in a high volume manufacturing of mobile telephones and made an artificial neural network model of the process. As input parameters to the model we have used process data logged by an automatic test equipment (ATE) and the result variables come from an Automatic Inspection system placed after the board manufacturing process. Using multivariate process modeling has enabled us to identify parameters, which contributes heavily to the quality of the product and can further be implemented to optimize the manufacturing process for system production faults.

Keywords: manufacturing process, high volume manufacturing, multivariate process modeling.

1. BACKGROUND

High volume manufacturing, providing products and manufacturing that best serve customers needs with mass production efficiency, has become an important topic for manufacturing industries. This work has been made to investigate an approach aiming to increase the optimization process in a consumer electronic production plant, with the special attention to estimate the significant features in a test data information flow.

The close monitoring of the operational performance of manufacturing processes, their associated instrumentation and control is seen to be of increasing strategic importance. The objective of monitoring process performance is to reduce the level of off-specification production and provide early warning and identification of important process related disturbances, malfunctions or faults.

Further author information:
P. Wide (correspondence): Phone: +46 19 303430; Fax: (+46)-19-303463, Email; peter.wide@ton.hoe.se;
S. Asp: stefan.asp@ton.hoe.se,

Part of the SPIE Conference on Sensors and Controls for Intelligent Machining and Agile Manufacturing
Boston, Massachusetts • November 1998
SPIE Vol. 3518 • 0277-786X/98/$10.00

Monitoring the performance of high volume manufacturing [1] processes using multivariate analysis [2, 3] and neural networks [4] is in many cases today a complexity of logistics and data handling. The production of mass customization [5, 6] has more and more become a new paradigm for the industries to provide products and production which best serve the customers' needs while maintaining high volume production efficiency. The basis of this new approach is aiming toward recognition of each customer as an individual and the subsequent production of a various "tailor-made" products. With this increasing capability and production flexibility built into modern manufacturing systems, companies with high production volumes can gain an advantage in optimization of the manufacturing process, by use of measurement technology and programmable software. In general, high volume manufacturing processes often increase the need for more sensor data which require new approaches of measurement technologies in order to increased the overall process knowledge. However, the analysis of huge data sets of process information has become more and more important, e.g. how do we extract the information features in order to optimize a process and reduce the overall data amount.

In this paper, the opportunities of improving the manufacturing process in a high volume manufacturing of mobile telephones is discussed. The objective of this approach is to proactively connect measured data information to the capabilities of classifying faults in the manufacturing process.

2. MODEL

The model is in this proposal focused on an illustrative and exemplifying part of the manufacturing process, e.g. the surface mounting unit. The process model exhibit two phases describing the system, observation parameters and variable parameters. As input parameters to the model we have used process data logged by an automatic test equipment (ATE) and the result variables come from an Automatic Inspection system placed after the board manufacturing.

The basic principle of the automatic inspection unit is illustrated in figure 1. The system involves a mounting machine and an inspection unit. The surface board is automatically applied in the surface mount machine and the components are mounted on both sides. The inspection system is located directly after the mounting unit and detects faults in the test process.

Figure 1. The board mounting, test and inspection process.

In this model, the errors and their reasons can be evaluated as well as how individual measurement tests are correlated to each other, i.e. soldering problems indicated in some measurements, calibration problem related to other measurements tests etc. These types of faults can further be classified by, for example an artificial neural network.

The test result variables measured by the automatic inspection and test system is for example:

- unsoldered connections
- solder bridge
- component missing
- wrong polarization
- tombstone
- etc.

By measuring the test variables, the future aim of this approach is to classify error types and predict parameter adjustments, resulting in an adaptive control of the manufacturing process. Different techniques can then be used, however, in this approach an evaluation by multivariable statistical analysis are used, as shown in figure 2, aiming to define significant data attributes in the test information by closer examination. The most significant data in the test data were redefined and further analyzed by an expert.

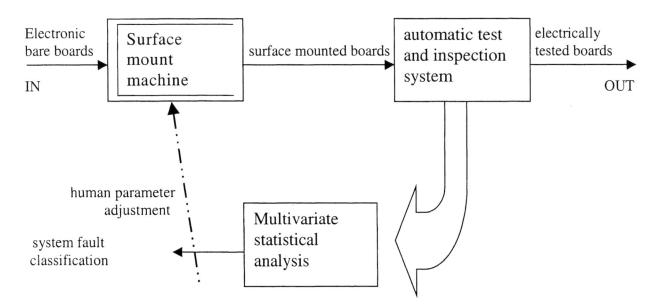

Figure 2. The proposed model.

The future intention of this approach is to implement a nonlinear model that predicts the optimal parameter adjustments of the manufacturing machines. There is also a possibility to evaluate how the input adjustable parameters of the surface mount machine is affected by secondary parameters, e.g. parameters that indirectly can be measured but not controlled by the surface mount machine adjustments.

The input adjustable parameters of the surface mount machine is for example:

- component pick-up rate
- rotation/polarization of component
- component placing force
- temperature in the soldering process
- etc.

3. PROCESSING OF MEASURED DATA

The classification of the measured data information corresponding to the manufacturing process data was logged by an automatic test equipment (ATE). Totally 63.030 mobile telephone boards was tested in this experiment. The resulting test variables were pre-processed in an Automatic Inspection system placed after the board manufacturing. A number of the tested boards were rejected due to test identification of disturbances, malfunctions or faults according to pre-defined process specifications. The faults were classified in 32 different categories and further analyzed by using the multivariate analysis method, PCA.

Principal Component Analysis [7], PCA, is used to monitor process performance and provide early warning and identification of important process parameters, e.g. disturbances, malfunctions or faults. PCA is a mathematical transform, which is used to explain variance in experimental data [8]. The measured data is structured in a matrix with N rows and K columns. The N rows correspond to the observations and the K columns correspond to the variables. The obtained matrix is modeled by projection methods, which approximate the data by projecting the information data to lower dimensions. The results are expressed as observation parameters, scores and variable parameters, loadings. To improve the interpretation of the analysis, plots of these parameters are of great importance giving a visual impression of the experimental data. The score plot shows the relation between the observations or experiments, e.g. the relationship between the data information corresponding to the mounting process data. Groupings of observations in the score plot can be used for classifications. A loading plot shows the relationship between the data, e.g. it indicate how much the different variables collected by the automatic inspection system influence the result.

PCA is a statistical mathematical method to transfer (often strongly correlated) variables $X_1,..., X_p$ to uncorrelated variables $Z_1 ,..., Z_p$. The components $Z_1 ,..., Z_p$ is a linear combination of $X_1,..., X_p$ which are chosen such as Z_1 is the component with the highest variance, Z_2 with the highest variance of the remaining data and so on. The data is transformed to uncorrelated data with the total variance kept, as described in equation 1.

$$\text{Var}[X_1] + \text{Var}[X_2] + ... + \text{Var}[X_p] = \text{Var}[Z_1] + \text{Var}[Z_2] + ... + \text{Var}[X_p] \tag{1}$$

If the last $p - k$ values is small, the following approximation can be made, according to equation 2.

$$\sum_{i=1}^{p} Z_i = \sum_{i=1}^{k} Z_i \tag{2}$$

to achieve a successful analysis, k is much smaller than p. By this approximation method a projection from p-dimensions to k-dimensions has been performed. This makes a regression analysis on the uncorrelated components $Z_1 ,..., Z_k$ possible without any colinearity problems.

PCA was used in this experiment to examine the measured data by extracting the main phenomena or systematic variability present in the test information. The residuals present the variability, which is interpreted as noise. By modeling the data in terms of a few significant principal components, plus error and residuals, there is a possibility to distinguish between weakly correlated attributes and strongly correlated data that obviously contribute very little to the discrimination process. The sensory attributes were standardized to unit variance prior to the analyses.

The total information was merged into a matrix, 32 fault types and 107 tests, the loading plot in figure 3 was obtained. It can be seen from the plot that at least three directions of measurement test no 84, 101 and 68 is not correlated to each other. A closer examination of the loading plot revealed that a large amount of measurement tests was strongly correlated and therefore contributed little to the discrimination process.

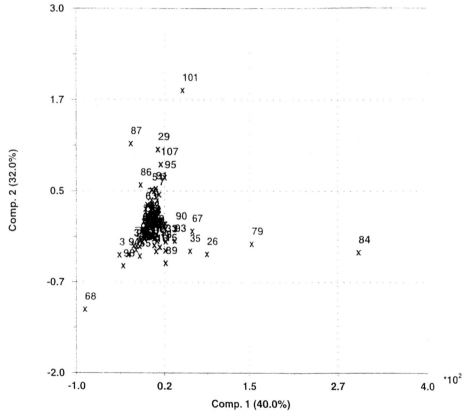

Figure 3. Loading plot of the total data set using principal component 1 and 2.

Hence, the importance of different features discriminating the process fault types is indicated and their correlation to a human expert opinion are obvious. A plot of variables, i.e. a two-dimensional score plot for the first principal component versus the second principal component is shown in figure 4. It can be seen that three clusters of fault types appear.

1   no 2,
2   no 17,
3   no 20.

In fact it can be shown by heuristics that the clusters indicate a strong correlation to corresponding system faults:

-   SMA soldering problems (1),
-   calibration problems (2),
-   others

An enlargement of the plot also indicates that the grouping fault types no 15, 11, 5 and 12 are related. In fact these fault types are strongly correlated to SMA process problems.

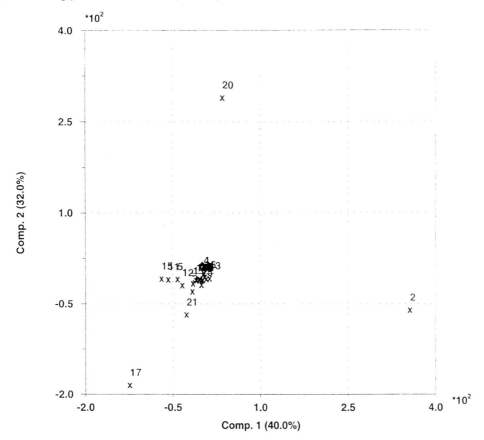

Figure 4. The score plot using principal components 1 and 2.

A closer examination of the Bi-plot, shown in figure 5, reveals for example that:

-   test measurement no 68 is strongly correlated to fault no 17,
-   test measurement no 84 is strongly correlated to fault no 2,
-   test measurement no 10 is strongly correlated to fault no 20,

This plot indicates a close correlation between a fault type and a corresponding measurement and vice versa.

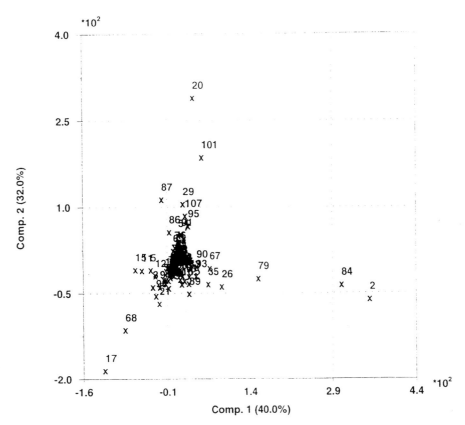

Figure 5. The Bi-plot showing principal components 1 and 2.

4. CONCLUSION AND DISCUSSION

This work shows the possibilities to classify inspection data from a high volume manufacturing of mobile telephones and to reduce the level of off-specification production, provide early warning and identification of important process related disturbances, malfunctions or faults.

Principal Component Analysis, PCA, is a method to evaluate multivariate data. The technique was in this approach used to examine the measured data by extracting the main phenomena of the observation, or systematic variability presented in the information. The residual represents the variability, which is interpreted as noise. By modeling the data in terms of a few principal components, plus error and residuals, there is a possibility to distinguish between weakly correlated and strongly correlated data that obviously contribute very little to the discrimination process. The PCA clearly shows that it is possible to separate the different type of system faults in the mounting process.

We can expect multivariate analysis methods to be of interest in the field of high volume manufacturing mainly as a featuring extraction of information in complex and huge data sets. The pre-processed data set may further be reanalyzed by using PCA information to reduce the strongly correlated observations. From these analysis, a subject of key data information may be identified and further classified in a model, i.e. artificial neural networks or Partial Least Squares, PLS.

This can with advantage be done by using classifiers with adaptive capability. This strategy will in the future be implemented in the proposed model as shown in figure 6.

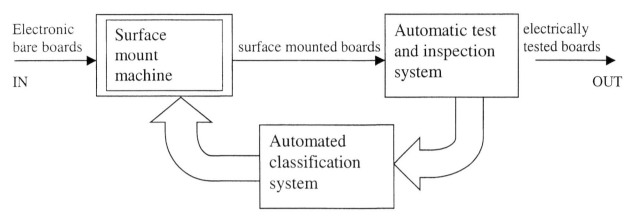

Figure 6. The fully automated process control model.

ACKNOWLEDGEMENTS

This work has been done at the Applied Autonomous Sensor System (AASS) laboratory at Örebro University and at Ericsson Mobile Communication plant in Kumla, Sweden. The work is a part of the joint project sponsored by Ericsson and the Department of Technology and Science whose support is gratefully acknowledged.

REFERENCES

1. M.M. Tseng, "Mass Customization- Opportunities and Challenges for High Value Added Products and Services", *proc. of the 4th Int. conf. in computer integrated manufacturing*, Singapore, October 21-24, 1997, pp. 34-42.
2. A.J. Morris and E. Martin, Process monitoring and fault detection through multivariate statistical process control, *proc. IFAC safeprocess'97*, vol. 1, pp. 1-14, 1997.
3. A. Simoglou, E.B. Martin, A. J. Morris, M. Wood and G. C. Jones, Multivariate statistical process control in chemical manufacturing, *proc. IFAC safeprocess'97*, vol. 1, pp. 21-28, 1997.
4. D. J. H. Wilson, G. W. Irwin and G. Lightbody, Nonlinear PLS-application to fault detection, *proc. IFAC safeprocess'97*, vol. 1, pp. 15-20, 1997.
5. S. Kotha, " Mass customization: Implementing the emerging paradigm for competitive advantage", *Strategic Management Journal* **16**, pp 21-42, 1995.
6. R. S. Lau, Mass Customization: the next industrial revolution", *Industrial Management* **37**, pp 18-19, 1995.
7. R.A. Johnson and D.W. Wichern, Applied multivariate statistical analysis, second edition, *Prentice-Hall International Editions*, New Jersey, 1992.
8. K. Espensen, T. Midtgaard and s. Schönkopf, "Multivariate analysis in practice", *CAMO AS*, 1994.

PRODUCTION OF ROTATIONAL PARTS IN SMALL-SERIES AND COMPUTER AIDED PLANNING OF ITS PRODUCTION ENGINEERING

Illés Dudás, Miklós Berta, István Cser
University of Miskolc, Department Production Engineering

ABSTRACT

Up-to-date manufacturing equipments of production of rotational parts in small series are lathe-centers and CNC grinding machines with high concentration of manufacturing operations. By the use of these machine tools it can be produced parts with requirements of increased accuracy and surface quality. In the lathe centers, wich containe the manufacturing procedures of lathes using statinary tools and of drilling-milling machine tools using rotational tools, it can also be produced the non-rotational surfaces (planes, flattering and holes on the faces, etc.) of rotational parts. The high concentration of manufacturing operations makes it necessary the planning and programing of the measuring, monitoring and quality control into the technological process during manufacturing operation.

In this way - taking into consideration the technological possibilites of lathe centers - the scope of computer aided technological planning's duties significantly increases.

It is trivial requirement to give only once (not in every manufacturing operation) the descriptions of the prefabricated parts and ready made parts. Starting taking into account these careful considerations we have been developing the planning system of technology of body of revolution on the base of GTIPROG/EC system [1] which useful for programing of lathe centers. Our paper deals with the results of development and the accuring problems.

Keywords: Production of Rotational Parts, Small-Series Production, Computer aided Planning, CA Programming of Lathe-Centers, Group Technology, CNC-Grinding, Quality Control, Flexible Manufacturing

1. TECHNOLOGICAL AND CONSTRUCTIONAL CHARACTERISTICS OF TURNING CENTRES AND THE REQUIREMENTS AGAINST PLANNING OF OPERATION FOLLOWING FROM THEM

Generally the red-tape operation elements of turning centres are also highly automated. The tool-change, the exchange and the turning over of feed magazine, the exchange and adjustment of chuck and chuck jaws, the adjusting and exchange of the gripper of workpiece-handling robot, the measurement of workpiece and tool are also automated.

The number of chuckings, their secondary time, and the required capacity of inter-operational magazine attachments are decreased by the concentration of operation.

Because of the decrease in the number of reference changes, the shape and positional accuracy of the machined elements is increased. The duplex and/or the compound-slide layout, as well as the tooling-up possibilities have a great

172

Part of the SPIE Conference on Sensors and Controls for Intelligent Machining and Agile Manufacturing
Boston, Massachusetts ● November 1998
SPIE Vol. 3518 ● 0277-786X/98/$10.00

influence on the subdivision of machining process into operations and on the sequence of operational elements. In some cases it is possible to overlap the operational elements, simultaneously carrying them out [2], [3].

The major phases of production design (denotation of operation elements, determination of their sequence of operation, choosing of tools, determination of cutting parameters, setting-up of tool co-ordination plan, designing of tool paths) of machining carried out on turning centres are mostly affected by the combination of the spindle and the saddle.

The most common instances concerning the production design and the checking of exclusions are represented by those turning centres (e.g. MAZAK) which have only one tool holder mounted on the cross-tool carriage, where stationary as well as rotating tools can be taken in. The tool magazines are conveyed by the base saddle, the manipulator and the tool holder are carried by the cross-tool carriage.

One of the most common variations of turning centres is the one-slide layout provided with two turrets. Numbers of times the combination of drum turret and tower turret is used. The tower turrets have 1-4-6-10 tool holders with tangential or radial tool clamping design. In case of one of the most commonly used compound-slide turning centres, the rotating tools are carried by one slide, and the stationary tools by the other. Those layouts are more complicated from the point of view of production design in which rotating as well as stationary tools can be mounted on each slide.

The rotating tool holders according to their machining position can be of radial and axial direction, furthermore they can be adjusted in the principal plane into arbitrarily chosen angular position or they are controllable along one or two rotational axes.

Generally the execution of boring and milling operations of workpieces to be manufactured on turning centres requires short operational lengths from aspect of tools, therefore the use of tools with short or abridged construction may be recommended in favour of more efficient machining. At the time of designation of tools or during the automatic tool selection we always have to endeavour to use the most rigid tool appropriate for the execution of a given machining task.

By the rotating tools applied on turning centres , various boring tasks not being in the rotational axis of the workpiece (boring of seating for entrainment, drilling, boring, counterboring, reaming, tapping) and various milling tasks (groove milling, plane milling) could be done.

The nature of operational elements is determined by the type of bearing area (end face, curved surface, cone), the direction of machining (rotation of main spindle or the axial and/or radial travel of tool), furthermore by the direction of tool clamping.

At some operational elements the machining can be executed repeatedly with uniform spacing (e.g. milling of regular polygons, boring on a given pitch circle etc.) due to the positioning ability of the main spindle. In case of a significant percentage of components, the complete machining of a component can be executed with one clamping because of concentration of operations. This user demand makes the solution of the problem of turning behind a shoulder necessary. The „reflecting" of travel cycles is also required by turning centres of such layout, where the second „main spindle" is located opposite to the first, i.e. mounted on one of the essential points of the tool holder or the tailstock, and therefore in this case the machining of the opposite side of the workpiece is taken place without the reversing of the workpiece.

The simultaneously working slides call for the resolving of the problem of production design of multiple machining.

The reliable and efficient operation of high priced turning centres and manufacturing cells and the quality and quantity demands of the more and more complicated components emphasize the importance of planning of supervisory and quality assurance functions.

During the planning of supervisory and quality assurance functions we have to deal with the resolving of tasks coming up before, during and after the machining.

The pre-machining supervision includes the dimension control of pre-products, the identification of necessary tools and inspection of their condition.

The supervision during machining covers the controlling of clamping force applied to clamp the workpiece, the supervision of cutting force, moment, machining performance, vibration and shape of chips, furthermore the measurement of accuracy to dimensions, configurational trueness and surface roughness during an operation and between operations, as well as the execution of tool change and conditional dimension correction of tools. The geometrical and shape tolerance of the completed workpiece will take place after the machining.

2. PROGRAMMING OF TURNING CENTRES

We have resolved the programming of turning centres – according to the above mentioned requirements – by the enhancement of GTIPROG-E system developed in the Industrial Technology Centre Automated Technical Design Ltd. for programming of traditional NC/CNC turning lathes.

The bibliography No. [4] and [5] provide further details concerning the performance, structure and technological services of GTIPROG-EC system.

The preponderant part of the component program containing the input data of the GTIPROG-EC system is made up by - besides the general identification data – the geometrical description of the blank and completed end-product. In the description of machining it is sufficient to specify the type of operation elements, the location of execution and the scheduling of execution. On the base of this information, the system determines the configuration of allowance, selects the tools necessary for the machining, arranges the tools into the tool positions depending from the construction of the machine tool (turret, magazine), computes the tool paths (Fig. 1.), and at last the postprocessor accomplishes the manufacturing documentation (Fig. 2.), and creates the control program in appropriate form and content demanded by the control.

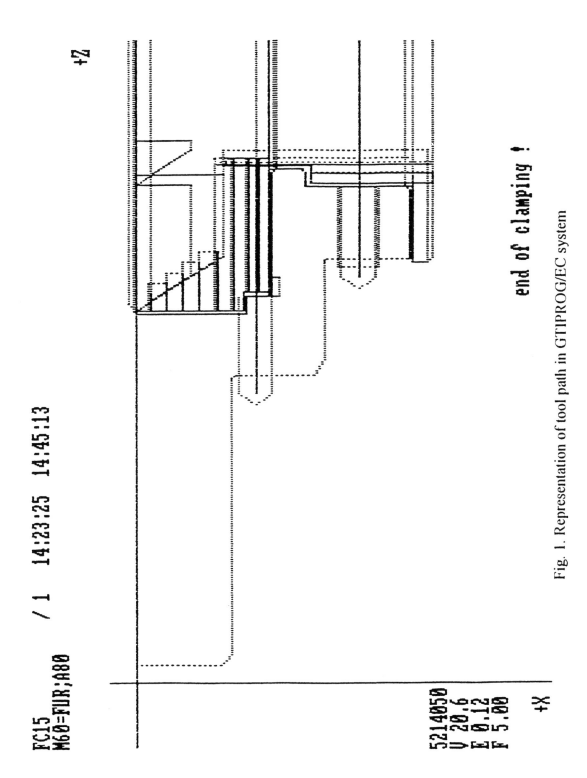

Fig. 1. Representation of tool path in GTIPROG/EC system

```
IBM PC & comp.    *****************************    GTIPROG  EC-04
*************     EPA-320/SINUMERIC SYSTEM 800/810T    **************

NAME OF PART      : TENGELYCSONK    FC15

LIST - FILE       : LST\FC15.DOC

PUNCHED TAPE FILE: LST\FC15.L1

NUMBER OF THE NC PROGRAM :  301

DATE              : 06-24-1998    14:51:39
```

```
              SERIAL NUMBER OF CLAMPING : 1
              ------------------------------
```

```
                                              N C   P R O G R A M
REVOL. NUMBER-INTERVAL AT THE BEGINING : 1    - - - - - - - - -
```

```
                                              % MPF 301
O P E R A T I O N   E L E M E N T S            N5 G40 G53 G97 M11
- - - - - - - - - - - - - - - - - -           :10 T1 D1 M06
                                              N15 G00 X0 M03 M08
     5 -   50 : DRILLING                      N20 Z150 S204
    55 -   80 :  HOLE ENLARGENING             N25 G01 Z137.751 F.115
    85 -  160 : EXTERNAL ROUGH FACING         N30 G04 F.5
   165 -  185 : EXTERNAL AXIAL ROUGH TURNING  N35 Z103.01 F.23
   190 -  390 : INTERNAL AXIAL ROUGH TURNING  N40 G04 F.5
   395 -  435 : EXTERNAL FINISH TURNING       N45 G00 Z150
   440 -  470 : EXTERNAL FINISH TURNING       N50 Z187
   475 -  520 : INTERNAL FINISH TURNING       :55 T2 D2 M06
   525 -  580 : INTERNAL RADIAL GROOVING      N60 G00 X0 M03
   585 -  630 : DRILLING                      N65 Z140.39 S157
   635 -  680 : TAPPING                       N70 G01 Z103.01 F.42
   685 -  715 : DRILLING                      N75 G00 Z140.39
                                              N80 Z157
                                              :85 T3 D3 M06
                                              N90 G00 X174 M03
T O O L - A R A N G E M E N T   P L A N           :
- - - - - - - - - - - - - - - - - - - - - -       :
```

TOOL IDENTIFI.	TOOL POSITION	CORRECTION	TOOL LENGTH	TOOL OVERHANG	DRILL DIAMET.	EDGE RADIUS
3214070	1	1	280.00	90.0	32.00	
3211000	2	2	310.00	90.0	50.00	
2101100	3	3	112.00	-90.0		.8
1101100	4	4	140.00	63.0		.8
2361000	11	5	112.00	-90.0		.8
2321000	12	6	112.00	-90.0		.8
1101000	5	7	140.00	63.0		.8
1411070	6	8	110.00	73.0		
5214040	7	10	134.00	0.0	10.2	
5512022	8	11	159.00	0.0	12.00	
5214050	9	13	184.00	0.0	10.00	

```
MACHINING TIME (min)      =   9.14
AUXILIANG. TIME (min)     =  11.45
        :
```

Fig. 2. Manufacturing documentation

3. ACHIEVEMENTS OF THE ENHANCEMENT OF THE SYSTEM

As a result of our recent developing activity, by changing the text data stored in the database we have extended the system to operate (communicate) in English, German and Hungarian, as well as to provide documentation in these languages. Students at the University of Miskolc Department of Machine Production Technology and at the Technical University of Budapest have acquired and have successfully been using this system for the accomplishment of their complex special subject tasks and for construction their final thesis.

4. REFERENCES

1. M. Berta – B. Futó – M. Juhász – Gy. Voloncs:
    „Programming of turning machining centres by microcomputer" (in Hungarian)
    MECHATRONINFO '88, MATE, Eger, 1988., p.: 339-350

2. I. Dudás – M. Berta – I. Cser:
    „Problems and conditions of computer integrated manufacturing" (in Hungarian)
    Gépgyártástechnológia, 1993. No. 5-6., p.: 205-209.

3. L. Horváth:
    „Planning of manufacturing technologies with computer systems" (in Hungarian)
    Budapest, 1995.

4. M. Berta – I. Cser – M. Juhász:
    „Turning centres programming by GTIPROG-E system"
    INTERTECHNO '90, Budapest, 1990., p.: 221–230

5. M. Berta – I. Cser:
    „Programming, operation planning and quality assurance of turning centres" (in Hungarian)
    8th International Conference on Tools, GTE, Miskolc, 1993., p.: 627-635.

Modeling of vibration of twist drills

Illés Dudás, and Gyula Varga

Department of Production Engineering, University of Miskolc,
H-3515, Miskolc-Egyetemváros, Hungary

ABSTRACT

Nowadays developing of the new technologies which decrease the unfavourable environmental effects of the traditional manufacturing processes and using them in the industrial production get even more into the focus. The development of environmentally clean manufacturing technologies requires careful and circumstantial analysis. In this paper the substantial measurements performed during experiments of environment - friendly drilling processes are shown including the examination of new and worn tool geometry, the geometry of the machined surfaces, the change of feed force and torque as well as the temperature of the contact zone between work and tool, an last but not least the analysis of the modified vibration too.

The mathematical model based on the known solvation method of partial differential equation is a good base model which can futher be developed. Nowadays a more general distributed parameter model that inclused both transverse and torsional vibration of the drill bit also seems desirable. The effects of damping and temperature must also be investigated.

Keywords: vibration analysis, environmentally clean manufacturing, modeling

1. INTRODUCTION

Drilling is one of the most important machining operation. Till this time the aim of the manufacturers was the use of the maximum value of coolant or lubricant. It was done in order to get as high drilling performance as possible. However nowadays the way of manufacturing a little bit changed because of the environment protection and the wish of machining more economical manner[1].

The coolants and lubricants endanger not only the environment but directly the health of the production workers as well. The increasing attention to environmental and health problems is reflected in the increasingly stricter legislation and national and international standards, so the speedy increase of the environmental protection tax can be excepted as well.

For these reason it is necessary to develop the environment - friendly, waste - free technologies with minimum quantity of coolant and lubricants or with the complete elimination of cutting fluids „dry" machining technologies. This new development field recently becomes a determinant one all over the world.

In the search for solutions and ways to improve machining processes it is essential to replace the conventional approach with new and innovative methods which allow a minimum environmental contamination to be achieved in conjunction with suitable technologies providing high process stability and reliability and acceptable economic conditions. In order to realise these requirements significant developments occur on the fields of coolants and lubricants, cooling technologies, tool materials and tool geometries[2, 3, 4].

The Department of Production Engineering took part in a European Community project, titled „Clean machining technology - decrease and substitution of coolants and lubricants in drilling". Other participants of the project are University of Dortmund as the coordinator of the project, Technical University of Magdeburg, University of Wroclaw and University of Plsen. Research reports[5] contain our scientific activities done so far.

As the introduction of every new manufacturing technology requires the deep previous analysis of several parameters so the introduction of environment friendly drilling as well.

For this reason a complex measuring task - among them measurement of different geometrical parameters as well as cutting force, torque, temperature and volume flow - was performed by us in order to adjust accurately the experimental conditions and analyse their effect.

What kind of degree will the consuption of twist drills increase? How the twist drill will wear? How the vibration of twist drills will change, etc? So it requires to work out a dynamic model for the transverse vibration of drill bit as well.

Part of the SPIE Conference on Sensors and Controls for Intelligent Machining and Agile Manufacturing
Boston, Massachusetts • November 1998
SPIE Vol. 3518 • 0277-786X/98/$10.00

In the posession of the model the effect of different circumstances can be examind. In this article our aim is to present a model which contains the effects of drill bit length, diameter and material properties.

2. EXPERIMENTAL CONDITIONS OF ENVIRONMENT FRIEND DRILLING

The environment friendly drilling experiments were performed by a program elaborated on the base of preliminary experiments. The technological parameters and values to be adjusted were determined using the method of Factorial Experiment Design[6].

Geometrical data of drilled holes:
  diameter of the holes was 10mm and the length of the machined through hole wasl =30mm.
Material of the workpiece:
  GG200 grey cast iron.
The used machine tool:
  machining centre, type MKC500.
Tools used for manufacturing:
  straight shank twist drills, diameter 10mm, produced by GÜHRING, satisfied the requirements mentioned above. The material of these drills were: HSS without any coating, Carbide (type HM and VHM), K10/K20 with different coatings (TiN, TiAlN and MoS_2) The twist drills had different edge geometry: pure edges (having straight lines) and sophisticated ones (having concave edges). The carbide material twist drills had inner cooling channels.
Coolants and lubricants:
  at the beginning of the experiments the emulsion of 5% with reduced volume was used (from 1,6 l/min till 0,3 l/min), after them for providing of the minimum quantity cooling lubrication environment-friendly oils (OMV-Oil X ULTRA-CF and OMV-Oil TB-CF) were used by reducing their volume (28cm³/h, 10 cm³/h, 0cm³/h). At last in case of "dry" drilling only pressed air of 0,2 MPa 160 l/min was used as coolant.

3. BACKGROUND

Many researchers have investigated the drill vibration and questions of stability[7, 8, 9] when machining with collant and lubricant. Fuji and his colleagues experimentally studied the effects of geometric parameters on transverse vibration in drilling. They developed a vibrational model which includes radial forces along the main cutting edge and the frictional forces due to the collision of the flank with the machined surface[8, 9]. Ema and his co-researchers experimentally examined that its frequency is equal to the bending natural frequency of the drill. This statement was done when the drill point was supported in the hole of the material to be drilled[7]. Ulsoy and Tekinalp[10] created a multiparameter model which model predicts the fundamental frequences of the drill. They took into consideration of cutting speed. Analysis of Tekinalp and Ulsoy[11] when using FEM gives a good correlation between experimental and calculated results. These models were valid for drilling with coolants and lubricants. However in the case when the drill has inner coolant ducts the rigidity and the second order inertial moments will change, so the vibration will be different.

On the other hand in case of drilling having no coolant and lubricant the value of thrust and torque will change because of the increased friction factor, and it has some effects to the vibration as well. Our model is based on the Lagrangian equation.

4. ELECTRIC MEASURING TECHNIQUE OF DYNAMIC CHARACTERISTICS OF THE DRILLING TOOLS

Beside the geometrical and kinematics machine errors the direction, the magnitude and the characteristics of the static and dynamic effects and because of these presence the elastic deformation of the drilling tool have influence on the discrepancy from the draw of the work produced on the different drilling machines, boring and turning machines or machining centre.

The stiffness of the covered and non-covered auger drill can be calculated with good approximate value but the stiffness and auttenuation behaviour of the machine main spindle can be estimated with higher approximate errors. The latest research methods for aiding the develop of the optimal tool construction can be good solution for this problem, however we worked out a measuring technique for inspection the real conditions of dynamic characteristics of the drilling tool[12].

The inaccurate static stiffness of the tool results in accuracy of the dimension of the produced work. The dynamic stiffness less than required can occur undesired vibration which superimposing can result in the surface irregularity of the work, the short of the lifetime of tool, excessive wear and fracture. Consequently the goodness of resistance to variable loading of the drill one of the most important qualification factors is requirement of the satisfying of increasing demand of he consumers and of the increasing of the cutting capacity.

5. MEASURING OF THE ELASTIC DEFORMATION OF THE DRILLING MACHINE

Specific elastic deformation measuring of the tool was performed in case of static and dynamic load. We consider the static deformation measuring of the drilling tool as the case of elastic deformation related to F= 0 Hz, so that we defined automatically the magnitude with the measuring of the dynamic elastic deformation. The specific elastic deformation or reciprocal stiffness means the displacement brought about by unit force[12].

The tool is interpreted as transfer circuit according to the concepts of control technique. So the transfer characteristic of the drill is characterised on the basic of the frequency transfer function of the elastic deformation. In accordance with it the qualification of the tool is performed in the view of the stability of the deformation processes and possibilities of forming of induced vibration.

To determine the elastic deformation and its reciprocal value, the dynamic stiffness brought about by dynamic load, clamping the drilling tool by its horizontal axis it was induced with variable force of increased frequency of sinusoidal type but with the max. amplitude and we measured the displacement amplitudes brought about by the induction in the direction of the force and perpendicularly to it.

The mark from the marker generator of low frequency was linked to electrodynamics load inductor with power amplifier. The gripping place of the tool was induced by bonded strain gauge force metre converter. We perceived the inducing vibration amplitudes with W10T inductive piezoelectric acceleration converter. The output of the DDM plus digital measuring amplifier was registered with LC II Macintosh computer.

We had direct possibility for representation of amplitude - phase locus with BEAM software and FFT vibration analysis. Simultaneous registration of answer back amplitude related to inducting force of sinusoidal amplitude made the transferring function possible to be determined with direct locus. With the aid of the applied electrical measuring technique methods we determined the vibration form and dynamic displacement - force transferring function of the drilling tool. The general equations which describe the relative elastic deformation can be determined in every position of the drilling tool. As the simulation of the loading effect at the gripping place the elastic displacement brought about with sinusoidal loading effect of variable direction and magnitude is determined by :

$$\vec{t} = \underline{\underline{D}} \cdot \vec{F}$$

Detailing:

$$[u; v; w] = \begin{bmatrix} D_{xu} & D_{yu} & D_{zu} \\ D_{xv} & D_{yv} & D_{zv} \\ D_{xw} & D_{yw} & D_{zw} \end{bmatrix} \cdot \begin{bmatrix} F_x \\ F_y \\ F_z \end{bmatrix}$$

Where:

$\vec{t}$: displacement vector of which component, displacement in the orthogonal coordinate system matched to the machine in the direction of u,v,w ,

$\underline{\underline{D}}$: 3x3 matrix of the displacement -force frequency characteristic in which from its own 9 frequency characteristic 3 comprises the direct and 6 the cross frequency characteristic in the main diagonal.

The first index signs the direction of the induction force, the second signs the translation direction of the displacement perception. At linear systems - as in the case of machine tools tested by us - the matrix is symmetrical, so.

180

$$D_{vx}=D_{yu}; \quad D_{xw}=D_{zu}; \quad D_{yw}=D_{zv}$$

$\vec{F}$: the vector of inducting force.

The accuracy of the guide of the drilling tool is influenced by the dynamic stiffness perpendicular to the direction of the drilling therefore during drilling we measured the vibration amplitude perpendicular to the axis of the drill with HBM TrK 5 non-contact inductive displacement transducers[12]. (Figure 1)

From the vibration characteristic we determined the resonance nodal points and amplitudes related to buckling half - wave. system.

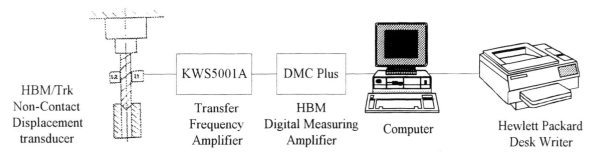

Figure 1

6. MODELING

Suppose the drill as a stepped shaft. The shank is a cilindrical part of the drill. The working part can be substitute with an another cylinder which diameter can be determined in the way which represents the same 2nd order inertial moment. The model considers the drill as a clamped-clamped.

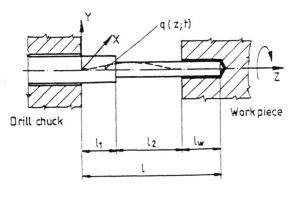

Figure 2

We will examine only l_1 and l_2 so the cross section A_1 and A_2 will be different, and q is the generalized coordinate.

For an infinitezimal length can be written for the l_1 length:

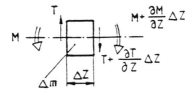

Figure 3

$$\Delta m = \rho \cdot A \cdot \Delta z$$

where. ρ - density of the drill material

The equation of theorem of momentum:

$$\rho \cdot A \cdot \Delta z \cdot \frac{\partial^2 q}{\partial t^2} = \frac{\partial T}{\partial z} \cdot \Delta z ,\qquad (1)$$

law of conversation of mement of momentum for the x axis:

$$0 = \frac{\partial M}{\partial z} \Delta z + T \Delta z ,\qquad (2)$$

where: T - shear forces
                M - moment

From (1) and (2):

$$\rho \cdot A \cdot \frac{\partial^2 q}{\partial t^2} - \frac{\partial^2 M}{\partial z^2} = 0 \qquad (3)$$

can be obtained.

Furthermore, let us denote v as the displacement of the center of gravity of the cross section and use the following approximantion:

$$\left|\frac{M}{IE}\right| \approx \frac{d^2 v}{dz^2} \qquad (4)$$

In this case instead of (3) the following equation can be written:

$$\rho \cdot A \cdot \frac{\partial^2 q}{\partial t^2} + \frac{\partial^2}{\partial z^2}\left(IE \cdot \frac{\partial^2 q}{\partial z^2} \right) = 0 \qquad (5)$$

Respectively for the l_1 and l_2 length IE will not depend on z.
The solution of (5) can be obtained by the Fourier-method:

$$q(z,t) = v(z) \cdot \tau(t) \qquad (6)$$

where: q is displacement into direction y.
Substitution into equation (5):

$$\frac{d^4 v}{dz^4} - k^4 \cdot v = 0 \qquad (7)$$

and

$$k^4 = \alpha^2 \frac{\rho A}{IE} ,$$

where: α^2 - const.

Solution:

$$v(z) = D_1 S_1(kz) + D_2 S_2(kz) + D_3 S_3(kz) + D_4 S_4(kz)$$

where:

$$S_1 = \frac{1}{2}(\text{ch } kz + \cos kz),$$
$$S_2 = \frac{1}{2}(\text{sh } kz + \sin kz),$$
$$S_3 = \frac{1}{2}(\text{ch } kz - \cos kz),$$
$$S_4 = \frac{1}{2}(\text{sh } kz - \sin kz).$$

(8)

are the Kruhlow functions.

The angular displacement:

$$\varphi(z) = k\left[D_1 S_4(kz) + D_2 S_1(kz) + D_3 S_2(kz) + D_4 S_3(kz)\right].$$

The moment:

$$M(z) = -IEk^2\left[D_1 S_3(kz) + D_2 S_4(kz) + D_3 S_1(kz) + D_4 S_2(kz)\right].$$

and the shear force

$$T(z) = IEk^3\left[D_1 S_2(kz) + D_2 S_3(kz) + D_3 S_4(kz) + D_4 S_1(kz)\right].$$

The D_1, D_2, D_3 and D_4 parameters can be determined from the boundary conditions.
It can be done to the end of the first and second length, l_1, and l_2. In this way the displacement and moment can be calculated.

7. RESULTS

The Report III.[5] contains of our experiments. We have seen that as the drilled length of the holes increased, the average value of cutting force increased as well.

The different forces caused different transverse vibration of the drill bits. Remark: BEAM program package provides the precise determination of average values of torque (and forces) in the steady state working condition. Nowadays cutting theory based on shear plane is combined with other cutting theories[13]. With these results the connection between torque, thrust and transverse vibration can be elaborated.

Vibrations of course play an important role in creation of hole quality. Increased vibration, when drill enters, can cause poor hole location accuracy, while in case of exit, excessive burr formation[14].

8. LITERATURE:

1. I. Dudás, I. Tolvaj, G. Varga, T. Csermely: „Measurement applied at the experiments of environmentally clean manufacturing operations", *Proc. of ISMTII'98, Fourth International Symposium on Measurement Technology and Intelligent Instruments, Miskolc-Egyetemvaros, Hungary,* pp. 487-492.

2. G. Byrne; E. Scholta: „Environmentally clean machining processes - A strategic approach", *Annals of the CIRP* vol. 42/1/1993. pp. 471-474.

3. T. Cselle: „Is Eco tooling on the way in? The pros and cons of dry machining techniqus. Modern Cutting Tools Technology" *GÜHRING 20.* Volume 14. pp. 6-8.

4. U. Heisel, M. Lutz, D. Spath, R. Wassmer, U. Walter: „Application of minimum quantity Cooling lubrication technology in cutting process". *Production Engineering* vol. II/1. 1994. pp. 49-54.

5. I. Dudás, G. Varga, T. Csermely, I. Tolvaj: „Experimentelle untersuchung des bohrprozess", Program STD2-EC. Titel des Projektes: *Umweltgerechte Zerspannungstechnik-Reduzie-rung und Ersatz von Fertigungsshilfsstoffen beim Bohren*, Universität Miskolc, Lehrstuhl für Maschinenbautechnologie, 3. Bericht, 1995. p. 80.

6. G. Varga: „Environment friend drilling-experiments by the use of factorial experiment design method", *Proceedings of the IXth International Conference on Tools, University of Miskolc,Miskolc, Hungary*, 3-5th September 1996. pp. 567-575.

7. S. Ema, M. Fujii, S. Marui: „Chatter vibration in drilling", *Transaction of ASME Journal Engineering for Ind.*, 1988. Vol. 110, pp. 309-314.

8. M. Fujii, E. Marui, S. Ema: „Whirling vibration in drilling, Part 2.: Influence of drill geometries, particularly of the drill flank, on the initiation of vibration", *Transaction of ASME Journal of Engineering for Ind.*, 1986. Vol. 108, pp. 163-168.

9. S. Ema, M. Fujii, S. Marui: „Whirling vibration in drilling, part 3.: Vibration analysis in drilling workpiece with a pilot hole, *Transaction of ASME Journal of Engineering for Ind.*, 1988, Vol. 110, pp. 315-321.

10. A. G. Ulsoy, O. Tekinalp: „Dinamic modeling of transverse drill bit vibrations", *CIRP Annals*, 1984, Vol., 33, Part I. pp. 253-258.

11. A. G. Ulsoy: „A lumped paramtere model for the transverse vibration of the drill bits", in Hardt D. E. and W. J. Book (eds), *Control of Manufacturing Process and Robotic Systems, ASME* 1983, pp. 15-25.

12. I. Dudas, T. Csermely: „Vibration analysis of drilling tools", *Proc. of ISMTII'98, Fourth International Symposium on Measurement Technology and Intelligent Instruments, Miskolc-Egyetemvaros, Hungary*, pp. 499-503.

13. E. J. Armarego: „Predictiv models for drilling thrust and torque - a comparison of three falnk configurations", *CIRP Annals*, 1984, Vol. 33, Part I. pp. 510.

14. D. F. Galloway: „Some experiments on the influence of various factors on drill performance". *Transaction of ASME Journal Engrng for Ind.*, 1957. Vol. 79, pp. 191-231.

Accurate machining and production geometry of complicated driving Pairs

Illés Dudás and Károly Bányai

University of Miskolc
Department of Production Engineering
Miskolc, Hungary

ABSTRACT

The intelligent automatization of the production of worm driving pairs has become a hot issue because of the requirements of the up-to-date high-grade production. In present production practice home and abroad only some elements have been realized, but a general system has not been developed.

Our paper presents the structure of a general system and some considerations and methods for the realization of some of its elements and subsystems. Some elements of the system we have already produced (CNC truing machine, measuring program, conceptional design programs) but the rest of the elements and their connection into the system are being worked out nowadays as our main research subject. We think that both the theoretical basis and methods, and the up-todate equipment developed for the realization, increase the productivity and the quality of the final product.

Keywords : intelligent manufacturing, expert system , worm gears, grinding machine, design, measurement

1. INTRODUCTION

The design and production of worm gearing with high performance have always raised newer and newer problems in the fields of constructional design and technological process planning.

With the increase of consumer demands many different types of driving pairs have appeared, beginning with cylindrical driving pairs having straight teeth. A lot of new demand were set to these new driving pairs, such as

- kinematical demands (intersecting axis driving, skew axis driving)
- increase of performance
- decrease of noise level
- etc.

One part of these demands requires changes in construction while the other part can be satisfied by production engineering developments.

The special character of the production of driving pairs is also shown by the fact that for the production of every type of driving pairs special, individual machine tool has been developed by machine tool producers because no universal machine tool can be used in this field (e.g. Oerlikon, Gleason type bevel gear toothing machine, Pfauter type worm gear milling machine, Klingelnberg thread grinding machine for worms).

These machine tools embody the expertise necessary for production - which represents the the knowledge base of the constructors - in their kinematical systems and automatized readjustment possibilities.
This potential advantage requires the design of the product, production planning and other components of production to be done in an intelligent automatized system.

The application field of intelligent automatization is based on the automatized process based control (visual recognition, measurement, analysis, stepping, etc.). Related to this, the application of intelligent instruments is required in the production, as well, assuring the communication among the elements.

Part of the SPIE Conference on Sensors and Controls for Intelligent Machining and Agile Manufacturing
Boston, Massachusetts • November 1998
SPIE Vol. 3518 • 0277-786X/98/$10.00

Although the whole process of design and production planning should be taken into account, here we can only deal with some of the elements mentioned below from the point of view of intelligent automatization.

2. IIS FOR DESIGN AND MANUFACTURE OF CYLINDRICAL WORM GEARS

In the previous points information agglomeration is compressively outlined which can indicate the direction toward the formation of the knowledge base of an expert system on the field of design, manufacturing and geometric qualification of helical gear-drives. The knowledge getting process carried out on the basis of the mentioned aspects can form the basis of the structure of the expert system.

In this section, the overall procedure is described first, and then the key parts of the IIS-WG (Intelligent Integrated System - Worm Gears) are described including the major functions of the expert system and artificial neural networks within the IIS-WG, numerical of tooth surfaces geometry and strength, and manufacturing.

2.1. Main Structure of the IIS-WG

Using this approach, the following activities are to be fully integrated:

a) conceptual design: formulation of product design specifications, concept generation and evaluation;
b) detail design: analysis, material selection, engineering drawing, design retrieval, etc;
c) manufacture: tooling, CNC programming;
d) measurement.

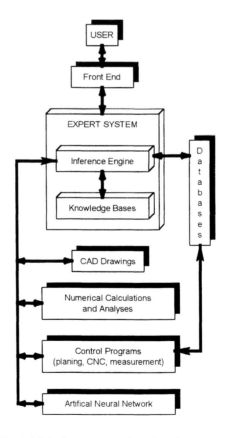

Fig. 1. Main Structure of the IIS-WG

The above can be classified into five categories: domain knowledge, numerical calculations, data processing, graphical presentation and drafting, and control of hardware (machines and devices). The domain knowledge is handled by the Expert systems and Neural Networks, while the rest are dealt with by CAD/CAM/CAE software and relevant hardware.

The main structure of the IIS approach is shown in figure 1. It consists of size basic elements: inference engine (IE), knowledge bases (KB), artificial neural networks (NN), numerical calculation and analysis facilities (NCA), databases (DB), and machines & devices (MD). The IE and KB forms the major part of the Expert System. The Expert System works as a coordinator to control and communicate with ANNs, NCA, DB and the contorl of MD.

2.2 Overall procedure

The overall procedure of the IIS-WG can be briefly explained as follows:

a) *design specifications* and *concept generation.* lhe user inputs design specifications first, which include input speed, speed ratio, power to be transmitted, central distance, etc. Using the data together with further necessary information derived from them, the design concepts are generated in terms of modules, number of starts of worm, number of teeth of wheel, etc.
b) *detail design.* The system selects materials from material database, carries out geometric calculations and strength analysis, designs the structure of the worm and the wheel
c) *re-design.* If any of the results obtained is not satisfied, then the system makes decision to modify the design parameters and goes back to redesign.
d) *CAD drawing and* databases. Once all the results arc satisfied, a CAD tool is invoked to produce the drawing of the designed worm and wheel pair, and all the results are saved into databases, which will be retrieved in the manufacturing phase.
e) *manufacturing.* The manufacturing phase includes cutting tool design, tool preparation including CNC manufacture and dressing; CNC manufacture of the thrcad surface of the worm and the worm shaft, and the manufacture of the wheel.
f) *measurement.* Within the manufacturing process, the tooth surface is measured using on-line equipment which is controlled by a computer. lhe results are analysed for the, control of tool dressing wheel.

3. CONCEPTION DESIGN OF WORM DRIVING PAIRS

The operational features of worm driving pairs are, among others, determined by the oil film formed between the mating surfaces. A method for the correction of mating relations and for increasing load capacity is to limit contact during mating to a hydrodynamically favourable region of the surfaces, that is, the localization of the bearing pattern.

Of all the mating relations the following characteristic features which are closely related to each other and are more or less characteristic of the type of the driving pair, are given special emphasis:

- the total length of the contact lines,
- the position and shape of the contact lines,
- the relation of the contact lines and relative velocities, - the dimension of the bearing pattern,
- the location/position of the bearing pattern etc.

These features essentially determine the formation of the loadable lubrication film, load capacity and furthermore the other working parameters. Although to some extent these properties are determined by the type (geometrical formation) of the driving pair, the appropriate choice of parameters typical of the type of the driving makes optimization possible. In this case the optimization can be accomplished in the possible interval (Fig. 2.).

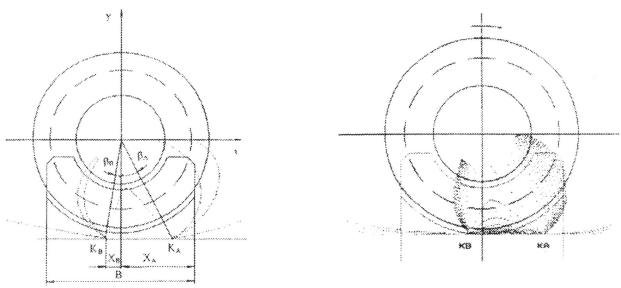

Fig. 2. Contact lines on the basis of the computacional model

4. PRODUCTION OF WORM DRIVING PAIRS

4.1. Setting up the production system

The functions of the elements and their interrelations are described, as if they created a flexible production cell so other functions and relations to other elements of the system are ignored.

The system structure is as follows:

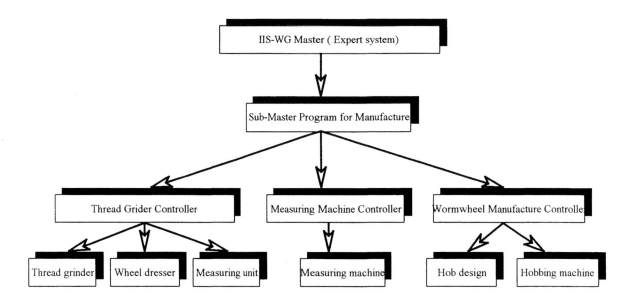

Fig. 3. The system structure

4.2. Grinding of helicoid surface

There are two fundamental problems with the at finishing manufacturing operation of conical helicoidal surfaces, which -in practice- hinder proper formation of the profile (from a technological point of view):

- Because of the wearing of the profile of the grinding wheel the profile and the diameter of the grinding wheel gradually changes. This is the reason why the produced profile of the worm is different from the theoretical profile, and from the original starting state as well.
- The changes of the diameter of the conical helicoidal surface along the axis result in the continuous changes of the worm profile (if the profile of the grinding wheel is constant).

For grinding the back surface of the conical pinion and the hob with nearly the same geometry there are three facilities.

a) Continous wheel controlling

On the base of the problem discussed above we would like to ensure the surface accuracy of the conical pinion, so that we should carry out the contionuous change of the wheel prifile for which a CNC wheel conrolling machine is required which is operated on the basis of an existing program package. This program package represents the mathematical backround of the enveloping and determines the wheel prifile in axial section. The CNC machine conrol the wheel always to the actual profile as the wheel passes along the axis. The disadvantage of this method is the high wheel consuming due to continuous wheel control.

b) Optimisation of the wheel profile

The method which meets the practical demands for accuracy and ensures the minimal wheel consuming is that the grinding wheel is controlled to the profile which produces the accurate pinion profile on a defined place between the smallest and the largest diameter and the profile distortion is under the required tolerance limit on the two outside parts too. The advantage of this method is that it can be easily accomplished not requiring high wheel consuming. But the disadvantage that depending on the dimensions of the pinion that machining can not always ensure to be under the tolerance limit. And when the pinion is devided into more parts there is break on the surface at the transitions (Fig. 4.).

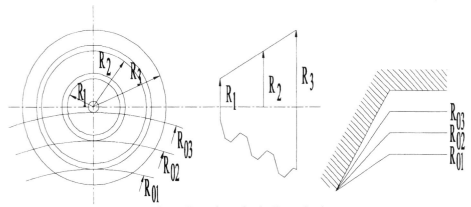
Fig. 4. Dressing of grinding wheel

c) Kinematic control of the grinding wheel

This method combine the advantages of the former two ways (accurate machining, minimal wheel consuming), but requires a very serious controling task which can be performed only with automatization. The substance of that is that the production of the accurate profile is realised not only with wheel profile controlling but with kinematic adjustment of the grinding wheel that is adjustment to the adequate position in terms of the enveloping. For that a grinding machine of new construction is required.

5. REQUIREMENTS OF THE THREAD GRINDING MACHINE

We can see from the above that the requirements of the tool machine which machines the typical surfaces of the tools suitable for the production of the screw surfaces with constant lead as well as their kinematic pair overstep the recent technical and controlling solution.

5.1. Kinematic requirements

- the essential requirement is to create a relative screw motion between the main drive and the work spindle.
- in case of screw surface of more starts the pitch for the set of start to be accurately realizable.
- The motions needed for back- off of the tool lateral and back surfaces to be provided (the rate , the track and the pitch of the back-off) . It means only radial back-off on the most machine.
- it should be suitable for machining both cylindrical and conical helicoid surfaces, so the objective table should be adjusted in certain angle or this possibility should be provided kinematically.
- The wheel controlling for the forming the wheel profile belonging to the given wheel diameter should be provided which should be able to be performed in certain periods independently of the machining cycle too.
- It sholud be suitable for automatic performing of more cycles with smaller lifting out between the individual cycles (at running back) and at the end of the cycle with larger lifting out (at withdrawal from the thread surface).
- the revolution of the work and the main spindle hould be variable infinitely which is required because of the wheel controlling during the machining and because of the roughing and finishing.

All of these requirements determine the kinematic construction of the machine and the formation of the (hydraulic) unit controlling motions.

5.2. Controlling requirements

In the respects of the controlling requirements we should consider that increasing the number of the shafts simultaneously controlled the cost of the controlling rises progresively (for example the cost of a five- axes controlling is many times greater than a $3 + 2$ axes controlling)

Therefore the appropriate performing of the function analysis may cut the controlling costs to a large extent.

Essentially we should consider the technical, manufacturing geometrical and manufacturing technological requirements.

An universal thread grinding machine should be suitable for machining a helicoid surface shown in fig.1. For that the following functions must be controlled:

- the revolution of the work spindle, probably against coordinates or time
- the controling of the motion of the grinding wheel house moving radial of the work axis
- the horizontal turning of the grinding wheel house around a given axis
- the horizontal shift of the wheel controller
- the vertical shift of the wheel controller

By means of the controlling these five axes the screw surface types (spiroid, globoid) can be ground.

For grinding the screw surface with changing lead it would be practical to control the longitudinal motion of the work table too.

Regarding the functins this five - axes controlling can be dissolved to the following:

- controlling of 3 axes for the kinematic formation of the screw surface development
- controlling of 2 axes for the adjustment of the wheel profile.

All of the further functions which are requirements for production of every screw surfaces can be accomplished with simple controlling and operation tasks.

6. DEVELOPMENT AND WORKING OUT OF A POTENTIAL SOLUTION

Considering the kinematic and controlling requirements listed above we are working on the development of a universal thread grinding machine.

We also had to reconstruct the block sheme, the structure of the system over the construction modifications the patent of which is under way (Fig. 5.).

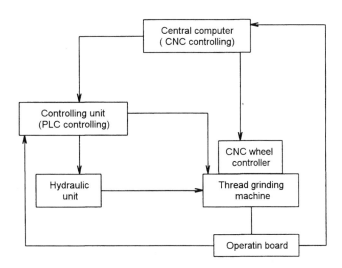

Fig. 5. Developed structure

We managed to solve partially one part of the controlling tasks. The base functions and the cycles were performed with PLC controlling.

The term of the geometrically accurate machining is the correct wheel profile for which there is an accepted patent technically built in the form of CNC wheel controlling machine installed with suitable softwares. We will not discuss it in details here. After constructional developing of the functions listed at the controlling tasks this universal thread grinding machine will bw suitable for the geometrically accurate machining of the screw surfaces shown in fig.1. with working out the software system supporting the controlling.

7. GEOMETRICAL QUALIFICATION (MEASUREMENT) OF CYLINDRICAL WORMS

The traditional controlling method of worms regards the helical surface control as a two dimensional problem. The helical surface, however, is a 3D form that is why we have to regard, it as a 3D task.
The measuring program of inspection on a coordinate measuring machine of general purpose has different requirements even theoretically, than software of coordinate measuring machine of special form and set-up.
The advance of coordinate measurement technique is caused by the fact that by the introduction of CIM systems including CAD/CAM and CAQ systems connected to the technological process planning the need arises for quick, precise and automated inspection methods of form surfaces.
In consequence of the advance of flexible manufacturing systems and CIM systems as well as the propagation of 3D measuring machines, there is increasing demand for the automated geometrical qualification of helicoid surfaces. The geometrical inspection and qualification of the most widely used cylindrical and conical helicoid surfaces - having constant pitch - on 3D coordinate measuring machine are an indispensable condition of the automated production of possible versions (various types, geometrical parameters) of helicoid surfaces.

The automated quality assurance incorporated in up-to-date manufacturing systems gives rise to a great deal of difficulties in respect of helicoid surfaces:

- there is an inverse proportionality between the accuracy of qualification and the time of data acquisition. So it is necessary to choose a method where the time of data acquisition is smaller than the transit time of the production of a cycle (because of the quick interference), however its accuracy assures the required tolerances,
- it would be advantageous not to make significant alterations in the working area and program of the measuring machine if there are changes in the types or/and dimensions of the products,
- the method of qualification has to be technology-oriented, on the one hand because of the possibility of alterations and on the other, because of the exploration of actual production errors (in case of helicoid surfaces the error of one parameter can cause the error of several other parameters, because they are closely related to one another).

In order to satisfy the requirements mentioned above it is necessary to have a measuring program which is general and where the appropriate changing of the different parameters means the different variations.

The geometrical dimensions and tolerances received on this way can be evaluated basically on 3D measuring machines since the helical surfaces are typically 3D surfaces. The foregoing conventional qualifications were carried out in a certain typical plane (axis plane, normal plane, inclined cylinder contact plane). The checking on 3D coordinate measuring machine provides the determination of the deviations in normal vector direction of the helical surface and on the other hand the uncovering of geometrical and kinematical errors of machining.
Thus oppositely to the foregoing conventional helical surface measuring it is applicable not only for the uncovering of failures defined in the different planes but it can provide the determination of the manufacturing errors (tool profile, tool-wearing, kinematics of the machine, alignment error) with the adequate processing of measuring data.

There are several methods both for inclusion and evaluation of measurement data (e.g. scanning, surface-regression, etc.). These are general-purpose methods, which do not utilize the advantage of the fact that the theoretical equation of the measured surface is known.
In this way it is necessary to take a great number of points, which makes the method very time-consuming. Using our method the number of measured points can be significantly reduced in addition to maintaining the measurement and evaluation accuracy.
After giving the number of measuring points the operator performing the measurement touches the helical surface „n" times with the feeler in the direction of the normal vectro by means of a handle. The distance between the points (of number „n") is to be the same.

After every touch the memory of the measuring machine stores the coordinates of the centre of the spherical feeler in the worm's own coordinate system. This method can be improved by setting two measuring points on the outer surface of the first and last teeth and the machine automatically measures the other points on the basis of the given parameters.
Given the two-parameter equations of the theoretical helical surfaces of different worm types, which are generally:

$$\vec{r}_{1F} = \begin{bmatrix} -B_1\sin(\vartheta) + r\cos(\vartheta) \\ B_1\cos(\vartheta) + r\sin(\vartheta) \\ u\sin(a_b) + p_a\vartheta \\ 1 \end{bmatrix} \tag{1}$$

This universal form gives:

- in the case of case of r = 0 Archimedian,
- in the case of $r = r_a = p_a ctg\beta - p_t > 0$ involute,
- in the case of $-r_a < r = r_0 < 0$ convolute screw surface.

In the case of $\delta_1 = 0$ (pitch angle) in all three instance the appropiate type of cylindrical worm is obtained as a result.

As the normal vector passes through the centre given at $\bar{r}_t$ (x, y, z) coordinates of feeler, the contact point of the theoretical helical surface can be determined. It is the common point of the line of n direction vector, passing through the centre of the feeler and the theoretical helical surface, i.e. the solution of these two equations

$$\left.\begin{aligned} \bar{r}_{lF}\left(\bar{r}_t - \bar{r}_{lF}\right) = 0 \\ \bar{r}_{lF} = \bar{r}_{lF}\left(\eta, \vartheta\right) \end{aligned}\right\} \qquad (2)$$

The set of equations is transcendent regarding the ϑ parameter, but it can be solved by computer algorithm (e.g. Newton-Raphson iteration).

The actual contact point is in the direction of the normal vector determined above and at a distance equal with the radius of the spherical feeler (r) from the centre of the feeler. Correcting the x, y, z coordinates of the centre of the feeler by the values Δx, Δy, Δz, the coordinates of a dual contact point are obtained

$$\left.\begin{aligned} x_m = x + \Delta x \\ y_m = y + \Delta y \\ z_m = z + \Delta z \end{aligned}\right\} \qquad (3)$$

$$\text{where} \quad \Delta x = \frac{n_x}{|n|}\, r; \qquad \Delta y = \frac{n_y}{|n|}\, r; \qquad \Delta z = \frac{n_z}{|n|}\, r; \qquad (4)$$

From the aspect of measurement technique these coordinates are only of approximate value, as the determination of the normal vector is performed with the initial parameters of the theoretical helical surface. The determination of the actual points needs correction because the parameters of the actual helical surface differ from the theoretical values.

The computer program adequate to the requirements above has been finished and it can carry out geometrical qualification according to the wishes. The analysis and comparison of these values to the values defined in the design give the basis of the feedback which modifies the manufacturing process and the setting values in order to minimise the deviations.
According to these the errors which can be evaluate on the conventional way can be originated to the following reasons:
- Pitch error: the kinematic error of the machine-tool or the error of the change gears
- Profile imperfection: the imperfection of the profile or alignment of the tool
- Axial pitch error: error of the dividing device of the machine-tool (in case of multiple start)

All these errors can be originated to the construction alignment and rigidity errors of the elements participating in the manufacturing process and these errors can be corrected in the function of the measured values.
The constant errors can be filtered out and ceased after the production of a couple of pieces and the variable errors (for example: tool wearing) can be corrected after the reach of the adequate level. Since the assembly is only manual thus the qualification of the dimensions and position error of the gearbox housing and the bearing positions is sufficient with the consideration of the tolerances determined during the simulation.

8. CONCLUSIONS

Our paper had shown the structure of a general system and some considerations and methods for the realization of some elements. subsystems. Some element of the system we have produced but the rest of the elements and their connection into the system is done nowadays as our main research subject. We think that both the theoretical basis and methods, and the up-todate equipment being developed for the realization, increase the productivity and the quality of the final product.

9. REFERENCES

1. I. Dudas, 1991, „Manufacturing of Helicoid Surfaces in CAD/CAM System", *Intenational Conference on Motion and Power Transmission, MPT'91, November 23-26 Hiroshima, Japan*

2. F. L. Litvin : „Gear Geometry and Applied Theory" , *PTR Prentice hall, Englewood Cliffs, New Jersey, 1994.*

3. D. Su, K. Jambunatthan, „A prototype knowledge-based integrated system for power transmission design ,in Advancement of Intelligen Production", *Eiji Usui (ed.) Elsevier Science B.V., 1994 pp. 45-50.*

4. I. Dudás, K. Bányai, „Manufacturing of helical surfaces in flexible production system', proceedings", *3rd International Conference on Automation, Robotics and Computer Vision, Singapore, 8-11. November, 1994, pp. 1036-1038.*

5. I. Dudás, Gy. Varga, K. Bányai, „Bearing Pattern Localization of Gearing", *International Conference of Gears, Dresden, Germany, 1996, pp. 427-441.*

6. I. Dudás, K. Bányai : „Simulational Analysis of the Effects of the Production Errors in Case of Worm Driving Pairs", *MTM '97 Conference, Tianjin, China, 3-6. Jul. 1997, pp: 620 - 624.*

7. I. Dudás, Zs. Bajáky : „Three Dimensional Measurement and Evaluation of Worms", *MTM'97, International Conference on Mechanical Transmissions and mechanisms, Tianjin, China, 1997 július 1-4.*

8. D. Su, I. Dudás : „Development of an intelligent Integrated System approach for design and Manufacture of worm gears", *9th International Conference on Tools', September 3-5. 1996. Miskolc, Hungary*

9. G. Niemann, H. Winter : „Maschinenelemente", *Band III. Springer Verlag, Berlin - Heidelberg - New York - Tokyo, 1983.*

10. M. Weck, Ch. Escher, K. Beulker : „Simulation and Optimization of Generation of Tooth Flank Modifications", *International Conference on Gears, 22-24 April, 1996 Dresden, Germany, pp. 883-895.*

11. F. L. Litvin, R. F. Handschuh : „Computerized Densing and Analysis of Face-milled, Uniform Tooth Heigt Spiral Bevel Gear Drives", *7th Internacional Power Transmission and Gearing Conferenc, San Diego, 1996, . pp. 485-492.*

12. G. D. Bibel , R. F. Handschuh : „Meshing of The Spiral Bevel Gearset with 3D Finite Element Analysis", *7th Internacional Power Transmission and Gearing Conferenc, San Diego, 1996, . pp. 703-708.*

Part B

MECHATRONICS

Introduction

Today's most advanced technological products are complicated, interdisciplinary endeavors. Mechanical, electrical, and computer control components are synergistically integrated to realize new functionalities that are not otherwise possible. In the past, most of the resources required to develop such a system were expended within the boundaries of the component technologies. Relatively little integration was required and each integration effort was a customized solution. The complexity of interdisciplinary systems has grown to a point where a significant portion of the total project resources are required solely for integration activities. The study of methodologies for integrating disparate disciplines has come to be known as mechatronics.

This is the first year that the Intelligent Systems and Advanced Manufacturing Symposium has incorporated a conference dedicated to mechatronics. As can be seen by the quality of the papers presented, this year's conference successfully introduced mechatronics technology into the SPIE ISAM forum. Next year, the focus of the conference will be more narrowly defined in the area of mechatronics for agile manufacturing. It is our hope that as the importance of mechatronics grows, the conference will grow as well.

Patrick F. Muir

SESSION 6

Mechatronics I

Analysis, Design and Control of a Novel, Optically-Commutated Adjustable-Speed Motor

Wyatt Newman, Ivan Risch, Yuandao Zhang, Steven Garverick, Michael Inerfield
Electrical Engineering and Computer Science Dept.
Case Western Reserve University, Cleveland, OH 44106

ABSTRACT

This paper describes the analysis, design and control of a novel, single-phase motor with a unique behavior resulting from the use of rotating power electronics mounted to the motor armature. Coils on the armature are selectively shorted by power MOSFET's which rotate with the armature, and torque is produced by interaction between currents induced in the shorted coils and the magnetic field produced by a stationary field coil. Control is limited to the timing of which armature coils are to be shorted as a function of dynamic conditions. Imposition of a choice of which coils to short is performed by powering stationary LED's, which are detected by rotating photodetectors. By illuminating stationary LED's according to some algorithm as a function of armature speed and angle, it is possible to modulate torque production and obtain torque or speed control, using only single-phase ac power and without the use of brushes or permanent magnets. An electro-mechanical model for this type of motor is presented and validated with respect to experimentation. The results show promise for achieving low-cost, adjustable-speed drives using this novel method of rotating electronics, optical communications, and computed commutation.

Keywords: Brushless motors, Electronic commutation, Adjustable-speed drives, Optical commutation, Single-phase motors, Universal motor, Dynamotor

1. INTRODUCTION

Advances in the capability and the economy of power semiconductors and microcontrollers inspires a re-examination of the traditional designs of electromagnetic drives. At present, there is a large technology gap between high-performance servo motor designs and common open-loop, single-phase drives. High-performance servo systems utilize power semiconductors, switching amplifiers, high-energy magnetic materials, precision angular feedback sensors and computer controls. Servo systems can achieve rapid and precise regulation of position, velocity or torque for applications such as numerically-controlled machining centers and robotics. At the other end of the spectrum are fractional horsepower drives designed to run open-loop from a single-phase sinusoidal voltage source (e.g., fan and pump motors powered directly by 60Hz, 120VAC). The latter drive is dramatically cheaper, but its lack of controllability makes it unsuitable for computer-controlled applications. Since computer control has become cheap and commonplace, there is a corresponding need for low-cost, controllable drives. In this paper, we describe a novel motor and controller design that shows promise for addressing this need.

Below, we describe our investigations in modeling and testing of a recently-patented novel motor concept, described in [1]. The approach is to modify a conventional, low-cost motor design by augmenting it with rotating power electronics [1, 2]. The rotating electronics include: power MOSFET's, a voltage rectifier and filter for supplying logic power to the rotating electronics, photodetectors that switch in response to illumination from the stationary frame, and digital logic. Stationary electronics include LED's that can illuminate the rotating photodetectors in selective angular ranges and a microcontroller to control the LED's. By enabling a given stationary LED, one or more of the photodetectors on the rotating electronics may be enabled, and these detectors enable corresponding MOSFET's on the rotating electronics. The MOSFET's are connected in pairs to coils on the armature, and by enabling a MOSFET pair, a corresponding armature coil is shorted. (All other armature coils remain open circuited). In this manner, it is possible to selectively short an arbitrary combination of armature coils by illuminating the associated phototransistors.

The above unusual arrangement offers the opportunity to alter the behavior of the motor by changing the pattern of LED illuminations as the motor runs. Note, though, that control of the motor is quite indirect. Illuminating a photodetector shorts a corresponding rotor winding—but deducing the instantaneous torque that results from such shorting is not trivial. Under the right circumstances, a shorted armature coil will build up an induced current, due to time-varying flux from the field coil, and this current can result in torque production in the desired direction. However, depending on the armature speed, the rotor angle, and the magnitude and time rate of change of the field current, it can also occur that little or no armature-coil current is induced, or that a current that is induced produces no torque, or that a current is induced but it produces a negative torque. It is thus important to develop a model for the electromechanical dynamics of this optically-commutated design in order to construct an appropriate algorithm for control.

In the following, we present the development of our model, compare simulations from our model to test data, and demonstrate that this unusual design is controllable and shows promise for realization of a low-cost adjustable-speed drive.

2. DESCRIPTION OF EXPERIMENTAL HARDWARE

The concept for this novel motor control approach is illustrated schematically in Fig 1, reprinted from [1]. A single field winding, driven by a sinusoidal voltage, produces a time-varying magnetic field that links multiple armature coils. The coils can be shorted selectively via optical switches, as suggested by the devices labeled "24".

If all of the coils were permanently shorted, the armature would be equivalent to that of a single-phase induction motor (though lacking the necessary means to enable a starting torque). In that case, behavior of the motor could be analyzed in familiar (e.g., as in [3,4]). However, the coils are only shorted on demand. If the coils are shorted as a pre-defined function of rotor angle (as suggested by Fig 1), this motor would seem to be similar to a brush-commutated motor, such as a universal series-wound motor [5]. An important difference, though, is that the currents in the armature coils selected by the brushes in a universal motor are driven directly by the external drive voltage, and the current in the field coil is equal to the current in the contacted armature coil. In contrast, the armature coils in the case of Fig 1 are merely shorted—not driven by a direct power source. Currents in the armature coils are thus produced solely by induction.

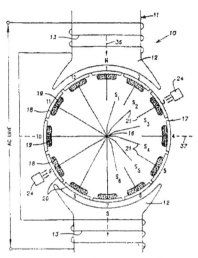

Fig 1: Schematic axial view of optically-commutated motor (reprinted from U.S. patent #5424625)

For our tests, two hardware implementations were utilized, both modifications of existing commercial universal motors. The first implementation was an "inverted" test rig, in which the armature was held stationary and the field was permitted to rotate. A slip ring was retrofit to enable supplying current to the rotating field winding. The original brush commutator of the universal motor was removed, and the leads for each of 8 coils wound on the armature were extended to be controlled by stationary electronics. The stationary electronics were restricted to shorting one or more armature coils, on demand under computer control, through MOSFET transistors. This test rig enabled us to experiment with alternative control schemes with only software changes. In addition, it allowed us to directly measure voltages in open-circuited armature coils, currents in close-circuited armature coils, and both voltage and current of the driven field coil. The rotating field housing was coupled via a pulley and toothed belt to a reactionless torque meter and a dc servo-motor load. This set-up provided static and dynamic torque vs speed measurements. Data from this inverted rig was used to tune and validate our simulation model of the electromechanical dynamics.

Our second implementation, shown in Fig 2, was a physical realization of the rotating electronics and optical commutation. Fig 2 shows a view of the wound armature, comprised of 4 coils wound in 16 slots. Four pairs of MOSFET coils were mounted on the circular circuit board on the left, and each MOSFET pair was wired to a respective armature coil. In addition, the MOSFET circuit board contained a voltage regulator, which was driven by voltages induced in the open-circuited armature coils and provided dc power for the rotating logic chips. The circular circuit board on the right contained the commutation logic (not visible from this view) and the photodetectors. Both circuit boards rotated with the armature. An additional circuit board contained stationary LED's mounted

Fig 2: Prototype armature; left circuit board comprises power switches and logic power supply; right board contains photodectors and logic

in distinct tangential sectors, and these LED's, which could be modulated under computer control, illuminated the rotating photodetectors across an axial gap.

3. MODELING AND SIMULATION

The electromagnetic dynamics of our motor can be described simply and compactly as:

$$v = Ri + \frac{d\lambda}{dt}$$ (Eqn 1)

Where v is a vector of voltages, i is a vector of currents, λ is a vector of flux linkages, and R is a matrix of resistances. For our inverted-motor apparatus, we have 9 coils to consider: one field coil and eight armature coils. Our vector of currents represents the 9 currents in our 9 coils, and the vector of voltages represents the 9 respective coil voltages. The vector of flux linkages can be expressed in terms of a matrix of mutual and self inductances, M, and the vector of currents, recognizing that all 81 terms of M are functions of armature angle, θ.

$$\lambda = Mi$$ (Eqn 2)

We note that the diagonal terms of the M matrix are the self inductances, and that the off-diagonal terms are symmetric: $M_{ij} = M_{ji}$. Further, by symmetry, the mutual inductances associated with armature coil "i" are identical to those associated with armature coil "j", but for a phase shift with respect to the dependance on rotor angle, θ. Substituting Eqn 2 into Eqn 1, we obtain the defining differential equation for currents:

$$v = Ri + Mdi/dt + (\partial M/\partial\theta)(d\theta/dt)i$$ (Eqn 3)

In Eqn 3, the inputs are the coil voltages, the rotor angle, and the rotor angular velocity, $d\theta/dt$. If we ignore magnetic saturation and hysteresis, Eqn 3 constitutes a ninth-order, non-homogeneous system of linear differential equations with variable coefficients[6]. One of the 9 voltages is the field voltage, which, for our intended operation, is 120Vac at 60Hz. The remaining voltages correspond to the 8 armature coils. For any armature coil that is shorted, we know that the corresponding voltage is 0. For any armature coil that is not shorted, we do not know the voltage *a priori*, but we do know that the corresponding coil current is 0. During a switching transient from one set of shorted coils to a new set of shorted coils, we must consider the fast magnetic coupling dynamics that induces rapid current changes. For a window of time in which there are no switching transients, however, Eqn 3 can be simplified. In our proposed mode of control, only one or two armature coils are shorted at any instant. For the case of one armature coil shorted, and for a window of time for which there are no coil switching transients, we can reduce our consideration to a second-order system comprised of the field-coil dynamics (subscript "f") and the dynamics of one armature coil (subscript "a"):

$$v_a = R_a i_a + L_a(\theta)\frac{di_a}{dt} + i_a\frac{dL_a(\theta)}{d\theta}\frac{d\theta}{dt} + M_{af}(\theta)\frac{di_f}{dt} + i_f\frac{dM_{af}(\theta)}{d\theta}\frac{d\theta}{dt}$$ (Eqn 4)

$$v_f = R_f i_f + L_f(\theta)\frac{di_f}{dt} + i_f\frac{dL_f(\theta)}{d\theta}\frac{d\theta}{dt} + M_{fa}(\theta)\frac{di_a}{dt} + i_a\frac{dM_{fa}(\theta)}{d\theta}\frac{d\theta}{dt}$$ (Eqn 5)

A prerequisite to modeling our full dynamics is that we correctly model the above simplified dynamics (coupled equations 4 and 5). As a first step, we identified the mutual inductance between the field coil and a chosen reference armature coil (defined as armature coil 1) as a function of angle. For this measurement, all armature coils were open circuited, a measured 60Hz sinusoidal current was driven through the field coil, and the induced voltage in the reference armature coil was measured for different armature angles. We defined a reference armature angle as the angle at which the mutual inductance between the field coil and armature coil 1 was zero, and we defined positive armature rotation as the direction in which the mutual inductance increased from 0 to positive values. Each armature coil had an identical mutual inductance function, but phase shifted by 22.5-deg for each successive armature coil. The resulting measurements of $M_{af}(\theta)$ revealed a trapezoidal mutual inductance profile. (Such a profile can be anticipated from a magnetic structure like that of Fig 1). Data from these measurements was used to define $M_{af}(\theta)$ in a look-up table within a numerical simulation of equations 4 and 5. The dynamic resistances (based on the in-phase component of voltage vs. current) of the field and armature coils were also measured and entered in the simulation.

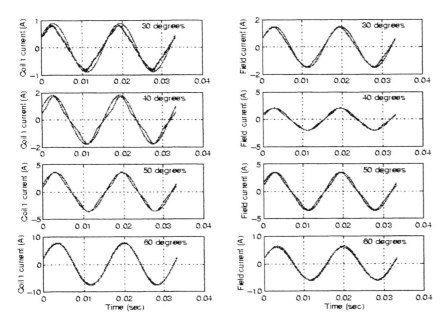

Based on this data, simulation of equations 4 and 5 was performed with the constraints $v_a = 0$ (shorted armature coil) and $d\theta/dt = 0$ (rotor stationary) at different fixed rotor angles. This condition (sinusoidal voltage excitation of the field coil and shorted armature coil) was tested experimentally and compared to the simulation results; the results are given in Fig 3. Given the close agreement, we can have confidence that the mutual inductance effects are well modeled.

Fig 3: Measured and simulated field and armature currents at different rotor angles

tabulated values for mutual inductance were analyzed to create additional look-up tables for the derivative of mutual inductance, $dM/d\theta$. (For our inverted test motor, the self inductances varied only slightly as a function of rotor angle, and thus these terms were dropped from Equations 4 and 5 in our simulation). Given a model of $dM/d\theta$, we next simulated and experimentally measured another simplified case: we imposed a regulated dc current through the field coil, permanently shorted our reference armature coil (with all other armature coils open), and externally rotated the armature at various fixed speeds. As a result of varying $M(\theta)$, the fixed field current induced a time-varying current in the shorted rotating armature coil. During times when the mutual inductance was increasing, the armature current decreased towards a negative asymptote; during times of decreasing mutual inductance, the armature current increased towards a positive asymptote; and during times of constant mutual inductance (the flat tops and bottoms of the trapezoidal mutual inductance profile), the armature current decayed towards zero. In all three cases, the approach towards the asymptotic value was determined by the L/R time constant. Our simulated and measured armature currents for this test are shown in Fig 4 for four different rotor speeds. The remarkably close agreement shown validates the precision of the model parameters excited by this test.

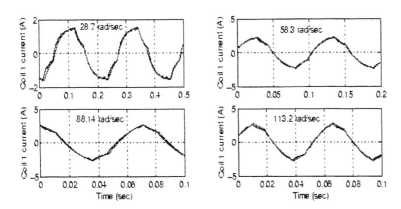

Fig 4: Measurements and simulation of back-EMF induced armature current and different speeds

While Figs 3 and 4 validate our modeling for a permanently shorted armature coil, we must extend our model to consider the effect of switching transients. In particular, it is desirable to short two armature coils simultaneously before open-circuiting any current-carrying armature coil. Ordinarily, open-circuiting a high-inductance, current-carrying coil results in large voltage transients that can lead to arcing or to breakdown and excessive heating in semiconductor switches. However, if a second shorted coil is coupled to the first coil through a high mutual inductance, open-circuiting the first coil results in a current being induced in the coupled coil, reducing the transient voltage and heating imposed on the first coil's switch. This transient is very fast, and it is hard to predict the efficiency of current recovery (i.e., the percentage of the original magnetic energy that is preserved by the second coil's response). Attempting to simulate this rapid transient would require an extremely short time step, and this would make the simulator impractical for examining longer-duration effects. Instead, we chose to obtain empirical data for the current recovery between consecutive armature coils due to switching and utilize this information within the simulator to bypass the fast transient. In operation, our simulator halts its normal progress when a switch is commanded, it rearranges the state variables (currents in each of the coils) based on the measured current recovery efficiency, then resumes the simulation with a new set of shorted armature coils with a new set of initial conditions. This approach permits both accurate and efficient simulation.

Fig 5 shows our simulation and measurement results with switching transients. Again, a regulated, fixed field current was imposed and various fixed rotor speeds were enforced, but for this case each armature coil was shorted for a range of 31.5 deg centered about 49 deg and 229 deg with respect to each coil's zero mutual-inductance angle. (Each coil was enabled twice per revolution, resulting in a sequence of a 13.5 deg range over which a single coil was enabled, followed by a range of 9 degrees over which two neighboring armature coils were enabled, repeated for all 8 coils twice per revolution).

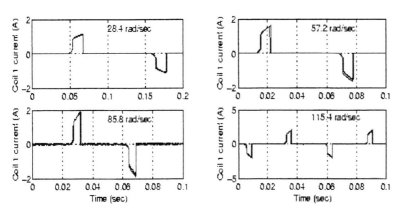

Fig 5: Measured and simulated armature currents with commutation at constant speed and dc field current

Fig 5 shows the current transients (both simulated and experimental) for armature coil 1 for four different rotor speeds. Initially when coil 1 was shorted, the current begab to rise from zero due to back-EMF. After 9 degrees of rotation, coil 8 was switched off, and coil 1 inherited most of the current that was formerly carried by coil 8, resulting in an apparent step change in coil-1's current. After this fast transient, coil-1's current continued to rise due to back-EMF. After 31.5 deg of rotation, coil 1 was open-circuited, and its current dropped rapidly (seemingly instantaneously) to zero. During this transient, coil 2 was shorted, inheriting much of the current formerly carried by coil 1, etc. Agreement between the simulation and the measurements was very close; the difference in barely discernable in the measurements vs simulations superimposed in Fig 5. This remarkable agreement validates our simulation approach.

It should be noted that the currents induced in the experiment of Fig 5 correspond to braking only. If a dc current were enforced through the field coil and if all armature coils were permanently shorted, then the motor would act as a dynamic brake, dissipating energy in the armature coils while absorbing mechanical power from the motor shaft. To make this device a motor instead of a brake, armature currents must be induced by a time-varying field current, and only those armature coils which would produce positive output power should be enabled. This effect can be visualized heuristically by considering the quasi-static torques that would result from shorting one armature coil while driving the field with an ac source. Time-varying field currents would induce currents in the shorted armature coil, provided the rotor angle were such that the mutual inductance were non-zero. The interaction between the field and armature currents, i_f and i_a, respectively, produces a torque, τ, which can be expressed as:

$$\tau = i_a i_f \partial M_{af} / \partial \theta \qquad \text{(Eqn 6)}$$

For quasi-static operation, we can ignore the effects of back-EMF and armature coil switching effects. In that case, a shorted armature coil can be viewed as a shorted secondary of a transformer. For a positive mutual inductance between the field and the shorted armature coil, the armature current response to a sinusoidal field current would be a sinusoid that is (ideally) 180-deg out of phase and with a magnitude proportional to the field current and the turns ratio. (The 180-deg shift results from the armature current tending to oppose the change in linked flux due to the varying field current). Consequently, for an instant in which the field current is positive and the mutual inductance is positive, the induced armature current would be negative.

By our definition, positive armature angles (between 0 and +180 deg) correspond to positive mutual inductances. Further, in the range −70 deg to +70 deg, the slope of the mutual inductance is positive. As a result, the quasi-static torque produced in the range 0 to 70 deg is negative, and the torque produced in the range −70deg to 0 deg is positive. The zero-degree angle is an attractive equilibrium point for shorted coil 1. By selectively shorting armature coils, one can always assure that only torques in the desired direction are produced, resulting in bi-directional motion, as well as either power output or power absorption, as desired.

Fig 6 shows the measured and simulated torque output for quasi-static operation. A sinusoidal field voltage was applied, and armature coils were selectively shorted for a range of 30.3 deg, each centered about 59 deg and 229 deg with respect to each coil's zero-mutual-inductance angle. Since the currents were time varying at 60 Hz, the resulting torques pulsated at 120 Hz. Each simulation point and each measured data point shown corresponds to the time-averaged torque at each measured armature angle. Agreement between the measured torque-angle profile and the predicted torque-angle profile is very good—within the experimental error due to friction and drive-belt slippage.

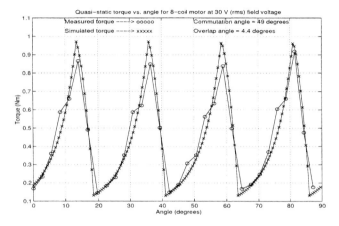

Fig 6: Plots of measured and simulated average quasi-static torque at 49 degrees commutation angle

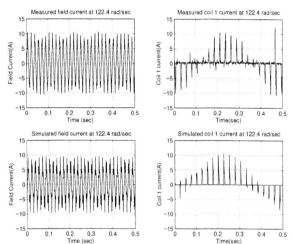

Fig 7: Measured and simulated coil-1 currents at 122 rad/sec

Finally, our simulation model of the motor dynamics was tested with full complexity. The field coil was excited with a 60Hz sinusoidal voltage and the armature coils were shorted over a range of 31.5 deg centered about 49 deg and 229 deg with respect to each coil's zero mutual-inductance angle. Figure 7 shows the simulated and measured field and armature currents for the case of a rotation of 122.4 rad/sec. The motor velocity was regulated by a coupled servo motor, which, in this case, acted as a power absorber while regulating speed. Since the frequency of armature commutation was not synchronous with the frequency of the field coil voltage excitation, the resulting current waveforms exhibited a beat phenomenon. Although the resulting waveforms were highly complex, the simulator clearly incorporated all of the necessary detail for predicting the dynamics.

The torque produced by this motor was time varying and highly complex (pulsating at 120Hz, in addition to other modulation effects). A prediction of the torque was computed from the simulation by computing the instantaneous field and armature currents times the corresponding slope of mutual inductance at the respective rotor angle, as per Eqn 6, and averaging this pulsating result over time. Relative to measured performance, the predictions for various speeds typically overestimated the torque by 10 to 20% (though some of this error may be attributable to bearing friction). Considering the complexity of the dynamics, this level of accuracy was considered to be highly successful.

Using our simulator, we were able to explore the torque-speed possibilities for this novel motor design as a function of commutation angle. The best condition found for optimizing average torque occurred (for our mutual inductance profile) when two armature coils were shorted at all times (i.e., each coil shorted over a sector of 45 deg, enabled twice per cycle). The optimal commutation angle for quasi-static torque production (e.g. starting torque) was near 49 deg. However, at higher speeds it was desirable to advance the commutation angle (switch earlier) to extend the torque-speed curve. (For further details, see [2]).

4. ADJUSTABLE SPEED CONTROL EXPERIMENTS

Having analyzed the electromechanical dynamics of our optically-commutated, selectively-shorted armature coil motor, we constructed a test motor with rotating electronics. This motor was evaluated both in terms of quasi-static torque and under control of a novel speed control algorithm. The electronics shown in Fig 2 were mounted on a 4-coil rotor. The rotor was wound with 152 turns per coil, distributed among four adjacent slot pairs. Windings for coils 1 and 3 were non-overlapping, and these windings were distributed such that all slots contained 38 turns. Coils 2 and 4 were wound on top of coils 1 and 3,

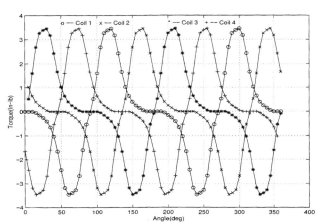

Fig 8: Quasi-static torque profiles for 4-coil, skewed-slot test motor with one armature coil shorted per profile

adding an additional 38 turns to every armature slot, and resulting in 50% overlap between each pair of adjacent armature coils. In addition, it was observed that the axial slots of the rotor, as shown in Fig 2, resulted in significant torque-angle distortion due to reluctance torques developed between the edges of the field poles and the rotor slots. To eliminate this undesirable effect, the rotor was modified to introduce a skew of 22.5 degrees over the length of the rotor (resulting in spiral rather than axial armature slots). The resulting design was tested with ac field voltage excitation with one armature coil shorted at a time. The device produced a torque as a function of angle as shown in Fig 8. With coil 1 shorted, the armature was attracted to stable poses of 0-deg and 180 deg. (Note, though, that the torsional stiffness about these stable poses was quite low). Coil 2 had stable poses of 45 deg and 225 deg, coil 3 had stable poses of 90 deg and 270 deg, and coil 4 had stable poses of 135 deg and 315 deg.

For coil 1 (marked with "o"), peak positive torque production occurred at angles of 120 deg and 300 deg, and negative peak torque production was at 60 deg and 240 deg. Useful positive torque was produced over nearly the entire range from 90 to 180 deg, and from 270 to 0 deg. With coil 2 shorted, positive torque was produced over the ranges -45 deg to +45 deg and 135 deg to 225 deg. Similarly, coils 3 and 4 produced positive torques, when shorted, over 90-deg ranges, phase shifted by an additional 45-deg each. Coil 1 had the strongest positive torque production of the 4 coils over the ranges from 127 deg to 172 deg and from 307 to 352 deg. Similarly, coils 2, 3 and 4 each had 2, 45-deg ranges per revolution in which they produced the highest positive torque. (A complementary set of ranges applied to maximum negative torque production). We define the

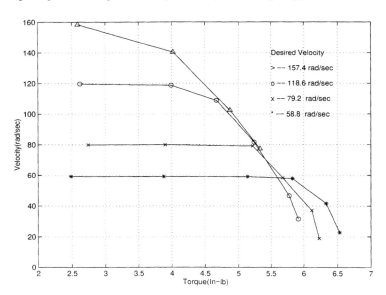

Fig 9: Measured velocity vs. torque load for the optically commutated motor with speed control

commutation angle as the center of the range of angles over which a coil is shorted. Based on the quasi-static measurements, the best 45-deg range over which to short a coil to maximize positive torque is centered on a commutation angle 31 deg in advance of the coil's stable equilibrium angles (for this example motor). For maximum negative torque production, the optimal commutation angle is +31 deg with respect to the equilibrium angles.

Using stationary LED's and rotating photodetectors, one can control the MOSFET's such that the armature coil with maximum torque production is always shorted. LED markers were installed on the stationary circuit board such that they illuminated the rotating photodetectors over the 45-deg angular ranges corresponding to the peak torque production of each coil. (An additional set could be illuminated over the optimal angular ranges for negative torque production).

When these LED's were continuously illuminated, the motor produced maximum average torque (correspondingly, maximum negative torque for the second set of LED's), at least at lower speeds. (At higher speeds, it was found that torque production was enhanced by advancing the commutation angle). Under this mode of control (fixed-angle commutation), the motor was a torquer, and its speed was dependent on its load. It is clear from Fig 8, however, that it is possible to choose alternative commutation angles to vary the torque production smoothly from maximum positive to maximum negative. This property can be exploited to achieve speed control.

A simple speed-control algorithm was constructed and tested. Measured results of the speed-controlled motor using optical commutation are given in Fig 9. For those speed commands for which the motor was capable of exerting the required load torque, the measured speed was nearly identical to the desired speed, demonstrating success of the speed control algorithm. When the combination of desired speed and torque exceeded the motor's capability, the motor defaulted to exerting the maximum torque possible, though inevitably resulting in a lower speed than desired (identical to the behavior of fixed-angle commutation).

Our results in speed control are still preliminary, but encouraging. One limitation observed was that the algorithm we invoked had poor transient response. Step changes in the torque load or step changes in the speed command resulted in oscillations that persisted for more than 10 seconds. In continuing work, we are examining alternative speed-control algorithms implemented in a low-cost microcontroller to achieve acceptable dynamic behavior. If successful, this design concept will lead to the realization of a new type of brushless adjustable-speed drive at significantly lower cost than current adjustable-speed drives.

5. SUMMARY AND FUTURE WORK

This paper has presented a detailed analysis of a novel motor design. The electromechanical dynamics are complex, but our simulations have demonstrated that we have correctly identified the important terms of the defining differential equations. Our simulations and our experiments have demonstrated that it is possible to achieve net positive torque from the unusual design described. The chief advantage to the design presented here is that torque or speed control can be achieved using a small number of low-cost components, offering the potential to create a low-cost, single-phase adjustable-speed drive.

While we have demonstrated feasibility of the proposed motor design, both in simulation and in prototype evaluations, the design is not yet optimized. The optimal copper distribution in the field and coil windings has not been determined. Also, more sophisticated speed control algorithms need to be developed for this motor. The speed controller should take advantage of the improved torque that can be obtained at higher speeds by advancing the commutation angle. In addition, better transient dynamics of the speed controller must be achieved. However, control algorithm changes will be achievable within the software of our microcontroller.

At present, alternative non-contact means of communication between the stationary frame and the rotating electronics are being explored, offering the possibility of greater flexibility of control algorithms implementations. In addition, the rotating electronic components are being replaced with surface-mount devices, where possible, reducing the size of the rotating electronics. Finally, we are extending the analysis to consideration of 3-phase motor designs, which should enable scaling up this low-cost adjustable-speed drive approach to higher-powered motors.

6. ACKNOWLEDGMENTS

This work was supported by the Cleveland Advanced Manufacturing Program (CAMP, Inc.) and by Dynamotors, Inc. The generous support of active involvement of Dynamotors president and founder, William Jones, is recognized and gratefully acknowledged.

7. REFERENCES

1) L. Haner, U.S. patent # 5,424,625.
2) I. P. Risch, "*Simulation Development for Design and Control of a Novel Single-Phase, Brushless Motor*", M.S. thesis, Case Western Reserve University, Dept. of Electrical Engineering and Applied Physics, August 1998.
3) H. H. Woodson and J. R. Melcher, *Electromechanical Dynamics*, Wiley & Sons, New York, 1968, Ch 4.
4) G. R. Slemon and A. Straughen, *Electric Machines*, Addison-Wesley, Reading, 1980, Ch10.
5) P. C. Sen. *Principles of Electric Machines and Power Electronics*. Wiley & Sons, Inc., New York, 1997, pg 409.
6) W. E. Boyce and R. C. DiPrima. *Elementary Differential Equations and Boundary Value Problems*. John Wiley & Sons, Inc., New York, 1969, pg 317.

Control of Ultra-High Precision Magnetic Leadscrew Using Recurrent Neural Networks

Timothy Chang[a], Tony Wong[a], Bhaskar Dani[a], Zhiming Ji[b], Mike Shimanovich[c], Reggie Caudill[c]

[a]Department of Electrical & Computer Engineering, NJIT, Newark, NJ 07102, USA

[b]Department of Mechanical Engineering, NJIT, Newark, NJ 07102, USA

[c]Department of Industrial & Manufacturing Engineering, NJIT, Newark, NJ 07102, USA

ABSTRACT

In this work, the problem of vibration control for a contactless magnetic leadscrew system is considered. A contactless drive system is a magnetic nut/leadscrew and air bearing assembly that operates on the principle of magnetic/aerodynamic suspension to position a load with high accuracy. However, the dynamics of such system is lightly damped, load dependent, and generally difficult to stabilize by conventional linear controllers. Therefore, the technique of recurrent neural network is applied to separate the oscillatory signals so that passband shaping can be carried out to regulate plant dynamics and to reject disturbances. This controller possesses a modular structure and is easy to implement. Experimental results also confirm the vibration suppression capabilities of this controller.

Keywords: Resonances, Vibration Control, Contactless Drive, Passband Control, recurrent neural network

1. INTRODUCTION

It is well recognized that ultra-high precision assembly/manufacturing (typically to 10 nanometers linear accuracy) is of strategic importance to industrial processes such as optoelectronics assembly, precision machining, and semiconductor manufacturing. In such processes, both the machine dynamics and operating environment are critical to the quality of the end product. "Hard" nonlinearities such as surface friction, backlash, and hysteresis are generally difficult to predict and compensate, resulting in significant degradation of the process performance.

To eliminate thread friction and wear and provide damping on the axis of motion, hydrostatic and aerostatic leadscrews are being used to replace conventional ball or roller leadscrews in manufacturing machines. For example, Landis Grinding Machines developed hydrostatic leadscrew for behind-the wheel dressing system with a claimed resolution of 10 nanometers; Satomi[1] studied the use of aerostatic leadscrew as positioning and guiding system for machine tools. These approaches use pressurized fluids to separate the meshed threads (i.e., mechanically coupled). On the other hand, magnetic coupling has also been investigated for achieving contactless drives. For example, Kikuchi[2] experimented with permanent magnet worm gear.

This paper presents an analysis and control of a contactless drive system Unlike the mechanically coupled leadscrew, the threads in this aerostatic leadscrew do not mesh into each other, but aligned through magnetic attraction instead. "Hard" nonlinearities are virtually eliminated. Magnetic coupling also makes it possible to produce finer pitch and achieve better resolution (currently about 10 nanometers). However, the lightly damped magnetic/aerostatic coupling results in a marginally stable open loop taht must be stabilized to eliminate ringing at the output.

Conventional approach towards the stabilization and regulation of loghtly damped system typically consists of two steps: 1) modelling and 2) controller synthesis where e.g. Kalman filter based stabilizers are designed. While such methodology may be effective in dealing with lumped parameter systems, application to the control of the magnetic leadscrew is generally inefficient owing to the uncertain plant dynamics and the excessively high control bandwidth requirements.

Controller design can be made more effective by recognizing two facts:

Send correspondence to Timothy Chang: changtn@admin.nit.edu

This work is supported, in part, by a NIST ATP Grant Number 70NANB5H1092 and the Multi-lifecycle Engineering and Research Center, NJIT

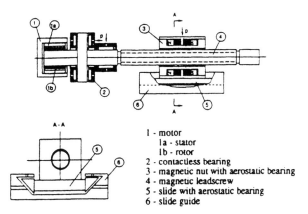

Figure 1. Experimental setup of the contactless drive system

1. Energy of a lightly damped flexible structure is mainly distributed in passbands that are band-limited.

2. Flexible systems typically have the following mathematical structure:

$$G(s) = \sum_i \frac{H_i s}{s^2 + 2\zeta_i \omega_i s + \omega_i^2} \tag{1}$$

where H_i is a position dependent gain (mode shape) and ζ_i, ω_i are, respectively, the damping factor and the natural frequency of the ith mode. In lightly damped systems, the natural frequency is approximately the same as the ringing frequency $\omega_i^d = \omega_i \sqrt{1 - \zeta_i^2}$ or resonant frequency $\omega_i^r = \omega_i \sqrt{1 - 2\zeta_i^2}$ that may be readily measured by either a frequency sweep or a white noise excitation test. The quantities ζ_i, H_i are, however, usually uncertain and cannot be determined accurately. The s term in (1) reflects the fact that rate sensors are used for pickoff measurement. It is absent if position sensor is used instead.

The organization of this paper is as follows: In Section 2, a dynamic model of the contactless drive system is derived. In Section 3, the properties of the open loop plant is analyzed. The recurrent neural network and passband shaping are introduced in Section 4. Controller design and experimental results are presented in Sections 5.

2. MODEL DEVELOPMENT

The contactless drive system is shown in Figure 1. This system consists of a contactless drive motor, a leadscrew, a magnetic nut, a thrust bearing, a slide, and a sensor measuring the absolute nut position.

The leadscrew and nut are made of soft magnetic material with fine rectangular thread, whose spacing is filled with non-magnetic epoxy. Permanent magnets are joined to the nut to supply energy to the magnetic circuit formed by leadscrew and nut pair. The operating point and the subsequent performance of the permanent magnets depend on the physical installation of the magnetic circuit and the magnetization of the magnetic circuit after assembly.

The aerostatic leadscrew system is supported on one end by a combination of externally pressurized air journal and thrust bearing. It is also supported by the nut, with the nut acting as an externally pressurized air journal bearing. The nut moves on a slide through a rectilinear air bearing.

A dynamic model of the motion in the in-feed (axial) direction has been derived in[3] and is sumarized below:

The absolute position of the shaft and the nut in the axial direction are defined as z_1 and z_2, respectively. The rotation of the shaft is defined as θ with the property that when $\theta = 0$, $z_1 = 0$ and $z_2 = 0$, the threads of the nut and the leadscrew are aligned. The linear motion of the nut caused by the rotation of the leadscrew shaft can be expressed as:

$$z_\theta = \frac{t_p}{2\pi}\theta$$

where t_p is the pitch of the leadscrew.

Let the tangential component of the total magnetic force on the shaft surface be given by F_t. The differential equation describing the rotation of the shaft is then derived as:

$$J\ddot{\theta} + b_\theta \dot{\theta} = T_m + F_t \cdot r \tag{2}$$

where r is defined as the radius of the leadscrew shaft which is driven by a contactless motor with torque T_m. The combined coefficient of viscous friction to the rotation in the air bearings is given by b_θ. The moment of inertia of the shaft about its axis be given by J.

The linear motion of the shaft in the axial direction is caused by the axial component of the total magnetic force, F_z, on the shaft, the restoring force F_B of thrust bearing, and viscous friction forces of the bearings. The differential equation for the motion of the leadscrew is therefore:

$$M_1 \ddot{z}_1 + b_1 \dot{z}_1 + F_B = F_z \tag{3}$$

where M_1 and b_1 are, respectively, the mass of the leadscrew and the viscous damping coefficient. Similarly, the linear motion of the nut in the axial direction is caused by the axial component of the total magnetic force, F_z, on the nut and it can be described by the following differential equation:

$$M_2 \ddot{z}_2 + b_2 (\dot{z}_2 - \frac{t_p}{2\pi}\dot{\theta} - \dot{z}_1) = -F_z + d \tag{4}$$

where M_2 and b_2 are, respectively, the mass of the nut (including a load) and the viscous damping coefficient. The disturbance d represents the effects of floor and motor vibrations.

The magnetic coupling force between the nut and screw shaft in the axial direction has been determined through experiments. It is observed that that two factors affect the magnetic force: 1) maximum break-through force F_{BT} and 2)the stiffness m_s and the magnetic force for axial coupling can be described by the following function:

$$\begin{aligned} F_z &= F_{BT} m_s \sin\left(2\pi \frac{z_2 - z_\theta - z_1}{t_p}\right), \quad 0 < (z_2 - z_\theta - z_1) < \frac{t_p}{2\pi m_s} \\ &= F_{BT}, \quad \frac{t_p}{2\pi m_s} < (z_2 - z_\theta - z_1) < \frac{t_p}{4} \end{aligned} \tag{5}$$

Equation (5) shows that the relative axial motion between the nut and the screw caused by external force tends to produce misalignment which in turn bends the magnetic flux lines at the gap and increases the magnetic resistance. Magnetic forces are automatically generated to restore the flux lines and the alignment of threads. The break through force F_{BT} occurs when the misalignment reaches $\frac{t_p}{4}$. If the external force exceeds F_{BT}, then the thread of one component will be pushed toward the spacing of the other component. In order to prevent thread jumping, the operating force should therefore be less than F_{BT}.

Similar to mechanically coupled leadscrews, the magnetic force in the tangential direction can be related to the magnetic force in the axial direction as:

$$F_t = \frac{t_p}{2\pi \cdot r} \cdot F_z \tag{6}$$

The stiffness and damping coefficients can be calculated based on the perturbed Reynolds equation with numerical method, or based on analogous electric circuits.[4]

The parameters of our experimental leadscrew as are follows: the inertia properties are $M_1 = 20kg$, $M_2 = 9kg$, and $J = 0.002kg \cdot m^2$; the shaft radius is $r = 12.5mm$, the thread pitch is $t_p = 0.1mm$, $F_{BT} = 30N$, $m_s = 4.1$, and the inlet air pressure for the bearings is $0.6MPa$. Based on the actual parameters, the restoring force of the thrust bearing is expressed as:

$$F_B = \frac{795.24}{10^{-5} - |z_1|} \cdot z_1 \tag{7}$$

3. MODEL ANALYSIS

For the purposes of analysis, a sixth order incremental model is derived by linearizing (2), (3), and (4) around $\theta = 0$, $z_1 = 0$, $z_2 = 0$:

$$T(s) = 2.5 \times 10^6 \frac{s^4 + 55s^3 + 4.3629 \times 10^6 s^2 + 2.1813 \times 10^8 s + 3.8919 \times 10^6}{s^6 + 155s^5 + 5.2271 \times 10^6 s^4 + 6.6300 \times 10^8 s^3 + 3.4344 \times 10^{12} s^2 + 1.7072 \times 10^{14} s - 9.9166 \times 10^7} \tag{8}$$

where $T(s)$ is the transfer from the force input at the nut to z_2. The open loop zeros are computed as $-2.5 \pm j2088$, -49.98, and -0.0178 while the open loop poles are: $-8.91 \pm j2110, -43.58 \pm j874.5, -50, 0$. The modes 0 and -50 are nearly cancelled, reflecting the fact that the leadscrew/motor dynamics are almost uncontrollable form the nut. The goal of control is to attentuate the nut resonance at 140Hz.

The bandpass nature of the resonant sections suggests the use of Hilbert transform to translate the energy bands down to baseband where bandwidth-conservative control system design[5] can be carried out for each resonant section. The control action for each section are naturally decoupled from each other in the steady-state due to the given frequency separation. Such decoupling gives rise to the modularity in the control system.

A definition of the Hilbert transform[6] is given in the next section, to be followed by a description of the plant structure.

4. PASSBAND CONTROL

4.1. Hilbert Transform

The Hilbert transform of a continuous time signal $x(t)$ is given by:

$$\hat{x}(t) = \frac{1}{\pi} \int_{-\infty}^{\infty} \frac{x(\tau)}{t - \tau} d\tau \tag{9}$$

and the inverse transform is given by:

$$x(t) = -\frac{1}{\pi} \int_{-\infty}^{\infty} \frac{\hat{x}(\tau)}{t - \tau} d\tau \tag{10}$$

where the integrals are understood to be Cauchy's principal values.

Denote $\hat{x}(t) = \mathcal{H}[x(t)]$ and $x(t) = \mathcal{H}^{-1}[\hat{x}(t)]$. The frequency domain relationship between $x(t)$ and $\hat{x}(t)$ is given by:

$$\hat{X}(\omega) = -j\,sgn(\omega)X(\omega) \tag{11}$$

where $\hat{X}(\omega)$ and $X(\omega)$ are, respectively, the Fourier transform of $\hat{x}(t)$ and $x(t)$.

4.2. Plant Definition

The uncertain plant is presently assumed to be linear, time-invariant, represented by the following state-space model:

$$\begin{aligned} \dot{x} &= Ax + Bu \\ z &= Cx \end{aligned} \tag{12}$$

Let the transfer function be given as:

$$G(s) = C(sI - A)^{-1}B = \sum_{i=1}^{N} G_i(s) \tag{13}$$

where

$$G_i(s) = \frac{c_{i1} + c_{i2}s}{s^2 + 2\zeta_i\omega_i s + \omega_i^2} \quad i = 1, 2, \ldots, N. \tag{14}$$

Denote $(x_i, \dot{x}_i)$ and y_i as the local state variables and the intermediate outputs of the ith subsystem:

$$Y_i(s) = G_i(s)U(s) \quad i = 1, 2, \ldots, N. \tag{15}$$

Since the open loop system is lightly damped, the subsystem output $y_i(t)$, $i = 1, 2, \ldots, N$ can be expressed as:

$$\begin{aligned} y_i(t) &= A_i(t)\sin(\omega_i^d t + \theta_i(t)) \\ &= y_i^c(t)\cos\omega_i^d t - y_i^s(t)\sin\omega_i^d t \quad i = 1, 2, \ldots, N \end{aligned} \tag{16}$$

where $y_i^c(t)$, $y_i^s(t) \in \Re$ are the low frequency in-phase and quadrature components of $y_i(t)$.

Let $amp(y_i(t)) = \sqrt{(y_i^c)^2 + (y_i^c)^2}$ be defined as the amplitude of $y_i(t)$ and let y_i^{ref} be defined as the reference signal. $amp(y_i(t))$ is obtained from $y_i(t)$ by standard demodulation techniques. Let the regulation error be defined as:

$$e_i(t) = amp(y_i(t)) - y_i^{ref} \quad i = 1, 2, \ldots, N \tag{17}$$

The control objectives are then

1. Stabilization: $amp(y_i(\infty)) = 0 \quad i = 1, 2, \ldots, N$

2. Regulation: $e_i(\infty) = 0 \quad i = 1, 2, \ldots, N$

3. Robustness: Properties 1) and 2) hold under small parametric perturbation in ζ_i, ω_i, c_{i1}, and c_{i2}, $i = 1, 2, \ldots, N$.

Condition 2 above clearly implies 1 (by setting y_i^{ref} to zero). It is also desired to achieve the control objectives with minimal plant information and control bandwidth.

Since it is observed that the energy content of the plant is distributed among the N passbands, each having a bandwidth of $2\zeta_i\omega_i$ and center frequency $\omega_i^r = \omega_i\sqrt{1 - 2\zeta_i^2}$. Therefore, Hilbert transform techniques can be applied to the N subsystems to obtain the equivalent low frequency models. A *bandwidth conservative* controller can then be synthesized without having to keep track of the carrier frequencies that may be too high for cost effective control systems design. It is noted that the conventional estimator based linear controllers do not take advantage of this property of lightly damped systems.

The next section introduce the low frequency equivalent models:

4.3. Low Frequency equivalent Model

Since the intermediate outputs of the subsystems are represented by:

$$y_i(t) = y_i^c(t) \cos \omega_i^d t - y_i^s(t) \sin \omega_i^d t \tag{18}$$

The section impulse response matrix $G_i(t) = \mathcal{L}^{-1} G_i(s)$, can also be decomposed into its low frequency in-phase and quadrature pair $G_i^c(t)$ and $G_i^s(t)$ in a similar manner:

$$G_i(t) = 2G_i^c(t) \cos \omega_i^d t - 2G_i^s(t) \sin \omega_i^d t \tag{19}$$

where the factor of 2 is introduced for notational convenience. It is obvious that $G_i^c(t)$ and $G_i^s(t)$ are stable iff $G_i(t)$ is stable. Furthermore,

$$
\begin{aligned}
y_i^c(t) &= G_i^c(t) * u_i^c(t) - G_i^s(t) * u_i^s(t) \\
y_i^s(t) &= G_i^s(t) * u_i^c(t) + G_i^c(t) * u_i^s(t)
\end{aligned}
$$

where $u_i^c(t), u_i^s(t)$ are the low frequency components of $u(t)$ aligned in the ith passband.

The baseband equivalent model of the ith subsystem is now obtained as:

$$Y_i^b(s) = G_i^b(s) U_i^b(s) \tag{20}$$

where

$$G_i^b(s) = \begin{bmatrix} G_i^c(s) & -G_i^s(s) \\ G_i^s(s) & G_i^c(s) \end{bmatrix} \tag{21}$$

and $Y_i^b = [Y_i^c \ Y_i^s]'$ and $U_i^b = [U_i^c \ U_i^s]'$. From (14), the low frequency equivalent model is:

$$G_i^b(s) = \frac{1}{2(s + \zeta_i \omega_i)} \begin{bmatrix} c_{i2} & \frac{c_{i2}\zeta_i \omega_i - c_{i1}}{\omega_i^d} \\ \frac{c_{i1} - c_{i2}\zeta_i \omega_i}{\omega_i^d} & c_{i2} \end{bmatrix} \quad i = 1, 2, \ldots, N \tag{22}$$

If the in-phase (cosine) component only is used for feedback control, i.e.

$$
\begin{aligned}
u_i^c(t) &= K y_i^c(t) \cos(\omega_i^d t) \\
&= K(c_{i2} \dot{x}_i + c_{i2} \zeta_i \omega_i x_i)
\end{aligned}
\tag{23}
$$

it can be readily shown that the closed loop eigenvalues are given by:

$$s^2 + (2\zeta_i \omega_i - K c_{i2})s + (\omega_i^2 - K c_{i2}\zeta_i \omega_i) = 0, \quad i = 1, 2, \ldots, N \tag{24}$$

Stabilization of the plant requires shifting all N poles into the left-half plane whereas regulation (sustained oscillation at a prescribed amplitude) requires precisely maintaining the poles at the $j\omega$-axis. In the next section, a nonlinear bandwidth conservative controller is synthesized based on the low frequency equivalent models.

4.4. Fixed Regulator Synthesis

Now since the in-phase component is used for feedback control (the quadrature component will also be utilized in later work), the low frequency equivalent transfer function for the ith subsystem is:

$$G_i^c(s) = \frac{c_{i2}}{2(s + \zeta_i \omega_i)} \tag{25}$$

A PI controller of the form

$$\epsilon_i (1 + \frac{K_i^I}{s}) \tag{26}$$

can be used. The resultant low frequency equivalent characteristics polynomials are:

$$s^2 + (\zeta_i \omega_i - \frac{c_{i2} \epsilon_i}{2})s - (\frac{c_{i2} \epsilon_i K_i^I}{2}) = 0 \quad i = 1, 2, \ldots, N \tag{27}$$

Thus knowledge of the sign of the high frequency gains c_{i2} is sufficient for robust stabilization of the closed loop system (parametric robustness of the regulator is evident from the above equation: the characteristics roots are always stable if ϵ_i is sufficiently large). Furthermore, regulation of mode oscillation amplitude is ensured by the integral control which supplies the *equivalent* closed loop transmission zero at the origin. For the magnetic leadscrew, the integral action can be set to zero.

In summary, the fixed, regulator consists of N identical modules, each comprising of: a demodulator, two multipliers (modulators), a gain adjust, a tuning gain ϵ_i, and a PI controller.

The successful functioning of the bandwidth conservative fixed regulator depends on the availability of the individual in-phase eigenfunctions $y_i^c(t)$ which are generally mixed at the output stage. An output mode separator is now applied to extract the $y_i^c(t)$'s by partial identification of the plant output matrix.

4.5. Neural Mode Separator (NMS)

The output mode separator originated in the communications community in applications such as interference cancellation [7], [8] and "blind separation" of signals [9],[10].

In the present work, statistical independence condition of the signals[9] is replaced by the following orthogonality condition:

$$\lim_{T \to \infty} \frac{1}{2T} \int_{-T}^{T} y_i(t) y_j(t) dt = m_{ij} \delta_{ij} \tag{28}$$

which is readily satisfied by the y_i's if ζ_i is sufficiently small.

The following algorithm[11] may be used to update the weights:

$$\dot{w}_{ij} = -\mu \alpha(\hat{y}_i) \beta(\hat{y}_j), \quad i \neq j, \ i,j \in [1, 2N] \tag{29}$$

The parameter μ represents the integral gain and $\alpha(\cdot)$, $\beta(\cdot)$ are odd, locally smooth functions. In particular, $\alpha(\cdot) = (\cdot)^3$ and $\beta(\cdot) = (\cdot)$ were proposed,[9] resulting in:

$$\dot{w}_{ij} = -\mu \hat{y}_i^3 \hat{y}_j, \quad i \neq j, \ i,j \in [1, 2N] \tag{30}$$

Expressing the equations in a matrix notation:

$$\begin{aligned} z &= Hy = Cx \\ \hat{y} &= WHy \end{aligned} \tag{31}$$

where

$$
W = \begin{bmatrix}
1 & w_{1,2} & w_{1,3} & \cdots & w_{1,2N} \\
w_{2,1} & 1 & w_{2,3} & \cdots & w_{2,2N} \\
\vdots & & & \cdots & \vdots \\
w_{2N,1} & w_{2N,2} & w_{2N,3} & \cdots & 1
\end{bmatrix},
\tag{32}
$$

the objective of the weight adaptation is to force $WH = P_N D$ where P_N is a general permutation matrix and D is a nonsingular diagonal matrix.

Convergence properties of the "general case" $(^7)$, $(^8)$ where the input signals are arbitrary, statistically independent signals is not known at present. However, for the case of the NMS whose inputs are eigenfunctions, the analysis is considerably simpler and tractable. This is because the integral equations (29) automatically filters out the high frequency components so that convergence analysis of the NMS reduces to analyzing the stability properties of a system with polynomial nonlinearities. The method of Lyapunov can then be applied to determine the stability of each equilibrium point and its corresponding domain of attraction.

To illustrate this point, consider the case of separating two eigenfunctions $\cos\omega_1 t$ and $\cos\omega_2 t$:

The input to the NMS are:

$$
\begin{aligned}
z_1 &= h_{11}\cos\omega_1 t + h_{12}\cos\omega_2 t \\
z_2 &= h_{21}\cos\omega_1 t + h_{22}\cos\omega_2 t
\end{aligned}
$$

then the weight updating equations are:

$$
\dot{w}_{ij} = \frac{3}{8}l_{ii}l_{ji}^3 + \frac{3}{4}l_{ij}l_{ji}^2 l_{jj} + \frac{3}{4}l_{ii}l_{ji}l_{jj}^2 + \frac{3}{8}l_{ij}l_{jj}^3 + \text{high frequency terms}
\tag{33}
$$

where $i \neq j, i,j \in [1,2]$, $l_{11} = h_{11} + w_{12}h_{21}$, $l_{12} = h_{12} + w_{12}h_{22}$, $l_{21} = h_{21} + w_{21}h_{11}$, and $l_{22} = h_{22} + w_{21}h_{12}$. The high frequency terms in (33) are negligible due to the lowpass nature of the integrators.

In this case, convergence of the NMS is governed by the stability of the NMS weight update equation (33) which has two stable equilibrium points:

$\begin{bmatrix} w_{12} \\ w_{21} \end{bmatrix} = \begin{bmatrix} -\frac{h_{12}}{h_{22}} \\ -\frac{h_{21}}{h_{11}} \end{bmatrix}$ and $\begin{bmatrix} w_{12} \\ w_{21} \end{bmatrix} = \begin{bmatrix} -\frac{h_{11}}{h_{21}} \\ -\frac{h_{22}}{h_{12}} \end{bmatrix}$ so that WH converges, respectively, to a diagonal matrix $\begin{bmatrix} h_{11} & 0 \\ 0 & h_{22} \end{bmatrix} \det H$ and a skew-diagonal matrix: $\begin{bmatrix} 0 & \frac{1}{h_{21}} \\ \frac{1}{h_{12}} & 0 \end{bmatrix} \det H^{-1}$

The *equivalent* high frequency gain is therefore $h_{22}\det H$ and $(h_{12}\det H)^{-1}$ respectively. Analysis of the stability in the large can be accommodated by constructing a suitable Lyapunov function (such as one with a quartic form) for each of the equilibrium points and its corresponding perturbed equations. In this way, the size of of domain of attraction can also be estimated. Analysis of the convergence and stability properties of the general (multiple input) case can be carried out in a similar manner.

Finally, it is noted that, for bandwidth conservation, it is possible to operate the NMS by undersampling the signals as the weight dynamics are basically determined by the baseband characteristics only.

4.6. Controller Structure

A block diagram showing the entire control system is given in Figure 2. Operation of the control system is presently based on two steps: 1) initial mode separation and 2) steady-state tracking.

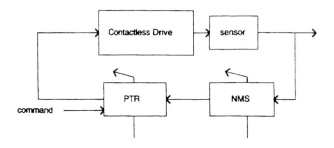

Figure 2. Structure of the neural network based controller

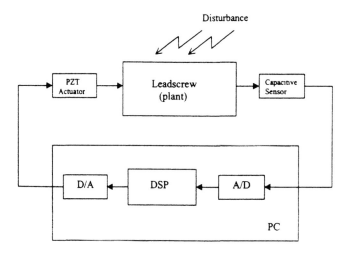

Figure 3. Experimental system

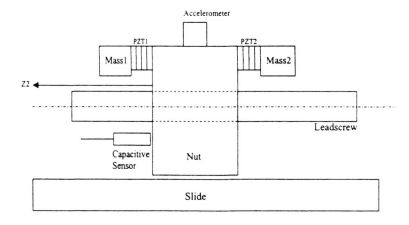

Figure 4. Sensor instrumentation at the nut

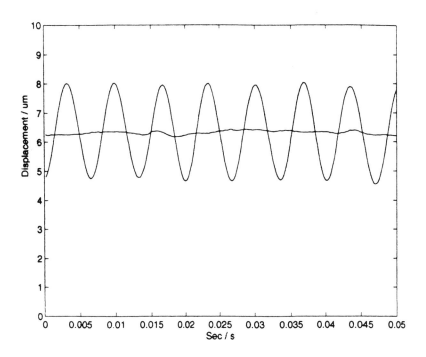

Figure 5. Nut Response: no load condition

5. EXPERIMENTAL RESULTS

A block diagram of the experimental system is shown in Figures 3 and 4:

The nut is instrumented with an accelerometer and a capacitance sensor that monitor $\ddot{z}_2$ and z_2 respectively. Two piezoelectric stacks, each with a 500g proof mass, are epoxied to the two ends of the nut. The piezoelectric stack on the left (PZT1) generates the disturbance motion while the stack on the right (PZT2) produces the control motion.

The experimental procedure consists of:

1. Inject a wideband random noise to PZT1 to excite the nut resonance.

2. Apply the neural network based control to stabilize the resonance.

3. Add an 1.5 kg load to the nut and re-test the closed loop system without adjusting the controller parameters.

The results are plotted in Figures 5, 6. It is observed that the oscillatory response due the nut resonance has been significantly attenuated. The load introduced a frequency drop of 18 Hz (from 150Hz to 132 Hz). The control system continue to perform satisfactorily. To further investigate the properties of the closed loop system. Fast Fourier Transform (FFT) of the nut response are taken. In both Figures 7 and 8, it is observed that the resonance at 150Hz (no load) and 132 Hz (1.5 kg load) is suppressed. In both plots, harmonics generated by the air compressor and building floor vibration are also visible. Such harmonics may be eliminated by using better mechanical isolation.

6. CONCLUSIONS

In this work, the problem of vibration control for a contactless drive system is considered. The dynamics of this system are first analyzed along with experimental measurements to generate a nonlinear plant model. Its properties are then studied by means by the linearized incremental model. It is shown that the plant is marginally stable, load dependent, and hard to control by conventional means. The technique of neural network/passband control is then introduced to deal with these difficulties. Experimental results confirm the vibration suppression capabilities of the passband controller. Finally, this controller is modular and easy to implement.

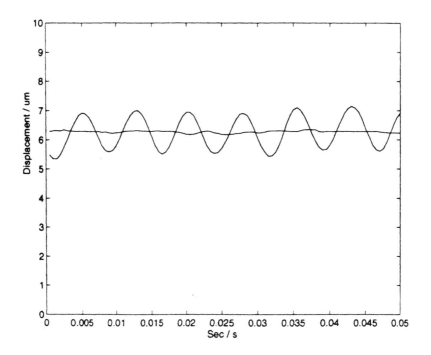

Figure 6. Nut Response: 1.5 kg load added

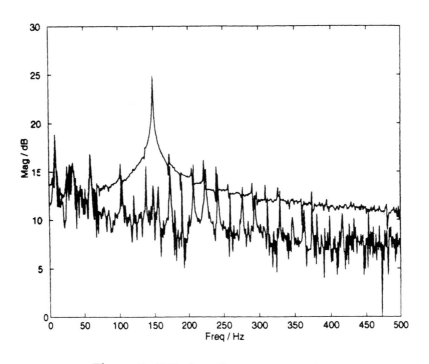

Figure 7. FFT of nut Response: no load condition

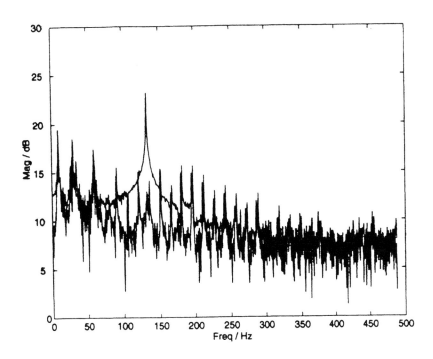

Figure 8. FFT of nut Response: 1.5 kg load added

REFERENCES

1. T. Satomi, "Studies on aerostatic lead screws," *World Congressof IFToMM* , pp. 1545–1548, 1987.

2. S. Kikuchi and K. Tsurumoto, "Design and characteristics of anew magnetic worm gear using permanent magnet," *IEEE Trans. onMagnetics* , pp. 2923–2925, 1993.

3. T. Chang, Z. Ji, M. Shimanovich, and R. Caudill, "Vibration control of contactless drive systems," *Proceedings to the 1996 IFAC World Congress* , 1996.

4. M. Shimanovich, "Development and application of hydrostatic spindle bearings in metal cutting machine tools," *Niimash (in Russian)* , 1972.

5. T. Chang, "Nonlinear tuning regulator for the control of lightly damped structures," *Proceedings of the 1993 American Control Conference* , pp. 1503–1507, 1993.

6. S. Haykin, "Communication systems , third ed.," *Wiley* , 1993.

7. Y. Bar-Ness and J. Rokah, "Cross-coupled bootstrapped interference canceler," *Proc. Int. Conf. on Ant. and Prop.* , pp. 292–295, 1981.

8. J. Carlin, Y. Bar-Ness, S. Gross, M. Steinberger, and W. Studdifor, "An if cross pol canceler for microwave radio," *Journal on Selected Area in Communication-Advances in Digital Communication by Radio* , pp. 502–514, 1987.

9. C. Jutten and J. Herault, "Blind separation of sources, part i: An adaptive algorithm based on neuromimetic architecture," *Signal Processing* , pp. 1–10, 1991.

10. E. Sorouchyari, "Blind separation of sources, part iii: Stability analysis," *Signal Processing* , pp. 21–29, 1991.

11. T. Chang and N. Ansari, "A learning controller for the regulation and stabilization of flexible structures," *Proceedings of the 1993 IEEE Conference on Decision and Control* , pp. 1268–1273, 1993.

Mechatronic long cane as a travel aid for the blind

Robert X. Gao and Xiaofeng Cai

Department of Mechanical and Industrial Engineering
University of Massachusetts
Amherst, MA 01003

ABSTRACT

Applying the principle of mechatronics, this paper presents design considerations for a new type of sensor-embedded "smart" long cane which can serve as an orientation and travel aid for the blind. The smart long cane uses a set of miniaturized ultrasonic sensors to detect obstacles along the travel path, and provide human voice feedback on the obstacle's height and distance to guide the cane user away from head collisions and subsequent injuries. Topics discussed include sensor array design, placement, and integration, structure of the embedded software, and ergonomic issues for the new cane design.

Keywords: smart long cane, travel aid, ultrasound sensors, wireless communication, ergonomics

1. INTRODUCTION

Among various forms of disability, blindness has been regarded as one of the most devastating that can strike people of all ages and significantly affect a victim's life. In the US, about two million people are blind or have severe low vision such that their visual acuity cannot be corrected to normal performance levels by conventional optical means. Each year, around 35,000 more adults become blind as a result of accidents or diseases such as cataracts, glaucoma, and diabetes[1-2]. According to an estimate of the World Health Organization [3], there are some 27-35 million blind people worldwide and at least an equal number of people of severe low vision. Of all the handicaps that blindness can cause, the loss of freedom in mobility is the most difficult to overcome. Extensive research efforts in the past decades have resulted in a wide range of electronic travel aids (ETAs)[4-8]. However, due to a number of technical and psychological barriers, the majority of blind people nowadays still use the long cane, which is a plain walking stick that provides an extended spatial sensing of about 0.5 meter ahead of the user, within an arc of about 120 degrees. Although the long cane is inexpensive, lightweight, easy to carry, and effective in detecting obstacles on the ground, such as uneven surfaces, holes, and steps, it has the severe deficiency of not able to detect overhanging obstacles along the travel path ahead of the cane user. As a result, the conventional long cane is not able to protect the user's body part above the waist height, and head injuries often occur due to collisions with overhanging obstacles such as low slung signposts, utility boxes, tree branches, or overhanging wires.

Based on the functionality of the existing ETAs, two fundamentally different approaches can be identified to the design and implementation of blind walking and orientation assistance devices. The first approach focuses on compensating as much as possible for the lost vision of the blind with sensory substitutions in order that they can perform like sighted people. A typical example is the SonicGuide[5], which is a head-mounted device that resembles a pair of glasses. The device emits ultrasound beams to about 5 meters in front of its carrier, within a field of about 50 degrees, and converts the reflected echoes into a complex sound pattern containing information about the distance, direction, and surface characteristics of the obstacle detected. Since the signal produced is too complex to interpret in a realistic walking situation, intensive training is needed for its effective use, which is time consuming and expensive. Furthermore, the complex nature of its signal display tends to cause information "overflow", which adds to the high stress inherently associated with blind walking. Because of these problems, ETAs of this type has not seen widespread acceptance.

Further author information -
R. X. G. (Correspondence): Email: gao@ecs.umass.edu; Phone: 413-545-0868; Fax: 413-545-1027
X. C: Email: xicai@ecs.umass.edu; Phone: 413-545-2362; Fax: 413-545-1027

The second approach of ETA design attempts to make use of a blind pedestrian's existing physical ability in walking, and provides a simply "go" or "no-go" warning signal to indicate whether it is safe or not to proceed along the travel path ahead. These devices are normally used in conjunction with other primary travel aids such as the conventional long cane or guide dog. Examples of these devices include the Mowat Sensor, the Nottingham Obstacle Detector (NOD), the Sonic Pathfinder, and the Laser Cane. A common feature shared by these travel aids is that obstacle warning is displayed either by an audible musical tone or by a pulse vibration whose frequency is related to the obstacle distance: higher frequency denotes shorter distance to an obstacle and vice versa. Although simple in form, these forms of signal display have the disadvantage of causing either bodily fatigue or wrong interpretation due to noise and other masking influences in the surrounding environment. More importantly, they are not compatible with the normal, realistic daily walking situation: musical tones or vibration pulses draw curiosity and attention to the blind user who would then feel observed and self-conscious.

The lack of effectiveness, reliability, ergonomic design, and easily understood feedback to the users has contributed to a surprisingly low acceptance rate of the ETAs developed over the past decades[9]. As a result, blind walking assistance has remained at a low tech level where the simple long cane, despite its deficiency in overhanging obstacle detection, continues to be the most widely used form of travel aid for the blind. This problem is worth study by the research community, especially in an era when information technologies are revolutionizing the way of communication and Internet is reaching out to every corner of the world.

The design and implementation of an effective, reliable, ergonomic, yet easy-to-use travel aid requires a multidisciplinary approach involving sensing, dynamics, signal processing, communication, microcomputers, human factors, system miniaturization, and structural integration. This approach is best supported by the mechatronic design philosophy, which emphasizes the synergistic integration of all the individual components for an optimized configuration of the final product. In this paper, the application of mechatronic principles to the design of a sensor-embedded long cane is presented. The new cane is designed to compensate for the lost vision of blind pedestrians by integrated human voice feedback that describes in key words the location of overhanging obstacles. In addition to technical considerations, the adoption of long cane as the basis for a new type of ETA is based on observations and surveys[10] of the blind community, which confirmed the tremendous popularity and symbolic importance of the long cane. This paper is focused on the design and placement strategy of an ultrasound sensor array for obstacle detection, the configuration of embedded hardware, and design considerations for the software structure.

2. SENSOR DESIGN AND PLACEMENT

To alert the cane user of an overhanging obstacle in the travel path ahead, the distance (D) and height (H) of the obstacle relative to the cane user need to be measured. Among various sensing principles applicable to the long cane situation, ultrasonic sensors have been selected because of their portability, ease of application, and relatively low cost. For the presented study, two types of ultrasonic sensors from Polaroid have been used, as illustrated in Fig. 1. The three sensors embedded into the upper section of the long cane (S_1 through S_3) are responsible for obstacle distance and height measurement. The measurement is based on the time-of-flight (TOF) principle, whereas Sensor S_2 first transmits a group of ultrasonic pulses at the beginning of each measurement cycle, and is then switched back to the receiving mode. If the pulses hit an obstacle that is located within the scanning range, they will be reflected back to the sensors S_1 through S_3 which are operated in the receiving mode. The time interval measured between the start of signal transmission from S_2 and receipt of the echo signals by the three sensors is a direct measure of the paths traveled by the ultrasonic waves L_1, L_2, and L_3, which are then calculated to determine the distance and height of the obstacle. Since the inclination angle (α) of the cane is a parameter for the calculation, and this angle varies because of the different body height of the cane users, the measurement needs to be adjusted for the instantaneous values of the angle. This is accomplished by the sensors S_4 and S_5 which are located on the lower portion of the long cane. The two groups of sensors (S_1 through S_3 and S_4 through S_5) were selected based on their specific functions: the former group is used for obstacle detection at a distance away from the users, thus they need to have a relatively long detection range with a narrow beam radiation angle to avoid false echoes from adjacent obstacles. In contrast, sensors S_4 and S_5 feature a short detection range at a wide beam angle to account for measurement errors caused by road surface unevenness, holes, etc.

The radiation directivity of an ultrasonic sensor is measured by its beam angle θ, as illustrated in Fig. 2. This angle is related to the wavelength λ of the ultrasound waves transmitted by the sensor and the sensor's physical dimension[11]. For a circular sensor with a diameter Φ, if the wavelength of the ultrasound waves transmitted is less than the sensor diameter (i.e. $\lambda < \Phi$), then the relationship is approximated by $\sin(\theta/2) \approx \lambda/\Phi$. For the condition $\lambda > \Phi$, the ultrasonic wave pattern will gradually become spherical in form. Therefore, a narrow beam angle and subsequently, high beam directivity is achieved by either selecting a sensor diameter Φ that is large relative to the ultrasonic wavelength λ, or increasing the radiation frequency f of the ultrasound wave, as the wavelength λ and the frequency f are related by $\lambda = v/f$, where v denotes the wave propagation velocity in the surrounding media.

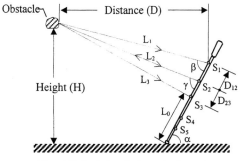

Fig. 1 Principle of obstacle detection

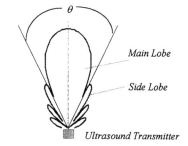

Fig. 2 Ultrasonic beam radiation pattern

In order for an ultrasound receiver to detect echo signals reflected by an obstacle, sufficient intensity of the ultrasound waves at the receiver site is required. Two major factors affect the ultrasonic wave intensity through its propagation. The first is the distance traveled by the ultrasound wave which is governed by the inverse square law and estimated at about 6 dB drop per doubled distance, regardless of the operation frequency. The second factor is the wave absorption by the propagation medium, which increases with elevated sensor operating frequency. In Fig. 3, the relationship among sensor size Φ, operation frequency f, and sensor detection range D is shown. For a fixed beam angle θ, if the operation frequency increases, the detectable range of the sensor will decrease, as well as the size of the sensor. While a smaller sensor is preferable for the structural integration into the long cane, a quick drop of signal intensity due to increased absorption by the medium is undesired. A weak signal is difficult to receive, vulnerable to background noise, and requires increased circuit complexity to process. Alternatively, if the sensor operation frequency is fixed, a smaller sensor will result in a shorter detection range. Therefore, for an optimized sensor design, a compromise needs to be made depending on the desirable obstacle detection range and beam angle, and acceptable sensor size and signal intensity reduction. In Fig. 4, the relationship between sensor beam angle and sensor size is illustrated. For a fixed frequency, an increasing ratio of λ/Φ indicates a decreasing sensor dimension.

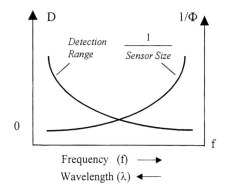

Fig. 3 Relationship among sensor size,
frequency, and detection range

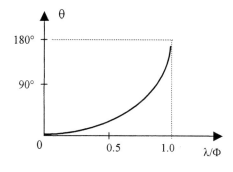

Fig. 4 Sensor beam angle vs. sensor size

To determine the location of the sensors on the long cane, two parameters need to be considered. The first one is the dynamic behavior of the structurally modified new cane. In realistic applications, the tip of the long cane will be used to tap on the ground to sense road surface conditions. This can be regarded as a forced vibration of the long cane system with a dynamic force applied to the tip of the cane. The dynamic force will be transmitted to the sensors as well as on-board electronics. Therefore, vibration analysis needs to be conducted to determine the locations of vibration nodes under various excitation frequencies. An appropriate location for a sensor is given where the sensor is least affected by the cane's vibration. Another factor affecting the sensor location is the relative spacing between each two adjacent sensors. Since an obstacle's distance and height are determined by measuring the propagation paths traveled by the ultrasonic waves L_1 through L_3 in conjunction with the sensor spacing D_{12} and D_{23}, as shown in Fig. 1, these two spacing will have an direct influence on the measurement accuracy. To quantify the influence of sensor spacing, the triangle L_1, L_2 and D_{12} was studied, where the three parameters are related by

$$L_1^2 + D_{12}^2 - L_2^2 = 2 \cdot L_1 \cdot D_{12} \cdot \cos \beta \tag{1}$$

Taking derivatives of both sides of the equation and assuming that the differential changes of L_1 and L_2 are equal in quantity, since they are measured by the same sensors, then following relationship between angle β and measured ultrasonic paths L_1 and L_2 can be determined:

$$\partial \beta = \frac{D_{12} \cdot \cos(\beta) + (L_1 - L_2)}{L_1 \cdot L_2 \cdot \sin(\beta)} \cdot \partial L_1 \tag{2}$$

Substituting the expressions for L_1 and L_2 as a function of obstacle distance and rearranging the equation yields the following relationship between the error coefficient value $f(D_{12})$ and sensor spacing D_{12}:

$$f(D_{12}) = \frac{L_1 - \sqrt{L_1^2 + D_{12}^2 - 0.45 L_1 \cdot D_{12}}}{0.97 \cdot D_{12}} \tag{3}$$

The dependency of the error coefficient value on sensor spacing is shown in Fig. 5, where sensor spacing D_{12} is measured by inches. For the presented study, the minimum error coefficient value was taken for placing the sensors S_1 and S_2. The spacing between sensors S_2 and S_3 is determined using the same procedure.

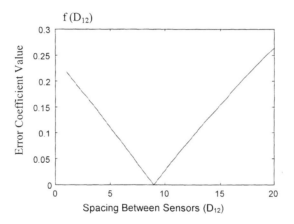

Fig. 5 Determination of optimum sensor spacing

3. CANE CONFIGURATION

Based on the results of long cane structural analyses and sensor experiments, the upper portion of the long cane was redesigned for the intended sensor integration. The new structure consists of two sections: an upper handle with a battery compartment, and a cylindrical holder for the sensor array. The handle has the same dimension as that of a conventional long cane, but is hollow inside to accommodate two 3V batteries. A flat surface was machined on one side of the handle to provide a reference position for the sensor orientation. In Fig. 6, an assembly diagram for the sensor holder portion of the new cane prototype is shown. While the focus of mechanical design was to maintain sufficient strength and structural stability, requirements from the integrated electronics and sensors were equally considered to allow for easy-assembly and easy access to the integrated components. The sensor holder portion is designed as a complete piece with three back cover plates. Each sensor was designed to be mounted first within a socket which provides the required sensor orientation angle with respect to the long cane surface. The socket is secured to the sensor holder. In addition to holding the sensors, the sockets also hold two miniaturized PCB boards on which data processing electronic components are mounted. The two

PCB boards were designed to separate the analog sensor driving circuit from the digital circuit containing a microcontroller. This arrangement allows for an easy maintenance of the electronics as well as flexible mechanical adaptation.

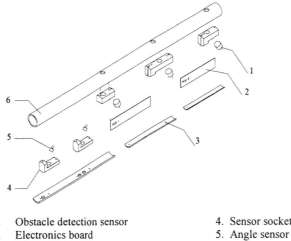

1. Obstacle detection sensor
2. Electronics board
3. Back cover plate
4. Sensor socket
5. Angle sensor
6. Sensor holder

Fig. 6 Assembly drawing of the sensor holder

4. SOFTWARE STRUCTURE

The distance and height information on an overhanging obstacle needs to be relayed in a real-time fashion from the cane-embedded sensor module to the blind cane user. Since wire connections may cause tripping, especially for a blind cane user, it is not compatible with the realistic blind walking situations. Therefore, telemetric data communication has been implemented for the presented study. The obstacle information is sent wirelessly from a cane-embedded signal transmitter to a user-carried signal receiver. The data communication is controlled by a dedicated microcontroller (PIC16C73A) on each end of the transmission line.

The system software for the wireless communication consists of two separate modules that execute data transmitting and receiving operations in a concurrent fashion.

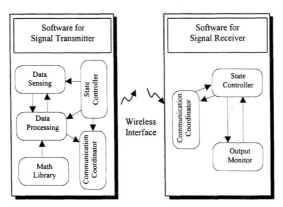

Fig. 7 Software structure for wireless data transmission

As is shown in Fig. 7, following major components are included in the signal transmitter and receiver software:

1) Communication Coordinator. The communication coordinator on each side of the transmission line coordinates the time sequence of wireless data transmission between the transmitter and the receiver. To ensure high efficiency, a simple messaging protocol is used. In addition to obstacle information such as the height and distance, a specific cane

identification number (CIN) is transmitted as part of the data structure. The CIN identifies the signal transmitter such that the receiver knows where the signal is coming from. This has practical significance as it prevents the receiver from receiving spurious data from either another signal source that is not related to the cane, or from a similar cane-embedded transmitter used by a nearby user. The communication coordinating software is configured such that at the beginning of each transmission cycle, the obstacle information is prefixed with a CIN. Upon signal receipt, the receiver will first compare the received CIN with its stored information. Only after a match is identified will further data processing and display procedures be conducted.

2) Math Library. The math library is established for the required signal processing and consists of three sub-modules for fix-point and float-point calculation and basic function evaluation. The float-point sub-module is designed to use 24-bit format which is based on a trade-off among accuracy, speed and resources requirement. The basic function sub-module contains a data look-up table with a linear interpolation algorithm to expedite certain calculation procedures.

3) State Controller. The state controllers were deigned to coordinate the seven different states under which the signal transmitter and receiver may be operating. As shown in Fig. 8, the seven states are: reset, self-diagnosis, data sensing, data fusion, data transmission, sleep, and alarm generation. The control variables used to determine the state of the controller are *Emergency Signal B* and *Obstacle Presentation I*. Based on the specific values of the variables and the current state, the controller will switch the system to a proper next state.

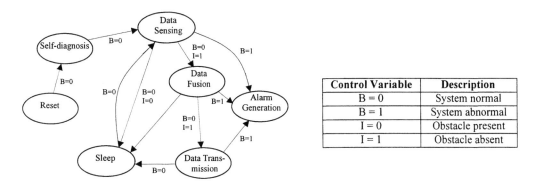

Control Variable	Description
B = 0	System normal
B = 1	System abnormal
I = 0	Obstacle present
I = 1	Obstacle absent

Fig. 8 State controller for signal communication control

5. ERGONOMICS AND SAFETY CONSIDERATIONS

In order for any new device to be readily accepted by its potential customers, it is essential that at the initial design stage, issues related to ergonomics, safety, and user friendliness be carefully considered. For a sensor-embedded new cane to be readily accepted by blind users, it has to be easy and convenient to operate, and is compatible with the user's walking habit and realistic daily walking situations. Two major aspects have been considered for the "smart" long cane design, which involves the mechanical and information interface. In Fig. 9, the system components related to the two aspects are shown.

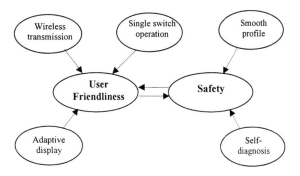

Fig. 9 Factors affecting ergonomics and safety considerations for the new cane design

To ensure reliable and proper functioning of the "smart" long cane, it needs to have an embedded self-diagnosis capability to alert the user of its own "health" status at the beginning of each operation cycle. Furthermore, to reduce the likelihood of mal-operation and user distraction, the number of mechanical switches and/or buttons needs to be reduced to a minimum. Considering that different users may walk at different speeds and the traffic situation and environment a blind pedestrian would encounter may change instantaneously, an adaptive optimization algorithm is implemented to control the signal output rate of the "smart" long cane[12]. Based on the user's walking speed and the history if prior obstacle identification, the signal display rate is adapted such that it is adequate but will not cause unnecessary tension and information overflow.

6. CONCLUSIONS AND FUTURE WORK

The mechatronics principles have been applied to the design of a new type of sensor-embedded "smart" long cane that can serve as an orientation and travel aid for the blind. The focus of study is to design various components involving mechanical, electrical, and computer engineering simultaneously and in a parallel fashion, to consider their interactions and their effects on the entire system, and to achieve their synergistic structural integration. A prototype for the new cane has been designed and implemented, and experimental studies are being conducted. The data will be used to modify the design for an improved version of the "smart" long cane. Future work includes optimization of the adaptive signal display algorithm, further reduction in system complexity and power consumption, and improved system miniaturization.

7. ACKNOWLEDGMENT

This work has been supported by the National Science Foundation under grant # BES-9402818. The authors would like to thank Mr. Szabolcs Sovenyi for his assistance in the sensor holder design and assembly drawing, and Mr. Charles Cichadnowicz for the prototype cane implementation.

8. REFERENCES

1. National Research Council, "Electronic travel aids: new directions for research", Washington, D.C., 1987.
2. National Federation of the Blind, "Do you know a blind person?", 1992
3. M. Lawrence, J. Lovie-Kitchin, and W. Brohier, "Low vision: a working paper for the world health organization", *Journal of Visual Impairment and Blindness*, pp. 7-9, 1992.
4. J. Borenstein and I. Ulrich, "The GuideCane – a computerized travel aid for the active guidance of blind pedestrians", *Proc. IEEE International Conference on Robotics and Automation*, Albuquerque, NM, Apr. 21-27, pp. 1283-1288, 1997.
5. J. Barth and E. Foulhe, "Preview: A neglected variable in orientation and mobility", *Journal of Visual Impairment and Blindness*, Vol. 73, No. 2, pp. 41-48, Feb., 1979.
6. S. Shoval, J. Borenstein, and Y. Koren, "Mobile robot obstacle avoidance in a computerized travel aid for the blind", *IEEE International Conference on Robotics and Automatons*, pp. 2023-2028, San Diego, CA, 1994.
7. L. Kay, "Electronic aids for blind persons: an interdisciplinary subject", *IEEE Proceedings*, Vol. 131, No. 7, pp. 559-576, 1984.
8. A. Heyes, "The sonic pathfinder: a new electronic travel aid", *Journal of Visual Impairment and Blindness*, Vol. 78, No. 5, pp. 200-202, May, 1984.
9. M. Sanders and E. McCormick, "Human factors in engineering and design", 7th Edition, McGraw-Hill, Inc., 1993.
10. R. Gao, interviews with *Eastern Blind Rehabilitation Center*, West Haven, CT, 1997, and with *Louisiana Center for the Blind*, Ruston, LA, 1994 and 1995.
11. Philips Components, "Piezoelectric ceramics: properties and applications", Eindhoven, The Netherlands, April, 1991.
12. X. Cai and R. Gao, "A microcontroller-based telemetric sensing module for the long cane", *Proc. The 9th International Conference on Signal Processing Applications & Technology (ICSPAT/98)*, pp. 183-187, Vol. 1, Toronto, Canada, September 13-16, 1998.

Mechatronics Education at Virginia Tech

John Bay[a], William Saunders[b], Charles Reinholtz,[b] Peter Pickett[c], and Lee Johnston[d]

[a]Bradley Department of Electrical Engineering
[b]Department of Mechanical Engineering
Virginia Polytechnic Institute and State University
Blacksburg, Virginia 24061

[c]Lexmark Corp, Lexington, KY.

[d]National Instruments, Austin, TX

ABSTRACT

The advent of more complex mechatronic systems in industry has introduced new opportunities for entry-level and practicing engineers. Today, a select group of engineers are reaching out to be more knowledgeable in a wide variety of technical areas, both mechanical and electrical. A new curriculum in mechatronics developed at Virginia Tech is starting to bring students from both the mechanical and electrical engineering departments together, providing them with an integrated perspective on electromechanical technologies and design. The course is cross-listed and team-taught by faculty from both departments. Students from different majors are grouped together throughout the course, each group containing at least one mechanical and one electrical engineering student. This gives group members the ability to learn from one another while working on labs and projects.

The senior, technical-elective mechatronics course is treated primarily as a design course. Because of the interdisciplinary nature of this design course, there are special demands on students' time as they learn 'out-of-area' technical topics. Therefore, the course is taught with asynchronous elements using a WWW site developed under the sponsorship of the NSF SUCCEED coalition. This helps the students to work at their own pace, within the confines of the semester. The site gives students access to class notes, homework assignments and solutions, and links to data sheets and application notes. It also provides multimedia instruction in the assembly of a custom-designed microcontroller board, called the VT84 prototyping board.

This paper is intended to provide potential mechatronics instructors and students with ideas for course development and to assess the success of our own efforts.

Keywords: Mechatronics, education, electromechanical systems.

INTRODUCTION

In the Fall Semester of 1996, an experimental course was taught at Virginia Polytechnic Institute and State University (Virginia Tech) for the first time. This new course, Mechatronics, was innovative in a number of regards:

- It was cross-listed between the electrical and mechanical engineering departments, and team-taught by faculty in those departments. While cross-listed courses themselves were not unusual, most existing cross-listed courses were arranged that way for administrative reasons, e.g., so that a

Part of the SPIE Conference on Mechatronics ● Boston, Massachusetts ● November 1998
SPIE Vol. 3518 ● 0277-786X/98/$10.00

227

department would only have responsibility for teaching it in alternate years. This course was designated a "true" cross-list, and both instructors were in class on most days.

- Students were recruited for the course such that a desired proportion was maintained between the electrical engineering and mechanical engineering majors. The intent was that they learn as much from each other as from the instructors.

- The course included both lecture and asynchronous laboratory components. Development of the asynchronous laboratory project was sponsored with external funds provided through the NSF SUCCEED Coalition and the Virginia Tech Center for Excellence in Undergraduate Teaching.

- Student design projects were initiated using a proposal-evaluation format, whereby student teams were allowed to create mechatronic systems limited only by their own imagination. The proposal preparation experience was welcomed by most students.

These features required as much work from the faculty as from the students, and represented a significant departure from the way courses were historically taught. The interdisciplinary collaboration alone was new to some of the participants, and required adjustments to the faculty's teaching methods, lecture notes, and class administration. Overall, these new methods for interdisciplinary course and administration were judged to be successful by the students, faculty, college administration, and industry observers. It is the purpose of this paper to disseminate interesting lessons learned to interested educators and observers.

JUSTIFICATION

Motivation for the development of the Mechatronics course came from several directions:

- A growing number of students have expressed some dissatisfaction with traditional lecture-based curricula in their departments. Through their own interactions with students in other majors, they often found interests in areas not taught in their home departments, but which required too many prerequisites or special approval to learn in other departments.

- The increasing involvement of students on interdisciplinary project teams has resulted in students from several engineering and non-engineering majors working on common projects [1], often on common technologies, although their coursework backgrounds were entirely different. For example, such design teams were already formed to enter the International Unmanned Ground Robotics contest, the FutureCar Challenge, and the SunRayce solar car competition. These students quickly recognized the value of these team projects and expressed concern about the lack of practical interdisciplinary design experience in the traditional curriculum.

- The college and department faculties began to stress interdisciplinary instruction upon the recommendations from internal curriculum review committees, industrial advisory boards, and the Accreditation Board for Engineering and Technology (ABET). Removing barriers to interdisciplinary faculty and student collaboration has become a priority at many universities.

- Industry sponsors, visitors, recruiters, and alumni have all expressed an interest in either four-year or graduate engineers who have acquired interdisciplinary or systems-level design experiences. These experiences include not only the exposure to diverse technologies, but also communications and presentation skills.

- The changing nature of products and processes in the past ten years needs to be addressed in the curriculum. Particularly, the prevalence of small microcontrollers in modern hardware design has facilitated and enhanced the mechatronic design principles introduced over twenty years ago in Japan. Engineers must train themselves to be versatile in this new interdisciplinary design environment where 'intelligent' or 'smart' products prevail.

All of these factors led to the development of the mechatronics course at Virginia Tech. Mechatronics is nominally a new topic of instruction, in the sense that it synthesizes state-of-the-art technologies into a coherent engineering science that may include embedded microcontrollers, advanced control and digital signal processing (DSP) techniques, digital communication systems, and sometimes microelectromechanical systems.

However, mechatronics might also be described as a back-to-basics approach to engineering that reverses the trend toward curriculum compression, compartmentalization and over-specialization. It revives the seemingly lost practice of educating engineers who have the ability to oversee and participate in the design, construction, and even commercialization of an entire product. There is one important distinction that must be made about this 'general engineer' in relation to generations of old. The general engineer of the twenty-first century must also possess state-of-the-art knowledge in technical areas that are emerging at unprecedented rates. Mechatronics provides an ideal framework to accommodate the educational demands required to train such highly-skilled, general engineers. The design-oriented organization of mechatronics is used as an outer layer that captures the generalized topics, allowing instructors to explore more in-depth discussions of various components according to their individual expertise and student interests at their own universities.

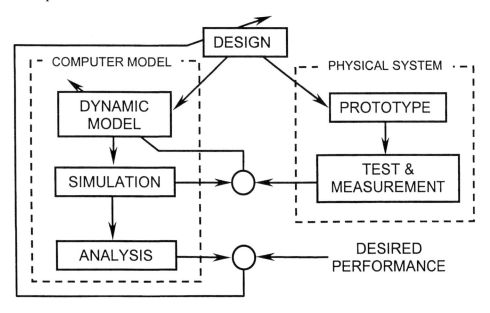

Figure 1. Integrated product design cycle.

In this sense, the course combines very traditional engineering expertise with in-depth material in the manner depicted by Figure 1. The block diagram represents the integrated analytical and experimental design flow that accompanies the entire design cycle of a new product. In recent years, engineering education has begun to focus on one or more of the blocks in this diagram at the expense of others. This trend has been forced either by the necessity to completely cover advanced topics within the constraints of semester syllabi and textbooks, department missions, or by the expertise of the faculty, who are often products of intensive dissertation research in very narrow fields of study. The result is the loss of perspective of the process as a whole. By constraining the technical content of the mechatronics course to those topics that are especially prevalent in electromechanical systems (see the next section), we have been able to consider the integrated product design paradigm as a whole. This is a systems-level design topic that should not be left to systems engineering courses alone. The next section discusses the specific syllabus topics that Virginia Tech faculty members have adopted as a reasonable blend for a mechatronics course at the advanced undergraduate level.

COURSE CONTENT

Mechatronics is well-known for its 'claim' to many different technical subjects. The challenge when designing a mechatronics course is to select the appropriate level of depth, for the appropriate topic areas. The syllabus of the lecture portion of the Virginia Tech course is as follows:

TOPIC	PORTION of COURSE
Microcontroller operation, interfacing, and programming	25%
Actuators and drive systems	15%
Sensors	15%
Dynamic modeling of electromechanical systems	15%
Signal acquisition and conditioning	10%
Control theory	10%
Programmable logic controllers	5%
Data communications	5%

The syllabus coverage of relevant topics reflects the emphasis that this mechatronics course places on the action components of a mechatronic system – the microcontroller, actuators, and sensors. Approximately half of the course is concerned with these subsystems. In the microcontroller section of the course, students learn fundamental computer architectures and study a particular microprocessor in detail – architecture and operation. During the lectures on actuators and sensors, the instructors present a large number of devices and contrast differences between theoretical and practical performances. The remainder of the lecture content is divided as shown above. Dynamic system modeling receives a great deal of emphasis, followed by traditional signals and systems topics, mostly as they relate to the use of the microcontroller for data acquisition and control during laboratory projects. Finally, the subjects of PLC devices and communication bus architectures are presented in limited detail.

After designing this syllabus, the instructors met some resistance from other faculty for the seemingly elementary and sometimes repetitious nature of these topics. For example, dynamic modeling, control theory, and microcontrollers are each topics that are taught in courses that are prerequisite to mechatronics. Furthermore, the time allotted to them in this course was judged to be insufficient for their complete coverage. However, it must be remembered that it is not the devices and methods themselves that are the topic of the course: it is the integration into a complex design that is the subject.

Although the basic architecture and operation of microcontrollers is taught (by necessity), the context of these lessons is the system in which they are employed. The speed, instruction set, I/O ports, and interrupt capabilities of the device are the key to their integration in a product. The interacting dynamics of a mechanical load, a motor, its power electronic drive, and the sensors (they have dynamics too!) cannot be understood without a basic understanding of their operation, and they cannot be understood in isolation.

Some of the topics are indeed new to the students, although they represent very basic knowledge for most engineers. For example, the lessons on sensors cover such technologies as piezoceramic devices, infrared and ultrasonic sensors, and encoders. Programmable logic controllers (PLCs) are taught in an industrial engineering class only, but most mechatronics students have not taken this course. Yet, when recruiters from industry come to campus seeking control systems engineers, it is often PLC programming that they seek as a qualification. These topics, too, are integrated at the systems-level coverage of electromechanical technologies.

It may also be argued that all these topics are very traditional engineering subjects. To the extent that they are covered in individual detail, this is largely true. However, their integration in the mechatronics course design overall provides both opportunities and constraints compared to a course in which these subjects might be individually taught. These opportunities and constraints derive largely from the same source: the diversity of the students. The opportunities lie in the student's ability to teach each other. The constraints derive from the frequent need to review material unfamiliar to some portion of the students, but their laboratory team collaborations can (and do) offset this disadvantage. While teaching microcontrollers, for example, it was found that mechanical engineers were uncomfortable with assembly language programming, while electrical engineers were more proficient. Likewise, mechanical engineers were much more skilled than electrical engineers at dynamic modeling. However, after a review of the fundamentals and an overview of the most important topics, the instructors proceeded to teach at the systems level (e.g., how the dynamics of an actuator dictate the design of a signal conditioner), while the students were expected to tutor each other as necessary. This is the primary purpose of assigning interdisciplinary lab teams and its successful implementation can provide substantial support of the brief lecture coverage for many topic areas.

THE VT84 BOARD and WEB SITE

The lessons in microcontroller technology occupy the largest single block of the syllabus. Although the electrical and computer engineers have had some exposure to microcomputer architectures and programming, none of the students have coursework experience with the particular processor selected for the course, the Microchip PIC 16C84.[*]

This chip was chosen primarily for its simplicity: it is a RISC machine with only 33 instructions to learn. It also has a pipelined instruction execution with a Harvard architecture. The Harvard architecture allows the program memory to be wider than the data memory, thereby allowing a single-byte instruction set, which, with the pipelined execution, allows almost all instructions to execute in a single clock cycle (instructions such as branches that affect the program counter being the only exceptions). This makes interfacing the device to real-time control projects relatively easy for the novice. The 16C84 is also a physically small device; we used the 18-pin DIP package so that we could

---

[*] Now discontinued and replaced by the backward-compatible 16F84, which substitutes FLASH memory for the 1K EEPROM program memory.

socket the chips for easy replacement. Another important feature of the chip is its in-circuit programmability and the development tools provided free by Microchip.

The processors were mounted on a custom-design microcontroller board called the VT84. The VT84 was designed by Lee Johnston, at that time a Virginia Tech student and teaching assistant. The board, shown in Figure 2 below, includes the processor and crystal oscillator, an analog-to-digital converter, a buffer, a serial communications interface, an H-bridge for driving motors, and the necessary passive components, switches, and connectors. It has one dual-row connector that is plugged into a standard laboratory breadboard for experimentation. A DB-9 connector and communications interface provide the interface to the RS-232 port of a PC. Through this port, assembled programs are downloaded with a custom-written data transmission program that runs under Microsoft Windows95.

The VT84 board is provided to the students in kit form. The students' first laboratory assignment for the semester is to populate the board (i.e. solder the parts to the board). This is facilitated by the course web site (see http://www.mechatronics.me.vt.edu), see Figure 3. On this site are step-by step instructions for mounting the components, proper soldering techniques, and links to sites through which they proceed to program the board and interface it to an input potentiometer and a DC motor.

The laboratory assignments all focus on the VT84 board and the device to which it can be interfaced. At first, the laboratory assignments are focused on familiarization and programming of the processor. This is greatly facilitated by Microchip's free MPLAB simulation program, in which the students can debug and simulate their programs, including input stimuli, interrupts, and timing. MPLAB works with MPASM to assemble debugged programs into download-able code that must then be demonstrated on the actual board.

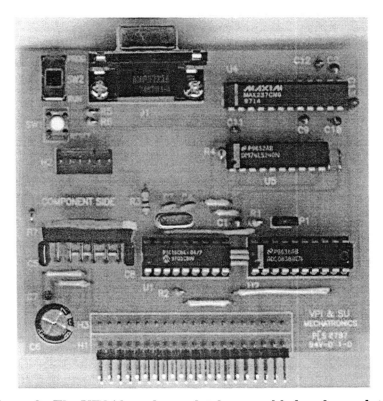

Figure 2. The VT84 board completely assembled and populated.

Subsequent assignments all lead toward the eventual use of the board as a digital PID controller that drives the DC motor with pulse-width modulated (PWM) commands to the H-bridge. The students, as guided by the web site, gradually learn to produce PWM signals of specific frequencies and duty cycles, read an input potentiometer and feedback potentiometer, process errors with a digital PID algorithm (which is taught in the lecture), and demonstrate their results in hardware. The web site is also a repository for on-line course notes. Although the VT84 kit costs the students approximately $65, the extensive use of the web site for class notes and assignments saves them the additional cost of a textbook.

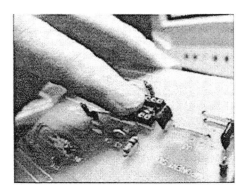

Figure 3. Sample image from VT84 assembly web site.

After these exercises there is one more assignment: the term project, which is discussed in the next section.

DESIGN PROJECTS

The capstone laboratory task presented to the student teams is the request for mechatronic designs and prototypes, of their own choosing, that may utilize the VT84 board and whatever other technologies they choose. The goal in assigning this project is to require the student to demonstrate creative mechatronic system design and development expertise outside of the guided environment that accompanied the other laboratory assignments.

To make the project resemble a real-world experience, the students must first submit written proposals to the instructors. These proposals are treated similarly to any competition that relies on formal proposals. The documents are examined for feasibility and completeness, with additional attention to matters of cost, difficulty, relevance, and inclusion of elements that will demonstrate a comprehensive understanding of more than just a single technology. During the past two years, a large number of the proposals were returned to the students for different levels of revision. Often, the reason for this rejection is that the proposed projects are too ambitious. Based on the instruction they receive in laboratory and classroom, and their overall inexperience with mechatronic systems, the tendency is for students to underestimate the interaction effects between the devices they select and the hardware they have previously used. For example, a common problem is to assume that the microcontroller outputs will drive an arbitrary load (such as solenoids). Of course, the student is then referred to his or her course notes, where the energy required by the mechanical model is used to calculate the current necessary from the voltage supply, and hence, the drive electronics necessary. Other common problems include underestimating the speed and memory capacity necessary from the microcontroller, the accuracy and precision of the feedback sensors, and the complexity of the code to be written (for example, writing multiplication routines for the PIC processor).

The following list illustrates the types of projects successfully demonstrated in Fall Semester, 1997:

- An AC induction motor controller.

- Automatic mini-blind adjuster that equalizes room light.

- Automatic vents to adjust room temperature.

- A prosthetic/robotic arm.

- A programmable robotic car (which required the use of two VT84 boards, see Figure 4 below).

Figure 4. Robot car with programming keypad and dual VT84 controllers.

SUMMARY AND CONCLUSIONS

The introduction of mechatronics at Virginia Tech has been a rewarding process for faculty and students at many different levels. Certainly, there are very tangible results that can be attributed to the mechatronics efforts. The new technical elective course offering is one such result. However, the intangible benefits seem to far outweigh such factual observations. The instructors have heard students say that mechatronics was the best course they have taken during their four-year program. Some corporate recruiters actually seek out students who have taken the course. The Virginia Tech student projects have certainly increased the technical capabilities of individual students as a result of taking the course, and the teaming quality has been favorably affected.

At this juncture, the most sensible questions about mechatronics seem to be related to exactly how this educational approach will be accepted in the next ten years and if accepted, how to deliver the vast array of topics that can be classified as part of mechatronics. The answers to these questions – for our university – are being discussed across the curriculum by faculty members in two different departments. Meanwhile, the students don't seem to care what the answers to these questions will be. They are happy as long as the mechatronics course is offered.

ACKNOWLEDGEMENTS

The mechatronics web-site development was supported by the National Science Foundation under a SUCCEED Coalition grant from North Carolina State University, number Subcon 91-0950-02 Amd51. The authors would also like to thank the departments of Electrical and Computer Engineering and Mechanical Engineering, and the Virginia Tech Center for Excellence in Undergraduate Teaching for additional support.

REFERENCES

[1]   Burgiss, M. J., C. F. Reinholtz, and J. S. Bay, "Education and Research Experience of the Autonomous Vehicle Team of Virginia Tech," *Proc. of the SPIE Conference on Intelligent Systems & Automated Manufacturing*, Pittsburgh, PA, pp. 295-305, October 1997.

SESSION 7

Mechatronics II

Miniaturized sensor module for a mechatronic bearing

Robert X. Gao and Priyaranjan Sahay

Department of Mechanical and Industrial Engineering
University of Massachusetts
Amherst, MA 01003

ABSTRACT

To assess the working condition of a rolling element bearing, the condition monitoring system should be located as close as possible to the bearing to take advantage of shorter signal transmission path, increased signal-to-noise ratio, and reduced complexity of the signal processing electronics. The advantages of integrated sensing are presented in this paper, with a focus on the design and analysis of a miniaturized sensor module. Mechatronic principles have been applied to treat the various subjects in a synergistic way. To complement analytical studies, experiments have been conducted on a scaled-up version of the sensor module to analyze the system dynamic response. The results obtained provided insight into the electromechanical interaction within the module as well as input for the system implementation using miniaturization technologies.

Keywords: sensor module, miniaturization, system dynamics, vibration analysis, experiments.

1. INTRODUCTION

Advanced mechanical systems are characterized by an extensive integration of "intelligence", represented by sensors, customized electronics, and microcontrollers, within their operational environment. This integration is essential to satisfying the increasing demands for better product quality, more functionality, higher reliability, and lower manufacturing cost. The past decade has seen an increasing trend of intelligence integration within various industrial and commercial products, from automobiles and machine tools to camcorders and toys. An important field that may take full advantage of intelligence integration is the bearing industry. This is largely due to the widespread applications of bearings which provide rotational freedom for machine systems. Very often the rotational motion plays a critical role in the safe operation of the overall system (e.g. wheels on a passenger train or landing gear of an airplane). Therefore, proper functioning of a bearing over its designed life cycle is of vital importance[1-6]. Since various adverse conditions may affect the normal functioning of a bearing, such as faulty installation, overloading, insufficient or excessive lubrication, premature and sudden failures of individual bearings often occur in real-world applications which may not only cause material damages, but even endanger human lives. This situation could be improved substantially, if the bearings at critical locations are equipped with integrated "intelligence" such that they can perform self-diagnosis in an on-line fashion. If predetermined threshold values representing a critical condition are exceeded, a warning signal can be generated to alert the system operator of potential failure[7-8].

The implementation of such a self-diagnosis mechanism requires the structural integration of a miniaturized sensor module into the vicinity of a bearing structure, ideally into the bearing itself, as schematically shown in Fig. 1. Compared to a sensor located at distant location, an integrated sensor is closer to the source of signal generation and thus has a shorter signal transmission path. This reduces the signal's vulnerability to noise contamination and thus requires less complex electronics for the signal processing. However, structural integration of a sensor module into a bearing is a challenging task. Mechanical loads and vibrations within the bearing operation environment can affect the performance of the electronic components mounded on the sensor module, or even cause them to fail, if they exceed the allowable stress and deflection of the electronic components. To ensure proper functioning of the integrated electronics, dynamic analysis and experimental studies of the integrated system needs to be conducted to evaluate various loading situations and their impact on the system performance.

Further author information -
R. X. G.: Email: gao@ecs.umass.edu; Phone: 413-545-0868; Fax: 413-545-1027
P.S.: Email: psahay@ecs.umass.edu; Phone: 413-545-2362; Fax: 413-545-1027

238

Part of the SPIE Conference on Mechatronics ● Boston, Massachusetts ● November 1998
SPIE Vol. 3518 ● 0277-786X/98/$10.00

To investigate the dynamic behavior of a miniaturized sensor module with dimensions in the millimeter range, experimental studies need to be designed carefully. This is due to the relatively large mass and dimension ratios between the dynamics measuring device (such as sensors or excitation equipment) and the sensor module to be measured. This is illustrated in Fig. 2, where the cross-section of a miniaturized sensor module for integrated bearing condition monitoring is shown (unit in millimeter). The large ratios may present a modifying effect that influences the dynamics of the module under tests and thus produce erroneous data. A practical solution to this problem is to first conduct experiments on a scaled-up version of the sensor model, and apply the data for subsequent design and analysis of the miniaturized version. This approach, taken by the presented study, has the cost-effective advantage that it provides the sensor designer with realistic data on how the miniaturized version would behave dynamically, before it is actually built by a special IC foundry.

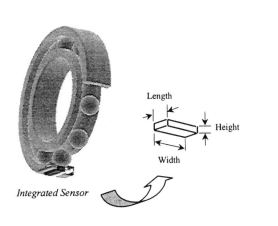

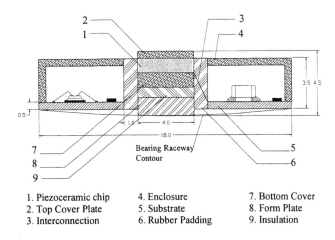

1. Piezoceramic chip   4. Enclosure   7. Bottom Cover
2. Top Cover Plate   5. Substrate   8. Form Plate
3. Interconnection   6. Rubber Padding   9. Insulation

Fig. 1 A bearing-integrated sensor module   Fig. 2 Cross-section of the sensor module

2. MECHANICAL ENVIRONMENT

As illustrated in Fig. 1, the miniaturized sensor module is designed for integration into the outer raceway of the bearing. This environment is characterized by periodic loading caused by the interaction between the rotating rolling elements and the raceway. The region where the sensor module is located can be described by a load zone where the load distribution is given

by the equation: $Q(\psi) = Q_{max} \left[1 - \frac{1}{2\varepsilon}(1 - \cos\psi) \right]^n$ for the angular region ($-\psi_l < \psi < \psi_l$). In this expression, ε is the load distribution factor and n is the load-deflection exponent[9]. Depending on the type of loading (radial, thrust, or combined load), the load distribution factor ε can be further expressed as a function of bearing geometry, diametral clearance, and load induced deflection. For ball bearings under pure radial load, $0 < \varepsilon < 0.5$, and n = 1.5. In Fig. 3, the load zone of a ball bearing caused by radial load is schematically shown.

For the presented study, a force sensor module is located at the center of the load zone to obtain maximum sensitivity. Based on the maximum load carrying capacity of the bearing that is specified by the manufacturer, the geometry of the slot made in the outer raceway, and deflection of the outer raceway under radial load, the maximum compressive load Q_{max} that is applied to the force sensing element can be determined. As illustrated in Fig. 2, the sensor module is designed such that only a portion of this load will be transmitted to the module substrate on which electronic components are mounted. The load that is applied to the substrate, and hence the electronics, is the horizontal component of Q_Ψ, whereas Q_Ψ is defined above. This situation is illustrated in Fig. 4. During bearing operation, a cyclic load is transmitted to the sensor module substrate and subsequently, to the electronic components. This load can be modeled as a function of $Q_{\Psi(H)}$, the horizontal component of Q_Ψ, and the bearing inner raceway rotational frequency ω (assuming a stationary outer race). It is essential to determine quantitatively how the cyclic mechanical load will affect the bonding between the leads of the integrated circuit chips and the module substrate. Excessive stress development within this region will cause the electronic chips to be disconnected from the substrate and fail to function properly. While numerical methods such as finite element analysis provides a useful tool for the study, the results need to be verified experimentally. This is because some important system parameters such as damping or stiffness are estimated for numerical analysis, which inherently involves uncertainties. Using results obtained for the experiments, the assumptions made can be modified to improve the modeling accuracy.

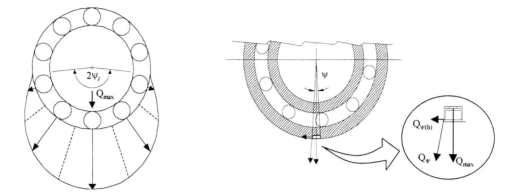

Fig. 3 Load distribution in a ball bearing   Fig. 4 Load application on the sensor module

3. EXPERIMENTAL STUDY

Experimental studies have been conducted on a scaled-up version of the sensor module which is three-times larger than the miniaturized version illustrated in Fig. 2. The scaled-up model consists of a copper-covered PCB substrate, IC chips, discrete electronic components, and a battery cell, as shown in Fig. 5. To study the dynamic load applied to the components, representative test points were selected on the model, as shown in Fig. 6. The test points were chosen at the corner of the module substrate, close to the rectangular hole on the substrate through which a piezoceramic sensing element is placed, and along the edge of the substrate board. Vibration amplitudes on these points were measured by a Kistler accelerometer model 8636B50. The specifications of the accelerometers include: sensor weight 5.5 g, measurement range ± 50 g, sensitivity 100mV/g, and bandwidth 0.5 Hz – 7 kHz.

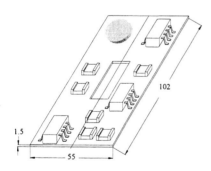
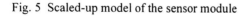
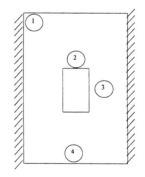

Fig. 5 Scaled-up model of the sensor module   Fig. 6 Representative test points on the substrate

The schematic given in Fig. 7 shows the experimental setup used to test the scaled-up model of the sensor module. The signal generator generated sinusoidal signals up to a frequency of 1,500 Hz. The signal was used to excite the electromechanical shaker, which then drove the sensor module mounted on the shaker. A mechanical fixture was fabricated to hold the substrate board. Electronic components were glued onto the substrate board at specified test point locations. The mechanical coupling between the components and the substrate board can be modeled by the vibration model in Fig. 8. The electronic component has a mass, M_1, and the lead act as spring with spring constant K_1 and damping coefficient C_1. Similarly, the substrate board has a damping coefficient C_2 with mass M_2. The effective spring coefficient of the board due to boundary conditions and material properties is modeled as K_2, which is a combined effect of contributing stiffness such as k_1, k_2, and k_3.

During experiments, the accelerometer was placed besides and directly on the selected test points of the model. The acceleration signal was processed by a charge amplifier, which was also connected to a digital oscilloscope for on-line data display. In Fig. 9, photos of the experimental setup were shown.

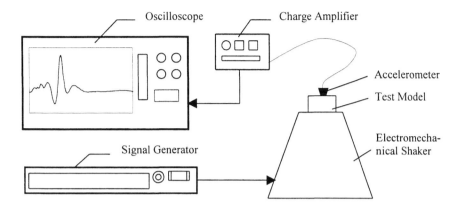

Fig. 7 Schematic of experimental setup

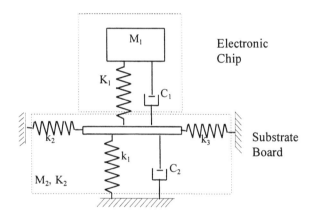

Fig. 8 Vibration model of the mechanical coupling between electronics and substrate board

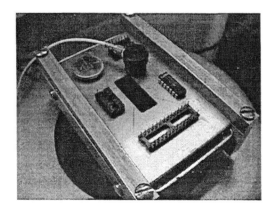 

Fig. 9 Photos of the experimental setup

4. EXPERIMENTAL RESULTS

The substrate board vibration at selected test points 1 through 4 are shown on Figures 10 and 11. The damping ratio of the substrate board system is determined through calculation of the logarithmic decrement δ_n. This is obtained to by measuring the vibration amplitude of the first peak X_0 and that after n cycles, X_n: $\delta_n = (1/n) \cdot \ln(X_0/X_n) = 2\pi\zeta / \sqrt{1-\zeta^2}$. The damping ratio of the system was found to be about 0.3.

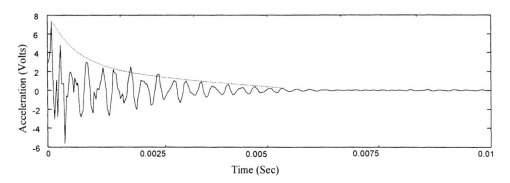

Fig. 10 Decaying oscillation of the substrate board with components on it

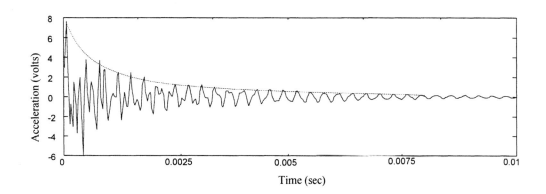

Fig. 11 Decaying oscillation of the substrate board without components on it

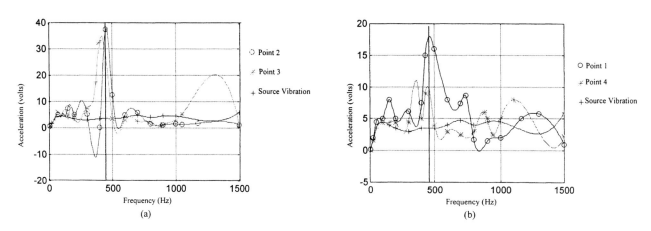

Fig. 12 Frequency response of the substrate board, with components, at test points 2 and 3 and 1 and 4

Another set of experiments was conducted to determine the frequency range within which the system can operates safely. If a slightly damped system such as the sensor module operates in the vicinity of its resonant frequency, the solder joints between the electronic components and the substrate board or the leads of the ICs can be easily broken due to the large vibration. This will cause the entire system to fail. A resonance situation of the integrated sensor module can be caused by a certain rotational speed of the bearing. From the result obtained, it was observed that the first resonant frequency occurs at around 430 Hz, as shown in Fig. 12. For an outer raceway integrated sensor module, this situation would occur only when the bearing is rotating at about 6,500 rpm. Since the bearing used for the presented study (SKF 6220) has a limiting speed of 3,000 rpm, no resonance-related problem is to be expected for the designed sensor module. However, this situation can change rapidly if the bearing has a defect which generates high frequency components. Therefore, proper damping needs to be designed into the sensor module to prevent resonance-related system failure from happening.

5. CONCLUSION AND FUTURE WORK

Proper design of a miniaturized sensor module for integrated bearing condition monitoring requires careful consideration of various aspects, which involve both mechanical and electrical engineering disciplines. A large-scaled version of a miniaturized sensor module was experimentally investigated to obtain insight into its dynamic behavior. Experimental data obtained provided input for the numerical modeling and analysis. Based on the results of this work, the design of the miniaturized sensor module will be modified to improve its vibration behavior. Future work will include thermal analysis and modeling to take into account heat generation from the electronic components.

6. ACKNOWLEDGMENT

This work has been supported by the National Science Foundation under CAREER DMI-9624353, and by the SKF Condition Monitoring company. The authors would like to thank Mr. Changting Wang for his assistance in the experiments.

7. REFERENCES

1. I. Farrel, "Vibration Analysis in the Press Section - Case Studies at Caledonian," Paper Technology, Vol. 35, No. 7, pp. 36-40, 1994.
2. N. Tandon and B. Nakra, "Defect Detection in Rolling Element Bearings by Acoustic Emission Method," *Journal of Acoustic Emission*, Vol. 9, No. 1, pp. 25-28, 1990.
3. D. Tepfer and L. Baldor, "Sikorsky Says Cause of Crash Was Subcontractor's Bearings", Connecticut Post, June 29, 1996.
4. S. Pandit, A. Joshi, and D. Paul, "Bearing Defect Detection using DDS and Wavelet Methods," *Proc. ASME Dynamics Systems and Control Division*, DSC-Vol. 58, pp. 341-348, 1996.
5. Y. Ueno, K. Mori, and N. Kasashima, "An On-line Diagnostic Method to Predict the Spalling on a Ball Bearing," *Proc. ASME Japan/USA Symposium on Flexible Automation*, Vol. 1, pp. 449-452, 1996.
6. C. Berggren, "Diagnosing Faults in Rolling Element Bearings Part 1: Assessing Bearing Condition," *Vibrations*, Vol. 4, No. 1, pp. 5-13, 1988.
7. R. Gao and P. Phalakshan, "Design Consideration for a Sensor-Integrated Roller Bearing", *Proc. ASME IMECE*, Rail Transportation Division, RTD-Vol. 10, pp. 81-86, 1995.
8. R. Gao, Y. Jin, and R. Warrington, "Microcomputer-based Real Time Bearing Monitor", *IEEE Transactions on Instrumentation and Measurement*, Vol. 43, pp. 216-219, 1994.
9. T. Harris, "Rolling Bearing Analysis", Third Edition, John Wiley & Sons, Inc., 1991.

Design of a mechatronic bearing through sensor integration

Robert X. Gao, Brian T. Holm-Hansen, and Changting Wang

Department of Mechanical and Industrial Engineering
University of Massachusetts
Amherst, MA 01003

ABSTRACT

Increasing demands for product safety and reliability requires the development and implementation of innovative condition monitoring mechanisms that are an integral part of the system to be monitored. Since an advanced condition monitoring system often consists of a variety of sensing, controlling, and actuating components, their effective and efficient integration requires the application of mechatronic design principles to achieve the desired synergy. This paper presents several aspects related to the design and implementation of a sensor-embedded mechatronic bearing, which can be used for the condition monitoring of various critical machine systems.

Keywords: mechatronic design, bearing condition monitoring, piezoceramic sensor, system integration

1. INTRODUCTION

A mechatronic system comprises mechanical, electrical, and control devices which are interconnected in their functionality. A modern jetliner is a good example. While flying under autopilot, the velocity and altitude of the aircraft are detected by various sensors. This information is processed by an onboard computer, and the computer flies the aircraft by manipulating its control surfaces. Through wireless communication with ground navigation stations, the current location of the aircraft is determined. The design of such a plane must simultaneously address mechanical and electronic issues. The dynamics of the aircraft determine the minimum speed at which data is acquired and control decisions are made, and the type of electrical components is determined by their operating conditions and requirements, which in turn is determined by the mechanical design. A mechatronic design philosophy is required.

In addition to control, another reason for integrating electronics into a system is for condition monitoring. The purpose is to prevent any unexpected failures by electronically monitoring the mechanical components. This has significance in many industrial and commercial applications, where unexpected machine components or system failure may not only cause severe economic losses (e.g. derailment of cargo trains due to wheel bearing overheating), but also even endanger human lives (when the rotor shaft bearing of a helicopter fails). Illustrated in Fig. 1 is the concept of a sensor-embedded "smart" bearing system that can be incorporated into a helicopter. The "smart" bearing has a miniaturized sensor module integrated into its outer raceway to measure the load and temperature conditions within the bearing. Since the data provided by the embedded sensor is taken directly from the location where a defect signal would originate, the amount of noise due to structure borne vibration is reduced. For load measurement, the output of an embedded force sensor can be divided into low and high frequency components. The low frequency components are dominated by the load carried by the sensor each time a rolling element passes over the embedded sensor, whereas the high frequency components are due to vibration caused by rolling contact[1-2]. If the bearing has a defect, then the defect could be detected in the high end of the vibration spectrum. For the presented study, this load and vibration measurement is accomplished by a single piezoceramic sensor which generates an electrical charge every time it is mechanically compressed. The charge generation can be generally described as:

$$[D] = [d][T] + [\varepsilon^T][E] \tag{1}$$

Further author information -
R. X. G.: Email: gao@ecs.umass.edu; Phone: 413-545-0868; Fax: 413-545-1027
B.H.H.: Email: bholmhan@ecs.umass.edu; Phone: 413-545-2362; Fax: 413-545-1027
C.W.: Email: cwang@ecs.umass.edu; Phone: 413-545-2362; Fax: 413-545-1027

244

Part of the SPIE Conference on Mechatronics ● Boston, Massachusetts ● November 1998
SPIE Vol. 3518 ● 0277-786X/98/$10.00

In Eq. (1), $[D]$ is the dielectric displacement, $[d]$ is the piezoelectric charge constant, $[T]$ is the applied stress, $[\varepsilon^T]$ is the dielectric permittivity, and $[E]$ is the applied electric field[3]. Referring to the coordinate system notation given in Fig. 2, the six stress components are written as T_i, $i = 1, 2, \cdots, 6$. With this notation, T_1 is a compressive stress on a face perpendicular to axis 1, and T_4 is a shear stress on a face parallel to axis 1.

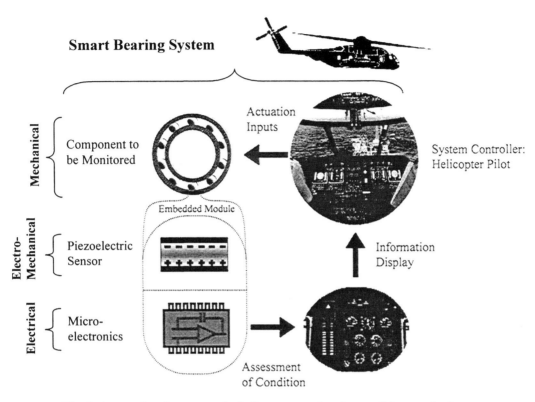

Fig. 1 A smart bearing system for helicopter rotor bearing condition monitoring

2. SENSOR MODEL

For a raceway-embedded sensor, the mechanical model is illustrated in Fig. 3. The section of the raceway over the embedded sensor is modeled as a beam which is clamped at the ends and supported by a spring at the center. The piezoceramic is compressed each time a rolling element passes over the slot. With the 3 axis of the sensor aligned vertically, electrodes located on the top and bottom surfaces and no electric field applied, Eq. (1) reduces to:

$$D_3 = d_{33}T_3 \qquad (2)$$

Assuming that the applied stress is due to a load F evenly applied over a face with surface area A, then $T_3 = F/A$. Multiplying both sides of equation (2) by A then gives:

$$Q = d_{33}F \qquad (3)$$

where Q is the electrical charge produced by the load F. The load on the sensor is determined by the load on the rolling element passing over it, and this is given by the Stribeck equation:

$$q(\psi) = q_{\max}\left[1 - \frac{1}{2\varepsilon}\left(1 - \cos\psi\right)\right]^n \qquad (4)$$

where $q_{max} = 5F_r/Z$, Z is the number of rolling elements, and ε is the load distribution factor[4]. From the model in Fig. 3, the load on the sensor is given by:

$$F = \frac{5Y_{33}AF_r\left[1-(1-\cos\psi_r)/2\varepsilon\right]^{\frac{10}{9}}\left(D^2-L^2\right)\cdot\tan^2(\psi_r)\cdot\left(2\sqrt{D^2-L^2}\tan(\psi_r)-3L\right)}{\left(192EIh-Y_{33}AL^3\right)\cdot Z} \tag{5}$$

where Y_{33} is the elastic modulus of the piezoceramic material, E is the elastic modulus of the bearing material, I is the moment of inertia of the cross-section of the modified raceway, D is the outside diameter of the bearing, and ψ_r is the location of a rolling element as it passes over the raceway slot. A charge amplifier is used to convert the sensor output Q, as given by Eqs. (3) and (5), to a voltage. For the output of the embedded sensor to be useful, the circuit design must take into account the characteristic frequencies of the bearing. The bandwidth of the electrical components must be compatible with the bandwidth of the mechanical components.

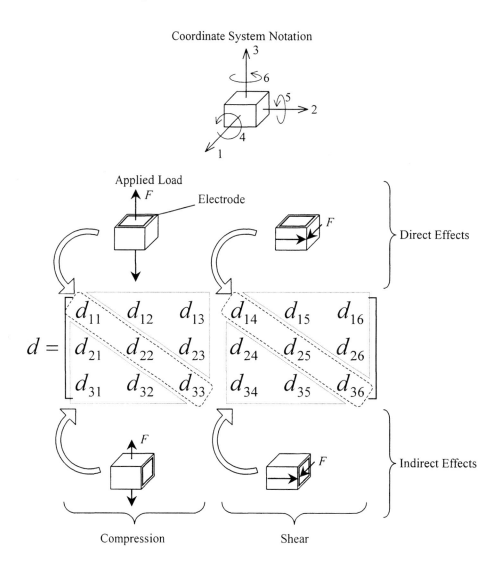

Fig. 2 Electromechanical behavior of a piezoceramic sensor

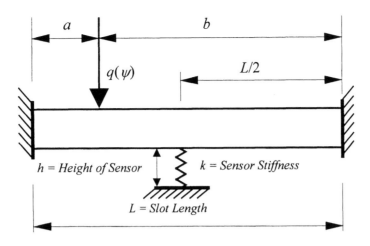

Fig. 3 Simplified mechanical model of a raceway embedded piezoceramic force sensor

3. SIGNAL FREQUENCIES

Several characteristic frequencies are of interest for the bearing condition monitoring. If the outer raceway is fixed and the inner raceway rotates at f, then the cage frequency is given by:

$$f_m = \frac{f}{2}(1 - d_b/d_m)$$ (6)

where d_b is the diameter of a rolling element, and d_m is the pitch diameter of the bearing. The frequency at which a rolling element passes over the raceway-integrated sensor is:

$$f_o = \frac{f}{2}(1 - d_b/d_m)Z$$ (7)

The frequency at which a rolling element passes over a point on the inner raceway is:

$$f_i = \frac{f}{2}(1 + d_b/d_m)Z$$ (8)

The rotational frequency of a rolling element is:

$$f_r = \frac{f}{2}\frac{d_m}{d_b}\left(1 - (d_b/d_m)^2\right)$$ (9)

For the presented study, a SKF 6220 ball bearing has been used which has the following dimensions: ball diameter $d_b \approx 24$ mm, bore diameter $d = 100$ mm, outer diameter $D = 180$ mm, pitch diameter $d_m = 140$ mm, and number of rolling elements $Z = 10$. With these dimensions, Eqs. (6) through (9) give $f_m/f = 0.41$, $f_o/f = 4.14$, $f_i/f = 5.86$, and $f_r/f = 2.83$. If the sensor is located in the outer raceway and used for load measurement, then the circuit must have a bandwidth which goes beyond 4 times the speed of the inner raceway in order to capture the first harmonic of a load signal. For a structural defect detection, the bandwidth must go beyond at least 6 times the speed of the inner raceway to capture the first harmonic of a defect signal. For practical purposes, several harmonics should be captured. To capture 10 harmonics of the vibration caused by an inner raceway defect, the bandwidth should be at least 60 times the maximum shaft speed.

If the shaft speed is given in Hertz and the charge amplifier has gain G, then the output of the embedded sensor module is given by:

$$V = Gd_{33}F$$ (10)

where F is given by Eq. (5) with $\psi_r = 2\pi f_m t = \pi f t(1-d_b/d_m)$. A simulated output of a sensor module embedded in a SKF bearing model 6220 is shown in Fig. 4, with the shaft rotating speed $f = 1.0$ Hz. The corresponding spectrum is shown in Fig. 5. Compared to the impulsive type of input that is caused by a defect, the load signal is relatively smooth. As shown in Fig. 5, most of the frequency content is in the lower end of the spectrum. Thus, if the bearing has a defect, then the sensor module output should have a spectrum which is dominated in the lower frequency range by the load and in the upper frequency range by the defect. The spectrum of the sensor module output for a bearing with an inner raceway defect is shown in Fig. 6. As expected, the lower frequency range is dominated by the load measurement, and the upper frequency range is dominated by harmonics of the defect frequency f_i. For an inner race defect, successive impacts occur at different locations in the load zone, and this causes the spectrum to be lobed. Figure 7 shows the spectrum of the sensor module output for a bearing with an outer raceway defect. The lower frequency range is again dominated by the load measurement, and the upper frequency range is dominated by harmonics of the defect frequency f_o.

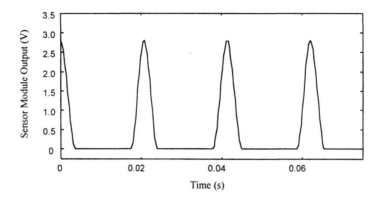

Fig. 4 Predicted output of an embedded sensor module

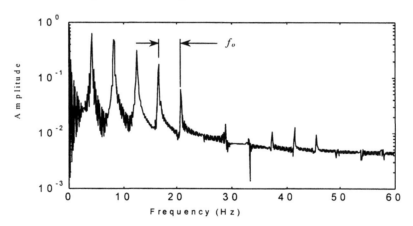

Fig. 5 Frequency spectrum of predicted sensor output

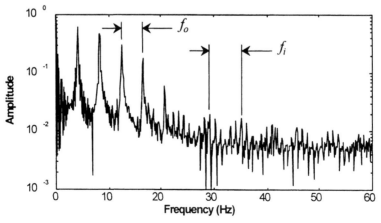

Fig. 6 Spectrum of predicted sensor output with an inner raceway defect

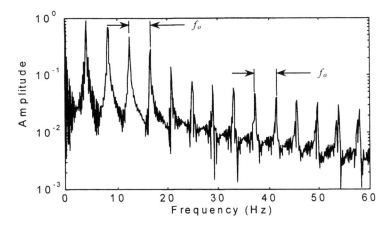

Fig. 7 Spectrum of predicted sensor output with an outer raceway defect

4. DATA COMMUNICATION AND USER INTERFACE

To enable effective data communication between the bearing embedded sensor module and external machine control system, a telemetric system has been designed. Telemetry refers to the process of information collection from a distant source by means of wireless data transmission using radio frequencies (RF). For many practical applications, the wireless approach offers greater flexibility and convenience in setting up a data acquisition system, and may be the only viable approach due to various boundary conditions that prevents a wired data transmission scheme (such as limited space available, physical interference with the processes, mobility or portability requirement, etc.). Figure 8 illustrates a data communication system for the bearing embedded sensor module through telemetry. The system operates in the ISM frequency band (920 MHz), and features a virtual instrument-based user interface.

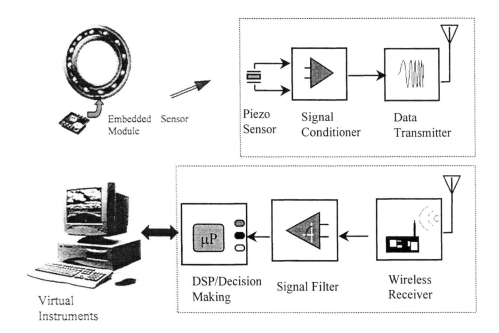

Fig. 8 Telemetric data communication system implemented for the embedded sensor module

A virtual instrument (VI) is a computer-based, software-driven test and measurement device. It utilizes the computational power of a generic computer's CPU and defines its specific functions through software programming. Various test and measurement functions can be realized by a virtual instrument, including control of information flow from a peripheral device over a standard interface to the central processing unit, analysis, processing, and display of acquired data, and data management. For the presented study, the VI system presents a communication link between the bearing embedded sensor module and the user. In addition to effectively display the acquired sensor data, data analysis in time and frequency domains need to be conducted by the VI to evaluate the bearing's dynamic response and inception of failure mode. A VI-based user interface "Integrated Bearing Defect Analyzer" is shown in Fig. 9. The upper left window of the analyzer shows real-time signals in the time domain, and the lower window shows the FFT analysis with normalized magnitude. The right hand side of the analyzer shows the configuration of the Analyzer. Users can choose which signal to display, what for an analysis tool (FFT, enveloping or wavelet) to apply, and the appropriate type of filter to be used. Others functions include real-time temperature display and threshold setting, filter cut-off frequencies, and sampling rate for data acquisition.

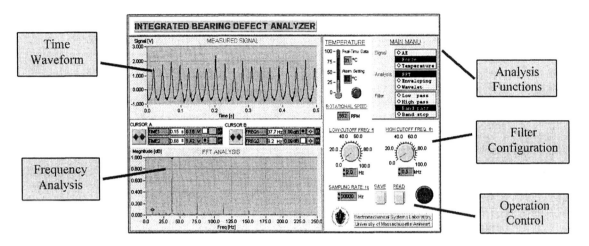

Fig. 9   A virtual instrument-based user interface for integrated bearing condition monitoring

5. CONCLUSION

Mechatronic design principles provide a systematic approach to effectively integrate various engineering aspects for the implementation of advanced machine condition monitoring system. In addition to bearing monitoring, the presented integrated sensing and control scheme can be applied to many other situations where reliable functioning of the system is of critical importance. Digital telemetric techniques are being explored to enhance the system's capability of multiple bearing condition monitoring.

6. ACKNOWLEDGMENT

This work has been supported by the National Science Foundation under CAREER DMI-9624353, and by the SKF Condition Monitoring company.

7. REFERENCES

1. B. Holm-Hansen and R. Gao, "Vibration analysis of a ball bearing with an integrated sensor", *Technical Papers of the North American Manufacturing Research Institution of SME, (NAMRC XXVI)*, pp. 131-136, Atlanta, GA, May 19-22, 1998.
2. B. Holm-Hansen and R. Gao, "Multiple defect analysis of a sensor integrated ball bearing", *Proc. 1998 ASME International Mechanical Engineering Congress and Exhibition, Dynamic Systems and Control Division*, Anaheim, CA, November 15-20, 1998.
3. J. Tichy and G. Gautschi, "Piezoelectric Measurement Technique", Springer-Verlag, 1980.
4. T. Harris, "Rolling Bearing Analysis", Third Edition, John Wiley & Sons, Inc., 1991.

Mechatronic objects for real-time control software development

Patrick F. Muir[a] and Jeremy W. Horner[b]

[a]Robotics Institute and the [b]Department of Electrical and Computer Engineering
Carnegie Mellon University, Pittsburgh, PA 15213

ABSTRACT

The design of real-time control software for a mechatronic system must be effectively integrated with the system hardware in order to achieve useful qualitative benefits beyond basic functionality. The sought-after benefits include: rapid development, flexibility, maintainability, extensibility, and reusability. In this work, we focus upon the interface between the device drivers and the control software with the aim to properly design this interface to best realize the aforementioned benefits. The results of this fundamental research include the development of an easily manageable set of four C++ object classes following an object-oriented approach to software design. These Universal Mechatronic Objects (UMOs) are applicable to a wide spectrum of actuators including dc motors, stepper motors, and solenoids; and sensors including pressure sensors, microswitches, and encoders. UMOs encapsulate the interface between the electrical subsystem and the control subsystem, providing the control software developer with a powerful abstraction that facilitates the development of hardware-independent control code and providing the electrical subsystem developer with an effective abstraction that facilitates the development of application-independent device drivers. Objects which are intuitively related to hardware components of the mechatronic system can be declared using the UMOs early in the system development process to facilitate the rapid concurrent development of both the electrical and the control subsystems.

Our UMOs were developed as part of a project to implement a real-time control system for a z-theta robotic manipulator. The z-theta manipulator is one component of the Minifactory project in the Microdynamic Systems Laboratory at Carnegie Mellon University. The goals of this agile assembly project include the reduction of factory setup and changeover times, plug-and-play type modularity, and the reuse of its components. The application of UMOs to the manipulator software development is shown to be consistent with these goals.

Keywords: object oriented programming, mechatronics, real-time control, mechatronic system design

1. INTRODUCTION

1.1 The growing role of mechatronics[1]

The development of systems incorporating mechanical, electrical, computer control and application software subsystems, is becoming commonplace. Today there are more solution options available to mechatronic system developers than ever before. Given a desired system functionality, there are often multiple solutions which will achieve the desired functionality using differing combinations of technologies. Instead of simply finding a satisfying solution, the opportunity to choose the "best" solution from among the alternatives is a reality. A solution which tightly integrates a set of highly interdependent components may be costly in terms of schedule and resources but result ultimately in the highest possible performance. On the other hand, a solution which is the straight-forward combination of existing technologies can minimize schedule and resource requirements, but does not take advantage of interdisciplinary synergies and results in suboptimal performance. We advocate a middle ground position in this paper, where interdisciplinary synergies are incorporated through proper configuration of subsystems, but the bulk of the development schedule and resources are devoted to realizing each subsystem from existing technologies. The intent being to achieve some desired synergies between subsystems while maintaining low resource and schedule requirements.

Specifically, we address mechatronic system development as a composition of subsystems which correspond roughly to the technical disciplines involved: mechanical, electrical, control and software engineering. Often a team approach is used, where each member is skilled in a relevant discipline. Given a functional specification for the system, and an understanding of the issues involved, compose the system from subsystems each of which can be reasonably achieved by the appropriate expert, then realize each of the subsystems and assemble the complete system. The synergy between subsystems of the system is built into the manner in which the system is composed from individual subsystems.

Once a synergistic set of subsystems has been configured, there remains the fundamental problem of specifying the interfaces between subsystems. As these integration and interfacing issues become more and more prevalent in research and

Part of the SPIE Conference on Mechatronics • Boston, Massachusetts • November 1998
SPIE Vol. 3518 • 0277-786X/98/$10.00

251

development projects, it is apparent that new mechatronics tools and methodologies will be needed to deal with them. In this paper, we present one such tool: Universal Mechatronic Objects (UMOs). These UMOs can be applied to any mechatronic system to form the interface between the electrical and the computer control subsystems and thereby act as an effective foundation upon which the control and application software can be built.

In the following discussions, we will refer to the person/team responsible for implementing the electrical and controls subsystems respectively as the *electrical developer* and the *controls developer*. The discussions do not specify how many team members need to participate; in fact, a single person could act as both electrical developer and controls developer for some projects. Advantages accrue through the application of UMOs independent of the team's size and makeup.

1.2 The electrical subsystem/control subsystem interface

We are focusing upon the interface between the electrical subsystem and the control subsystem in this work. Figure 1 depicts the various hardware and software layers involved. The first software layer above the hardware consists of device drivers which interact directly with the computing hardware. The device drivers are considered part of the *electrical* subsystem because their development requires intimate knowledge of how the actuators and sensors are interfaced to the computing hardware. It is then efficient use of resources; therefore, that an electrical developer compose the device drivers. The control developer will need to read the sensors and write to the actuators, but need not be concerned with the details of how this reading and writing is accomplished.

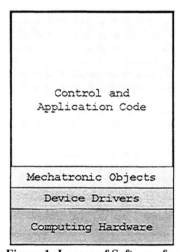

Figure 1: Layers of Software for a Mechatronic System

As can be seen in Figure 1, mechatronic objects are shown to be the interface between the device drivers (i.e., the electrical subsystem) and the control software (i.e., the control subsystem). Given this arrangement, we discuss in Section 4, how we designed the mechatronic objects to encapsulate the access functions for actuators and sensors so that the hardware-dependent details of the device drivers are hidden from view of the control developer. Further, the application-specific details of the control algorithms and application software are hidden from view of the electrical developer. The assembly of the mechatronic objects can be accomplished by the team member responsible for system integration, (i.e., a mechatronics engineer perhaps), early in the project, before either the electrical or control developers begin their work. Periodically throughout the course of the project the mechatronic objects can be re-evaluated based upon progress thus far. We propose that by defining the boundary between the electrical and control subsystems by the use of a standard set of UMOs, the entire project will proceed more quickly, efficiently and reliably toward the desired functional system realization.

1.3 Object oriented programming

We are advocating that an object oriented paradigm is appropriate for the definition of the electrical/control subsystem boundary. Object oriented programming, in contrast with more traditional structured programming methodologies is modular in a way which allows the assembly of all variables and functions relating to a concept. For example, an actuator (sensor) has associated with it certain variables and functions which all must be present for the programmer to use it effectively, but which are not necessary if the actuator (sensor) is not used. The required variables, called *member variables*, might include the actuator's name, the last value commanded to the actuator, and a variable whose value indicates whether the actuator is synchronous or asynchronous. The required functions, called *member functions*, might include an initialize function that sets-up the actuator for use, a write function, and a finalize function that is called when the program is about to exit. In such a case, it is useful to encapsulate these variables and functions into a single module, called an *object*. The C++ language has been designed to facilitate OOP with the built-in type *class*. An object that is derived from a particular class is called an *instance* of the class.

One advantage of the use of C++ and Object Oriented Programming (OOP) is the notion of inheritance. We can define a class which encapsulates all of the member variables and functions required for a wide spectrum of actuators and is entirely independent of any particular actuator. Then we can derive an instance of the class for each *particular* actuator in our system. Each of these actuator objects will *inherit* the member variables and functions of the parent class with no additional coding. The modularity enforced through the application of OOP allows software to be constructed so that improvements can be implemented through *local* modifications only. Thus for example, if changes are made to the device driver code, no changes will be necessary in the control code and visa versa. Also, because the programming objects (i.e, actuators and sensors) relate directly with the actual system components (i.e., actuators and sensors), no new abstract concepts need to be mastered. Further benefits will accrue if UMOs are applied consistently across multiple projects incorporating a wide variety of hardware because control software from one project can be readily reused on another.

1.4 Paper organization

We present our reasoning and implementation of UMOs as follows. Section 2 enters into a discussion of the motivations for our research in the area. Desired characteristics of both the system development process and the resulting system are introduced to motivate our work. Following this, Section 3 describes prior work which is relevant to the topic. Our four UMOs are detailed in Section 4. Here we provide complete printouts of C++ code which may be included and used in the software for any mechatronic system. Then in Section 5, we describe our application of UMO's to the development of a z-theta robot manipulator. This manipulator is an important component of an on-going project to develop a modular reconfigurable system for automated precision assembly called Minifactory. Finally, in Section 6, we conclude with a short discussion of the results.

2. MOTIVATION

2.1 Introduction

There are several possible approaches for interfacing the electrical and control subsystems. Consider this simple but prevalent situation: A mechatronic system incorprates a DC motor driven by an amplifier that is interfaced to the control computer by a Digital-to-Analog Converter (DAC) circuit. A control function is implemented to compute the voltage to next be applied to the motor. How do we write the software to command this voltage?

One solution would be to write an inline device driver within the control function that outputs an arbitrary 8-bit value to the DAC. Then, convert the voltage value into an appropriate 8-bit value and execute the device driver with the computed 8-bit value. This solution would function, but has many undesired characteristics. Firstly, the inline device driver code must be repeated in all of the functions which utilize the DAC which increases the size of the code unnecessarily. The control developer also needs to understand the operation of the DAC so as to convert his desired voltage into an appropriate 8-bit value. The more technology each team member must master, the greater are the chances for errors. It would be advantageous for the control developer to be able to write his code without needing to understand parts of the electrical subsystem. If ever the device driver needed to be changed, (for example, if a bug is found in the driver), then all copies of the device driver need to be located and changed. Such practices are prone to errors resulting from inconsistent coding of the device drivers.

An improvement on the aforementioned solution would be to write the device driver as a macro and allow the compiler to insert inline code everywhere the macro is invoked from the single master definition. This method ensures that all applications of the function are consistent, but does nothing to relieve the control developer from mastering parts of the electrical subsystem.

An even better solution might be to encapsulate the device driver in a function. This single function can then be called at runtime by the control software and any other software that uses the DAC. The device driver function could require a parameter which specifies the desired motor voltage in volts so that the control developer need not understand how to convert his voltage into an appropriate 8-bit value for the DAC. This solution is a widely-practiced method of solving the problem, because venders of DAC cards often provide device drivers with their products (as do vendors of many other types of interface cards). However, this solution still requires the control developer to know that a DAC is utilized in the commanding of the voltage to the motor. This issue may not seem very important in the case of one DAC and one motor, but with typical systems, multiple actuators with multiple types of interface circuits (e.g., digital IO (DIO), quadrature counters, ADC, and DAC circuits) are present and the control engineer is required to match IO channels to actuators and sensors and understand which electrical components are involved with each command of a voltage to a motor. Further, there is often more than one way to command a particular interface circuit to produce the same result (e.g., writing bits, bytes, or words) and sometimes values must be written in associated registers in order to achieve the results desired (e.g., data direction registers, output enable bits, etc.) This solution simply requires the control developer to master too much of the electrical system which has presumably already has been mastered by the electrical developer. And what if some part of the electrical subsystem is reconfigured? The control code must then also be changed.

Now consider a solution arrived at by proper application of the object-oriented paradigm. The *DAC-Amplifier-DC Motor* combination is declared as an object. Even though this object is not detailed until Section 4, we can describe the effects of its use here. If the object is one of a *standard* set of UMOs, the control developer may already be familiar with the interface which it presents, so he can apply it with no additional knowledge of how the results will be achieved. The solution is simply for the control engineer to include a standard header file in the file containing the control software, and at the point where he needs to command the voltage to motor he calls the member function `motor.write(voltage)` where `motor` is the name of the particular motor and `voltage` is the desired motor voltage. Similarly the electrical developer may already be familiar with the UMOs and he knows that he must write a device driver segment that takes as input a voltage in volts and executes all the conversions and low-level bit twiddling required to get that voltage to appear at the motor. This scenario is indeed an improvement over the prior methods. The control developer doesn't have to understand the operation of the DAC. In fact, he need not know that a DAC and amplifier are used. Even if the DAC and amplifier are replaced half-way through the project by a DIO and an amplifier with a direct digital input, the control engineer need not be concerned. Furthermore, the control developer can start working on his control software before the circuits are built, before the motor arrives, even before the electrical developer who will be writing the device driver joins the team. Likewise, the electrical developer can work independently. Moreover, there will be no disagreements over how values are passed between subsystems because this is part of the definition of the UMOs and is available for inspection by all beforehand.

We do not wish to imply that the control subsystem can be written in all cases without accounting for the transfer functions of the actual electronics used. However, it has been our experience that in most practical cases the *form* of the control software can be designed independent of the drive hardware and only gains need be adjusted for use with differing drive electronics and interface circuits.

Our intention here is merely to introduce some of the important issues relating to the specification of the electrical/control interface. In Sections 4 through 6, we provide complete declarations of the UMOs and the reasoning behind them.

3. PRIOR WORK

The subject of our work can be succinctly described as the application of OOP to the software interface between the device drivers and the control software for mechatronic projects. In this narrowly defined area, we are not aware of any similar works. However, prior publications in the areas of object-oriented programming (OOP) and the C++ programming language, OOP applied to control system design, and OOP applied to robotics projects are closely related precursors to our work. Here we review a representative sampling of these works.

Object oriented programming is a topic of much discussion and progress in the last few years. The advantages of OOP over more traditional structured programming methods is by now well documented [2, 3]. Although object oriented design can be implemented using several different programming languages, C++ is the language of choice [4, 5] for most of the literature that we have reviewed because of its many built-in features which facilitate OOP. As will be seen in Section 4, the salient characteristics of actuators and sensors can be mapped directly to member variables and member functions of object classes in C++ by application of the object oriented paradigm.

For the realization of industrial control systems, Ericsson [6] advocates the application of the object-oriented paradigm to all phases of control system development including functional specification, design, and implementation. He illuminates the application of an object oriented formalism in translating verbal system specifications into object definitions at a high level of abstraction. His work does not address individual actuators and sensors.

Pereira [7] similarly applies the object oriented paradigm to the development phases of a real-time industrial automation application. His assignment of physical equipment to software objects encompasses the lowest levels including individual actuators and sensors. However, his work introduces specific objects as they are needed by the system at hand and does not develop universal classes which are useful for a spectrum of actuators and sensors as we do. A software layer between the system hardware and the application software is introduced to perform device driver functions but no special interface is identified between the device drivers and the control code.

There is a growing list of projects employing OOP technologies in robotics. One of the earliest works was the development of a Robot Independent Programming Environment [8] (RIPE) at Sandia National Laboratories. The RIPE incorporated a four level programming structure and a hierarchy of generic parent classes. Their device driver level included such complex devices as bar code readers and gantry robots and so can not be equated to the much simpler, lower-level device drivers referred to in our work. The object classes within the higher software levels are documented but not for the lower levels. No generic actuator or sensor classes were published. Further, the interface between the lowest-level device drivers and the control code is given no special significance.

OOP has been applied to production control systems [9]. In the referenced work, the objects are intelligent manufacturing objects each of which represent a complicated piece of production machinary, such as a CNC turning machine. The authors do not model individual actuator or sensors. Their work focuses upon the scheduling, controlling and monitoring of the manufacturing objects.

Our research differs from these previous works. First and foremost, we are unique in our identification of the device-driver/control software interface as a boundary between engineering disciplines. As such, the design of the interface becomes a fundamentally important *mechatronic* issue. We have gone several steps beyond this realization to arrive at a universal set of objects (i.e., the UMOs) which can be applied to any mechatronic project to provide a functional, reusable, intuitive interface layer of software that facilitates system development. Also, our application of the object oriented paradigm is, in general, at a lower level than is previously documented.

Our results are similar to these previous works insofar as the benefits which accrue through the application of OOP. Ericsson[6] sites the intuition, reusability, useful abstraction, and faster development benefits that accrue. Pereira[7] concludes that information encapsulation, robustness, and reusability are some of the advantages realized. Miller and Lennox[8] site the benefits: reusability, extensibility, reliability and portability. Gausemeier[9], et.al. list the advantages of the application of OOP as flexibility, ability to distribute and scale the system, portability, and reusability.

4. UNIVERSAL MECHATRONIC OBJECTS

4.1 Introduction

We detail the design and application of our set of four UMOs in this section. Section 4.2 delves into a discussion of the characteristics which are desired for the electrical/control software interface. We review the reasoning which led us to decide what level of modularity is appropriate for mechatronic objects in Section 4.3. The nomenclature used for referring to different types of mechatronic objects is explained in Section 4.4. Then in Section 4.5, the UMOs are presented including complete listings of actual C++ code.

4.2 Desired characteristics for an electrical/control interface

The discussions in Section 2 illuminate some of the characteristics of a good electrical/control subsystem interface. Here we list all of the characteristics that we have identified to be useful for this interface. The interface should be:

- **functional** - the code must function as an interface between the electrical and control software subsystems.
- **universal** - the code must apply to a broad spectrum of actuators and sensors, and their associated electronics.
- **modular -** the code corresponding to a conceptual entity must be easily manipulated as a single unit.
- **intuitive** - the code must be easy to understand and apply, providing an appropriate level of abstraction.
- **complete** - the code should unambiguously define all aspects of the interface.
- **concise** - the code should incorporate only those features that are typically required in most applications.
- **extensible** - the code should allow future addition of custom member variables or functions.
- **efficient** - a reasonable attempt should be made to avoid excessive computational overhead.
- **compact** - a reasonable attempt should be made to avoid excessive memory requirements.

It should be noted that reuseablity derives directly from the universal and modular characteristics of the code. Reusability is the practical benefit that accrues when the code embodies both universal and modular characteristics. Similarly, rapid development and maintainability are practical benefits that result from the modular, concise, and intuitive characteristics of the code.

4.3 What are the objects?

The applicability of OOP techniques to a particular problem can be ascertained by the amount of commonality between the concepts in the problem space. It is, therefore, useful to identify the concepts and the commonalities involved in the device-driver/control software interface. Figure 2 depicts the generic interconnection of actuators and sensors within a mechatronic system.

Actuators, such as motors, solenoids, speakers, relays, LEDs, and valves receive controlled power for their operation by driver electronics of some type. For a DC servo motor, this may be a large, complex motor amplifier. For an LED, the drive electronics may consist simply of a current-limiting resistor. In order for the computer software to control the actuator, an output circuit is used. For motor amplifiers that require an analog voltage command, the output circuit would be a DAC. If the actuator is an LED or a relay, the output circuit would be a DIO.

In an analogous fashion, sensors, such as switches, temperature, pressure, humidity, position, velocity, acceleration and force sensors require filter electronics and an input circuit. For example, a shaft encoder requires a quadrature decoder/counter in order to count the number of pulses generated by the encoder. In this case, the input circuit is a DIO channel consisting of 8 or more parallel bits. For a microswitch, the filter electronics may consist simply of a current limiting resistor, and the input circuit is a single DIO bit.

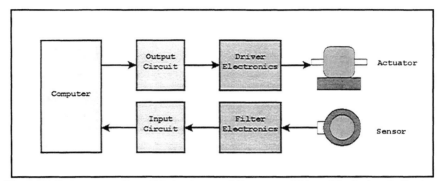

Figure 2: Interconnection of Actuators and Sensors within a Mechatronic System

The concepts that we select to be objects in our code should correspond to the concepts which have commonality that can be exploited to our benefit. Suppose we select a motor to be an object. The electrical interface to a motor consists of wires connected to its internal coils. A brushed motor has one set of two wires. A three-phase brushless motor may have 3, 4 or 6 input wires depending upon how it is internally wired. A stepper motor may have 4, 6 or 8 wires. We could similarly list differing control functions required by different motors. Clearly there is not much commonality evident in the selection of a motor as an object. The same is true if we were to select a specific sensor, such as an encoder, as an object.

Now consider grouping the drive electronics with the motor as an object. An amplifier for a brushless DC motor and one for a brushed DC motor may both accept DC analog voltages in the range -10V to 10V as inputs. Thus, we have more commonality at this level of abstraction than when assigning motors and encoders as objects. However, there are other difficulties at this level. Some DC servo motor amplifiers require digital inputs, some stepper motor drivers require a step bit and a direction bit, and others require a serial RS232 connection to command the motor. If we were to group individual sensors with their respective filter electronics, we would similarly find that some produce analog outputs in various configurations and others provide various configurations of digital outputs. We must conclude that this level of abstraction is also inadequate.

Consider grouping together the combination of a specific motor, drive electronics, and output circuit and call this an object. The interface to this object is now at the level of memory-mapped input/output circuitry. The command for an LED, solenoid, or valve is a single output bit. The command for a stepper motor is a set of bits. The command for a DC servo motor, brushed motor, AC motor or any other motor is a set of bits. By grouping a sensor with its filter electronics and input circuit we similarly find that in all cases the interface is a set of bits. This is a natural consequence of the fact that actuators and sensors are memory-mapped within the computer and thus accessed by reading and/or writing to memory locations. For this reason, there is a great deal of commonality at this level of abstraction. We have chosen to use this level of abstraction for our UMOs.

Listing 1: Common Type Definitions
```
//common.h
#ifndef COMMON_H
#define COMMON_H

typedef enum {ZERO, ONE, ON, OFF, RIGHT, LEFT, UP, DOWN, HIGH, LOW, FRONT, BACK,\
              CW, CCW, ENABLE, DISABLE, PASS, FAIL, COMPLETE, INCOMPLETE} binary_enum;
typedef enum {Z_ENCODER_COUNTER_INPUT, T_ENCODER_COUNTER_INPUT,\
              C_PRESSURE_SENSOR_INPUT, G_PRESSURE_SENSOR_INPUT, Z_MOTOR_DAC_OUTPUT,\
              T_MOTOR_STEP_OUTPUT, T_MOTOR_DIRECTION_OUTPUT, Z_ENCODER_ZERO_OUTPUT,\
              T_ENCODER_ZERO_OUTPUT, C_VACUUM_SOLENOID_OUTPUT, G_VACUUM_SOLENOID_OUTPUT,\
              G_PRESSURE_SOLENOID_OUTPUT, TIMER_INPUT} io_enum;
typedef enum {VOLTS, DEGREES, SAMPLING_PERIODS, MICRONS} units_enum;

#endif  COMMON_H
```

4.4 Nomenclature

The following naming conventions will be applied throughout the remainder of the paper to simplify our presentation. We will refer to the combination of a particular actuator with its associated drive electronics and output circuit simply as an "actuator". Likewise, we will refer to the combination of a particular sensor with its associated filter electronics and input circuit simply as a "sensor". Using this terminology, we must always be sure to identify all three components when describing an actuator or sensor. It is not complete to specify that an actuator is a DC motor; because a DC Motor which is driven by a PWM Amplifier through a single DIO bit requires a different interface than the same motor when it is driven by an analog amplifier through a DAC. We will use hyphenated notation as a shorthand method for referring to actuator and sensor configurations. For example, the two actuators just described can be denoted as *DIO-PWMamplifier-DCmotor* and *DAC-AnalogAmplifier-DCmotor* and a typical sensor encountered would be denoted as *ADC-LowPassFilter-Microphone*.

Listing 2: Universal Mechatronic Object Declarations: Actuators

```
//ioLib.h
#ifndef IOLIB_H
#define IOLIB_H
#include "common.h"
//---------------------------------------------------------------------------
class binary_actuator
{
private:
  bool is_synchronous; //True if the actuator is synchronous, false if asynchronous
  binary_enum current_command; //If synchronous, the most recent value commanded
  binary_enum current_value; //Most recent value written to the actuator
  binary_enum default_value; //Value written to the actuator for reset
  binary_enum one_name; //The name for the 1 state, e.g. "on"
  binary_enum zero_name; //The name for the 0 state, e.g. "off"
public:
  io_enum name;
  binary_actuator(io_enum name_parameter, bool is_synchronous_parameter,\
                  binary_enum default_value_parameter, binary_enum one_name_parameter,\
                  binary_enum zero_name_parameter);
  ~binary_actuator();
  reset(); //Resets asynchronously the actuator
  bool write(binary_enum value);  //Commands a value to the actuator
  bool update(); //Writes the most recently commanded value to the actuator
  binary_enum read(); //Returns the value most recently commanded
}; //---------------------------------------------------------------------------
class digital_actuator
{
private:
  bool is_synchronous; //True if the actuator is synchronous, false if asynchronous
  float current_command; //If synchronous, the most recent value commanded
  float current_value; //Most recent value written to the actuator
  float default_value; //Value written to the actuator for reset
  float min_value; //Smallest value that can be commanded to the actuator
  float max_value; //Largest value that can be commanded to the actuator
  float resolution; //Smallest command increment
  float zero_offset; //Command producing zero output
public:
  io_enum name;
  units_enum units; //All values have these units
  digital_actuator(io_enum name_parameter, units_enum units_parameter,\
                  bool is_synchronous_parameter, float default_value_parameter,\
                  float min_value_parameter, float max_value_parameter,\
                  float resolution_parameter, float zero_offset_parameter);
  ~digital_actuator();
  reset(); //Resets asynchronously the actuator
  bool write(float value); //Commands a value to the actuator, returns true if ok
  bool update(); //Writes the most recently commanded value to the actuator
  float read(); //Returns the value most recently written to the actuator
};
```

In practice, software that is written to be easily understandable for accessing actuators which require only one output bit is significantly different than software that is intuitive for accessing those requiring a group of bits. The difference is that the binary state of the IO bit for actuators which use only one bit has a *logical* meaning whereas, for all other actuators the group of IO bits has a *numeric* meaning. For this reason, we refer to actuators which require a single output bit as *binary actuators* and those requiring a group of output bits are referred to as *digital actuators*. Similarly, Sensors requiring only one input bit are referred to as *binary sensors* and those requiring a group of input bits are *digital sensors*. In Section 4.5, it will become apparent why the software for a binary device is different from that for a digital device.

Our set of four UMOs (i.e., the binary actuator, digital actuator, binary sensor and digital sensor) is sufficient for modeling all devices which have a single interface value, for this reason we refer to this set of four mechatronic objects as the *atomic objects*. Some devices must be modeled as an combination of atomic objects. For example, a *DIO-StepperDrive-StepperMotor* actually requires two binary actuator objects, one binary actuator acts as the step signal and the second binary actuator acts as the direction signal. Another example would be a servo axis consisting of a *DAC-Amplifier-DCmotor* for axis drive and a *DIO-QuadratureCounter-Encoder* for axis feedback. We refer to mechatronic objects such as these which are formed as the combination of other mechatronic objects as *compound objects*.

```
                    Listing 3: Universal Mechatronic Object Declarations: Sensors
//ioLib.h continued

//------------------------------------------------------------------------------
class binary_sensor
{
private:
  bool is_synchronous; //True if the sensor is synchronous, false if asynchronous
  binary_enum current_value; //the most recent value read
  binary_enum one_name; //the name for the 1 state, e.g. "on"
  binary_enum zero_name; //the name for the 0 state, e.g. "off"
public:
  io_enum name;
  binary_sensor(io_enum name_parameter, bool is_synchronous_parameter,\
                binary_enum one_name_parameter, binary_enum zero_name_parameter);
  ~binary_sensor();
  binary_enum read(); //Reads a value from the sensor
  bool sample(); //Reads directly from the sensor and stores in current_value
  reset(); //Resets asynchronously the sensor
}; //---------------------------------------------------------------------------
class digital_sensor
{
private:
  bool is_synchronous; //True if the sensor is synchronous, false if asynchronous
  float current_value; //If synchronous, most recent value read
  float min_value; //Smallest value that can be read
  float max_value; //Largest value that can be read
  float resolution; //Smallest value change that can be read;
  float zero_offset; //Value read corresponding to zero
public:
  io_enum name;
  units_enum units; //All values have these same units
  digital_sensor(io_enum name_parameter, units_enum units_parameter,\
                 bool is_synchronous_parameter, float min_value_parameter,\
                 float max_value_parameter, float resolution_parameter,\
                 float zero_offset_parameter);
  ~digital_sensor();
  float read(); //Reads a value from the sensor
  bool sample(); //Reads directly from the sensor and stores in current_value
  reset(); //Resets asynchronously the sensor
}; //----------------------------------------------------------------------------
#endif  //IOLIB_H
```

4.5 Mechatronic Object Declarations

We now present and discuss the declaration of the mechatronic objects. Listing 1 is an excerpt from a header file named `common.h` because the type declarations therein are common to all of the other files. This listing contains the enumerated type `binary_enum` which contains all of the names which may be used to denote the two states of a binary actuator or binary sensor. The use of words, such as "on" and "off" to represent the two states of a binary actuator is far more intuitive than the use of the numbers 1 and 0. Similarly, the enumerated type `io_enum` facilitates the use of intuitive names for referring to actuators and sensors. We could have used the standard type `string` for naming them, but the computational overhead associated with the manipulation of strings is not warranted. The enumerated type `units_enum` enables the use of names for specifying the units for actuator and sensor values. This listing was taken from the code for the z-theta manipulator, so the actual enumerated entries may be different for a different mechatronic system. The use of these types will become obvious in the following code listings.

```
Listing 4: Code Structure for Device Drivers
//ioMan.cc
#include "ioMan.h"
#include "common.h"
//---------------------------------------------------------------------------
void IO_initialize(io_enum name_parameter)
{ switch(name_parameter)
  { case FIRST I/O_NAME: INITIALIZATION CODE FOR FIRST I/O; break;
    case SECOND I/O NAME: INITIALIZATION CODE FOR SECOND I/O; break;
    :
    case LAST I/O NAME: INITIALIZATION CODE FOR LAST I/O; break;
    default: cout << "No initialize function for that name." << endl;
};};
//---------------------------------------------------------------------------
void IO_finalize(io_enum name_parameter)
{ switch(name_parameter)
  { case FIRST I/O_NAME: FINALIZATION CODE FOR FIRST I/O; break;
    case SECOND I/O NAME: FINALIZATION CODE FOR SECOND I/O; break;
    :
    case LAST I/O NAME: FINALIZATION CODE FOR LAST I/O; break;
    default: cout << "No finalize function for that name." << endl;
}; };
//---------------------------------------------------------------------------
void IO_reset(io_enum name_parameter)
{ switch(name_parameter)
  { case FIRST I/O_NAME: RESET CODE FOR FIRST I/O; break;
    case SECOND I/O NAME: RESET CODE FOR SECOND I/O; break;
    :
    case LAST I/O NAME: RESET  CODE FOR LAST I/O; break;
    default: cout << "No reset function for that name." << endl;
}; };
//---------------------------------------------------------------------------
long IO_read(io_enum name_parameter)
{ switch(name_parameter)
  { case FIRST SENSOR NAME: READ CODE FOR FIRST SENSOR; return(VALUE);
    case SECOND SENSOR NAME: READ  CODE FOR SECOND SENSOR; return(VALUE);
    :
    case LAST SENSOR NAME: READ  CODE FOR LAST SENSOR; return(VALUE);
    default: cout << "No read function for that name." << endl; return(0);
}; };
//---------------------------------------------------------------------------
void IO_write(io_enum name_parameter,long value_parameter)
{ switch(name_parameter)
  { case FIRST ACTUATOR NAME: WRITE CODE FOR FIRST ACTUATOR; break;
    case SECOND ACTUATOR NAME: WRITE  CODE FOR SECOND ACTUATOR; break;
    :
    case LAST ACTUATOR NAME: WRITE  CODE FOR LAST ACTUATOR; break;
    default: cout << "No write function for that name." << endl; break;
}; };
```

Listing 2 displays the declaration of binary and digital actuators. Listing 3 displays declarations for binary and digital sensors. Taken together these two listings form the basis for all mechatronic objects.

Looking at the class `binary_actuator`, we find six *private* member variables. These member variables are private, meaning that they can not, and need not, be accessed by any of the device driver or control software. The Boolean variable `is_synchronous` is either true or false indicating whether or not the particular actuator should be commanded synchronously each sampling period, or should be commanded immediately whenever the `write` function is called. The member variable `current_value` stores the last value that was written using the `write` function. `One_name` and `zero_name` are the names of the states corresponding to 1 or 0 binary values. The `default_value` is the name of the state in which the actuator will be initialized or reset to. The remaining variable, `current_command`, is the value that was last commanded to the actuator hardware. Note that if the actuator is asynchronous, the `current_command` will be assigned the `current_value` as soon as the `write` function is called. Whereas, a synchronous actuator will not change its `current_command` until the next time `update` is called, even if `write` has been called one or more times.

The only public member variable is the actuator's name. The `name` is used within the device drivers to make the proper correspondences between device driver code segments and mechatronic objects. The member function having the same name as the class, `binary_actuator`, is called the *constructor* according to C++ terminology. This is the function that gets called when the user declares a new object of this class, which explains why one parameter for each of the member variables is passed to the function. Upon calling the constructor a new object is created and the member variables are assigned to be equal to the parameters passed. The actuator is also initialized when the constructor is called. The function `~binary_actuator` is the *destructor*. This function is called to free up the resources allocated to the object after it is no longer needed. The function `reset` simply calls the device driver code segment `io_reset` which typically sets the value of the actuator to its default value, but may be programmed by the electrical developer for other duties as well. The function `update` commands the `current_value` to the actuator hardware and thus only applys to synchronous actuators. The `write` function gives the actuator a new value and returns true if it was successful. The `read` function returns the value of `current_command`.

The private member variables for the digital actuator differ from those of the binary actuator by the lack of `one_name` and `zero_name` and the addition of `min_value`, `max_value`, `resolution`, and `zero_offset`. `Min_value` and `max_value` correspond respectively to the minimum and maximum values that can be commanded to the actuator. The variable `resolution` denotes the command change corresponding to a one bit change. The `zero_offset` is the value that must be commanded to the actuator to obtain a zero response. There is one additional public member variable called `units` whose meaning is self-evident. The ability to specify the units of the actuator commands allows the control developer the ability to program using the units which are best suited for each particular actuator. Whereas all values within a `binary_actuator` are of type `binary_enum` and are interpreted using the specified values of `one-name` and `zero-name`, all values within a `digital_actuator` are of type `float` and are interpreted according to the `units` member variable.

A binary sensor is declared similar to a binary actuator except that no `default_value` or `command_value` are needed. Sensors do not have a `write` function nor an `update` function. In contrast, a `sample` function is included which applies only to synchronous sensors. The `read` function only reads the state of the actual hardware if the sensor is declared as asynchronous. Otherwise a call to `read` will return the `current_value`; the `current_value` itself will not be set from the actual hardware until the next execution of the `sample` function. Digital sensors behave like binary sensors insofar as sampling and reading are concerned, and like digital actuators in the way that units are used.

It is worth mentioning that the four classes could be declared hierarchically with a *device* class having the member variables `is_synchronous` and `name` and the function `reset`, because these are common to all the classes. Derived from the parent *device* class could be *binary_device* and *digital_device* classes which respectively declare additional commonalities. Then at a third level, the four atomic objects could be declared with only the member variables and functions not already declared by their respective parent classes. We have chosen not to make the declarations in such a hierarchical fashion because it has been reported[10] that the use of inheritance in this way incurs additional processor overhead that degrades the real-time performance, and because it tends to make the classes less intuitive. However, the user, at his discretion could rewrite the classes hierarchically and still enjoy all of the other benefits described in this paper.

The declarations for the mechatronic objects should be included in the control developer's code. The electrical developer has a different interface to deal with. In order for the mechatronic objects to access the device drivers properly, the device drivers must adhere to the simple format shown in Listing 4. The electrical developer must program four device driver code segments for each atomic actuator or sensor. Three of the required code segments are `IO_initialize`, `IO_finalize`, and `IO_reset`. Additionally, for each actuator he must provide `IO_write` and for each sensor he must provide `IO_read`. Once written, these code segments are simply inserted into the appropriate case statements shown in Listing 4. The code segment `IO_initialize` prepares an atomic object for use. Conversely, `IO_finalize` performs any tasks which are required when the object is retired from use.

Early in the development of a mechatronic system the integrator must declare each of the actuators and sensors in the system as an object. Compound objects must be modeled as an combination of atomic objects. For example, a servo axis might consist of a *D/A-Amplifier-DCmotor* for axis drive and a *DIO-QuadratureCounter-Encoder* for axis feedback. A compound object is declared by *aggregating* its component objects as will be shown in Section 5. One way to understand the roles of atomic and compound objects is by analogy with C++ types. The C++ language provides built-in types which can be applied directly, such as `char`, `int` and `float`. The user then is able to aggregate multiple chars, ints or floats within a `struct` to model compound data structures. Analogously, the UMO provides four built-in atomic objects (binary_actuator, digital_actuator, binary_sensor and digital_sensor) and the user is able to aggregate atomic objects in order to model combinations of these.

Once they are declared, each actuator (sensor) will *inherit* all of the member variables and functions defined by the *UMO*. This provides a powerful standard interface for use by the control developer even before any device drivers are written. In other words, the UMO's provide an abstraction for the control developer which allows the computer control software to be written in a portable, hardware-independent manner. Further, the electrical developer can compose the device drivers and format them to interface with the UMO's in a straightforward standard way as well. Thereby, the UMO's provide an abstraction for the electrical developer which allows the device driver software to be written in an application-independent manner. Central to the advantages of UMOs is the ability of the electrical and control developers to proceed with the development of their respective subsystems independently and in parallel. We propose that in practice this will result in a reduction in the total time for system development when compared with the traditional practice of not clearly defining this interface at all.

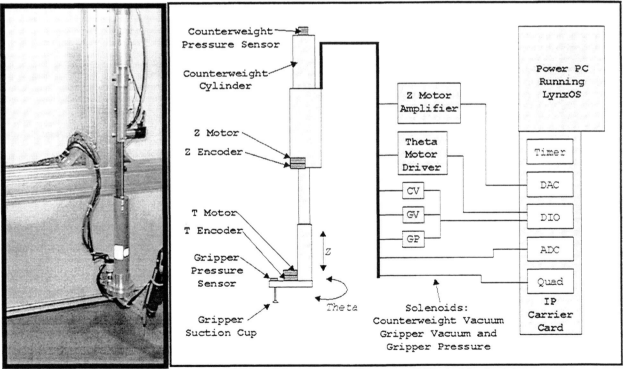

Figure 3: Photograph and Block Diagram of the Prototype Z-Theta Manipulator

5. CASE STUDY: Z-THETA MANIPULATOR

5.1 Minifactory Overview

Minifactory[11] is an on-going project within the Microdynamic Systems Laboratory in the Robotics Institute at Carnegie Mellon University. The goal of the project is to develop a modular system for automated precision assembly. The system concept centers around the operation of small table-top *courier* robots which carry subassemblies from one overhead processing station to another so as to realize the assembly of a product. It is envisioned that most processing stations will incorporate a *z-theta manipulator* for manipulation of parts. We have applied the UMOs described in this report to the control of a prototype z-theta manipulator.

5.2 Overhead Manipulator Hardware

Figure 3 shows a photograph and a block diagram of the major mechatronic components of our prototype z-theta manipulator. The control computer is a PowerPC running the Lynx real-time operating system. There is a carrier card plugged into the PC that allows the installation of up to 6 Industry Pack (IP) interface circuits. We utilize timer, digital to analog converter, digital input/output, analog to digital converter, and quadrature counter IP modules.

The z-axis has an associated servo motor, motor driver, and encoder with zero pulse. The theta-axis has an associated stepper motor[1], stepper driver with step and direction inputs, and encoder. There is a pneumatic counterbalance cylinder with an associated pressure sensor and vacuum solenoid. Gripping of parts is accomplished by an end-mounted suction cup which has an associated vacuum solenoid and pressure sensor for gripping parts, and a pressure solenoid for releasing parts. Note that the video camera in the photograph was connected directly to a video monitor for part viewing and is not considered in the following discussion.

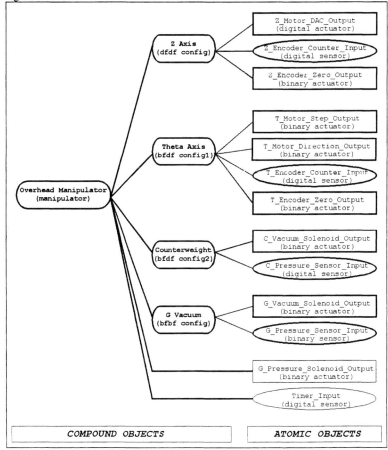

Figure 4: Heirarchy of Mechatronic Objects for the Z-Theta Manipulator

---

[1] Because the prototype manipulator was intended as a testbed for control and application software development, this step motor and step/direction driver configuration was sufficient. However, a dc motor with PWM amplifier is planned for our second-generation manipulator design to enable more precise positioning.

5.3 Overhead Manipulator Objects

A straightforward mapping of actuators, sensors and their associated electronics and interface circuits to objects using the UMOs was performed and the results are diagrammed in Figure 4. Atomic actuators are diagrammed by rectangles, atomic sensors as ovals, and compound objects as rounded rectangles. It is evident that most of the objects are declared as atomic objects. Four compound objects are associated with the z, theta, counterweight, and gripper control groups. The remaining compound object represents the entire manipulator and aggregates both atomic and compound objects.

Notice that there is not a one-for-one mapping of hardware devices and objects. The *DIO-QuadratureCounter-Encoder* on the z-axis has two objects associated with it. One is a digital sensor representing the encoder count and the other is a binary actuator representing the control bit that allows the quadrature counter to zero when a zero pulse is detected by the encoder. Similarly, the *DIO-StepperDriver-StepperMotor* on the theta-axis requires one binary actuator to represent the step input and a second binary actuator to represent the direction bit. It would not be proper to declare the *DIO-stepperDriver-StepperMotor* as a 2-bit digital actuator because the two control bits do not represent the *numeric* value of a control signal. Notice that the counterweight pressure sensor is modeled as a digital sensor; whereas, the gripper pressure sensor is modeled as a binary sensor. This is correct because the counterweight pressure sensor has an analog output voltage that is read using the ADC. The gripper pressure sensor is a two-state threshold device that is read through one bit of the DIO.

The `Timer_Input` object is a good example of how to use a sensor object to synchronize the software execution to hardware that produces interrupts. The `IO_initialize` device driver segment for `Timer_Input` sets up a counter to produce interrupts every sampling period; in this case every millisecond. The `read` function of the `Timer_Input` can be called from the control software using the C++ line of code: `missed=Overhead_Manipulator.timer->read()`. This line of code causes the `IO_read` device driver segment for `Timer_Input` to run. The `IO_read` segment blocks, allowing other processes to run, until an interrupt from the timer occurs, then it simply returns a zero to the calling software. If at least one interrupt has already occurred since the last time `read` was called, the function returns immediately with an integer representing the number of interrupts which were missed. Thus, even though there is no physical sensor involved in sampling period timing, a digital sensor object can be used to interface with the timer.

Listing 5: Declarations of Mechatronic Objects for the Overhead Manipulator

```
digital_actuator z_motor_dac_output(Z_MOTOR_DAC_OUTPUT,VOLTS,true,\
                         0.0,10.0,10.0,(10.0/2047.0),0.0);
binary_actuator t_motor_step_output(T_MOTOR_STEP_OUTPUT,true,DOWN,UP,DOWN);
binary_actuator t_motor_direction_output(T_MOTOR_DIRECTION_OUTPUT,true,CW,CW,CCW);
binary_actuator z_encoder_zero_output(Z_ENCODER_ZERO_OUTPUT,false,DISABLE,ENABLE,DISABLE);
binary_actuator t_encoder_zero_output(T_ENCODER_ZERO_OUTPUT,true,DISABLE,ENABLE,DISABLE);
binary_actuator c_vacuum_solenoid_output(C_VACUUM_SOLENOID_OUTPUT,true,OFF,ON,OFF);
binary_actuator g_vacuum_solenoid_output(G_VACUUM_SOLENOID_OUTPUT,true,OFF,ON,OFF);
binary_actuator g_pressure_solenoid_output(G_PRESSURE_SOLENOID_OUTPUT,true,OFF,ON,OFF);
digital_sensor z_encoder_counter_input(Z_ENCODER_COUNTER_INPUT,MICRONS,true,\
                         55000.0,129000.0,4.64357,-147871.0);
digital_sensor t_encoder_counter_input(T_ENCODER_COUNTER_INPUT,DEGREES,true,\
                         -270.0,270.0,0.000529483,227.4438);
digital_sensor c_pressure_sensor_input(C_PRESSURE_SENSOR_INPUT,VOLTS,true,\
                         0.0,1000.0,1.0,0.0);
digital_sensor timer_input(TIMER_INPUT,SAMPLING_PERIODS,false,0.0,99999.9,1.0,0.0);
binary_sensor g_pressure_sensor_input(G_PRESSURE_SENSOR_INPUT,true,FAIL,PASS);
dfdf_config z_axis(&z_motor_dac_output,&z_encoder_counter_input,&z_encoder_zero_output);
bfdf_config1
t_axis(&t_motor_step_output,&t_encoder_counter_input,&t_motor_direction_output,\
                         &t_encoder_zero_output);
bfdf_config2 counterweight(&c_vacuum_solenoid_output,&c_pressure_sensor_input);
bfbf_config g_vacuum(&g_vacuum_solenoid_output,&g_pressure_sensor_input);
manipulator overhead_manipulator(&z_axis,&t_axis,&counterweight,&g_vacuum,\
                         &g_pressure_solenoid_output,&timer_input);
```

5.4 Overhead Manipulator Software

Listing 5 shows the actual declarations of these objects. The compound objects in the system must be customized. One representative example is shown in Listing 6. The remaining compound objects are not included for lack of space, but can be reproduced easily using the one listed as an example. The compound objects only require three member functions:

reset, update and sample. Each of these functions simply calls the functions of the same name for each of its components. For example, the update member function for `Overhead_Manipulator` simply calls the update functions for its components which are or which contain actuators: `Z-Axis`, `Theta_Axis`, `Counterweight`, `G_vacuum`, and `G_Pressure_Solenoid_Output`. In this way, one call to the function `overhead_manipulator.update` will recursively update all the actuators in the system. Similarly, all of the sensors can be sampled using `overhead_manipulator.sample`.

Listing 6: One of the Compound Objects for the Z-Theta manipulator

```
class bfbf_config //binary_feedforward_binary_feedback_configuration
{public:
  binary_actuator* feedforward_device;
  binary_sensor* feedback_device;
  bfbf_config(binary_actuator* feedforward_device_parameter,\
          binary_sensor* feedback_device_parameter);
  update();
  sample();
  reset();   };
```

The complete set of manipulator objects forms the foundation for the control and application code for the system. One way to write modular control functions would be to develop the control functions as member functions of the appropriate mechatronic objects. For example, a function that steps the theta motor one step would be a member function of the object `T_Motor_Step_Output`. A function that returns the motor to a specific position would require access to the theta motor step and direction and the encoder, so it would be written as a member function of the theta_axis object. In this manner, the hierarchical organization of the mechatronic objects can be used to organize the control functions as well.

6. DISCUSSION

We have developed a set of four software objects, collectively referred to as Universal Mechatronic Objects, which provides the foundation for the development of control and application software for any mechatronic system. The flexibility of the UMOs to model a spectrum of actuators and sensors derives from the observation that, at the lowest level, actuators and sensors are accessed by the computer as memory-mapped IO devices. There is a close intuitive correspondence between actual hardware components and the mechatronic objects which facilitates rapid development and easy maintenance of the control software. The UMOs encapsulate the interface between the device-drivers and the control software providing an abstraction to the control developer which is hardware-independent, and thereby facilitating the portability and reuseability of the control code. We envision that this property may allow future systems to generate control code *automatically*. Consistent application of UMOs across several different mechatronic systems will allow software authors and maintainers to develop a familiarity with the objects which can further improve their efficiency, in contrast to the current tendency to develop custom code for each new system.

We have argued that the application of UMOs lead to many desired benefits during the development of a mechatronic system. Quantifiable results are difficult to obtain due to the nature of the benefits. In order to further this work, we are disseminating the UMOs to the interested users. We were unable to include the entire source code for the definitions of the UMOs in this paper because of a lack of space. Moreover, reuse of the code from hardcopy is time consuming and error prone. To facilitate the widespread use of UMOs we will make them and other associated code accessible over the internet at www.cs.cmu.edu/~muir/mechatronics.

7. ACKNOWLEDGEMENTS

This work has been supported by the National Science Foundation under grants DMI-9523156 and DMI-9527190. We would like to thank Ralph Hollis, Minifactory project lead and head of the Microdynamic Systems Laboratory, for his helpful suggestions and support over the course of this work. We would also like to acknowledge Ben Brown for the electromechanical design and construction of the z-theta manipulator and Al Rizzi for the PowerPC setup and the coding of the low-level device drivers for the z-theta manipulator.

8.REFERENCES

1. P.F. Muir, "The Growing Role of Mechatronics in System Realization," *SPIE's International Technical Working Group Newsletter: Robotics and Machine Perception*, Volume 7, Issue 2, August 1998, pp. 4-5.

2. D.G. Firesmith, *Object-Oriented Requirements Analysis and Logical Design*, John Wiley & Sons, New York, 1993.

3. T. Love, *Object Lessons: Lessons Learned in Object-Oriented Development Projects*, Sigs Books, New York, 1993.

4. B.R. Rao, *C++ and the OOP Paradigm*, McGraw-Hill, Inc., New York, NY, 1992.

5. B. Stroustrup, The C++ Programming Language, Third Edition, Addison-Wesley, Reading, MA, 1997.

6. G. Ericsson, "Functional Specification of Industrial Control Systems: An Object-Oriented Approach," *Proceedings of the Third IEEE Conference on Control Applications*, Glasgow, Scotland, UK, August 1994, pp. 1347-1352.

7. C.E. Pereira, "Applying Object-Oriented Concepts to the Development of Real-Time Industrial Automation Systems," *Proceedings of the Third Workshop on Object-Oriented Real-Time Dependable Systems*, 1997, pp. 264-270.

8. D. J. Miller and R.C. Lennox, "An Object-Oriented Environment for Robot System Architectures," *Proceedings of the 1990 IEEE International Conference on Robotics and Automation*, pp. 352-361.

9. J. Gausemeier, K.H. Gerdes and S. Leschka, "Cell Control by Intelligent Objects: A New Dimension of Production Control Systems," *Proceedings of the 1994 IEEE/RSJ/GI International Conference on Intelligent Robots and Systems*, Munich, germany, September 1994, pp. 47-55.

10. G. Glass and B. Schuchert, *The STL Primer*, Prentice Hall PTR, NJ, 1995.

11. R.L. Hollis and A. Quaid, "An Architecture for Agile Assembly," *American Society of Precision Engineering 10th Annual Meeting*, Austin, TX, October 1995.

Open architecture controller for semiconductor assembly system

Tae Won Kim   and   Deok Soo Han

Wire Bonder Team, Precision Machinery Div., Samsung Aerospace Ind.
145-3 Sangdaewon 1-dong, Jungwon-ku, Sungnam City, Kyungki-do 462-121, KOREA

ABSTRACT

To develop a next-generation manufacturing system with flexibility, it is necessary to define H/W and S/W architecture based on an open architecture concept.   To satisfy the open architecture concept, in this paper, H/W is divided into three parts for hard real-time task, soft real-time task, and non-real-time task.   And, S/W also is divided into three layered level for application level, system level, and device level.   Due to the modulization of H/W and S/W, it is easily possible to modify and/or upgrade the control system including S/W and H/W according to user requirements.   Especially, it is also possible to develop a new control system by modifying a part of application and device level.   To show the validity of the proposed method, a detail control concept of wire bonder with the open architecture concept is described.

Keywords : open architecture, real-time control, embedded system, wire bonder

1. INTRODUCTION

To develop a next-generation manufacturing system with flexibility, while minimizing life-cycle cost for the machine controller, as well as for developing the control system itself, it is necessary to define hardware and software architectures based on an open architecture concept[1].

Controller elements, a modularity concept, and higher level requirements for various elements of an open modular architecture controller are stated to convey the definitions of open, architecture controller in the context of automotive applications. Satisfying these requirements will make an open, modular controller to be economical, maintainable, open, modular and scalable, and thus, meet the manufacturing needs in the automotive industry. Expected benefits of having open, modular architecture controllers include reduced initial investments, low life cycle costs, maximized machine uptime, minimized machine downtime, easy maintenance of machines and controllers, easy integration of commercial and user proprietary technologies, plug and play of various hardware and software components, efficient reconfiguration of controllers to support new processes, and incorporation of new technologies.

Because of the need to support a wide range of applications and the continual pressure to be more cost competitive, automotive companies are migrating toward controllers that provide agility and flexibility. In the future, it will no longer be acceptable to take the approach of replacing existing controllers with newer and better models when a few new functions need to be added.

Although it is very difficult to form a universal agreement on the definition of an open system, (1)*vendor-neutrality*, and (2)*component-integrability* can be thought of as two fundamental features of an open system. Vendor-neutrality is necessary because an open system should be designed based on well-established standards that are independent of a single proprietary vendor. Component-integrability is required for the portability and incremental expandability of any open system[2].

In addition to the openness requirement, an OAC must provide guaranteed real-time performance that is one of the fundamental features of automated manufacturing systems. A control task in a manufacturing system consists of several sub-tasks, such as sensing machine status, several levels of control algorithms, and controlling actuators. Some of these tasks are periodically executed and others aperiodically. However, all of them must meet certain timing constraints. In a real-time system, such as a manufacturing system, it is sometimes meaningless to monitor/control the process if these time constraints are not met. However, the issue of meeting real-time constraints has not been adequately addressed in previous research on OAC. Thus, to develop an advanced manufacturing controller, we must achieve two goals. *The first goal is to build a flexible open system to meet the need of integrating advanced machine monitoring and control technologies in a modular manner. The second goal is to build a system with guaranteed response time for tasks at different levels of hierarchy and real-time interfaces between machine application task components in an advanced manufacturing system.*

Section 2 describes the needs of automotive manufacturing applications, and open architecture researches are reviewed in Section 3. Section 4 summarizes requirements for open architecture controller, and Section 5 discusses the configuration of our working machine, SWB-100G. Section 6 introduces design concept of proposed open architecture controller.

2. APPLICATION NEEDS

The wide range of manufacturing applications in the auto industry impose different capability and functionality demands on equipment controllers. These applications are generally categorized into two major classes[1]:

(1) Computer Numerical Control (CNC) type applications requiring coordinated-axis motions and the control of a small number of discrete I/O points such as machining operations, and

(2) Programmable logic control (PLC), discrete event-oriented type applications requiring mostly sequential logic solving, with some non coordinated motions such as transfer line operations.

Within each, the operation requirements can vary greatly.

In case of semiconductor assembly machine such as die bonder and wire bonder, it requires both of two types applications. To be specific, the wire bonder is incorporated with CNC type application for fine control of the XY table and the indexer motor, discrete input sensors, and discrete output actuators, and PLC type applications for bonding sequence, leadframe feeding system and so on.

Also, needs of automotive manufacturing applications can be examined in the following categories:

● **Cost**

It is critical that the life cycle cost- to-benefit ratio associated with controls is minimized. Some factors affecting life cycle economics are:

- costs of wiring, interconnections, and making changes in physical equipment configuration;
- costs of machine down time due to controller failures;
- costs of training personnel in operation, maintenance, programming, making changes and upgrades;
- costs of opportunities lost by not performing upgrades because it is difficult to enhance the functionality of the proprietary equipment without replacing them;
- costs associated with not having the ability to reuse and easily integrate available and proven hardware and software components, tools, and aids.

These factors must be considered when decisions are made to select controllers for particular applications.

Even though life cycle cost is emphasized, the initial implementation cost of an open, modular control system is still an important factor. It is desirable to have the initial cost lower than that of a proprietary control system for equivalent functionality. One of the purposes of specifying open architecture controllers is to have the ability to integrate and leverage multi-vendor control solutions. With wider choices of products, lower cost to performance ratio can be achieved for required functions. Control systems should leverage the rapid technology advancements in the general purpose computing industry in order to improve the overall cost to performance ratio.

● **Flexibility**

Because of rapid changes in market demands, manufacturing systems in the automotive industry is needed to have the flexibility to adjust the product and volume mix. Such adjustments include model changeovers, as well as changes to productions schedules due to unexpected interruptions of production and sudden shifts of customer demands. Controllers of these systems must support changes with minimal change over delay, yet maintain performance requirements. The controllers should also allow users to easily add to or upgrade controller functionality without relying on technology vendors and controller suppliers.

● **Connectivity**

Most machines on the factory floor are generally required to be connected to the manufacturing information system in the plant. Controllers of these machines should allow easy integration of appropriate hardware and software tools to support such connection with minimal cost and effort. It is preferable that off-the-shelf third party components are available to be integrated in the controller for this purpose so that the use of higher cost proprietary technology can be avoided.

Factory floor systems generally have I/O systems, controllers should have integrated diagnostic capability and help functions for both the controllers and the machines being controlled to assist in preventive maintenance and troubleshooting activities. Since different diagnostic functions may be needed for different machines and/or applications, controllers should have tools available for users to develop customized diagnostic functions easily.

● **Maintenance**

In order to minimize the downtime of manufacturing systems, controllers should have integrated diagnostic capability and help functions for both the controllers and the machines being controlled to assist in preventive maintenance and troubleshooting activities. And the controller should support robust plant floor operation (maximum uptime), expeditious repair (minimal downtime), and easy maintenance (extensive support from controller suppliers, small spare part inventory, integrated self-diagnostic and help functions, etc.)

● **Training**

Retraining the workforce to work with an open architecture controller could be a significant cost issue. The controller architecture should be designed to provide an intuitive, user-friendly environment so that the cost of training can be minimized.

3. OPEN ARCHITECTURE RESEARCHES

The major research efforts in the area of open architecture control (OAC) systems include the following:

- The OSACA (Open System Architecture for Controls within Automation systems; ESPRIT III project 6379) project[3] may be one of the largest-scale projects for OAC, in which almost all of the standardization matters including network, application software as well as hardware, have been considered.

- The National Institute of Standards and Technology (NIST) proposed and used the RCS (Real-Time Control System) reference model architecture over the past 15 years[4].

- The Next Generation Controller Program (NGC), based on the RCS reference model, co-sponsored by the National Center for Manufacturing Sciences (NCMS), the U.S. Air Force and Martin Marietta, organized industry requirements and prepared a Specification for an Open Systems Architecture Standard (SOSAS)[5].

- The Enhanced Machine Controller Architecture (ECA) is the next step beyond NGC/SOSAS by NIST. In the ECA project, an open machine tool has been implemented based on the NGC/SOSAS and RCS reference model[6].

- Other research projects like as the Chimera project at Carnegie Mellon University[7], the Multiprocessor Database Architecture for Real-Time Systems (MDARTS)[8] at the University of Michigan, and the Hierarchical Open Architecture Multi-Processor Motion Control System(HOAM-CNC)[9] at the University of British Columbia, have demonstrated a variety of approaches to OAC.

4. REQUIREMENTS FOR OPEN ARCHITECTURE CONTROLLER

To meet the goals stated in Sec.1, we have to consider the following requirements for an open architecture controller.

- The controller architecture must incorporate hardware and software products commercially available and be built to industrial standard specifications.
- The controller infrastructure must have the ability to perform all tasks in a deterministic fashion and satisfy specific timing requirements of an application.
- Controller hardware bus structure must be a standard in the marketplace. VME-bus or some other form of PC bus architecture such as ISA, EISA, or PCI is preferred.
- The overall cost of the controller must be minimized.

- The controller must provide the flexibility for integration of user proprietary technologies.

- The controller must provide appropriate, multi-level security access procedures for using and modifying system and application software programs.

- The information of the controller must be kept simple.

- The information management scheme must support built-in operating and information integrity and ensure that data is valid for all tasks executed in the system. For example, I/O update must be completed before the data is used by other elements in the controller.

- The information management must support proper authorization and priority schemes.

- The information must meet the real-time requirements of the system.

- The interface of the information must be simple and allow data sharing and update from other controller components, e.g. the motion control component of the system.

- The controller architecture must support both messaging and direct memory access capabilities for information exchange.

- The human interface must have the ability to interface with other elements in the controller, using a "well accepted" messaging scheme, such as DDE in a Windows environment.

- The controller architecture must support standard output to server drives, either digital or analog drives.

- The controller architecture must have the flexibility of keeping the trajectory planning and servo control as an entity or separating them.

- The controller architecture must have a common motion control interface that supports multiple vendor products.

- The controller architecture must allow for easily integration of additional axes when required.

- The discrete I/O system of the controller requires an editing and display method that resides underneath the control systems graphical user interface and interfaces with the human interface element of the controller.

- The controller architecture must have the capability to interface with various I/O systems, including those commonly used I/O systems on the market.

- The controller architecture must provide the capability that allows users to modify I/O logic while the I/O logic is being executed, i.e., the on-line editing function.

- The controller architecture must have the flexibility of integrating special functions such as traces or historical records of discrete I/O events.

- The sensor interface must provide a scheme for sensor configuration, initialization, and calibration.

- Sensor data must have pre-defined format that can be processed by the controller.

5. DESIGN OF OPEN ARCHITECTURE CONTROLLER

5.1 Mechanical Configuration

The mechanical configuration of our working machine, SWB-100G[10], is shown in Fig.5-1.   It consists of Linear Stepping Motor(LSM)-based XY table, bonding head incorporating with EFO, USG(Ultrasonic Generator) and optic system with CCD camera, programmable LIU (Load/Indexer/Unloader) and so on.   Almost all of mechanical parts are operated by electrical actuators such as motor or solenoid.   Thus, how to control component and/or synchronize the operating sequence is most important to make the machine properly work.

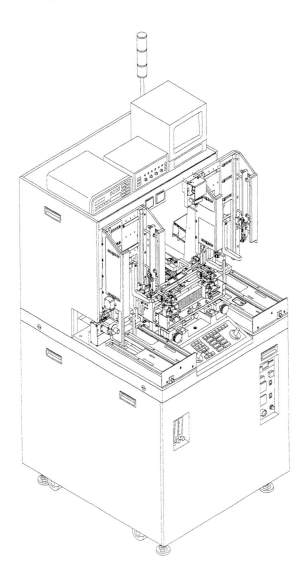

Fig. 5-1. The mechanical configuration of SWB-100G

5.2 H/W Configuration

As described in Sec. 1, this paper is devoted to design an OAC for wire bonder. Thus, the SAOAC (Samsung Aerospace Open Architecture Controller) is designed to meet two basic requirements: *openness* to meet the need of integrating advanced machine monitoring and control technologies, and ***real-time operation*** to guarantee response times of tasks at different levels of abstraction between task components in an advanced semiconductor manufacturing machine.

The base hardware configuration of SAOAC is a distributed system in which processing units are connected through a real-time link/bus. This distributed system enables the use of a range of hardware configurations. Anything from a small micro-controller to a medium-size computer can be a processing node in a particular configuration. However, regardless of their size and functionality, they operate within a unified software hierarchy and maintain communication compatibility with real-time guarantee. To build a heterogeneous configuration while keeping vendor-neutrality, no specific hardware platform is defined for the SAOAC. However, each processing unit is based on an industry standard architecture and built with standard off-the-shelf components such as the VME-bus. Fig. 5-2 shows a typical example of the SAOAC configuration. There are three kinds of processing units in this configuration: *MMI (Man-Machine Interface) unit*, *real-time computing unit*, and *real-time control unit*. The MMI unit is usually used for non-real-time tasks such as programming and non-real-time system monitoring. The real-time computing unit deals with real-time control and monitoring tasks such as real-time data-logging, diagnosis, scheduling, and soft-real-time controls such as operation of indexer motor and/or loader/unloader motors. The real-time control unit performs fine-grain real-time tasks including servo-level control and data-acquisition.

In a distributed system like SAOAC, the communication channel between processing nodes plays an important role for real-time performance as well as its openness. Although there are several communication protocols used for manufacturing automation (e.g, Mini-MAP, CAN and FieldBus), to send periodic, sporadic, and non-real-time messages over a single network in a bounded time, SAOAC adopts the VME bus as a real-time communication link between processing units. Because all units can be installed in a VME-rack and this configuration is very familiar with us. The H/W configuration of proposed controller is shown in Fig.5-2.

The functions of each H/W module of Fig. 5-2 are described as follows;

● CPU Board

It is composed of Motorola MC68040 CPU. It takes charge of supervisory control of all modules in SWB-100G. The main functions are described as follows;

- coordinate I/O modules in Logic I/F,

- communicate with PRS(Pattern Recognition System) for recognition of image

- communicate with DSP board for motion control

- control the non-real-time type motors connected in Motor Control board

● **Logic I/F**

It consists of various I/O modules.   Each I/O module represents a sensor or actuator.   The I/O module interfaces are used by CPU board to check and/or operate sensors and actuators, respectively.

● **DSP Board**

It is composed of TMS320C31 DSP.   It consists of three axis control modules for XY LSM (Linear Stepping Motor) for X and Y directional motion, and VCM (Voice Coil Motor) for Z directional motion.   Each axis control module requires positioning sensor such as encoder.   In SWB-100G, optical encoder sensor and proximity sensor are used for precise control of XY table and VCM, respectively.   The resolution of XY and Z directional control is 0.15625 μm for each direction.

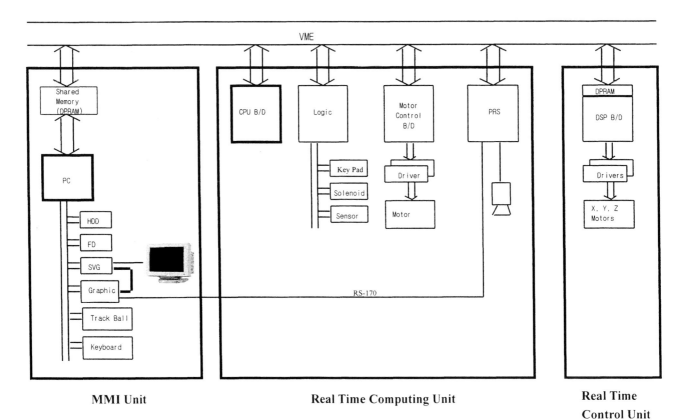

Fig. 5-2. H/W configuration of SWB-100G

● **Motor Control Board**

It controls non-real-time type motors such as indexer motors, step motors for loader/unloader elevators, and other motors.

● **PRS(Pattern Recognition System)**

It is an image processing board.   It can capture the real live video image, recognize the taught features, and returns the result as a position in the image plane.   It can be connected to CPU board via serial cable or VME-bus.

5-3. Software Configuration

To enable the writing of highly portable application programs, which should be completely isolated from the hardware configuration, the software hierarchy of SAOAC consists of three major layers: (1) *application layer*, (2) *object management layer*, and (3) *device driver layer* as shown in Fig.5-3. The application layer is composed of application programs, functional modules, and abstract machine models. Application programs are top-level software that includes the user interface, programming, and monitoring. To make this application program portable, abstract machine models and highly modular functional modules are used, which are independent of hardware configuration. The functional modules and abstract machine models are managed by an application integrator, with which functional modules written for a specific application can be reused or extended for other applications.

An abstract machine model corresponds to a real machine's hardware. This abstract machine model contains a specification of the machine itself as well as the data acquired at run-time. The run-time data are managed by the real-time object manager while ensuring the pre-defined response time. Since an application program as well as functional modules, interact only with the abstract machine models, they are isolated from the hardware. This isolation enables the modules to possess modularity and reusability.

The second software layer of the SAOAC, the object management layer, consists of virtual device driver, system configurator, real-time object manager, and real-time operating system. The main role of the system configurator is a mapping between hardware-independent application software (including functional modules and abstract components) and real hardware such as controlled plants and remote processing modules. If the controlled plant is connected to the local I/O interface hardware, the virtual device driver is used, of which a hardware-specific device driver would eventually have an inherent interface scheme. If the controlled plant is connected to the remote processing modules or any functional module wanting to use the data from the remote processing module, the system configurator uses a network driver for that data. Because   these   mappings by the system configurator are also isolated from writing application programs, they maximize software modularity and reusability. The real-time object manager provides system services tuned to the domain of object-oriented machine control applications. These services extend the micro-kernel operating system services and include domain-specific scheduling of tasks and resources. The object manager also supports persistency and configuration definition. The real-time object manager is designed on top of a commercially-available real-time operating system which has a micro-kernel architecture and a POSIX-compliant interface.

The third software layer of the SAOAC, the device driver layer, is the only hardware dependent part.

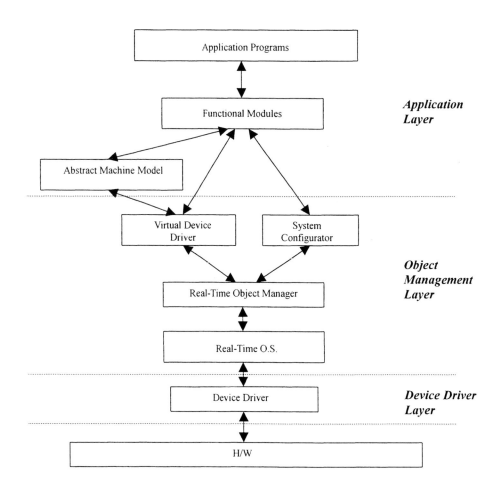

Fig. 5-3. Software hierarchy of SAOAC

6. CONCLUDING REMARKS

In this paper, SAOAC (Samsung Aerospace Open Architecture Controller) is proposed by considering the openness and real-time processing. To develop the next generation controller, the SAOAC achieved three goals. First, our system is fully open, because it does not depend on a specific hardware or software component. Second, our system provides guaranteed real-time operation, an important requirement for advanced manufacturing. Third, our system can integrate a wide range of monitoring or control features in a modular manner.

It is noted that the proposed concept of SAOAC can be implemented to other industrial controller such as die bonder or SMD mounter with small amount of changes, since the architecture was designed by considering openness and flexibility (extendability).

7. REFERENCES

[1] C.Bailo, G.Alderson, and J.Yen, Requirements of Open, Modular Architecture Controllers for Applications in the Automotive Industry, Dec. 1994

[2] J.Park, S.Birla, K.G.Shin, Z.J.Pasek, G.Ulsoy, Y.Shan, and Y.Koren, "An Open Architecture Testbed for Real-Time Monitoring and Control of Machining Processes," Proc. of *American Control Conference*, Seattle, U.S.A, Jun. 1995

[3] G.Pritschow, "Automation technology - on the way to an open system architecture," *Robotics & Computer-Integrated Manufacturing*, Vol.7, No 1, pp.103-111, 1990

[4 F.M.Proctor, B.Damazo, C.Yang, and S.Frechette, Open architecture for machine control, NISTIR-5307, Technical report, National Institute of Standards and Technology, Dec. 1993

[5] Manufacturing Technology Directorate Wright laboratory, Next Generation Controller Specification for an Open Systems Architecture Standard, WI-TR-94-8033, Sep. 1994

[6] F.M.Proctor and J.Michaloski, Enhanced machine controller architecture overview, NISTIR-5331, Technical report, National Institute of Standards and Technology, Dec. 1993

[7] D.B.Steward, R.A.Volpe, and P.K.Khosla, Design of dynamically reconfigurable real-time software using port-based objeccts, CMU-RI-TR-93-11, Technical report, Carnegie Mellon Univ, Jul. 1993

[8] V.B.Lortz and K.G.Shin, MDARTS: A multiprocessor database architecture for real-time systems, CSE-TR-155-93, Technical report, The Univ. of Michigan, Mar. 1993

[9] Y.Altitas and W.K.Munasinghe, "A hierarchical open-architecture CNC system for machine tools," Annals of the CIRP, The Univ. of Michigan, Vol.43, No.1, pp.349-354, 1994

[10] Samsung Aerospace Ind., Maintenance Manual for SWB-100G, 1997

SESSION 8

Mechatronics III

Optimal Input Shaper Design
And
Application to High Speed Robotic Workcells

Timothy Chang, Kedar Godbole, Edwin Hou
Department of Electrical & Computer Engineering
New Jersey Institute of Technology
Newark, NJ 07102

ABSTRACT

This work addresses the design of optimal input shaper and its application to the motion control of a robotic workcell. An optimal shaper is proposed to tradeoff performance and robustness according to assembly specifications of the workcell. The optimal shaper, along with standard shaper designs such as Zero Vibration (ZV), Zero Vibration and Derivative (ZVD), and Extra Insensitive (EI) are applied to conduct cycle time testing on a two-axis Adept Technology Robotic Workcell. The performance of each shaper is evaluated with respect to residual vibration, robustness, and speed. Specifically, the workcell performance for various unknown loading conditions is observed. It is shown that the optimal shaper produces the best overall results.

Keywords: robot control , workcell, optimal shaper, cycle time test

1. INTRODUCTION

A major goal in the control of robotic workcell is the reduction of cycle time so that cell throughput can be maximized. For linear workcells where the robots are of the Cartesian-type, reduction of cycle time requires 1) the improvement of steady state accuracy and 2) transient response. Conventional robot controllers, to a large extend, utilize PID control and its variants. Despite the well established robustness and steady state characteristics of the PID control, the resultant closed loop response tends to be oscillatory and hence can significantly slow down the overall system performance.

In recent years, the method of input shaping has been introduced ([1], [2], [3]). Input Shaping is a feedforward control strategy that involves the modification of the command input to get the desired output from the system. The main concern for applying input shaping to robotic workcell control is its inherently low robustness which is compounded by the fact that the operating conditions in a work cell can vary quite significantly. The basic Zero Vibration (ZV) design cancels system vibration by means of carefully timing and proportioning the command so that the successive output oscillations are mutually cancelled. In frequency domain, the input shaper can be viewed as supplying the zeros to cancel the elastic poles of the plant. A number of improved designs have emerged: Zero Vibration and Derivative (ZVD) and Extra Insensitive (EI). These designs enhance the robustness of the ZV design by placing extra zeros at or around the elastic poles but invariably leading to slower response or increased residual vibration. In this paper, an optimal shaper is introduced to obtain optimal trade off between performance and robustness. A comparative study of the four shaper designs will be made and evaluated experimentally.

The organization of the remainder of this paper is as follows: Section 2 provides a description of the experimental system and the robot models. Section 3 presents a mathematical analysis of input shaping and a description of the optimal shaper design. Section 4 presents the experimental results of the ZV, ZVD, EI and optimal shaper.

2. SYSTEM HARDWARE DESCRIPTION

This section provides a brief description of the experimental hardware used for the testing and verification of the algorithms. Detailed description of the hardware and the software platforms may be found in [4]. The experimental system consists of a two-axis Cartesian robot, an Adept VME based controller, a DSP development system hosted in a standard Pentium computer, and an encoder interface card, which also resides in the PC. A block diagram of the system is shown in Figure 1.

The VME controller is used only as a supervisory system and is not involved in the actual control loop. The position of the robot module is determined by keeping track of the encoder, a function performed by the encoder interface card. The encoder interface card has four 24 bit counters and thus can keep track of four encoders, however, only two of them are used in our system (one for each axis). The position is maintained by the counters and the counters are read off, to obtain the position of the robot module. This position reading is then transferred by the PC to the DSP system which computes the control output and outputs the command to the servo amplifiers that drive the axis motors. The DSP system is a development system from 'Dalanco-Spry', and has a TMS320C31 DSP running at 50MHz. The DSP board has ADCs, DACs and also 128K words of memory for code/data. The DSP provides the number crunching power for the fast execution of control algorithms which is critical for the proper control of the robot.

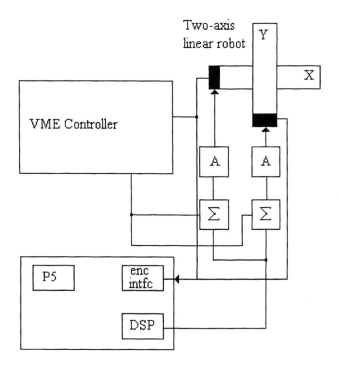

Figure 1 System Block Diagram.

2.1 Linear Robot System

The robot consists of two linear modules, a type H module and a smaller type M module mounted on the type H module. The module basically is a precision ground ball-screw drive mechanism, with linear guides for the slide. Both the H and M-modules have a 20 mm pitch, 10 micron repeatability, and 1.2m/s top speed.

2.2 Dynamic Model Derivation for the Robot Module

With the matching power amplifier for the motor, the robot module can be viewed as a DC servomotor with an inertial load attached to it. Since the leadscrew is a ball-screw mechanism, the frictional effects are small and can be neglected. The mass on the slider can be reflected onto the motor shaft as a rotational inertia. Thus the problem is reduced to modeling the DC servo motor problem, and the translation of the linear quantities into the angular quantities. The lowest order transfer function describing the gross motion of the robots is of the form:

$$\frac{X(s)}{V(s)} = \frac{a}{s(s+b)} \qquad (1)$$

2.3 Actual Model Parameter Measurements

Actual tests to determine the models for the robot modules were performed. The test results are presented in Table 1 and 2. Note that the actual numbers reflect the transfer function for everything from the DAC to the encoder.

Table 1 Test results for the X module.

load (kg)	a	b
0	4.9308 e03	7.1577
1	4.7268 e03	7.2422
2	4.6199 e03	7.4321
3	4.4956 e03	7.5245
4	4.4118 e03	7.9568
5	4.3671 e03	8.1109

Table 2 Test results for the Y module.

load (kg)	a	b
0	1.6559 e04	0.8372
1	1.6205 e04	1.1220
2	1.5028 e04	1.3247
3	1.3403 e04	1.3861
4	1.2870 e04	1.4722
5	1.2193 e04	1.5999

3. INPUT SHAPING

Input shaping is an open loop scheme which involves pre-shaping the actuator input such that the oscillation is ended after the input has reached its final value. This is based on the cancellation of the responses to a sequence of impulses. Input Shaping involves the convolution of the input with a sequence of impulses of suitable amplitude and spaced appropriately in time with the command input. For exact cancellation to occur the amplitudes of the impulses and the delay must be designed properly and must also be precise. Impulse amplitudes are a function of system damping while the delays depend on the damping as well as the natural system frequency. This means that any input shaping scheme must be designed with some robustness built in, otherwise there will not be an exact cancellation of the impulse responses as the system parameters change with changes in load, or friction etc. An input shaping scheme is illustrated in Figure 2.

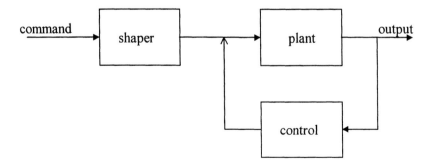

Figure 2 Input Shaping Scheme.

3.1 Mathematical Analysis of the Input Shaping Scheme

A brief mathematical overview of the input shaping scheme is presented. The analysis of the two-impulse case is considered. A linear system, may be modeled as first and second order sections. Consider a second order system,

$$G(s) = \frac{\omega_n^2}{\left(s^2 + 2\zeta\omega_n s + \omega_n^2\right)} \tag{2}$$

The unit impulse response of this system $y(t)$ is

$$y(t) = \frac{\omega_n}{\sqrt{1-\zeta^2}} e^{-\zeta\omega_n(t-t_0)} \sin\left(\left(\omega_0\sqrt{1-\zeta^2}\right)(t-t_0)\right) u(t-t_0) \tag{3}$$

Let y_1 be the response to impulse $A_1\delta(t-t_1)$ and y_2 be the response to impulse $A_2\delta(t-t_2)$. Then the total response is

$$y = y_1 + y_2 \tag{4}$$

where

$$y_1(t) = \frac{\omega_n A_1}{\sqrt{1-\zeta^2}} e^{-\zeta\omega_n(t-t_1)} \sin\left(\left(\omega_0\sqrt{1-\zeta^2}\right)(t-t_1)\right) u(t-t_1) \tag{5}$$

and

$$y_2(t) = \frac{\omega_n A_2}{\sqrt{1-\zeta^2}} e^{-\zeta\omega_n(t-t_2)} \sin\left(\left(\omega_0\sqrt{1-\zeta^2}\right)(t-t_2)\right) u(t-t_2) \tag{6}$$

Let

$$B_1 = \frac{A_1\omega_n}{\sqrt{1-\zeta^2}} \tag{7}$$

and

$$B_2 = \frac{A_2\omega_n}{\sqrt{1-\zeta^2}} \tag{8}$$

and also

$$\omega_d = \omega_0\sqrt{1-\zeta^2}. \tag{9}$$

Then the total response can be written as

$$y(t_N) = B_1 e^{-\zeta\omega_n t_N} e^{\zeta\omega_n t_1} \sin\left(\left(\omega_0\sqrt{1-\zeta^2}\right)(t_N - t_1)\right) + B_2 e^{-\zeta\omega_n t_N} e^{\zeta\omega_n t_2} \sin\left(\left(\omega_0\sqrt{1-\zeta^2}\right)(t_N - t_2)\right) \tag{10}$$

The residual vibration can therefore be expressed as:

$$|y(t_N)| = e^{-\zeta\omega_n t_N}\left\{\sqrt{\left(\sum_{i=1}^{2} B_i e^{\zeta\omega_n t_i} \cos\left(\omega_d\left(t_N - t_1\right)\right)\right)^2 + \left(\sum_{i=1}^{2} B_i e^{\zeta\omega_n t_i} \sin\left(\omega_d\left(t_N - t_1\right)\right)\right)^2}\right\} \quad \text{(for } t_n > t_1, t_2\text{).} \tag{11}$$

Now $|y(t_N)|$ depends upon A_1, A_2, t_1, t_2. We desire that there be no residual vibration. So if we solve for A_1, A_2, t_1, t_2, then with $t_1 = 0$ we have

$$A_1 = \frac{1}{1+K}$$

$$A_2 = 1 - A_1 = \frac{K}{1+K} \tag{12}$$

where $\quad K = e^{\frac{-\pi\zeta}{\sqrt{1-\zeta^2}}}\quad$ and $\quad \Delta T = \frac{\pi}{\omega_0\sqrt{1-\zeta^2}}$.

This is the Zero Vibration (ZV) shaper. The impulse sequence is shown in Figure 3.

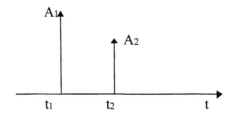

Figure 3 ZV Shaper.

For the ZVD shaper,

$$A_1 = 1/(1+2K+K^2),$$

$$A_2 = 2K/(1+2K+K^2),$$

$$A_3 = K^2/(1+2K+K^2),$$

$$T_1 = 0, \ T_2 = \Delta T, \ T_3 = 2\Delta T.$$

(13)

while the impulse sequence is shown in Figure 4.

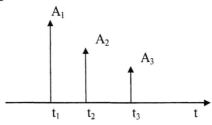

Figure 4 ZVD Shaper.

For the EI shaper , the curve fit formulae are [5] given by:

$$A_1 = 0.2494 + 0.2496V + 0.8001\zeta + 1.233V\zeta + 0.4960\zeta^2 + 3.173V\zeta^2$$

$$A_2 = 1 - A_1 - A_3$$

$$A_3 = 0.2515 + 0.2147V - 0.832\ 5\zeta + 1.415V\zeta + 0.8518\zeta^2 - 4.901V\zeta^2$$

(14)

$$T_2 = (0.5000 + 0.4616V\zeta + 4.262V\zeta^2 + 1.756V\zeta^3 + 8.578V^2\zeta^2 - 108.6V^2\zeta^2 + 337.0V^2\zeta^3)T_d$$

$$T_3 = T_d$$

The principal advantage of the ZVD and EI shapers is increased robustness. The ZV shaper has only two switch times and is faster, but its performance deteriorates rapidly if the natural frequency or the damping in the system changes. The ZVD and EI shapers are more robust, but since they have three switches, they are slower, requiring more time for the output to settle to the reference value. If the system parameters are well defined and do not vary significantly then the ZV shaper is the better choice. However if the system parameters are subject to change, then the ZVD or the EI shaper is to be preferred. To further understand the differing robustness of these shapers, it is useful to look at the frequency domain interpretation.

3.2 Frequency Domain Interpretation of Input Shaping

The ZV shaper performs a pole zero cancellation as shown in Figure 5. Obviously if this cancellation is not exact then there will be residual vibration.

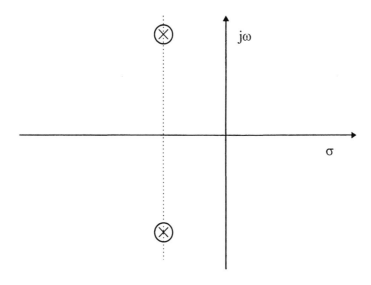

Figure 5 Pole Zero Cancellation in ZV Shaper.

The ZVD shaper adds two zeros for each pole and so increased robustness is observed.

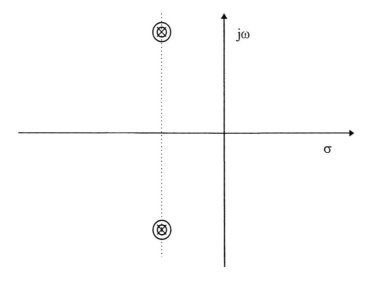

Figure 6 Pole Zero Cancellation in ZVD Shaper.

It is noted that the EI shaper will not have zero vibration for zero deviation of the system parameters, but offers increased overall robustness.

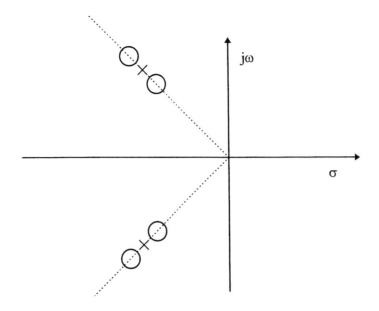

Figure 7 Pole Zero Cancellation in EI Shaper.

3.3 Synthesis of New Optimal Shaper Designs

For the previous shaping methods (ZV, ZVD, EI), no special weighting is assigned to the nominal plant parameters. In some cases we may have some knowledge of the statistical nature of plant parameter variation, and it may be useful to incorporate this knowledge into the shaper design to minimize the expected level of residual vibration. We consider two types of distributions:

1. Uniform: The natural frequency ω has the probability density function

$$f(\omega) = \frac{1}{\omega_L - \omega_R}, \omega \in [\omega_L, \omega_R] \tag{15}$$

and is assumed to be uniformly distributed in the interval $[\omega_L, \omega_R]$.

2. Gaussian: The natural frequency ω has the probability density function

$$f(\omega) = \frac{1}{\sqrt{2\pi}\sigma} e^{\frac{-(\omega-\omega_0)^2}{2\sigma^2}}, \omega \in R \tag{16}$$

where ω_0 is the nominal frequency.

In both cases the objective is to derive an optimal shaper design that suitably balances the performance and robustness. In EI shaper design, the robustness criterion has been the maximization of the frequency range while keeping the residual vibration to less than a pre-specified percentage (e.g. 5%). Variations in the damping coefficient can also be taken into account by defining the joint probability density functions. This method has the following advantages:

1. Frequency interval is selectable.
2. Frequency interval can be weighted (such as by a probability density function).
3. Robustness with respect to the damping factor variation is preserved.
4. Standard shaper designs such as ZVD and EI can be derived as special cases.

The optimal shaper is designed by performing the nonlinear optimization of a performance index rather than the solution of equations. The performance index may be defined as

$$J = \int_{\xi_L}^{\xi_R} \int_{\omega_L}^{\omega_R} V(\omega,\xi)f(\omega,\xi)d\omega d\xi \tag{17}$$

where f is a joint probability density function and the optimization variables are the switch times, and the impulse amplitudes.

Alternatively a simpler performance index such as:

$$J = \int_{\omega_L}^{\omega_R} V(\omega,\xi)f(\omega)d\omega \tag{18}$$

may be used along with a damping constraint to ensure the robustness of the solution with respect to the damping variations.

A procedure based on simulated annealing is utilized to locate the optimal shaper. Simulated annealing is a technique for solving nonlinear optimization problems by mimicking the physical process of thermal annealing. To solve an optimization problem with a simulated annealing algorithm, the problem is first converted into a system consisting of
  1. states - which are solutions of the problem,
  2. energy of a state - the cost function,
  3. a temperature - a control parameter,
  4. a new state generation mechanism - a function for generating new solutions
  5. a cooling schedule - a function for controlling the temperature.

For the optimal shaper problem, the amplitudes (A_1, A_2), and the switch times (t_1, t_2) of the shaper are used as the state. New states are generated by randomly perturbing these four parameters and the size of the perturbations is based on an adaptive scheme that varies with the temperature (T_i). This allows the search to proceed aggressively in the beginning and a more finer search at the end. The performance index J is the cost function and the cooling schedule follows $T_{i+1} = 0.9 * T_i$. The initial state can be random or is the solution of one of the other shapers. In all instances, the simulated annealing converges to a solution.

3.4 Implementation of Input Shaping on the Robot System

From Tables 1 and 2 we obtain parameters for the X and Y modules. The system parameters are used for the calculation of the shaper parameters. All shapers are designed for a nominal load of 1 kg. The shapers were implemented with the parameters shown in Table 3.

Table 3 Shaper Parameters.

Module	Shaper	A1	A2	A3	T1	T2	T3
X	ZV	0.5582	0.4418		0	0.0949	
Y	ZV	0.5199	0.4801		0	0.0489	
X	ZVD	0.3116	0.4932	0.1952	0	0.0949	0.1898
Y	ZVD	0.2703	0.4992	0.2305	0	0.0489	0.0978
X	EI	0.3299	0.4612	0.2089	0	0.0949	0.1899
Y	EI	0.2845	0.4722	0.2433	0	0.0489	0.0979
X	Optimal	0.4719	0.1339	0.3942	0	0.0139	0.1002
Y	Optimal	0.2595	0.4965	0.2440	0	0.0513	0.1026

4. TEST RESULTS

The four shaper designs defined in Table 3 are implemented on the TMS320C31 based DSP system. Each shaper commands the robots to execute a U-shaped test trajectory and return to the initial position as shown in Figure 8. The results are plotted in Figures 9-12 as XY-plots with all units expressed in millimeters. Maximum deviation from the test trajectory in the X and Y directions are summarized in Tables 4 and 5. Completion time and RMS errors are tabulated in Tables 6 and 7.

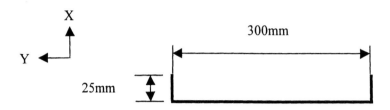

Figure 8 Command Trajectory for the Robot.

4.1 Results for the ZV Shaper

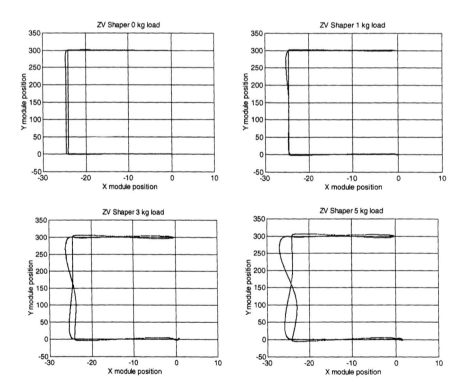

Figure 9 Cycle Time Test Results with ZV Shaper.

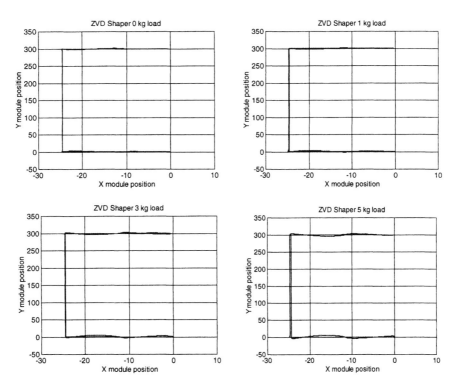

Figure 10 ZVD Shaper Test Run #3.

4.2 Results for the EI Shaper

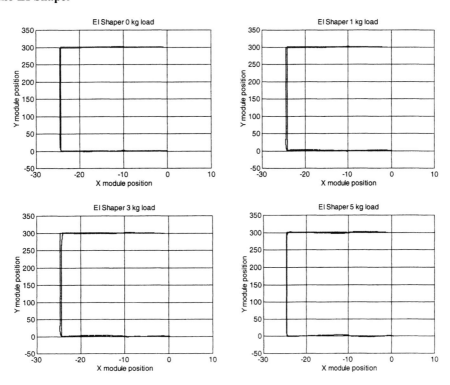

Figure 11 EI Shaper Test Run #3.

4.3 Results for the Optimal Shaper

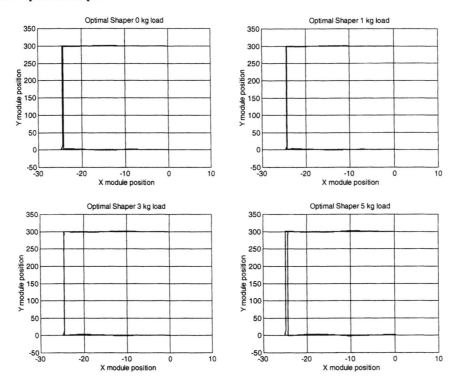

Figure 12 Optimal Shaper Test Run #3.

Table 4 Maximum Deviation from Command Trajectory X-module (in mm).

load (kg)	ZV	ZVD	EI	Optimal
0	0.8	0.6	0.65	0.75
1	0.7	0.5	0.7	0.7
3	1.5	0.5	0.65	0.5
5	2.7	0.55	0.4	0.7

Table 5 Maximum Deviation from Command Trajectory Y-module (in mm).

load (kg)	ZV	ZVD	EI	Optimal
0	1.6	1.2	2.5	2.0
1	2.2	1.2	2.5	2.0
3	5.5	3.1	2.2	2.1
5	5.5	3.5	2.5	2.2

Table 6 Completion Time for One Run Along the Trajectory (in sec).

load (kg)	ZV	ZVD	EI	Optimal
0	0.87	1.16	1.2	1.18
1	0.82	1.18	1.1	1.16
3	0.90	1.18	1.1	1.16
5	0.95	1.18	1.2	1.15

Table 7 RMS Errors for the Shaper Designs.

load (kg)	ZV	ZVD	EI	Optimal
0	132.5837	187.3340	239.2080	224.9403
1	291.2664	216.7372	306.7621	223.5067
3	732.0741	508.6997	279.6754	226.9504
5	938.3214	605.1436	370.8576	311.8987

From Tables 4-7, the following conclusions are drawn: The ZV shaper is the fastest (in terms of completion time) but also the least robust. The EI shaper is relatively fast and robust, but has a high RMS error, especially at the nominal condition (1 kg). The optimal shaper provides high speed of response, robustness, as well as low RMS error.

5. CONCLUSIONS

In this work, input shaping is demonstrated as a feed-forward strategy for cancellation of residual oscillation. The effects of system parameter variation on the cancellation are examined. The performance of the ZV shaper is seen to deteriorate rapidly with deviations in the plant parameters. ZVD, EI and optimal shapers are seen to be more robust with respect to the system parameter variations, and the deterioration in the performance is restricted. The ZVD, EI and optimal shaping strategies are more robust, however they are slower. The ZV shaper is the fastest and if the system model is very well known, it would be the best fit. The command shaping is utilized to command the robot over a U-shaped trajectory, and significant improvements in speed are obtained.

6. SELECTED REFERENCES

1. L. Pao, T. N. Chang, and E. Hou. "Input Shaper Designs for Minimizing the Expected Level of Residual Vibration in Flexible Structures," *Proceedings of the 1997 American Control Conference*, Albuquerque, NM, June 1997.
2. N. Singer and W. Seering. "Preshaping Command Inputs to Reduce System Vibration," *ASME Journal of Dynamic Systems, Measurement and Control*, 112(1), 1990.
3. W.J. Book, "Controlled Motion in an Elastic World," *ASME Journal of Dynamic Systems, Measurement and Control*, 115(2), 1993.
4. T.N. Chang, K. Godbole, M. Eren, Z. Ji, and R. Caudill, "Development and Implementation of An Application Programming Interface for PC/DSP Based Motion Control System," to appear at the 1998 SPIE Symposium on Intelligent Systems and Advanced Manufacturing, Boston.
5. L. Pao, private communications, 1997.
6. Dalanco Spry. *Model 310 Data Acquisition and Signal Processing Board for the IBM PC and Compatibles*, 1993
7. Texas Instruments. *TMS320C3x Floating Point Optimizing C Compiler User's Guide*, 1995.
8. Technology 80 Inc. *Model 5312B 4-Axis Quadrature Encoder- PC Technical Reference*, 1995.
9. Technology 80 Inc. *Model 5312 Software Developer's Guide*, 1995.
10. Adept Technology Inc. *Adept MV Controller User's Guide*, 1995.
11. Adept Technology Inc. *Adept MV Controller Developer's Guide*, 1995.
12. Adept Technology Inc. *Adept Advanced Servo Library Reference Guide*, 1995.

The application of adaptive texture filters to the automated visual inspection of antibiotic susceptibility tests

Z. Zhang[a], S. Snowden[b], J.C. Wang[c], and D. Kind[d]

[acd]Manufacturing Engineering and Industrial Management, Department of Engineering
University of Liverpool, Liverpool L69 3BX, UK

[b]Instruments Department, Mast Group Limited, Mast House, Derby Road, Bootle
Liverpool, L20 1EA, UK

ABSTRACT

Computer vision systems have been used in recent years to perform automated antibiotic susceptibility tests based on the disk-diffusion method. However, certain organisms do not reflect light very well. As such, the reliability of such automated inspection systems is sometimes not as high as expected. This paper proposes to use texture analysis to improve the quality of test images and thereby simplify the inspection tasks. Adaptive texture filters are used to maximise the difference between regions of interest in a test image and the background, enabling a thresholding operation to be carried out easily. The principles of adaptive filtering for texture analysis are discussed. A training algorithm is presented to generate optimised filters for generic texture inspection problems. An experimental study is carried out to investigate the performance of this technique in highlighting poorly reflecting organisms in antibiotic susceptibility tests.

Keywords: Computer Vision, Texture Analysis, Image Processing, Mechatronics, Antibiotic Susceptibility Tests

1. INTRODUCTION

All microbiology laboratories perform antibiotic susceptibility tests to determine the best chemotherapy for a patient. There are a number of methods to perform this test, but the dominant method is known as the disc diffusion method. An organism is grown on a petri-dish filled with a given agar containing the required nutrients to aid the organisms growth. On to this inoculated plate small paper discs are placed which have been impregnated with a known amount of an antibiotic. Once the plate has been incubated and the organism allowed to grow, zones of inhibition will appear around the paper disc where the organism was unable to grow. The diameter of this zone, when compared to a look-up table will provide the clinician with the data required to prescribe a particular course of drugs to kill the infection.

This is a relatively simple problem of measuring a stripe from the disc to the zone edge, presently performed by a computer vision system. Unfortunately certain organisms (Streptococci, Haemophilus) do not reflect light too well, and therefore appear as no more than noise on a digital image. This work proposes to use adaptive filters to discriminate between the coarse texture of the organism and the smoother texture of the media lacking growth. This would potentially highlight the organism allowing easy measurement of the zone of inhibition. This technique can then be applied to the existing system as a step in fully automating the diagnostic process.

2. ADAPTIVE CONVOLUTION FILTERS FOR TEXTURE ANALYSIS

Convolution filters have been used with considerable success for texture discrimination[1,2,3]. They are computationally less expensive compared to the conventional methods for texture analysis such as co-occurrence matrices[4].

Further author information -
Z.Z.(correspondence): Email: zhengwen.zhang@liv.ac.uk; WWW: http://www.liv.ac.uk/~indstud/staff/dzhang/dzhang.html;
Telephone: (44) (0) 151-7944685; Fax: (44) (0) 151-7944693

292

Part of the SPIE Conference on Mechatronics • Boston, Massachusetts • November 1998
SPIE Vol. 3518 • 0277-786X/98/$10.00

The application of a square convolution mask to a digitised image is represented by the following operation:

$$H(i, j) = \sum_{x=-k}^{x=k} \sum_{y=-k}^{y=k} W(x, y) P(i + x, j + y) \tag{1}$$

where the operator W is a convolution mask, P is grey level of pixel (i+x, j+y) in the original image, and $H(i,j)$ represents the result of convolution at pixel (i,j). The mask elements (weights), $W(x,y)$, are generally signed integers and satisfy a zero-sum constraint, which results in a zero response in areas of uniform intensity and removes any DC bias from the image. The mask in the above equation is of size (2k+1)x(2k+1) elements.

Fig. 1. Processing steps of a convolution filter channel

A convolution filtering channel for texture analysis comprises three processing steps, as shown in Fig. 1. First, an image is convolved with a convolution mask. Second, the absolute values of the convolution outputs are calculated to produce an intermediate image. Third, a smoothing operation (i.e., moving window average) is applied to the intermediate image to produce the filtered image. The combination of absolute and smoothing operations constitutes the "texture energy" measure proposed by Laws[5].

$$E(i, j) = \frac{1}{s^2} \sum_{p'=0}^{s-1} \sum_{q'=0}^{s-1} | H(i - \frac{s-1}{2} + p', j - \frac{s-1}{2} + q')| \tag{2}$$

where $E(i, j)$ represents the output of the filtering channel, i.e., the texture energy, at pixel (i, j). The size of the smoothing (average) window is sxs.

For general texture classification problems, a number of such filtering channels would be used to process the original image to produce a number of filtered images. As a result, each pixel in the original image will have a number of corresponding output values, one from each of the filtered images. These values are used to form a multi-dimensional feature vector which is used by a classifier to determine the texture identity of the pixel.

When the task is to discriminate between two textures, i.e., to discriminate between a foreground and a background texture (a requirement in most inspection applications), a single filtering channel could be used in conjunction with a thresholding operation to perform the task. The texture identity of each pixel could be obtained by comparing the corresponding output value from the filtering channel with a threshold. This may be represented by the equation below.

$$Pixel(i, j) \in \begin{cases} Class\ A & if E(i, j) \geq T \\[1em] Class\ B & if E(i, j) < T \end{cases} \tag{3}$$

where A and B represent two texture classes involved in the classification task and T is the threshold value.

The problem becomes how to find a filtering mask which produces greater outputs (texture energy) on one texture and smaller ones on the other, so that the two textures can be separated in the filtered image by a thresholding operation.

3. FILTER OPTIMISATION FOR INSPECTION PROBLEMS

Although the feature extraction properties of filters are widely understood, defining the discriminate features in any given application can prove difficult and the discriminate features are usually only found through experimentation, a disadvantage for real world applications. One of the more notable approaches to finding an optimal solution is the Monte-Carlo approach[6,7]. An algorithm developed based on this approach for the optimisation of single channel filters for inspection applications is detailed below.

Given two images a and b of size $m \times m$ as the samples for textures A and B respectively, mask generation is formulated as a task of finding the optimised values of mask elements (i.e., $W(x,y)$, $x,y=0,1,2,...,2k+1$) so that filter outputs (texture energy) on pixels of image a are maximised and those on pixels of image b minimised. This is achieved by an adaptive training process based on Monte Carlo method. The scheme works by iteratively changing mask values to maximise a merit function calculated as the normalised distance between the average texture energy values resulting from a single mask on texture samples a and b respectively.

$$M = \frac{\frac{1}{m^2}\left(\sum_{i=0}^{m-1}\sum_{j=0}^{m-1} E_a(i,j)\right) - \frac{1}{m^2}\left(\sum_{i=0}^{m-1}\sum_{j=0}^{m-1} E_b(i,j)\right)}{|W|} \qquad (4)$$

where

$$|W| = \sqrt{\sum W_{i,j}^2}$$

represents the scale of the mask, $E_a(i,j)$ and $E_b(i,j)$ are the filter outputs (texture energies) on the $(i,j)^{th}$ pixel of sample image a and b respectively, M the merit function.

The free variables, i.e., the mask elements, are adapted iteratively in the form of a heuristic random walk. Masks are constrained to be zero-sum and to have integer elements between -100 and 100 only. A brief description of the optimisation process is given below.

At the beginning of the training process, an initial *random mask* is produced. This mask is applied to the training samples a and b and the resulting value of merit function calculated. The mask is now regarded as the *current best mask*. The algorithm then attempts to improve upon this mask in an iterative loop. At each iteration, a *new random mask* satisfying the given constraints is generated and the resulting value of merit function computed. A third mask, referred to as the *learnt mask*, is then computed by averaging the *current best mask* and the *new random mask*, weighted according to their corresponding values of merit function.

$$W_l = \frac{M_c W_c + M_r W_r}{M_c + M_r} \qquad (5)$$

where W_c, W_r, W_l represent the *current best mask*, the *new random mask*, and the *learnt mask* respectively. M_c and M_r are the values of merit function corresponding to mask W_c and W_r.

The final step in the loop is to compare the values of merit function achieved by the three masks and to define the one giving the highest merit value as the *current best mask* for next iteration.

$$W_c^{(t+1)} = \begin{cases} W_c^t & if \quad M_c = \max(M_c, M_r, M_l) \\ W_r^t & if \quad M_r = \max(M_c, M_r, M_l) \\ W_l^t & if \quad M_l = \max(M_c, M_r, M_l) \end{cases} \qquad (6)$$

where t is the index for successive iterations, M_l is the merit value achieved by the *learnt mask*. The process repeats for a pre-determined number of iterations or continues until a pre-set merit value is achieved.

The performance of the *current best mask* improves over iterations in the training process due to following principles. If two masks are both giving high values for the merit function, there is some probability that they are both close to the optimum, and they are therefore both versions of a same mask subjected to different small perturbations. In electronic signal processing, perturbations of unknown origin are considered as random noise, and noisy signals are averaged to produce a better estimate of the unperturbed signal. In principle, the noisy signals could be weighted inversely as the amplitude of the noise to give maximum noise suppression. In the mask training algorithm, masks are averaged with the weights being their corresponding merit function values in order to obtain a better estimation of the optimum mask.

An additional option of the algorithm is to add "fine tuning" to the training process. This is achieved by replacing Equation (5) with

$$W_l = \frac{nM_cW_c + M_rW_r}{nM_c + M_r} \tag{7}$$

where n is a tuning factor which is varied during the mask training process. At the beginning of the process, n is set to 1, which means that the current best mask is weighted equally with the newly generated random mask. As training proceeds, n is gradually increased to give the *current best mask* a higher weighting than the *new random mask*, so that the adjustment to the *current best mask* at each iteration is relatively small. The inclusion of such a control in the training process is necessary for inspection problems. At the beginning of the training process, the direction of the filter vector is relatively away from the direction of neighbourhood vectors of the texture sample. A lower n value will enable global random search to take place rapidly. As training proceeds however, the direction of the filter vector gets closer to the required direction. A large adjustment to the filter vector will tend to move it further away from the required direction. What is required at this stage is "fine tuning". Higher n values provide a mechanism to control the fine tuning process. Fig. 2. shows the flow chart of the mask optimisation algorithm.

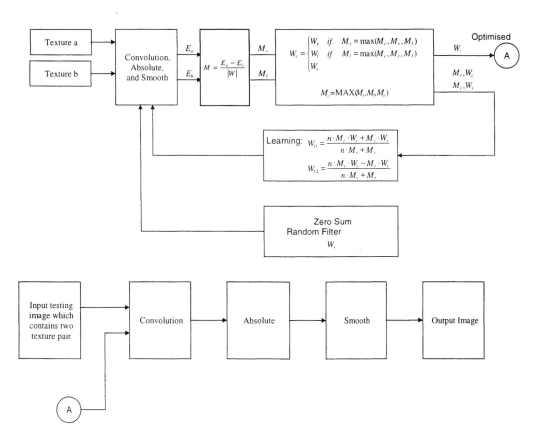

Fig. 2. The mask optimisation algorithm

4. TESTS ON BENCHMARK TEXTURES

The proposed technique in Section 2 and 3 was first tested on four images constructed from a number of textures in the Brodatz album[8]. The textures used here have been widely used by other researchers as benchmark textures. In our test images, all textures have been histogram equalised so that their grey level distributions have identical means and variances. This is to ensure that the resulting separation is achieved from textural differences rather than intensity differences.

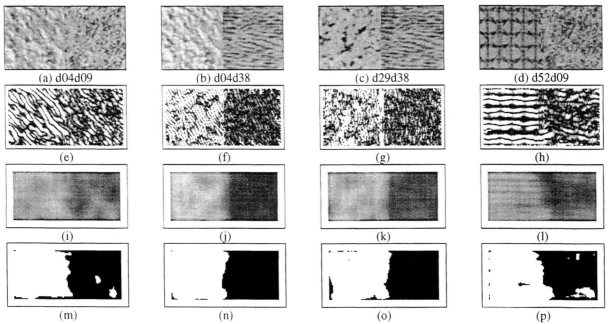

(a) d04d09	(b) d04d38	(c) d29d38	(d) d52d09
(e)	(f)	(g)	(h)
(i)	(j)	(k)	(l)
(m)	(n)	(o)	(p)

Fig. 3. Test of adaptive texture filters on benchmark textures

Fig. 3(a), (b), (c) and (d) show four pairs of textures. The first texture pair consists of two textures D4 and D9 from Brodatz' album. The second pair consists of D4 and D38, the third D29 and D38, and the fourth D52 and D9. The experiment is carried out in two steps. In the first step, the training algorithm detailed in Section 3 is used to find a filtering mask to discriminate between the two textures constituting each individual texture pair. In the second step, the trained filters are applied to the images shown in Fig.3 (a) to (d). The resulting images after convolution and absolute operations are shown in Fig.3 (e) to (h). Those after the smoothing operation are shown in Fig.3 (i) to (l), which are then thresholded to produce the segmented images shown in Fig.3 (m) to (p). It may be seen from this experiment that the algorithm has successfully found filtering masks to discriminate between the given textures.

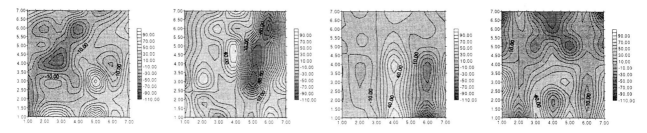

Fig. 4. The profiles of filters optimised for textures shown in Fig. 3.

Fig. 4 shows the resulting filters from the optimisation process in a 3D plot where the brightness shadings represent the magnitudes of mask elements at various locations. The size of the mask shown is 7x7.

5. APPLICATION IN ANTIBIOTIC SUSCEPTIBILITY TESTS

The technique proposed in Sections 2 and 3 has also been tested on practical antibiotic susceptibility problems. Fig.5 (a) shows a poorly lighted petri-dish image captured by the test instrument. It may be seen from the image that some zones are brighter than the background, some darker, and some very similar to the background. It is very difficult to segment the zones from the background using direct thresholding. Fig. 5 (b) shows the result of a direct attempt to threshold the image, which is very poor.

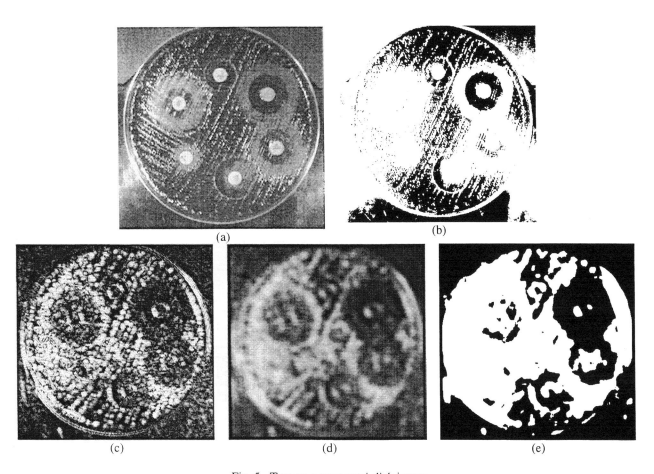

Fig. 5. Test on a poor petri-dish image

In order to improve this image, a texture filter (7x7) was trained with the technique proposed in Section 3 to distinguish between the zone areas considered as one texture and the background areas considered as another texture. Fig. 5 (c) shows the result after convolution and absolute operations when the trained filter was applied to the test image. It may be seen that some improvements over the original image was made. All zone areas have become comparatively darker than the background, although there are still a lot of noises in the image. A smoothing operation was then carried out to remove some of the noises from the image. The result is shown in Fig. 5(d). In Fig. 5(e), an attempt was made to threshold the image after convolution and smoothing. It was found that there were improvements compared to the result of direct thresholding shown in Fig. 5(b) but the improvements were not significant to justify the practical use of the technique in a test instrument. Further analysis revealed that texture differences between background and zone areas were very small. Work is therefore being carried out to investigate other approaches to using texture filters to improve the quality of such images and these will be reported in future publications.

6. DISCUSSIONS AND CONCLUSIONS

This paper introduces the application of image processing in antibiotic susceptibility tests and outlines a texture analysis method for highlighting poorly reflecting samples in test images. The principles of adaptive filtering for texture analysis are discussed and an algorithm presented to perform filter optimisation. The performance of the optimised filters on practical antibiotic susceptibility test problems was investigated. It was found that the proposed technique can perform texture inspection tasks successfully but its effectiveness in highlighting poorly reflecting samples in antibiotic test images is not as good as expected. Further work is being carried out to investigate other possibilities of using texture filters to improve the quality of such images.

7. RERFERENCES

1. D. Dunn, W. E. Higgins, and J. Wakeley, "Texture Segmentation Using 2D Gabor Elementary Functions", *IEEE Transactions on Pattern Analysis and Machine Intelligence,* Vol. 16, No.2, pp. 130-149, 1994.
2. X. Michel, R. Leonard, and A. Gersho, "Unsupervised Segmentation of Texture Images", *Proceedings of SPIE,* Vol. 1001, Visual Communications and Image Processing'88, pp. 582-590, 1988.
3. M. Clark and A. C. Bovik, "Experiments in Segmenting Texton Patterns Using localised Spatial Filters", *Pattern Recognition,* Vol. 22, No. 6, pp. 707-717, 1989.
4. R. M. Haralick, "Statistical and Structural Approaches to Texture", *Proceedings of the IEEE,* Vol.67, No.5, pp. 786-804, 1979
5. K. I. Laws, "Textured image segmentation", Ph.D. dissertation, *Univ. of Southern California*, 1980.
6. K. Benke and D. Skinner, "Segmentation of Visually Similar Textures by Convlution Filtering", *The Australian Computer Journal*, Vol. 19, No. 3, pp. 134-139, 1987.
7. K. Benke, D. Skinner, and M. Chung, "Application of Adaptive Convolution Masking to the Automation of Visual Inspection", *IEEE Transaction on Robotics and Automation*, Vol. 6, No. 1., pp. 123-127, 1990.
8. P. Brodatz, "*A photographic Album for Artists and Designers*", Dover, New York, 1966.

Configuration control of a modular arm with N active links

Jerome Foret[a], Wei Tech Ang[a], Ming Xie[a], Jean-Guy Fontaine[b]

[a] Nanyang Technological University Singapore, M.P.E. Autonomous Vehicle Lab

[b] Ecole National Superieur d'Ingenieur de Bourges France

ABSTRACT

This paper presents a new class of solution to the inverse kinematics for a modular arm with N-active links. Due to the design advantage of the active link, we bring the inverse kinematics problem from a 3D space to a 2D space. Based on the proposed methodology, a class of simple solutions can be quickly and easily obtained. Simulation results prove the validity of the solutions. Results with real modular arm are also included in the paper.

Keywords: Inverse kinematics, modular manipulator and active link

1. INTRODUCTION

This paper deals with a modular arm composed of N active links used in a hand-eye coordination platform. Hand-eye coordination can be considered as a type intelligent behaviour which is characterised by three inter-related components: a)perception, b)decision and c)action.

Hand-eye coordination has been actively studied under the research topic of visual servoing [2,3,4,6,14,15]. In order to demonstrate Hand-eye coordination behaviour in real time, two critical issues have to be solved: a)How to generate motion control commands from images and b) How to achieve real-time performance depends on the solution of inverse kinematics. This is not simple problem for kinematically redundant arm of N links. In [5,7,8,10,11,13,17...24], the solution are applicable to real time systems but remain analytical. In [1,9,10,12,17], the discussions have been focused on optimisation of posture using singularity analysis.

This paper presents a new strategy of deriving simple solutions to inverse kinematics of a modular arm with N active links. The key idea is to make use of the design advantage of active links to bring the inverse kinematics problem from a 3D space to a 2D space. This allows us to obtain geometrical closed-form solutions more efficiently.

This paper is organised as follows: Section 2 shows the design concept of active link and the resulting model that we have developed [2]. Section 3 defines the problem on which this paper focuses. In section 4, we present the derivation of the geometrical inverse kinematics and Section 5 gives simulation and experimental results. Section 6 concludes this paper with highlights of the future works.

2. DEFINITION AND PROPERTIES OF AN ACTIVE LINK

2.1. Design of One Active Link

In robotics, there are two perspectives in looking at a robot arm, mechanically it is a manipulator that performs tasks; mathematically it can be regarded as a kinematic chain composed of co-ordinate frames that represent links and joints. There has been little interaction between mechanical design works and theoretical works. The emphasis of the mechanical design of robot arm is usually the mechanical requirements (e.g. torque, stiffness, workspace etc.).

With the advent of new requirements on manipulator modularity and reconfigurability, researchers have started to re-think the design solutions for robot arm. Despite many designs have evolved, the focus has been on the achievement of hardware flexibility in terms of modularity and reconfigurability, but the link between design and inverse kinematics solution is still absent.

Part of the SPIE Conference on Mechatronics • Boston, Massachusetts • November 1998
SPIE Vol. 3518 • 0277-786X/98/$10.00

299

In our study, we propose a unique entity that integrates link and joint - Active Link, as the basic building block for our modular robot arm. An ideal Active Link would be one that has three DOF as shown in Figure 2.1.

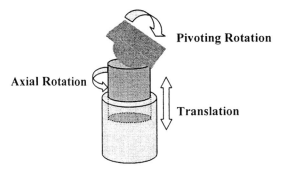

Figure 2.1: 3 DOF Active Link

However, when design practicality and mechanical limitations are carefully thought about, we set the translation parameter to be a constant (i.e. abandon the translational DOF). The proposed design of Active Link is shown in Figure 2.2.

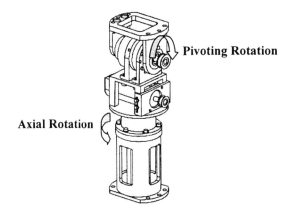

Figure 2.2: Active Link with 2 DOF

We denote by N the number of link and by n the number of DOF. The active links will be serially connected to make up the robot arm. If an application requires higher flexibility and mobility, additional modules can be added to provide more degrees of freedom; conversely, the DOF of the manipulator can be scaled down when the application is simple i.e. the degree of freedom is scaleable. The manipulator is full rank when N=3 (n=6) and if N>3 the kinematic chain becomes redundant (n>6). Based on this design concept, we can build an open kinematic chain composed of three or more Active Links. Currently, we have designed three sizes of Active Links to cater for different torque and mechanical stiffness requirements.

2.2. Properties of the Modular Arm with N Active Links

Kinematically, an Active Link can be represented as a set of three frames:

$$L_i = \{\theta_i^a, \theta_i^p, l_i\} \tag{2.1}$$

Where:

θ_i^a represents the axial rotation of link i,

θ_i^p represents pivoting rotation of link i,

l_i represents the translation of link i.

Figure 2.3a and 2.3b show the attachment of the three frames on a general and actual Active Link respectively.

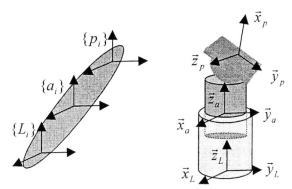

Figure 2.3.a A general Active Link   **Figure 2.3.b An actual Active Link**

One important design characteristic of the Active Links is that the link offset between the co-ordinate frames is always zero. This unique characteristic will enable the inverse kinematics problem to be mapped from a 3D problem to a 2D problem.

Based on Figure 2.4, the forward kinematics of a modular arm with N-Active Link may be given as follow:

$$^W(x,y,z,1)^T = {}^W M_E \bullet {}^E(x,y,z,1)^T \tag{2.2}$$

$$^W(\alpha,\beta,\gamma,0)^T = {}^W M_E \bullet {}^E(\alpha,\beta,\gamma,0)^T \tag{2.3}$$

$$^W M_E = {}^W M_{L_0} \bullet \left\{ \prod_{i=0}^{N-2} \left({}^{L_i} M_{a_i}(\theta_i^a) \bullet {}^{a_i} M_{p_i}(\theta_i^P) \bullet {}^{p_i} M_{L_{i+1}} \right) \right\} \bullet {}^{L_{N-1}} M_E \tag{2.4}$$

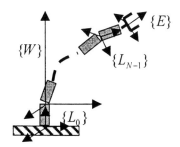

Figure 2.4: Modular Manipulator with N ACTIVE LINK

Where {W} is the world co-ordinate frame, {E} the one attached to the end-effector, $\{L_0\}$ the frame attached to link 0 and $\{L_{N-1}\}$ the one attached to the last link.

It is to note that the modular manipulator will be composed of N Active Links and one end-effector with one DOF (axial rotation) hence, the minimum manipulator will have n=2N+1=7 DOF, with 1DOF redundant. As a result, our study here focuses on redundant manipulators only.

3. PROBLEM DEFINITION

Based of the forward kinematics given in the previous section, the general way to obtain the inverse kinematics may be expressed as:

$$^{W}X = f(q) \tag{3.1}$$

$$^{W}\dot{X} = J(q) \bullet \dot{q} \tag{3.2}$$

Where in (3.1) and (3.2) ^{W}X and $^{W}\dot{X}$ are respectively the position and the velocity (6×1 vectors) of the end-effector expressed w.r.t. the world coordinate frame {W}, f( ) is a 6×1 vector, J( ) is the usual Jacobian of the system and q and $\dot{q}$ are the joint angle and velocity vectors (n×1) of the manipulator. The common way of writing the inverse kinematics of the system is to find an analytical solution for inverting the Jacobian and adding the missing equations using the internal mobilities of the redundant kinematic chain:

$$\dot{q} = J^{+}\left(^{W}X\right) \bullet {}^{W}\dot{X} + \left(I - J^{+}J\right) \bullet \dot{q}_{\text{int}} \tag{3.3}$$

Where in Equation (3.3), $J^{+}( )$ is the pseudo-inverse of the Jacobian J( ) and $\dot{q}_{\text{int}}$ is a r×1 (r= Number of Redundancy) joints velocity vector. We propose here another way of writing the inverse kinematics by first inverting Equation (3.1):

$$q = g^{ext}\left(^{W}X\right) + g^{\text{int}}\left(^{W}X\right) \tag{3.4}$$

And then by differentiation of the previous mapping:

$$\dot{q} = J^{ext}\left(^{W}X, q\right)^{-1} \bullet {}^{W}\dot{X} + \frac{dg^{\text{int}}\left(^{W}X\right)}{dt} \tag{3.5}$$

In the previous formulas the indexes *ext* and *int* represent the solution of minimum norm and the internal mobilities respectively. The choice of this representation is motivated by the fact that the solution of minimum norm also corresponds to the solution for the minimum manipulator as described in Section 2. The following figure represents the home position of the manipulator and notations used to describe both the modular arm and the desired position and orientation of the end-effector:

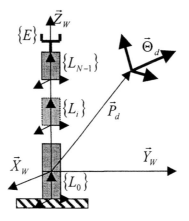

Figure 3.1: Home Position and Desired Position and orientation

Where inputs of inverse kinematics are the desired position and orientation of the wrist (that is directly derived from the one of the tool tip): $\left(\vec{P}_{d}, \vec{\Theta}_{d}\right) = {}^{W}X$ and outputs are the link's parameters: L = {$(\theta_{i}^{a}$, θ_{i}^{a}, $l_{i})$, i=0, ..., N-1}.

4. INVERSE KINEMATICS

As described in section 3 the aim is to find the inverse kinematics given by Equation (3.4). The proposed solution attempts to control the modular arm in any configuration (i.e. any number of link, at least 3). We are able to achieve this due to the unique design characteristics of the Active Links by having zero link offset between co-ordinate frames. We derive the inverse kinematics problem as follow:

a) Translating the 3D problem into a 2D problem by meeting the two following conditions:

- **Geometric Condition** (necessary): using link 0 to move links 1 to (N-1) perpendicular to normal of the constrain plane (defined by $\left(\vec{P}_d, \vec{\Theta}_d\right)$).

- **Kinematic Condition** (sufficient): using link 1 to leave the others pivoting axes parallel to the normal of the constrain plane.

b) Finding the solution in the plane corresponding to the 2 links configuration;

c) Optimizing the posture of the manipulator using the internal mobility;

d) Orientating the terminal using simple geometrical properties.

4.1. Constraint Plane Determination

Links 0 and 1 are used to meet the geometric and kinematic conditions. The parameters attached to those links are computed to define the homogenious transformatrion between {cp} (frame attache to the constrain plane) and {W} denoted by:

$$^{W}M_{cp}(\theta_0^a, \theta_0^p, \theta_1^a) = {}^{W}M_{L_0} {}^{L_0}M_{a_0} {}^{a_0}M_{p_0} {}^{p_0}M_{L_1} {}^{L_1}M_{a_1} {}^{a_1}M_{cp} \qquad (4.1)$$

Where in the present case $^{W}M_{L_0} = {}^{p_0}M_{L_1} = {}^{a_1}M_{cp} = I_{4\times4}$ and $I_{4\times4}$ is a 4×4 identity matrix and others matrices are defined in section 2.2.

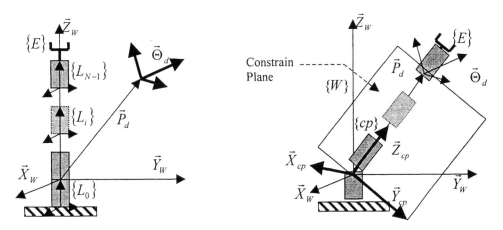

Figure 4.1: From 3D to 2D Problem. Definition of the constraint plane

According to Figure 4.1 the geometric condition is met by computing:

$$\theta_0^a = \arctan\left(\frac{P_{dy}}{P_{dx}}\right) \qquad (4.2)$$

$$\theta_0^a = \arccos\left(\frac{P_{dz}}{\left\|\vec{P}_d\right\|}\right) \qquad (4.3)$$

To meet the kinematic condition, we define

$$\vec{x}_{a_1}^{\text{int}} = {}^{W}M_{cp}(\theta_0^a, \theta_0^p, 0) \bullet (1,0,0,1)^T \qquad (4.4)$$

And θ_1^a becomes:

$$\theta_1^a = \arccos\left(\frac{\vec{x}_{a_1}^{\text{int}} \bullet \vec{X}_{cp}}{\left\|\vec{x}_{a_1}^{\text{int}}\right\| \bullet \left\|\vec{X}_{cp}\right\|}\right) \qquad (4.5)$$

Based on this 2D approach, next section focuses on finding a solution for positioning the end-effector in the constraint plane.

4.2. Positioning the end-effector

Once the modular arm is moved into the constraint plane, using 2 meta-links configuration, the inverse kinematics mapping can be easily derived. According to Figure 4.2 the angle values involved are computed for positioning the end-effector to the desired position, the orientation will be left to the latest stage.

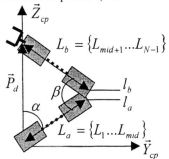

Figure 4.2: Positioning the Terminal in the Constrain Plane

In Figure 4.1 *mid* is the index used to define the two meta-links L_a and L_b (of length l_a and l_b respectively) defined as a set of Active Links and the angle values to be computed in order to reach the desired position are:

$$\alpha = \arccos\left(\frac{l_a^2 + \left\|\vec{P}_d\right\|^2 - l_b^2}{2l_a\left\|\vec{P}_d\right\|}\right) \qquad (4.6)$$

$$\beta = \pi - \theta_{mid}^p = \arccos\left(\frac{l_a^2 + l_b^2 - \left\|\vec{P}_d\right\|^2}{2l_al_b}\right) \qquad (4.7)$$

We can not set $\theta_0^p = \alpha$ because the geometric and kinematic conditions would not be met. But as the relation between {cp} and {W} is known, we compute the updated values for links 0 and 1 as:

$$\theta_0^{a,up} = \arctan\left(\frac{^W\vec{z}_{p_1} \bullet (0,1,0)^T}{^W\vec{z}_{p_1} \bullet (1,0,0)^T}\right) \qquad (4.8)$$

$$\theta_0^{p,up} = \arccos\left(\frac{^W\vec{z}_{p_1} \bullet (0,0,1)^T}{\left\|^W\vec{z}_{p_1}\right\|}\right) \qquad (4.9)$$

$$\theta_1^{a,up} = \arccos\left(\frac{\vec{x}_{a1}^{int} \bullet {}^w\vec{X}_{cp}}{\left\|\vec{x}_{a1}^{int}\right\| \bullet \left\|^w\vec{X}_{cp}\right\|}\right) \qquad (4.8)$$

Where:

$$^W\vec{z}_{p_1} = {}^W M_{cp}(\theta_0^a,\theta_0^p,\theta_1^a) \bullet R(\alpha) \bullet (0,0,1,1)^T \qquad (4.11)$$

$$\vec{x}_{a_1}^{int} = {}^W M_{cp}(\theta_0^{a,up},\theta_0^{p,up},0) \bullet R(\alpha) \bullet (1,0,0,1)^T \qquad (4.12)$$

And:

$$R(\alpha) = \begin{bmatrix} 1 & 0 & 0 & 0 \\ 0 & \cos(\alpha) & -\sin(\alpha) & 0 \\ 0 & \sin(\alpha) & \cos(\alpha) & 0 \\ 0 & 0 & 0 & 1 \end{bmatrix} \qquad (4.13)$$

The next section optimises the posture of the arm with respect to the singularities. This solution has to be performed for the minimum configuration of N=3 even it does not allow any possible optimisation.

4.3. Posture optimisation

Obviously the previous solution is only feasible if β is big enough not to reach the limit value of θ_{mid}^p but in most cases this limit is difficult to avoid. Moreover, this solution involves singularities that decrease the manipulability index of the manipulator. Nevertheless, this solution still has to be computed because it corresponds to the minimum manipulator solution. For manipulators composed of more that 3 Active Links, we propose an iterative algorithm that makes the previous configuration evolve in order to reach an optimum manipulability index. A function reflecting singularities is proposed maintain the computation simple. Minimising this function will optimise the posture of the arm.

Due to the particular design and because the problem is translated to a plane the internal singularities of the manipulator can be easily measured by regarding the relative position of two consecutive links. The following figure gives a simple illustration of this property:

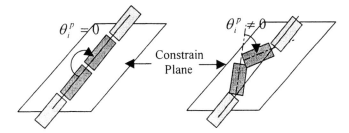

Figure 4.3.a: Singular Configuration, loss of mobility **Figure 4.3.b: Non Singular Configuration, no loss of mobility**

From this illustration we propose the following criteria to relate the state of the manipulator with respect to singularities:

$$S = \frac{\sum_{i=1}^{N-1}\left|\cos(\theta_i^p)\right|}{N-2} \qquad (4.14)$$

The minimisation of Equation (4.14) will provide the optimisation of the configuration of the arm. To do so we propose an iterative algorithm schematised on Figure 4.4:

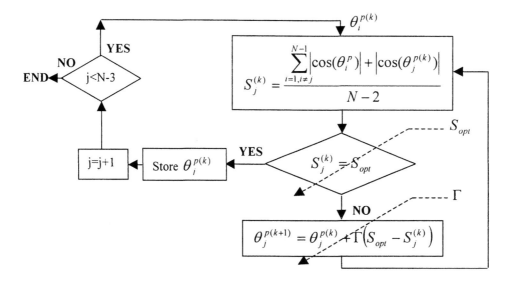

Figure 4.4: Flowchart for Iterative Optimisation Algorithm

Where, in Figure 4.4, the values for S_{opt} and Γ have to be set in order to make the error $S_{opt} - S_j^{(k)}$ to converge to zero. More precisely S_{opt} depends on the number of links and the position to be reached and Γ depends on the gradient of the index S and also depends on the limit value of θ_j^p. According to Figure 4.4, each time one $\theta_j^{p(k)}$ has to be optimized the corresponding index $S_j^{(k)}$ is evaluated and compared to S_{opt}. The updated value $\theta_j^{p(k+1)}$ is proportional to this difference and Γ is the coefficient of this proportion. Once $\theta_j^{p(k)} = \theta_j^{p,opt}$ we compute the two following angles in order to maintain the end-effector in the desired position. The final posture of the manipulator can be represented in the constraint plane as shown on the next figure:

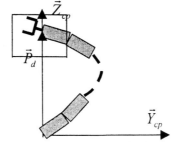

Figure 4.5: Final Configuration of the Manipulator

Once the end-effector is at the desired position, the desired orientation has to be reached. Next section presents the simple method to meet this point.

4.5. Orientating the terminal

Figure 4.6.a is a zoom of the square drawn on Figure 4.5:

Figure 4.6.a: Orientation after Optimization Process   **Figure 4.6.b: Final Orientation after rotation of angle** α

In order to reach the desired orientation α is computed as follow:

$$\alpha = \arccos\left(\frac{\vec{P}_d \bullet \vec{\Theta}_d}{\|\vec{P}_d\| \bullet \|\vec{\Theta}_d\|}\right) - \sum_{i=0}^{N-2} \theta_i^p \qquad (4.15)$$

We recall that from Equations (4.7), (4.8), (4.9), (4.10) and (4.15), g^{ext} is entirely known and from the optimization algorithm described previously, g^{int} is also defined. We notice that only five parameters are used to give the minimum norm solution, in fact one more DOF has to be performed in order to compute the complete solution. This last DOF corresponds to the axial rotation attached to the terminal since the desired orientation is written as, not only one vector but also one angle (i.e. quaternion). More over if the singularity avoidance is not the only constrain desired (ex. obstacle avoidance), the others can be given in terms of tilt angles for several constrain planes. As example let consider the minimum manipulator: the constraint plane defined by $\left(\vec{P}_d, \vec{\Theta}_d\right)$ can be changed in $\left(\vec{P}_d, \vec{V}\right)$ where $\vec{V}$ is such that the previous constrain plane rotates around $\vec{P}_d$.

Next section validates the method by few examples of the posture adopted by the arm for different position and orientation desired. Pictures of the minimum manipulator designed by [2] are also presented.

5. SIMULATION AND EXPERIMENTAL RESULTS

This section shows the modular arm for different desired position and different number of Active Link: first through the graphic interface build under Mathematica software and second using the real manipulator corresponding to the minimum manipulator. The simulation results are presented for manipulators composed of Active Link with same length, this doesn't touch the generality of the method but requires less computational capacity. To validate experimental results, we compare them to simulation results.

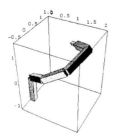

Figure 5.1: Posture of a modular arm with 5 ACTIVE LINK to reach: DESIRED POSITION:{1.2, 1.1, 2}:REACHED POSITION:{1.2, 1.1, 2., 1.}

Figure 5.1: Posture of a modular arm with 11 A.L close to its singular position: DESIRED POSITION:{5.364, 5.02, 5.08}:REACHED POSITION:{5.364, 5.02, 5.08, 1.}

The two examples have been computed with the same source code, we notice that the orientation is not entirely taken in account because it is not the main point of the method.

Next figure shows the manipulator on a path (circle) and is compared to the real arm on the same path:

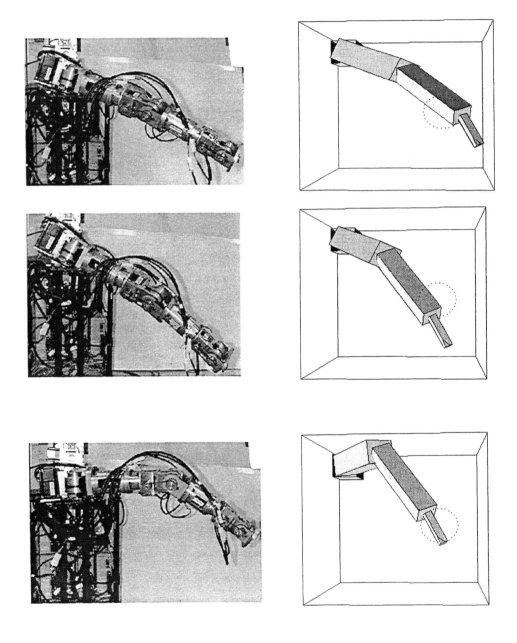

Figure 5.3: Real arm compared to the simulated one following a circle.

6. Conclusion and Future Works

To conclude this article we remind the key points on which the method exposed is based on: using the design[2] it is always possible to find a plane to translate the 3D problem into a 2D one. This involves tow conditions (geometric and kinematic) that have to be respected. From a simple solution into this plane we derive a optimized one and orientating the terminal then becomes very easy to compute. The future works are mainly to apply this method first for Hand-Eye coordination platform and second for long distance tele-robotics. It is also desired to improve the method by using the modular concept for more general open kinematic chain.

7. References

[1] K.Leeser D.Tonnsend, Control and Exploitation of Kinematic Redundancy in Torque Controllable Manipulator via Multiple Jacobian Superposition, *Proc. Of the Int. Conf. on Field and Service Robot*, pp. 442-448, FSR 1997

[2] W.T.Ang M.Xie, Mobile Robotic Hand-Eye Coordination in Platform. Design and Modeling, *Proc. Of the Int. Conf. on Field and Service Robot*, pp. 319-326, FSR 1997

[3] Y. Toda Y. Konishi H. Ishigaki, Positioning Control of Robot Manipulator using Visual sensor, *Iint. Conf. On Automation Robotics Control and Vision*, pp. 814-818, Dec. 1996

[4] F. Chaumette P. Rives B. Espiau, Positioning of a Robot with respect to an Object, Tracking it and Estimating its Velocity by Visual Servoing, *IEEE Int. Conf. Robotics and Automation*, Vol. 3, pp. 2238-2253, Sacramento Calif, 1991

[5] D. R. Meldrum G. Rodriguez G. F. Franklin, An Order (N) Recursive Inversion of the Jacobian for N-Link Serial Manipulator, *IEEE Int. Conf. Robotics and Automation*, pp. 1175-1180, Sacramento Calif., April1991

[6] W. Jamg Z. Bien, Feature-Based Visual Servoing of an Eye-In-Hand Robot with Improved Tracking Performance, *IEEE Proc. Of Int. Conf. On Robotics and Automation*, pp. 22545-2260, Sacramento Calif. April 1991

[7] B. M. Kent W. E. Red, Inverse Kinematics for Globally Orienting o Robot End-Effector using the Secondary Degrees-of Freedom.

[8] G. R. Pennock A. T. Yang, Application of Dual-Number Matrices to the Inverse Kinematics Problem of Robot Manipulator, *Journal of Mechanisms Transmission and Automation in Design* , June 1985.

[9] K. S. Hong Y. M. Kim C. Choi K. Sin, Inverse Kinematics of a Serial Manipulator: Kinematic Redundancy and Two Approches for Closed-Form Solution, *IEEE Int. Conf. Robotics and Automation*, pp. 780-785, New Mexico, April 1997

[10] K. Anderson J. Angeles, Kinematic Inversion of Robotic Manipulators in the Presence of Redundancies, *Int. Journal of Robotic Research*, Vol. 8, No. 6, pp. 80-97, 1989

[11] J. Angeles A. Rojas, Manipulator Inverse Kinematics via Condition-Number Minimization and Continuation, *Int. Journal of Robotics and Automation*, Vol. 2 No. 2, pp.61-69, 1987

[12] M. Kirkanski, Symbolic Singular Values Decomposition for Simple Redundant Manipulator and its Application on Robot Control, *Int. Journal of Robotic Research*, Vol. 14, N0. 4, pp. 382-398, Aug. 1995.

[13] R. Menseur K.L. Doty, A Fast Algorithm For Inverse Kinematics Analysis of Robot Manipulators, *Int. Journal of Robotic Research*, Vol. 7, No. 3, pp. 52-63, June 1988

[14] M. Xie, Towards Visual Intelligence of Service Robot, Proc. Of the Fourth, *Int. Conf. Automaution Roboitcs Control and Vision*, pp. 2217-2221, Singapore, Dec. 1996.

[15] M. Xie, Visual Servo Control with Uncalibrated Vision: A Theory and Experiments, *Journal of the Institution of Engineering Singapore*, Vol. 37, No. 1. 1997.

[16] H Y. Lee C. Woernle M. Hiller, A Complete Solution for Inverse Kinematics Problem of General 6R Robot Manipulator, *ASME Journ. Of Mechanical Design*, Vol. 113, pp.481-486, Dec. 1991

[17] H. Y. Lee W. Walischmiller, Position Analysis and Singularity Identification of an Industrial Robot, 1997

[18] S. Chiaverini, Singularity-Robust Task-Priority Redundancy for Real-Time Kinematic Control of Robot Manipulators, *IEEE Trans. Robot. Automation*, Vol.13, No. 3, June 1997,.

[19] K. Kreutz-Delgado M. Long H. Seraji (MIT), Kinematic Analysis of &-DOF Manipulator, *Int. Jour. of Robotics and Automation*, Vol. 11, No. 5, pp. 469-481, Oct. 1992.

[20] H. Seraji, Configuration Control of Redundant Manipulators: Theory and Implementation, *IEEE Trans. On Robotics and Automation*, Vol. 5, No. 4, pp. 472-490, Aug. 1989

[21] D. Lim H. Seraji (MIT), Configuration Control of Mobile Dexterous Robot: Real-Time Implementation and Experimentation, *Int. Jour. of Robotics Research*, Vol.16, No. 5, pp. 601-618, Oct. 1997

[22] H. Seraji, M.K. Long T.S. Lee, Motion Control of 7-DOF Arms: The Configuration Control Approach., *IEEE Trans. on Robotics and Automation*, Vol. 9, No. 2, pp. 125-138, April 1993

[23] H. Seraji, R. Colbaough, Improved Configuration Control for Redundant Robots, *Jour. Robotics System*, pp. 897-928, 1990.

[24] K. Tchong, R. Muszynski, Singular Inverse Kinematic Problem for Robotic Manipulator: A Normal Form Approach, *IEEE Trans. On Robotics and Automation*, Vol. 14, No. 1, pp. 93-104, Feb. 1998

Addendum

The following papers were announced for publication in this proceedings but have been withdrawn or are unavailable.

[3518-14]   **Integrating 3D scanning, CAD, and rapid prototyping systems**
              E. M. C. Childers, M. M. Trivedi, N. T. Lassiter, Univ. of California/San Diego

[3518-15]   **Online monitoring of robotic spot welding (in three parts): automatic tip drissing, electrode condition, and predicting weld cable failure**
              G. Swaggerty, CSI Online Products

[3518-16]   **MIP project: a demonstrator IMS**
              J. W. Perram, H. G. Petersen, P. T. Ruhoff, B. B. Kristensen, L. K. Baekdal, B. N. Jorgensen, I. Balslev, N. O. Bernsen, M. Masoodian, Odense Univ. (Denmark)

[3518-23]   **Control of a CNC machining center using the indirect measurement of a cutting force**
              D. S. Kwon, J. I. Song, Korea Advanced Institute of Science and Technology; J. H. Son, DAEWOO Motors Inc. (Korea); S. K. Kim, Samsung Electronics Co., Ltd. (Korea)

[3518-35]   **Model-based trajectory tracking control of wheeled mobile robots (WMRs)**
              R. Rajagopalan, K. G. Thanjavur, Concordia Univ. (Canada)

Author Index